Analogy-Making as Perception

Neural Network Modeling and Connectionism
Jeffrey L. Elman, editor

Connectionist Modeling and Brain Function: The Developing Interface
Stephen José Hanson and Carl R. Olson, editors

Neural Network Design and the Complexity of Learning
J. Stephen Judd

Neural Networks for Control
W. Thomas Miller, Richard S. Sutton, and Paul J. Werbos, editors

The Perception of Multiple Objects: A Connectionist Approach
Michael C. Mozer

Neural Computation of Pattern Motion: Modeling Stages of Motion Analysis in the Primate Visual Cortex
Margaret Euphrasia Sereno

Subsymbolic Natural Language Processing: An Integrated Model of Scripts, Lexicon, and Memory
Risto Miikkulainen

Analogy-Making as Perception: A Computer Model
Melanie Mitchell

Mechanisms of Implicit Learning: Connectionist Models of Sequence Processing
Axel Cleeremans

Analogy-Making as Perception

A Computer Model

Melanie Mitchell

A Bradford Book
The MIT Press
Cambridge, Massachusetts
London, England

Printed and bound in the United States of America.

Library of Congress Cataloging-in-Publication Data

Mitchell, Melanie.
   Analogy-making as perception : a computer model / Melanie
Mitchell.
      p.   cm. — (Neural network modeling and connectionism)
   "A Bradford book."
   Includes bibliographical references and index.
   ISBN 978-0-262-51544-3 (pb.:alk.paper)
   1. Analogy—Computer simulation.   2. Perception—Computer
simulation.   3. Artificial intelligence.   I. Title.   II. Series.
BF446.M57   1993
153.7—dc20   92-38045
                                                           CIP

Contents

Series Foreword

The goal of this series is to identify and bring to the public the best work in the exciting field of neural network and connectionist modeling. The series includes monographs based on dissertations, extended reports of work by leaders in the field, edited volumes and collections on topics of special interest, major reference works, and undergraduate and graduate texts. The field is highly interdisciplinary, and works published in the series will touch on a wide variety of topics ranging from low-level vision to the philosophical foundations of theories of representation.

Jeffrey L. Elman, editor

Associate editors:

James Anderson, Brown University

Andrew Barto, University of Massachusetts, Amherst

Gary Dell, University of Illinois

Jerome Feldman, University of California, Berkeley

Stephen Grossberg, Boston University

Stephen Hanson, Princeton University

Geoffrey Hinton, University of Toronto

Michael Jordon, Massachusetts Institute of Technology

James McClelland, Carnegie Mellon University

Domenico Parisi, Instituto di Psicologia del CNR

David Rumelhart, Stanford University

Terrence Sejnowski, Salk Institute

Paul Smolensky, University of Colorado

Stephen P. Stich, Rutgers University

David Touretzky, Carnegie Mellon University

David Zipser, University of California, San Diego

Foreword

Melanie Mitchell and Douglas Hofstadter's Copycat program, described in this book, is a marvelous piece of work which I find very inspiring. In addition to its novel insights into the nature of analogy, Copycat offers an intriguing alternative to deterministic symbol processing.

This work will be of broad interest in cognitive science and AI, especially for readers concerned with analogy-making, perception, or new approaches to modeling thought. Although the book's audience is diverse enough to merit inclusion in any of several MIT Press series, it was my suggestion that it be published in the series on Neural Network Modeling and Connectionism. For the benefit of both connectionist modelers and the many advocates of competing approaches, I would like to explain why this work is of particular importance.

Connectionist research has so far explored two key regions of the space of parallel models of computation. We know how to encode propositional information in localist (structured) networks, and how to do certain primitive types of inference in those networks by spreading activation. But a purely localist approach has many limitations, such as a lack of powerful learning algorithms. It is also awkward to dynamically create new structures in a localist network, or to modify existing ones. And it is hard to get multiple pieces of information to interact.

A second large region of computational space contains the "distributed" connectionist models, whose strengths and weaknesses differ from those of their localist cousins. Distributed models at present possess only a weak inference capability, based on either nonlinear interpolation between training points (perceptrons, back-propagation, etc.) or parallel relaxation (e.g., Boltzmann machines.) Current distributed models deal poorly with problems having a complex combinatorial structure, but they can dynamically create new structures as novel activity patterns over their hidden units, and they can learn to imitate many types of behavior.

Copycat opens up a third, largely unexplored region of the space of possible models. Because it is not constrained to use neuron-like units, its designers could posit more powerful symbol manipulation primitives which are cashed out as pieces of Lisp code. This left them free to focus on more abstract concerns, namely the sort of flexible symbolic inference required for conceptual slippage and analogy-making.

Copycat is not a "classical AI" type program, although it does use Lisp procedures to manipulate structured symbolic data. Its reliance on stochastic search to find solutions to analogy problems is a radical innovation. Its use of spreading activation through a Slipnet to guide that search gives the model a partly localist flavor, but on the other hand, since the components of the symbol structures it creates are simultaneously active units, which interact in hard-to-predict ways, the model has a distributed flavor as well. Copycat thus exemplifies a new approach to symbol processing, but one that is very much in harmony with what connectionists have been trying to achieve.

Dr. Mitchell writes in a straightforward, easy-to-read style, and provides many illustrations of actual Copycat runs. She is to be commended for her candor in describing the program's limitations as thoroughly as its successes. Her book will surely be a beacon for many future explorers of this new region of computational space. One could not ask for a better guide.

David S. Touretzky
Carnegie Mellon University

Acknowledgments

My thesis advisor, Douglas Hofstadter, was the prime mover behind the Copycat project: he created the domain and formulated the program's architecture, and he has guided and collaborated with me in every aspect of my work. Any success this project has had is due primarily to his original and insightful thinking about thought. It was his book *Gödel, Escher, Bach* that originally convinced me to go into this field, and he has continued to be an inspiring teacher as well as a constant friend and supporter. His influence will without doubt be strong and pervasive in all my future work.

Two other professors at the University of Michigan have inspired and influenced me in significant ways: John Holland has taught me a great deal about complex systems, adaptation, and how to build computer models, and Stephen Kaplan has strongly influenced how I look at cognition. Both have had lasting effects on my view of what it is to be a scientist.

The other members of my doctoral committee—Arthur Burks, Keki Irani, Steven Lytinen, and Edward Smith—gave me many important suggestions for my research and for this book. Edward Smith and David Pisoni helped me think about how to demonstrate the model's psychological validity, and John Logan of Indiana University helped me run some experiments.

Robert French was my closest comrade in graduate school. He has provided invaluable assistance on the Copycat project, and has also been a continual source of friendship, intellectual companionship, and moral support.

This project has been assisted and influenced in many ways by the other past and present members of Douglas Hofstadter's research group, including David Chalmers, Gray Clossman, Daniel Defays, Liane Gabora (who wrote the statistics-gathering program for Copycat), Greg Huber, Helga Keller, Kevin Kinnell, David Leake, Roy Leban, Alejandro López, James Marshall, Gary McGraw, David Rogers, Peter Suber, and Henry Velick. Other fellow past and present graduate students and faculty at Michigan and elsewhere have helped me in various ways in thinking about the issues and in improving the manuscript. These include Jonathan Amsterdam, Robert Axelrod, John Barnden, Lashon Booker, Michael Cohen, Stephanie Forrest, Dedre Gentner, James Levenick, Wayne Loofbourrow, Arthur Markman, Mitchel Resnick, Rick Riolo, Carl Simon, and Mark Weaver. In particular, James Levenick read most of the chapters and provided many valuable comments.

David Touretzky and Keith Holyoak served as reviewers for The MIT Press, and their comments were exceptionally helpful. Thanks also to Paul Bethge, Teri Mendelsohn, and Harry Stanton for their help in transforming a dissertation into a book.

I am very grateful to my parents, Norma and Jack Mitchell, for their unending love and support, as well as for their weekly "pep talks," which helped enormously to keep up my morale while I was writing my dissertation. My aunt, Faith Dunne, was also a constant source of good advice and loving prodding throughout that process.

Finally, I want to thank David Moser, in part for many discussions about this project and for many helpful comments on the manuscript, but more important, for being my most patient listener, my most enthusiastic supporter, and my dearest friend and companion.

My research on this project has been financially supported by a University of Michigan Regents' Fellowship, by a Michigan Society of Fellows Postdoctoral Scholarship, and by grants to Douglas Hofstadter's research group from the National Science Foundation (grant DCR 8410409), from the University of Michigan, from Mitchell Kapor, Ellen Poss, and the Lotus Development Corporation, from Apple Computer, Inc., and from Indiana University.

Analogy-Making as Perception

Chapter 1

Introduction

A native talent for perceiving analogies is ... the leading fact in genius of every order.
—William James, *The Principles of Psychology* (1890/1950, p. 530)

How, when one is faced with a situation, does understanding come about in the mind? How are we guided by a multitude of initially unconnected and novel perceptions of an entity or a situation to a coherent and familiar mental description, such as "coffee cup," "the letter A," "in the style of Bach," or "the Vietnam of Central America"? How are such representations structured so that they are flexible, fluid, and thus adaptable to many different situations, rather than brittle, rigid, and inextensible?

The thesis of this book is that analogy-making lies at the core of such understanding processes, and that analogy-making is itself a process of high-level perception. Here, "high-level perception" refers to the recognition of objects, situations, or events at various levels of abstraction higher than that of syntactic sensations tied to particular sensory modalities; it is to be distinguished from modality-specific mechanisms such as those of low-level vision. Another term for it would be "abstract recognition," referring to the recognition mechanisms we use when, say, we read a newspaper article about officials performing secret acts, shredding documents, or lying to Congress and characterize these events as "a coverup" or "another Watergate."

This book describes a computer program, called Copycat, that models analogy-making as a high-level perception process in which conceptual fluidity of the kind described above emerges from complex, subconscious interaction between perception and concepts. The Copycat project was originally conceived by Douglas Hofstadter (1984a, 1985a) as part of a continuing research program in cognitive science, the long-term goal of which is to understand the mechanisms underlying the fluidity of concepts: their overlapping and associative nature, their blurry boundaries, their dynamic and graded (rather than static and all-or-nothing) relevance in a given situation, their flexibility as a function of context—in short, their fluid rather than rigid adaptability to different situations. Such fluidity is a hallmark of human thought, and its source is not well understood.

Hofstadter and his research group have been investigating this fluidity of concepts for many years and in a number of different domains, including pattern recognition, analogies, counterfactuals, speech and action errors, humor, translation between languages, and the creation and recognition of different styles in such domains as typefaces, music, and art (Hofstadter 1987). What is striking is that some of the same mental mechanisms seem to underlie these seemingly disparate mental activities. In particular, central to all of them is the phenomenon of *conceptual slippage*, in which, under pressure, certain concepts in a mental representation are not held fixed but are allowed to "slip" — that is, to be replaced by conceptually related concepts in response to various kinds of pressures present in the situation at hand.

For example, consider the question "Who is the first lady of Great Britain?" (Hofstadter 1985a). A straightforward description of the American first lady is "wife of the president"; however, this description will not work in the case of Great Britain, since, for one thing, Great Britain has no president. Thus, the usual description of "first lady" cannot be applied literally (unless you want to rigidly assert that Great Britain has no first lady since it has no president). Rather, one must treat the concept liberally, allowing some slippage. For instance, you might feel that the "president" of Great Britain is the prime minister. The question of the first lady of Great Britain was even more complicated a few years back, when the prime minister was a woman, Margaret Thatcher. Then, many people were willing to say that the first lady (in other words, the prime minister's "wife") was Mrs. Thatcher's husband, Denis. Thus, given the pressure of certain differences between the United States and Great Britain, people allowed the concepts *president* and *wife* to slip into *prime minister* and *husband*, respectively; these different concepts were seen to play the same roles in their respective situations. (People have also suggested numerous other candidates for the British first lady, including Queen Elizabeth, her husband Prince Philip, and Thatcher herself.) This notion of fluidly exporting mental representations (such as "wife of the president") from one situation to another — sometimes requiring certain concepts to slip under pressure into related concepts — is fundamental to the mental phenomena that my colleagues and I are attempting to model.

Underlying this entire research program is a belief in the ubiquity and the centrality of high-level perception and conceptual slippage in all aspects of thought, from basic and ordinary acts of recognition and categorization to rare and seemingly mystical feats of insight and creativity. Thus, we believe that it is extremely important for researchers in cognitive science to isolate and study these phenomena. The Copycat project is one attempt to do so.

High-level perception is intimately tied up with concepts: it is the act of applying previously stored concepts to describe and chunk parts of a new situation in order to build up a coherent mental representation. (Here the term "situation" can refer to something as concrete as a coffee cup or to something much more complex and abstract, such as a certain political or social event.) But since every situation is different, recognition is not a mere matter of rigidly applying predefined, static concepts to describe aspects of an uninterpreted situation. An essential part of the recognition process is a mutual accommodation of one's concepts and one's developing mental representation of the situation at hand (as in the example above, where the concept of "first lady" and the mental representation of Denis Thatcher had to be reshaped in order to fit each other).

The process of recognizing concrete and abstract situations is more general than what is often referred to as *categorization*. That term often implies that the situation is assigned to a single previously stored and easily verbalizable category (such as "coffee cup" or "coverup"). However, the "category" of a situation is often difficult to verbalize, yet recognizable nonetheless. Situations that abstractly remind one of other situations are often very clear examples of this. For example, a friend told me about a 45-minute airline flight he took from Pittsburgh to Detroit before which the plane had been kept on the ground in Pittsburgh for 90 minutes so that a delayed shipment of soft drinks could be brought on board. The wait for the soft drinks defeated the whole purpose of the drinks, which was to make the trip seem shorter and more comfortable. This story instantly reminded me of how the University of Michigan Physical Plant Department had fixed a decorative fountain on campus that often overflowed by installing a large float valve, which stopped the flow of water when the water level got too high. This had made the fountain resemble a huge toilet tank, which of course completely defeated its purpose, which was to be aesthetically pleasing and thus make the campus look more beautiful. I spontaneously recognized that the airplane situation was in the same quite abstract and difficult-to-verbalize category as the fountain situation—something like "situations in which an action taken to remedy a problem actually defeats the main purpose of the thing affected by the problem." (Several examples of such reminding experiences are discussed in Schank 1983.)

This example illustrates the blurry line between what we call categorization and what we call analogy-making. Was my reminding experience a feat of analogy-making or a feat of categorization? There is no clear distinction between the two. When a child learns that the words "mouth" and "drink" apply to a huge number of different objects and situations, is it categorization or analogy-making? Is a person who describes Nicaragua as "another Vietnam" or the Iran-Contra scandal as "Reagan's Watergate" categorizing or making analogies? One makes an analogy when one perceives non-identical objects or situations as being "the same" at some abstract level. Analogy-making is thus intimately related to recognition and categorization, for the essence of recognizing a cup (or a face, or a wave equation, or a symphony in the style of Mozart) is perceiving it to be "the same" at some level as other instances of that category. Very similar, if not identical, mental mechanisms seem to underlie analogy-making, recognition, and categorization.

Turner (1988, p. 4) makes a similar point: "Deeply entrenched analogical connections we no longer find inventive. We regard them as straightforward category connections." He characterizes the difference between analogical and categorical connections among concepts as a difference in the "degree of entrenchment" in the conceptual system rather than a difference in kind. Holyoak (1984) also makes a related point when he hypothesizes that analogical thinking may underlie the acquisition of schemas (abstract categories).

High-level perception thus encompasses recognition, categorization, and analogy-making, and its central feature is the fluid application of one's existing concepts to new situations, often via conceptual slippage. The "first lady" example illustrates very strikingly how people use concepts with a great deal of flexibility. The concept "first lady" is ordinarily taken to mean "the wife of the president"; thus, it is easy to find the counterpart of the American first lady in, say, Mexico, where there currently is a married male president. However, exporting the concept to Great Britain in the days when Margaret Thatcher was prime minister required some flexibility: it required certain concepts (*president* and *wife*) to slip into related concepts rather than being rigidly fixed.

A reader might protest at this point that it is not necessary for concepts to slip if we simply generalize the original definition of "first lady" to "spouse of the head of state." However, more examples make it clear that the concept "first lady," like other real-world concepts, cannot be crammed into so small a space. Hofstadter (1985a) gives two other examples that elegantly demonstrate this: When Pierre Trudeau was prime minister of Canada many people considered his former wife, Margaret, to be Canada's first lady, and for a long time during Jean-Claude Duvalier's reign in Haiti the title of first lady belonged to Simone Duvalier, his mother and the wife of the late former president François Duvalier. How are we to generalize "first lady" now? Does it mean "spouse or parent, present or former, of head of state, present or former" (Hofstadter 1985a, p. 548)? Even if such a verbose and awkward description were plausible, other undeniable instances of first ladies would force further amendments (e.g., in some Muslim countries the king has more than one wife; in the Philippines many people would have said that Corazón Aquino held the titles of president and first lady simultaneously).[1]

Another problem with attempting to abstract away any differences by using a generalized definition such as "spouse of the head of state" is that, by adopting such a generalization, you lose the sense that Denis Thatcher was not a normal first lady; you lose the sense of tension that comes from the strong feeling that the role should be filled by a woman. Such a sense of tension is essential to assessing the quality or interest of an analogy. Also, important information is lost in a generalization (e.g., *spouse*) that is present in a conceptual slippage (e.g., *wife* slips to *husband*). In order to complete or extend an analogy one often has to keep track of how certain concepts slipped.

The above examples are related to Lakoff's (1987) discussion of "radial" categories (e.g., "mother"); and perhaps an analysis similar to those presented by Lakoff could be applied to the concept of "first lady," the meaning of which comes from the interaction of several different "models," such as *wife of the president* and *most distinguished woman in a particular field*. (Greta Garbo has been called the "first lady of film," and Ella Fitzgerald the "first lady of jazz.") But the main point of presenting this example is to illustrate how subtly flexible and "slippery" real-world concepts can be and how hopeless it is to try to come up with a definition or rule that will cover all past, present, and future cases. The view underlying this research project is that the only way to flexibly understand or categorize new situations is via analogy, often with conceptual slippage required. This brings out once again the close relation between categorization and analogy-making.

The "first lady" examples illustrate a central idea of this research: a view of concepts in which each concept consists of a central region surrounded by a halo of associated concepts that are potential slippages. For example, *husband* is in the halo of the concept *wife*, and in some situations (such as identifying the first lady of Great Britain) the description *wife* can slip to the description *husband*. That is, *husband* in one situation can be seen as playing the same role as *wife* in the other situation. The halo of potential slippages changes in response to context: a particular slippage is possible only with the right sort of pressure. For example, in a country with a married male head of state one would be extremely unlikely to slip *wife* to *husband* in the description of first lady and identify someone's *husband* as the first lady of that country. This slippage can take place only under certain pressures, such as in the case where the head of state is a married *woman*.

Conceptual slippage is ubiquitous in thought, and in some aspects of thought it can be seen especially clearly. For example, our speech and our actions are permeated with errors involving conceptual slippages, such as word substitutions ("Please fix the window—uh, I mean *mirror*" or "Are my legs—uh, I mean my *tires*—touching the curb?") and action errors (stopping one's car and unbuckling one's watch instead of one's seat belt; trying to look up the word "February" in the B section of a dictionary because February, like B, is the second in a series).[2] Slippages are also apparent in the counterfactual statements people constantly make. You accidentally drop a milk bottle onto the floor, breaking it, and think "I wish I had dropped the orange juice jug instead, since it's made of plastic." Concepts tend to slip to close neighbors. For example, *milk bottle* slips to *orange juice jug* rather than to, say, *tablecloth*—it is very unlikely that you would think "I wish I had dropped the tablecloth instead; *it* wouldn't have broken." But of course the closeness—as well as the *availability* of other concepts as potential slippages from a given concept—depends on the situation. What slips, and how, depends on the interaction of specific *pressures* on the perceiver of the situation. The Copycat program is an attempt to model this context-dependent nature of conceptual slippage, to show how pressures in specific situations interact with concepts to provoke appropriate slippages. (See Hofstadter 1979 [chapter 19] and Kahneman and Miller 1986 on slippage in counterfactual thinking, Hofstadter and Gabora 1990 on slippage in humor, and Hofstadter 1982, French and Henry 1988, and Moser 1991 on slippage in translation between languages.)

The Copycat project concerns analogy-making, which provides a particularly clear window on the ways in which conceptual slippage takes place. Since analogy-making is all about perceiving resemblances between things that are different, an analogy puts pressure on concepts to slip into related concepts, as in the analogies involving first ladies. Different people use the word "analogy" to mean different things, but when the term is taken in a very broad sense, to include all types of similarity comparisons ("this object is like that object", or "this situation is like that situation"), one cannot overestimate its ubiquity and importance at all levels of thought, from the most common and mundane acts of categorization to the most rare and significant feats of creation and discovery. Many researchers, e.g. Gentner (1983), would hesitate to label categorization as a kind of analogy-making; however, as was illustrated above, it is somewhat hard to draw a line between the two. As Gentner (1983) has pointed out, there is a spectrum of similarity comparisons. The point here is that the mechanisms underlying these various mental activities are, if not the same, then at least very closely related.

The following are some examples of analogy-making (or, in some cases, its close cousins) ranging from the everyday and mundane to the rare and exalted (though not necessarily in perfect order):

- A child learns the difference between cups and glasses, and can use the two words to correctly identify different objects.
- A child learns to recognize cats, dogs, boys, girls, etc. in books as well as in real life.
- A person is consistently and easily able to recognize the letter A in spite of the fact that it appears in a vast variety of shapes and styles, both in professionally designed typefaces and in different people's handwriting. There is something about all these A's that is essentially the same.
- A person is consistently and easily able to recognize that all the letters in a certain typeface (say, Helvetica) are in the same style; there is something about the letters that is essentially the same.
- Jean says to Simon "I call my parents once a week." Simon replies "Me too"—meaning, of course, not that he calls Jean's parents once a week, but that he calls his own parents.
- A woman says to her male colleague "I've been working so hard lately, I haven't been able to get enough time to spend with my husband"; he replies "Yeah, me neither." He doesn't mean that he has no time to spend with her husband, or with his own husband, or even with his own wife (he's not married); he means that he has no time for his girlfriend.
- People use the last two syllables from "alcoholic" to create new concepts, such as *workaholic*, *chocoholic*, *sexaholic*, and *shopaholic*.
- An advertisement describes Perrier as "the Cadillac of bottled waters." A newspaper article describes teaching as "the Beirut of professions." An opinion piece describes Saddam Hussein as "the Noriega of the Middle East."
- Nicaragua (or El Salvador) is called "another Vietnam." Cambodia is called "Vietnam's Vietnam." The Iran-Contra affair is called "Reagan's Watergate," and newspapers even dub it "Contragate."
- President Ronald Reagan calls the Nicaraguan Contras "Freedom Fighters" and likens them to "our Founding Fathers" in the American Revolution.
- A newspaper article portrays Denis Thatcher as the "first lady of Great Britain."
- A jury acquits a man accused of rape because they decide that the victim was wearing "provocative" clothes and was "asking to be raped." The National Organization for Women protests, asserting that this is like saying that a person wearing an expensive watch is asking to be robbed.
- Britain and Argentina go to war over the Falklands (or las Malvinas), a set of small islands located near the coast of Argentina and populated by British settlers. Greece sides with Britain because of its own conflict with Turkey over Cyprus, an island near the coast of Turkey, the majority of whose population is ethnically Greek.

• A classical-music lover hears an unfamiliar piece on the radio and easily attributes it to Mozart. An early-music enthusiast hears a piece for baroque orchestra and can easily identify which country the composer was from. A studio composer arranges the Beatles' rock hit "Hey Jude" in "easy listening" style to be played on Muzak radio stations.

• The linguist Zhao Yuanren translates *Alice's Adventures in Wonderland* into Chinese, adapting the puns and other wordplay so that they work smoothly in Chinese while retaining the essence of the English original.

• The physicist Hideki Yukawa attempts to explain the nuclear force by using an analogy with the electromagnetic force. On this basis, he postulates a mediating particle for the nuclear force similar to the photon, which mediates the electromagnetic force. However, the new particle would have to mediate conversion of uncharged particles (neutrons) into charged particles (protons), and vice versa, which photons could not do. So certain slippages have to be made from the electromagnetic force to the nuclear force:

non-converter (photon) $\Rightarrow$ *converter* (new particle),

which implies

uncharged (photon) $\Rightarrow$ *charged* (new particle),

which in turn implies

massless (photon) $\Rightarrow$ *massive* (new particle),

which requires a slippage from one type of equation to another:

massless equation $\Rightarrow$ *massive equation*.

Yukawa uses these slippages to predict properties of the hypothesized particle (now known as a *pion*). The particle is subsequently discovered, and the predicted properties are verified (Yukawa 1973a,b).

• Johann Sebastian Bach takes a simple aria and creates a set of thirty variations on it (the "Goldberg Variations"). Each variation is quite different and complex, and many involve constraints not present in the original aria, but each contains something of the essence of the original in either its melodic or its harmonic structure.

In an important sense, all of these count as examples of analogy-making. All are illustrations, at different levels of impressiveness, of the fluid rather than rigid nature of concepts and perception, by which the *essence* of a situation (be it a cup, a printed A, a family situation, a profession, a political situation, a piece of music or literature, a scientific idea, or whatever) can be distilled and fluidly transported to a different situation. Thus, though these examples range over a wide spectrum, there are fundamental psychological issues common to all of them. They reflect in different ways the same set of mental abilities: those of high-level perception and conceptual fluidity. The Copycat project is an attempt to extract and isolate some of these common issues and abilities and to propose a set of ideas about the underlying mental mechanisms. This proposal takes the form of a computer program that can make analogies in a microworld that contains many of these issues in an idealized form.

Furthermore, the above examples give some indication of the ubiquity and the range of analogy-making in human thought. The human analogy-making capacity is far more than a mere tool used in the context of problem-solving, or a servant to a "reasoning engine". It is a central mechanism of cognition; it pervades thought at all levels, both conscious and unconscious, and cannot be turned on and off at will. (This view of the centrality of analogy in thought is complemented by the work of Lakoff and Johnson [1980] and Lakoff [1987], who argue, using a vast array of linguistic metaphors, that we understand all abstract and complex concepts—such as "love"—by analogies to more direct perceptual experiences.)

The Copycat project is an attempt to model certain aspects of concepts, but it differs in focus from much of the current psychological research on concepts and categories, which generally deals with *prototypes, exemplars, graded structure*, and other notions related to the internal structure of individual categories (Rosch and Lloyd 1978; Smith and Medin 1981; Lakoff 1987). In the Copycat project we are more concerned with the dynamics of the activation and association of concepts as *active symbols* in the brain (Hofstadter 1979, chapter 11; Hofstadter 1985d) and with how such symbols are flexibly to describe and relate different situations. The nature of this focus will become clearer in chapters 2 and 3, where the psychological issues addressed by this project are spelled out and the computer model is described.[3]

Two previous projects, Jumbo (carried out by Hofstadter) and (Seek-Whence) (carried out by Hofstadter and his graduate students Marsha Meridith and Gray Clossman), investigated certain aspects of high-level perception and conceptual slippage, but each of those projects had a number of limitations (which will be discussed in subsequent chapters). The particular goal of the Copycat project is to further develop ideas from these projects by building a model of how perception interacts with concepts to engender appropriate—and sometimes creative—conceptual slippages in the realm of analogy-making, a realm in which the necessity of constructing fluid and adaptable mental representations is particularly apparent.

The Copycat program interprets and makes analogies between situations in an idealized microworld involving letter-string analogy problems. The program's architecture brings together many ideas, some inspired by other attempts at modeling perception and some inspired by naturally occurring self-organizing systems. These ideas include the following:

- A parallel and self-organizing approach to building perceptual descriptions via the interaction of large numbers of independent "perceptual agents," with no global executive controlling the system's processing. This was inspired in part by the self-organizing mechanisms of metabolic processes in living cells and by the Hearsay-II speech-understanding program of Erman et al. (1980).

- A model of concepts in which a concept's "halo" of potential slippages is not explicitly defined but rather emerges in response to what is perceived in the situation at hand. In this model, concepts attain various levels of activation in response to what is perceived, resulting in the *shaded*—rather than black-and-white—levels of "presence" or "relevance" of various concepts in the situation at hand. Activated concepts spread activation to conceptual neighbors, and a concept's proximity to other concepts (and thus its potential availability for slippage from other concepts) is dynamic and context-sensitive (changing according to current perceptions). Such a model has aspects in common with certain types of semantic networks (since concepts are modeled by nodes and links in a network) as well as with connectionist networks (since the degree of activation of nodes, the degree of association between nodes, and the constitution of concepts themselves are emergent outcomes of the interaction of the network as a whole with what is being perceived in the environment).

· An interaction of bottom-up (environment-driven) and top-down (concept-driven) modes of constructing perceptual descriptions, and a gradual transition from dominance of a bottom-up mode to dominance of a top-down mode, as organizing themes emerge from what has already been perceived.

· A notion of a *parallel terraced scan*, in which many different avenues of interpreting situations are explored simultaneously, each at a speed and to a depth proportional to moment-to-moment evaluations of its promise.

· The use of *temperature* as a feedback device to measure the amount and quality of global organization. This measure is then used to control the degree of randomness with which decisions are made in the system. The effect is to speed up the exploration of more promising avenues with respect to less promising ones as more and more information is obtained about them.

· A notion of *statistically emergent* high-level behavior, in which the system's low-level activities (involving mutually competitive and supporting actions by large numbers of independent perceptual agents) are permeated with nondeterminism, but more deterministic high-level behavior (e.g., the composition of concepts, the parallel terraced scan, and the actual analogies created by the program) emerges from the statistics of the low-level nondeterminism.

Chapter 2

High-Level Perception, Conceptual Slippage, and Analogy-Making in a Microworld

2.1 Copycat's Microworld

The Copycat project has attempted to isolate many of the central issues in high-level perception and analogy-making, to strip each of them down to its essence, and to construct a computer model that deals with these issues in this idealized form. This research methodology is similar to that used by physicists, who typically attempt to solve an idealized version of a problem that nonetheless captures the essence of the original problem. In the basic sciences, particularly in physics, such a methodology is indispensable for gaining insight into deep underlying principles, because phenomena in the real world are often too complex to approach directly. For the same reason, we believe that this methodology is also indispensable for approaching problems in cognitive science: much insight into mental mechanisms can be gained by looking at problems in a more stripped-down form, avoiding the real-world complexity that would make the construction of models intractable.

Using this "isolate and idealize" strategy, Hofstadter (1984a,b; 1985a) has developed an idealized microworld for studying many of the essential features of high-level perception and analogy-making. The basic objects in this world are the 26 letters of the alphabet. Analogy problems are constructed out of strings of letters, as in the following:

1. **abc** $\Rightarrow$ **abd**
   ijk $\Rightarrow$?

That is, one is given the change from the string **abc** to the string **abd** and asked to "do the same thing" to the string **ijk** (i.e., one is asked to be a "copycat" — to copy the initial change, but using the material of the target string). The strings in such problems are meant to represent idealized situations consisting of objects, relationships between objects, and events; in this way they serve as metaphors for more complex real-world situations. The *initial string* **abc** and the *target string* **ijk** are frameworks, each with its own objects and relationships. The change of **abc** to the *modified string* **abd** highlights a fragment of the first framework; the challenge is to find "the same fragment" in the second framework (the target string) and to highlight and modify it in "the same way." What has been highlighted, how it has been highlighted, and what "the same way" means in the second framework are all up to the analogy-maker (human or machine) to decide.

The knowledge available to an analogy-maker in this microworld is fairly limited. The 26 letters are known, but only as members of a platonic linear sequence; shapes of letters, sounds, words, and all other linguistic and graphic facts are unknown. The only relations explicitly known are predecessor and successor relations between immediate neighbors in the alphabet. Ordinal positions in the alphabet (e.g., the fact that *S* is the 19th letter) are not known. Italic capitals (e.g., *S*) denote the 26 abstract *categories* (or *types*) of the alphabet, and never appear in strings; bold lower-case letters (e.g., **a**, **b**, and **c**) denote *instances* (or *tokens*) of those categories, and appear only in strings. *A* and *Z*, being alphabetic extremities, are salient landmarks of equal importance. The alphabet is not circular; that is, *A* has no predecessor and *Z* has no successor. The alphabet is known equally well backward and forward (i.e., the fact that *N* is the letter before *O* is as accessible as the fact that *P* is the letter after *O*). In addition, strings (such as **abc** or **kkjjii**) can be parsed equally well from left to right and from right to left. The analogy-maker can count, but is reluctant to count above 3 or so, and has a common-sense notion of grouping by sameness or by alphabetical adjacency (forward or backward with equal ease).

As can be seen from the description above, the knowledge assumed for this microdomain not only is limited; it is also different from that of people with respect to letter strings. (People can count far above 3, people usually know the alphabet better forward than backward, English speakers read from left to right, and so on.) The idea here is not to construct a model of how people solve letter-string analogy problems *per se*, but rather to construct a *domain* that, though idealized, captures much of the essence of real-world analogy-making, so it can be used in developing a more general model. That is, Copycat's alphabetic microworld is meant to be a tool for exploring general issues of cognition rather than issues specific to the domain of letters and strings. Thus, there is a balance to be achieved in constructing such a microworld: we want people to be able to understand and solve the letter-string problems without needing too much instruction about the restrictions of the domain; however, we also want to avoid having features in the domain that are specific to the letter-string problems themselves (e.g., a left-to-right bias in reading) but extraneous to the real issues of high-level perception and analogy-making that we are investigating. In addition, we exclude complex mathematical knowledge because we are trying to get at subconscious recognition processes rather than highly conscious "expert" activities (such as calculating that the distance from *A* to *E* is twice as large as the distance from *M* to *O*).

For problem 1 above, a reasonable description of the **abc** ⇒ **abd** change is "Replace the rightmost letter by its successor," and straightforward application of this rule to the target string **ijk** yields the common-sense answer **ijl**. A more literal description (almost never given by people) is "Replace the rightmost letter by a *D*," which yields the answer **ijd**. (This answer seems so literal-minded that many people laugh when it is suggested to them.) Even more literal-minded answers are **ijk** ("Replace any *C* by a *D*," and, since there are no instances of *C* in **ijk**, just leave the target string alone) and **abd** ("Replace any string by **abd**"). However, these answers are very rarely given by people. People are very good at describing things at a level of generality appropriate for the purposes of living in the real world, and this sense of what is appropriate in the real world automatically carries over to the abstract letter-string domain. Even though—technically—there are no "right" and "wrong" answers in a domain so divorced from real-world concerns, people rather consistently agree on a single answer or a small set of answers as being the best response(s) to a given problem. People's mental mechanisms have evolved for perception and analogy-making in the real world, but these mechanisms are still in operation even when the domain is artificial. Thus, artificial domains such as the letter-string domain can be used to study general mental mechanisms. (The information given here about "what people do" on these problems comes from numerous informal and formal surveys of people's answers to various letter-string analogy problems. The results of the formal surveys are given in chapters 4 and 5 and summarized in chapter 6.)

In problem 1 above, the rule "Replace the rightmost letter by its successor," describing the initial change **abc** ⇒ **abd**, can be applied straightforwardly to the target string **ijk**. However, other problems are not so simple. For instance, consider the same initial change and an alternate target string:

2. **abc** ⇒ **abd**
   iijjkk ⇒ ?

Here a straightforward, literal application of the original rule would yield **iijjkl**, which ignores the strong similarity between **abc** and **iijjkk** when the latter is seen as consisting of three *groups of letters* rather than as six *letters*. If one perceives the role of *letter* in **abc** as played by *group* in **iijjkk**, then in making a mapping between **abc** and **iijjkk** one is forced to let the concept *letter* slip into the similar concept *group*. The rule for changing the target string becomes "Replace the rightmost *group* by its successor," which yields the answer **iijjll**. Coming up with such a rule and a corresponding answer is a good example, in the letter-string world, of mental fluidity (as contrasted with the mental rigidity that gives rise to **iijjkl**).

Now consider the following variant:

3. **abc** ⇒ **abd**
   kji ⇒ ?

Here a literal application of the original rule would yield **kjj**, which again ignores a more abstract similarity between **abc** and **kji**. An alternative some people prefer is **lji** ("Replace the *leftmost* letter by its successor"), which is based on seeing **abc** as a left-to-right string and **kji** as a right-to-left string (where each string increases alphabetically). This opposite-direction view requires a slippage from the concept *right* to the concept *left*, which in turn gives rise to the slippage *rightmost* ⇒ *leftmost*. Another answer given by many people is **kjh** ("Replace the rightmost letter by its *predecessor*"), in which **abc** is seen as increasing and **kji** as decreasing (both viewed as moving rightward), requiring a slippage from *successor* to *predecessor*.

The same arguments would apply to the problem **abc** ⇒ **abd**, **kjih** ⇒ ?, in which initial string **abc** is of length 3 and the target string **kjih** is of length 4. In the microdomain, as in real-world analogy-making, it is not necessary for there to be a one-to-one mapping between the objects of the two situations; an analogy can be made in spite of the fact that some objects, such as the **b** in **abc** and the **j** and **i** in **kjih**, have no clear counterparts in the other situation (just as one can make an analogy between the "first family" of the United States and that of Great Britain without having to find a British counterpart for the American president's pet).

Still other kinds of slippages can be seen in the answers to the following three problems.

    4. **abc** $\Rightarrow$ **abd**

       ace $\Rightarrow$ **?**

Applying the original rule literally to problem 4 yields the answer **acf**, which does not take into account the "double successor" structure of **ace** (C is the double successor of A, etc.). If **ace** is seen as similar to **abc** because **abc** is a "successor group" and **ace** is a "double-successor group," then the answer is **acg** ("Replace the rightmost letter by its *double successor*"). As was mentioned above, the only relations explicitly known to analogy-makers in this microworld are immediate successor and predecessor relations; thus, in order to arrive at the answer **ace**, an analogy-maker would have to create the concept *double successor* on the fly, for the purpose of making this analogy.

    5. **abc** $\Rightarrow$ **abd**

       mrrjjj $\Rightarrow$ **?**

The answer that people give most often to problem 5 is **mrrkkk**, but this does not take into account the abstract similarity between **abc** and **mrrjjj**: **abc** increases *alphabetically*, whereas **mrrjjj** consists of groups whose lengths increase *numerically*. If this similarity is perceived, then the answer is **mrrjjjj**, which reflects the view that the role played by *letter* in **abc** is played by *group-length* in **mrrjjj**, and which requires a slippage from one to the other ("Replace the rightmost *group-length* by its successor"). Even though people don't often produce this answer, when given a choice some feel that it is a better answer than **mrrkkk**. People occasionally give the answer **mrrkkkk**, replacing both the group length and the letter category of the rightmost group by their successors. This answer confounds aspects of the two situations. The strings **abc** and **mrrjjj** are similar, since they both are woven together by the "fabric" of successorship; however, this similarity is abstract, since in one case the fabric is successor relations between letters and in the other case it is successor relations between group lengths. It thus seems strange to insist on retaining the notion of letter successorship in the group-length situation, where it no longer applies. It is as if a translator decided to tell the story of *War and Peace* in the context of the American Civil War but gave the (now American) characters the names Natasha and Alexey, refusing to let this aspect of the original novel slip. An even stranger translation would leave the names in the original Cyrillic letters, which might correspond to the answer **mrrdddd**. (Hofstadter has given the name "frame blends" to such mixtures of flexible and rigid thinking, which seem to be extremely common in thought and which are at the root of much humor of various kinds. See Hofstadter and Gabora 1990.)

People have also proposed answers such as **mrryyyy**, where the three **j**'s are replaced by four copies of a randomly chosen letter—here **y**. The reasoning is that since the successorship fabric in **mrrjjj** has nothing to do with the specific letters *M*, *R*, and *J*, it doesn't matter *which* letter value is used to replace the **j**'s. Such reasoning is too sophisticated for the current version of Copycat, which does not have the concept "randomly chosen letter." But even if Copycat could produce such an answer, I would still argue that **mrrjjjj** is the best answer to this problem. The letters *M*, *R*, and *J* serve as the medium for expressing the message "1-2-3," and I feel that the best solution is one that *preserves* that medium in expressing the modified message "1-2-4." Otherwise, why wouldn't **uggyyyy** be just as good as, if not better than, **mrryyyy**? Yet no one has ever proposed such an answer.

6. **abc ⇒ abd**
   aababc ⇒ ?

In problem 6 it is hard to make sense of the target string, and most people answer **aababd**, applying the rule "Replace the rightmost letter by its successor" directly. But if **aababc** is parsed as **a–ab–abc**, then a strong though abstract similarity to the initial string **abc** emerges in which the "rightmost letter" of **aababc** is the group **abc**, and its "successor" is **abcd**, yielding the answer **aababcd**.

I hope that the preceding problems help to make the case that although the analogies in this microworld involve only a small number of concepts, some of them require considerable flexibility and insight. Problem 7 is a particularly clear example of such an analogy.

7. **abc ⇒ abd**
   xyz ⇒ ?

At first glance this problem is essentially the same as problem 1 (with target string **ijk**), but there is a snag: *Z* has no successor. Most people answer **xya**, but in Copycat's microworld the alphabet is not circular and thus the program could not come up with this answer. We intentionally excluded it because one of the goals of the project is to model the process by which people deal with impasses. This problem forces an impasse that requires analogy-makers to restructure their initial view, possibly making conceptual slippages that were not initially considered, and thus to discover a different way of understanding the situation.

People give a number of different responses to this problem, including **xy** ("Replace the **z** by nothing at all"), **xyd** ("Replace the **z** by the literal letter **d**"—given the impasse, this answer seems less rigid and more reasonable than did **ijd** for problem 1), **xyy** ("If you can't take the **z**'s *successor*, then the next best thing is to take its *predecessor*"), and a number of other answers. However, there is one particular way of viewing problem 7 that, to many people, seems like a genuine insight, whether or not they come up with it themselves. The essential idea is that **abc** and **xyz** are "mirror images"—**xyz** is "wedged" against the end of the alphabet, and **abc** is similarly wedged against the beginning. Thus the **z** in **xyz** and the **a** in **abc** can be seen to correspond, and then one naturally feels that the **x** and the **c** correspond as well. Underlying these object correspondences is a set of slippages that are conceptually parallel: *alphabetic-first* $\Rightarrow$ *alphabetic-last*, *rightmost* $\Rightarrow$ *leftmost*, and *successor* $\Rightarrow$ *predecessor*. Taken together, these slippages convert the original rule into a rule adapted to the target string **xyz**: "Replace the *leftmost* letter by its *predecessor*." This yields a surprising but strong answer: **wyz**.

Copycat's microworld was designed to bring out very general issues—issues that transcend any specific conceptual domain. In that sense, the microworld was designed to "stand for" other domains. Thus, one is intended to conceive of, say, the *successor* (or *predecessor*) relation as an idealized version of *any* non-identity relationship in a real-world domain, such as "parent-of," "neighbor-of," "friend-of," "employed-by," or "close-to." A *successor group* (e.g., **abc**) then plays the role of any conceptual chunk based on such a relationship, such as "family," "neighborhood," "community," "workplace," or "region." Of course, the inclusion of "sameness" needs no defense; sameness is obviously a universal concept, much as is *opposite*. Although any real-world domain clearly contains many more than two basic types of relationships, two already suffice to make an inexhaustible variety of structures and events of arbitrary complexity.

The seven problems discussed above give some idea of Copycat's microworld, but they are only a small sample from a vast space of interesting analogy problems involving letter strings (chapter 5 and appendix A contain additional sample problems). These problems capture something of the flavor of the "first lady" examples given in chapter 1, illustrating how analogy-making requires fluid rather than rigid concepts: the process of making an analogy between two situations puts pressure on certain concepts in one situation (e.g., *president* and *wife*, or *rightmost*, *letter*, and *successor*), forcing them to slip into associated concepts in the other situation.

The current version of the Copycat program can deal only with problems in which the initial change involves the replacement of only one letter, which is why all the examples given above use the initial change **abc** $\Rightarrow$ **abd** (of course, the *answer* can involve a change of more than one letter, as in problems 2, 5, and 6). But this is a limitation of the program as it now stands. In principle, the domain is much larger.

2.2 Abilities Required for High-Level Perception and Analogy-Making

It is important to emphasize once again that the goal of this project is not to model specifically how people solve these letter-string analogy problems (it is clear that the microworld involves only a very small fraction of what people know about letters and what knowledge they might use in solving these problems), but rather to propose and model mechanisms for high-level perception and analogy-making in general. Analogy-making can be characterized very broadly as distilling the *essence* of one situation and *adapting* it (via conceptual slippage) to fit another situation. The letter-string analogy problems were designed to isolate and make very clear some of the mental abilities that are required for this process of understanding and perceiving similarity between situations. These abilities include the following (which, though listed separately, are of course strongly interrelated).

Mentally constructing a coherently structured whole out of initially unattached parts
This description is very broad, and could be given as a definition of "recognition." It applies not just to modality-specific recognition processes (such as interpreting visual scenes, recognizing faces, or comprehending utterances), but also to more abstract kinds of recognition (such as the recognition of *a coverup* or *a symphony in the style of Mozart*). The letter-string problems in Copycat's microworld are given to the program basically unlabeled; only bare-bones descriptions of each letter are given. Relationships and correspondences between letters are not given ahead of time, and it is up to the program to take the initially unattached letters and to weave them together into meaningful groupings and correspondences. The other abilities listed below are necessary for doing this.

Describing objects, relations, and events at the "appropriate" level of abstraction
What is "appropriate" depends on the situation, of course. People tend to agree on how abstract the description of a situation should be; that is, they agree on which things should be perceived in terms of the roles they play and which should be perceived more literally. For example, if one sees the Iran-Contra affair as "another Watergate," one focuses on Ronald Reagan in his role as "president" (and thus the counterpart of Richard Nixon) rather than, more literally, as "a man named Ronald Reagan." There is often competition among different possible descriptions: one could describe Oliver North as "a lieutenant colonel" (no lieutenant colonels played a significant role in Watergate), or as "the one who shredded the documents" (perhaps viewing *him* as the counterpart of Nixon, if one views the latter as "the one who erased the tapes"). Or one might view North as "the scapegoat who was following orders from higher up," seeing him as the counterpart of the Watergate burglars. Situations in the real world contain many different facets, and there is always competition among the various ways of perceiving these facets. Sometimes literal descriptions will be appropriate: Washington, for example, is literally the same in both the Watergate and Iran-Contra situations.

This tension between literal descriptions and abstract roles is very evident in Copycat's letter-string analogy problems. For example, in problem 1 (**abc ⇒ abd**, **ijk ⇒** ?) should the **c** in **abc** be described literally as "a *C*," or more abstractly in terms of its role as "the rightmost letter"? (There are, of course, other possible roles one could perceive the **c** as playing: "the third letter in the string," "the highest letter in the alphabetic sequence," "the successor of the **b**," and so on.) Likewise, should the **d** in **abd** be described as "a *D*," or should the successor relationship with respect to the **c** be perceived? The answers to these questions depend on the context. For the given problem, the description "Replace the rightmost letter by its successor" or "Replace the highest letter in the sequence by the next letter in the sequence" seems most appropriate (and these are almost always the ones given by people when they are asked to describe the change), since one wants to give a description of a given situation that one can fairly easily export to other situations, though without being too abstract and thus losing too much information. But consider the following problem:

1a. **abc ⇒ abd**
    xcg ⇒ ?

Here it might seem more reasonable than in the original problem to describe the **c** in **abc** at "face value" (i.e., using the rule "Replace *C* by *D*"), since there is an instance of *C* in the target string as well and since the target string lacks the successorship structure of the initial string. Such a view would yield the answer **xdg**, whereas the "Replace the rightmost letter by its successor" view would yield the answer **xch**.

An intermediate case is the following:

> 1b. **abc** ⇒ **abd**
>   **abcd** ⇒ ?

There is a tantalizing instance of *C* in the target string, tempting us to answer **abdd**; however, there is also an abstract description applying to both **abc** and **abcd**: both are increasing sequences beginning with *A*. The latter view lobbies for the answer **abce**, which is usually preferred by people.

Other variants, such as 1c and 1d, illustrate the variations and gradations in these pressures:

> 1c. **abc** ⇒ **abd**
>   **cde** ⇒ ?

> 1d. **abc** ⇒ **abd**
>   **cba** ⇒ ?

The point is that this central issue of perceiving roles versus literal descriptions and describing elements of situations at "appropriate" levels of abstraction can be captured to some extent in the letter-string domain, small and restricted as it is. Moreover, as can be seen from the preceding examples, one can explore this issue in great detail in the microworld by constructing *families* of analogy problems (as in 1a–1d, where each member of a family varies a certain pressure along a certain dimension). Copycat's behavior on several such families of problems (including problems 1a–1d) will be described in chapter 5.

Chunking certain elements of a situation while viewing others individually
Chunking is fundamental to perception at all levels. For instance, visually recognizing a chair requires mental chunking and labeling of its various parts (e.g., seat, back, arms). Aurally interpreting a spoken sentence requires mental chunking of phonemes, syllables, words, and so on. Similarly, in more abstract forms of perception, making sense of a situation and making analogies between situations requires determining which parts should be viewed (and perhaps mapped onto the other situation) as single units. For example, in Watergate, one might chunk Haldeman and Ehrlichman as a unit, and then map that unit to a North-Poindexter unit in the Iran-Contra situation, or one might perceive Congress as a single unit in both situations. (Similarly, a recent article about the biomedical researcher Jonas Salk quoted a critic as saying "He's no Watson-and-Crick.") The chunking issue arises frequently in letter-string problems—for example, in problem 2 (**abc** ⇒ **abd**, **iijjkk** ⇒ ?) and, more complexly, in problem 6 (**abc** ⇒ **abd**, **aababc** ⇒ ?), where discovering a useful parsing for the target string is rather difficult.

Focusing on relevant aspects and ignoring irrelevant or superficial aspects of situations
Any complex situation has a huge number of perceptible aspects, only some of which are relevant to a useful understanding of it. The ability to figure out which features are important and which can be ignored is fundamental to perception and analogy-making. For example, when looking for the Watergate counterpart of Ronald Reagan, do we care that Reagan has a wife named "Nancy"? When asking who played the role of Fawn Hall, do we pay attention to the fact that her boss (Oliver North) was a Marine? Do we care who was on the Senate investigating committee? This issue also plays a fundamental role in analogy-making in the letter-string domain. For example, in **abc** ⇒ **abd**, **kjih** ⇒ ?, do we care that there are three letters in **abc** and four letters in **kjih**? Does the **b** in **abc** have to correspond to anything in **kjih**? And is it important to take into account that the rightmost letter of **abc** is an instance of *C*? Elements of situations do not come pre-labeled with the "right" description attached. Likewise, they usually do not come pre-labeled as "important" or "relevant," though we often have *a priori* knowledge about what kinds of things are likely to be important or relevant. The perceiver is required to use both *a priori* knowledge and what has already been perceived about a given situation to determine which aspects are important and essential and which are irrelevant and superficial.

A very important point must be made here. The phrase "the ability to figure out which features are important and which can be ignored," used in the preceding paragraph, misstates the issue somewhat. The problem is not, by any means, merely one in which many possible aspects of the situation are set before you and you have to chose the ones to use in creating an interpretation or analogy. Perception does not merely involve deciding which *clearly apparent* aspects of a situation should be ignored and which should be taken into account. It also involves the process by which *not clearly apparent* aspects—concepts that were initially considered to be irrelevant, or which were not even considered to be part of the situation in the first place—*become* apparent and relevant in response to pressures that emerge as the understanding process takes place. In other words: Sometimes, under certain pressures, concepts come into play that you initially did not even suspect were part of the situation in any way.

As an example of these ideas, suppose you invite your good friend Greg to dinner and he doesn't show up on time. What do you do? At first, simple, standard explanations and actions come to mind: he was briefly delayed; he ran into traffic; he had trouble parking. But as half an hour passes, then an hour, then two, the explanations and actions you think of become more and more extraordinary. The following might come to mind: call his office (no answer); call his apartment (no answer); check your calendar to make sure the dinner date is tonight (it is); rack your brain trying to remember if he warned you he might be late (you have no such memory); call friends of his to see if they know where he is (they don't); call his parents in Philadelphia (they haven't heard from him in weeks); call the police (they suggest checking the hospital); call the hospital (he's not there); go to his apartment (he's not there); ask his neighbors if they've seen him lately (they last saw him this morning); drive along routes he would likely have taken (he's nowhere to be seen); buy a megaphone and call out his name as you drive along; call several airlines to see if he's on a plane leaving town tonight; turn on the TV to see if you can spot him sitting in the audience of his favorite talk show; check the date on today's newspaper to see if you've accidentally traveled several days into the future through a time warp; and so on. Though the last few are outlandish, most of these thoughts did occur to my friends and me when we were in such a situation. The point is that as time goes by and pressure builds up, one's thoughts go farther and farther out on a limb. One considers things that one never would have considered initially, letting seemingly unquestionable aspects of the situation slip under mounting pressure: Did I dream that I invited him? Did we have a falling-out that I forgot about? Did he leave town and not tell me?

Not only are certain concepts explicitly present in one's mental representation of a situation (e.g., you consciously believe that Greg was driving); there are also implicit associations with those concepts, most of which stay well below the level of awareness. In view of Greg's lateness, the thought that he is driving might easily evoke an image of his having trouble parking (a strong association). However, it is less likely that, early on, you will imagine him in a car accident. This weaker association is potentially there, but will not be brought into the picture without pressure (he is quite late, it is dark outside, etc.). This illustrates a general point: Wildly strange ideas (or even ideas slightly past one's defaults) do not continually occur to a normal person for no good reason; a person to whom this happens is classified as crazy. Time and cognitive resources being limited, one must resist nonstandard ways of looking at situations when there is no strong pressure to do so. You don't check the street sign on your corner every morning to make sure the name hasn't changed. You don't check under your car for a hidden bomb every time you want to drive. Likewise, counterintuitive ideas in science come about only in response to strong pressures. For example, had the Michelson-Morley experiment come out the other way (i.e., had it proved there is an ether) and had Einstein still proposed special relativity, with all its deeply counterintuitive notions, it would have been seen as just a fascinating crackpot theory, not a great scientific advance. Not only is pressure needed for one to bring in previously uninvolved concepts in trying to make sense of a situation, but the concepts brought in are related to the source of the pressure. (This bears on the discussion in the previous chapter concerning what kinds of slippages are made in counterfactual thinking. These ideas overlap with Kahneman and Miller's [1986] treatment of counterfactuals.)

In short: Flexibility in thought requires the potential for unexpected concepts to be brought into one's understanding of a situation, but only in response to pressure. An *a priori* absolute exclusion of a whole class of concepts initially assumed to be irrelevant is too rigid; one might then be prevented from coming up with unexpected new ways of looking at things. On the other hand, limitations of space and time make it impossible for *all* one's concepts to be made equally available for use in forming mental representations. A premise of the model being proposed here is that the presence or absence of a concept in a situation is not black-and-white. Rather, all one's concepts should have the *potential* to become relevant in any situation. However, owing to the need for cognitive economy, they cannot all be made available all the time or to the same degree. Instead, one must somehow manage to keep seemingly irrelevant concepts pretty much in the background most of the time, without absolutely and irrevocably excluding them.

These issues of graded relevance and availability of concepts in different situations come up often in the letter-string domain. For example, consider problem 5:

5. abc $\Rightarrow$ abd
   mrrjjj $\Rightarrow$?

You want to make use of the salient fact that **abc** is an alphabetically increasing sequence, but how? This internal "fabric" of **abc** is a very appealing and seemingly central aspect of the string, but at first glance no such fabric seems to weave **mrrjjj** together. So either (like most people) you settle for **mrrkkk** (or possibly **mrrjjk**), or you look more deeply. But where to look when there are so many possibilities? The interesting thing about this problem is that there happens to be an aspect of **mrrjjj** lurking beneath the surface that, once recognized, yields what many people feel is a more satisfying answer. As was discussed above, if you ignore the *letters* in **mrrjjj** and look instead at *group lengths*, the desired successorship fabric is found: the lengths of groups increase as "1-2-3." Once this hidden connection between **abc** and **mrrjjj** is discovered, the rule describing **abc** $\Rightarrow$ **abd** can be adapted to **mrrjjj** as "Replace the length of the rightmost group by its successor," which yields "1-2-4" at the abstract level, or, more concretely, **mrrjjjj**. But bringing the nonstandard concept of *length* into the picture requires strong pressures. These pressures include the top-down pressure to perceive successor relations in **mrrjjj** once they have been noticed in **abc**, the fact that once groups of letters are perceived in **mrrjjj** the notion of *length* becomes weakly active and lingers in the background, and the decreased resistance to bringing in nonstandard concepts after more standard ones have failed to yield progress in making sense of the situation at hand. Thus, this problem demonstrates how a previously irrelevant, unnoticed aspect of a situation emerges as relevant in response to pressures.

Taking certain descriptions literally and letting others slip when perceiving correspondences between aspects of two situations
As was shown by the "first lady" examples in chapter 1, even when roles (such as "wife of the president") have been perceived in a situation (e.g., the United States) they cannot always be exported smoothly to a new situation (e.g., Great Britain). Either the roles have to be abstracted further ("spouse of the head of state") or slippages have to be made (*president* $\Rightarrow$ *prime minister, wife* $\Rightarrow$ *husband*). The process of perceiving correspondences between situations involves fights among pressures to use descriptions literally, to make descriptions more abstract, and to let descriptions slip into related descriptions. (Notice that there is a distinction between *ignoring* certain aspects of a situation because they are deemed to be irrelevant and letting one's descriptions of certain aspects *slip* precisely because they *are* relevant but do not apply in their current form to the new situation.) The letter-string domain was designed primarily to focus on the question of how different pressures interact to trigger appropriate slippages. Problems 2–7 illustrate several different translations of the same rule

("Replace the rightmost letter by its successor"), each involving slippages triggered by different pressures that come up in the perception of the different target strings.

Exploring many plausible avenues of possible interpretations while avoiding a search through a combinatorial explosion of implausible possibilities
A serious problem in trying to model perception is figuring out how to deal with the combinatorial explosion of possibilities in interpreting a situation. Competition must exist; however, since the number of possible ways of interpreting a situation and making correspondences between situations is so large, not all possibilities can be explored fully (in fact, most cannot be explored at all). This potential combinatorial explosion exists even for the simple situations in the letter-string domain (for example, in problem 6 there are quite a number of possible ways in which the string **aababc** could be structured and mapped onto the string **abc**)—though, of course, to a much lesser degree than for real-world situations. In any case, since the goal of the Copycat project is to propose and test mechanisms for high-level perception and analogy-making *in general* rather than specifically in the letter-string domain, we must make sure that the program does not take advantage of the small size of the microworld. Instead, the program must, as people do, have ways of circumventing exhaustive search of any kind. To do so, it is necessary to use information as soon as it is obtained to narrow the exploration of possibilities. For example, in making an analogy between the Watergate and Iran-Contra scandals, if you decide that the notion of "erasing tapes" in the Watergate situation corresponds to "shredding documents" in the Iran-Contra situation, then this view should make a mapping between Rosemary Woods (Nixon's personal secretary, who erased tapes) and Fawn Hall (North's secretary, who shredded documents) more worthy of consideration than a mapping between, say, Woods and Reagan's personal secretary. Likewise, when one is solving problem 3 (**abc** ⇒ **abd**, **kji** ⇒ ?), if *successorship* has been identified as a seemingly useful notion in the initial string, there should be top-down pressure to consider it in the target string as well. And if you perceive the two strings as increasing alphabetically but in different spatial directions (and thus make the slippage *right* ⇒ *left*), then a mapping between **c** and **k** (with the slippage *rightmost* ⇒ *leftmost*) becomes much more compelling, and consideration of a **c–i** mapping less likely. The process of using information as it is obtained not only involves allowing what is noticed to activate and reshape existing concepts in a bottom-up manner, but also involves allowing existing concepts to direct perception in a top-down manner. This interaction of bottom-up and top-down modes of processing is an essential part of the Copycat program.

The notion of competing pressures
The abilities discussed above all illustrate how analogy-making necessarily entails competition among the huge number of possible ways of interpreting a situation and of seeing similarities between situations. As can be seen in the various examples given above, a fundamental notion here is that of competing *pressures* acting on the analogy-maker. Certain pressures are always strong in any analogy: for example, there is always a pressure to map salient things (such as "the president") onto other salient things, a pressure to map identical

things (and very similar things) onto each other, and a pressure to use abstract descriptions (or roles) rather than literal descriptions. Other situation-specific pressures arise during the process of analogy-making, and any interesting analogy is the result of interaction and competition among these possibly conflicting pressures. The Copycat program is a model of this interaction and competition among mental pressures, and the letter-string microworld provides an arena in which all these various pressures arise in particularly clear ways. Also, the strengths of pressures can be minutely varied by constructing families of analogies such as the family given in 1a–1d above.

2.3 Retrieval

In Copycat's domain, both analogues (the initial and target strings) are given ahead of time, and some part of the initial string (e.g., **abc**) is highlighted by the presence of the modified string (e.g., **abd**), in which something has changed. This contrasts with the usual way in which people make analogies: they are confronted with a situation, and either that reminds them of another situation with which they make an analogy (e.g., my "without-beverages-flight/overflowing-fountain" analogy from the previous chapter) or they construct a fictional situation that is analogous to the original situation in order to understand or to make some point about the original situation (e.g., the analogy between "provocative" clothing and an expensive watch). This problem of how people are reminded of situations or construct hypothetical situations has to do with the question of how memories are stored and retrieved. The Copycat project does not deal with this question directly, although many of the issues it does deal with—e.g., categorization, perception of similarity, slippage, and competition among interacting pressures—are closely related to questions about memory and retrieval. A faith underlying this research is that, for the time being, the problem of how people understand and make analogies between *given* situations can be investigated separately from the problem of how people are reminded of one thing by another, though many of the same issues will be investigated, and research on the former will thus yield insights useful to research on the latter, and vice versa. This faith is shared by most cognitive scientists working on models of analogy-making (including Gentner [1983], Holyoak and Thagard [1989], and Kedar-Cabelli [1988b], among others), though the process of memory retrieval in the context of analogy-making has been investigated by a number of researchers (including Gick and Holyoak [1983], Schank and Leake [1989], and Thagard et al. [1990]).

2.4 Defense of the Microworld

The following are the most frequently raised objections to the use of letter-string analogy problems for the purpose of constructing a model of analogy-making.

"The problems are too simple and have no relation to real-world analogy-making."
I hope the discussion in the previous section has (at least partially) demonstrated the relation between the letter-string problems and "real-world" analogy-making. Although the letter-string analogies are abstract and idealized, this

lack of "real-world" flavor is in some ways advantageous: it is very clear exactly what knowledge the program does have, and people are less likely to mistakenly believe that the program has an understanding of complex real-world concepts when it doesn't or that the program's behavior is more intelligent than it really is. It is sometimes too easy to ascribe intelligence to a program on the basis of its seeming ability to deal with concepts about which we humans know a lot but about which the program actually knows almost nothing. This has been a recurring problem in artificial-intelligence research (see, e.g., Woods 1975 and McDermott 1981). The point of working in a microdomain in cognitive science is to isolate a phenomenon (such as analogy-making), strip it down to its bare bones, and get rid of its extraneous real-world trappings while retaining its essence so that it can be investigated more clearly.

"They are not real analogies; they are more like the proportional analogies on standardized tests or like sequence-extrapolation problems."
There is a large difference between the usual "proportional" analogy problems on standardized tests such as the Scholastic Aptitude Test (e.g., "foot : shoe :: hand : ?") and Copycat's letter-string analogies. Copycat's problems could be stated in the same form (e.g., **abc : abd :: iijjkk : ?**); however, unlike the three-word SAT analogies, each string has quite a lot of internal structure to it, with many possible correspondences between parts of the first and third strings instead of just one global correspondence between two atomic entities (e.g., "foot" and "hand"). The letter strings are more like multi-part situations than like single words. A better comparison would be with the geometric analogy problems of Evans (1968). Copycat's task has also been compared to sequence extrapolation. Problems based on the initial change **abc ⇒ abd** have the flavor of sequence extrapolation, but the program is by no means limited to solving such problems. But even the **abc ⇒ abd** problems are quite different from typical sequence-extrapolation problems, most of which use mathematical formulas that have little to do with the kinds of perceptual processes we are investigating. Other computer models of pattern perception and sequence extrapolation in strings of letters have been constructed (see, e.g., Simon and Kotovsky 1963), but the patterns used have generally not explored the range of issues discussed in the previous section. (One exception is the Seek-Whence program of Hofstadter and Meredith [Meredith 1986], which dealt with many of these issues.)

"Each problem is purposeless, and none has any use in real-world problem-solving, so it is impossible to decide among rival answers to any problem."
This objection seems to me to have two parts: (1) Is it possible to give any answer to these letter-string analogy problems? (2) How can we say that, for a given analogy problem in this domain, one answer is any better than another? The first part comes from the claim that, because there is no notion of "purpose" in these letter-string problems (i.e., the analogies are not being used for solving real-world problems), there are no grounds for giving any answer. This objection seems to me to be easily refuted by the fact that people quite readily give answers to the letter-string problems and often have very strong opinions about the merit of their answer versus other answers. Moreover, in daily life,

people make countless "purposeless" analogies all the time; the human mind is continually perceiving, categorizing, and noticing all kinds of concrete and abstract similarities. Several examples of such ubiquitous analogies were given in the previous chapter. A conscious purpose, if there is one, is one pressure among many, and usually is one of the factors that serve to highlight certain aspects of the source analogue (Burstein and Adelson 1987; Kedar-Cabelli 1988b). For example, Kedar-Cabelli discusses how one could decide which features of a ceramic mug should be taken into account when making an analogy with a Styrofoam cup, given that the purpose is to determine whether or not the latter could be used to drink hot liquids. But one could certainly make an analogy between the mug and the cup (in the sense that they could be seen as essentially similar) without that specific purpose in mind, since both have features that are salient *a priori* and relationships that one notices even in the absence of any conscious purpose. Likewise, **abc** and **ijk**, say, have intrinsic similarities that are noticed even when there is no conscious purpose for doing so. A conscious purpose, being part of an overall context (often a relatively important part), serves to enhance the relevance of certain features. In the letter-string domain, the change of the initial string into the modified string (e.g., **abc** $\Rightarrow$ **abd**) plays a similar role in that it highlights certain aspects of the initial string and helps indicate what aspects of the strings one should take into account when making an analogy (e.g., the spatial positions—such as *rightmost* and *leftmost*—of elements in the string).

This notion of a conscious *purpose* as a *sine qua non* for analogy-making comes, I believe, from a somewhat narrow view in which analogy-making is seen as a tool to be used in problem-solving, rather than as a ubiquitous and pervasive mode of thought that blends smoothly into recognition and categorization. No one would argue that recognition and categorization are done only when there is a conscious purpose. Recognition and categorization are activities that for us are as automatic as breathing—this automatic processing has evolved in order to ensure our survival in the world. Analogy-making is a result of the same automatic mechanisms.

The second part of the objection (about the possibility of judging the relative merit of answers) can also be countered in the same way: People *do* have preferences when answering these problems. They see certain answers as strong and others as weak or even ridiculous. Of course, there is not always universal agreement on a single "right" answer to a given problem. Although there are generally a small number of answers that people will give to a problem, preference *within* that set depends on individual taste.

In the real world, the analogies people find compelling are analogies that take into account the essential features of situations and that strip away superficial and irrelevant aspects. Often, the more hidden or deep the shared essence, the more interesting and compelling the analogy. What is "essential" in a situation often has a very definite meaning in the real world: it is what one *must* perceive in order to survive and succeed in one's environment. In an artificial domain, such as that of the letter-string analogy problems, there is no such objective way of determining which answers are good and which are bad. But even so, people feel that certain ways of looking at a given problem are better than other ways, because they are using perceptual mechanisms that evolved to deal with real situations in the real world. These mechanisms do not get turned on and off simply because the domain is seemingly artificial and content-free and because our survival does not depend on our actions. (This fact is implicitly acknowledged by the general acceptance of abstract visual analogy problems for use on intelligence tests. Most people agree that the solution of such problems has *something* to do with intelligence.) Thus, since analogy problems in this artificial letter-string domain have an "essence" to be perceived, people perceive it and are able to base their answers on it.

2.5 Specific Goals of the Copycat Project, and Judging the Program's Performance

Two general goals for the Copycat project are that the program act with intelligence (albeit of a limited kind in a limited domain) and that its internal architecture and external behavior make it a plausible model of the aspects of *human* intelligence that we are investigating. These two facets are, of course, not simple to separate. It could be argued (and I believe it is in part true) that the more intelligently the program acts, the more plausible it is as a model of human intelligence. However, it is certainly possible for a program to act with considerable intelligence—in a limited domain—but for its intelligence to arise from internal mechanisms that are very different from those of the human mind. A salient example of this is the recent rise of chess-playing programs to near-grandmaster capability. These programs play chess by searching through a huge number of possible moves from a given board configuration, many moves into the future, and then selecting the move that promises the best future outcome. Psychologists agree that human chess experts do not play in this way; rather, they rely upon high-level pattern-spotting abilities to recognize certain abstract patterns on the board, and they then move in ways appropriate to those patterns (deGroot 1965). Chess-playing programs act intelligently, but their intelligence comes from a very different source. However, chess is a very limited domain, and it is not at all clear that a program whose intelligence was more wide-ranging, and that included very fundamental human abilities such as categorization and analogy-making, could operate on principles very different from those underlying human intelligence.

A major goal of the field of artificial intelligence is to discover the general principles of intelligence, not necessarily its specific instantiation in brains. For instance, some AI researchers gain inspiration from other natural systems, such as biological evolution (Holland 1986) or the immune system (Farmer, Packard, and Perelson 1986). The goal of psychology, on the other hand, is to understand the mechanisms of human (or animal) intelligence and behavior. Thus, the Copycat project is part artificial intelligence and part psychology. One motivation is the desire to understand in general how flexibility and adaptability—the hallmarks of intelligence—come about in complex systems (and metaphors from both biology and society have been used in designing Copycat's architecture). Another motivation is the desire to understand the nature of high-level perception and concepts specifically in humans. These two very long-term goals are intimately related; it may be that one cannot be accomplished without the other. The hope is not merely that Copycat acts intelligently, but that it does so *because* it uses mechanisms like those of human intelligence, thus more directly shedding some light on what these mechanisms are. Copycat as it currently stands is, of course, a far cry from human intelligence, even in its very limited domain. But the hope is that, in spite of its limitations, Copycat captures something significant about the mechanisms of human perception and analogy-making, and that even where it is wrong it captures enough to be interestingly and usefully wrong. The hope is that the mechanisms being proposed have enough truth to them that the program's successes and failures say something interesting and helpful about what is right and wrong with these mechanisms.

How are we to assess the program's performance with regard to both its AI and its psychological aspects?

There are three performance criteria to be addressed:

• To what extent is Copycat able to a solve a range of problems in its domain that capture the central issues we are studying, coming up with solutions that that demonstrate the possession of fluid concepts?

• To what extent are Copycat's internal mechanisms general and psychologically plausible? By "general" I mean not dependent on the small size or the specific details of the letter-string domain, but able to work in more complex, real-world domains. By "psychologically plausible" I mean not at odds with known psychological facts, and not employing implausible processes, such as exhaustive search through all possible interpretations of a given situation.

• To what extent are the more specific behaviors of the program (e.g., the range of the answers it gets to a particular problem, the relative time it takes to get certain answers, or certain identifiable stages in its processing, such as "hitting a snag" in **abc** $\Rightarrow$ **abd**, **xyz** $\Rightarrow$?) plausible behaviors for a human?

2.5.1 Demonstrating the Range of Copycat's Abilities

The domain of letter-string analogy problems is rich and open-ended; a large number of issues in recognition and analogy-making can be explored in it. I think it is plausible to postulate that any computer program that could fully match human ability in this domain would be well along the way to being a generally intelligent program. The current version of Copycat is, of course, far from this. However, the various letter-string analogy problems discussed in this chapter do capture a number of central issues in high-level perception and analogy-making, and the ability to solve a large range of such problems would demonstrate that Copycat has a fair amount of conceptual fluidity—that it is able to make appropriate conceptual slippages in a number of different situations.

Problems 1–3, 5, and 7 were chosen by me as targets for the current version of Copycat. (Problems 4 and 6 are beyond the capabilities of the current version of Copycat, which can get the solution **aababcd** to problem 6 (**abc** $\Rightarrow$ **abd**, **aababc** $\Rightarrow$?) in principle but which in practice gets this solution about once in several thousand runs.) It is generally too difficult for the program to discover and maintain the necessary parsing of the target string (**a–ab–abc**). Copycat is currently unable to get the solution **acg** to problem 4 (**abc ⇒ abd, ace ⇒ ?**) even in principle, since it lacks the ability to construct new temporary concepts such as *double successor*.)

The results of the program's performance on these problems, given in chapter 4, demonstrate most of its current capabilities.

The point, of course, is not merely to get Copycat to solve a particular set of five problems, but to construct a program that is able to deal with the general issues that are contained (in idealized form) in those problems. Each of the five problems requires different kinds of perceptual structures to be built and different kinds of conceptual slippages to be made, so the fact that the program (whose mechanisms are meant to be general, not specific to the letter-string domain) can deal with these five cases demonstrates that its concepts do have considerable fluidity in adapting to different situations in its microworld.

Since the program uses general mechanisms to solve these problems, it can also solve a large number of other problems. Each of the five target problems can be modified in many different ways; a set of such modifications produces a family of problems in which pressures are varied along different axes (as in problems 1a–1d). Copycat's performance on 24 variants of the original five problems, displayed in chapter 5, shows how robust and flexible the program is when it is stretched to deal with problems that it was not specifically designed to work on.

2.5.2 Demonstrating the Generality and Plausibility of Copycat's Internal Mechanisms

As was discussed in chapter 1, Copycat's architecture brings together a number of ideas for modeling the mechanisms underlying high-level perception and conceptual slippage. Although Copycat makes analogies only in the letter-string world, these mechanisms are meant to be general. They are not meant to rely on any specific details of the letter-string world, on the fact that there are only a small number of concepts in the microworld, or on the fact that the situations with which the program is faced are relatively simple. The mechanisms are also meant to be psychologically plausible.

2.5.3 Comparing Copycat's Behavior with Human Behavior

The range of the program's abilities and the generality and psychological plausibility of the proposed mechanisms can lend some credence to Copycat as a model of human psychological processes, but it is of course desirable to obtain further evidence that the mechanisms we are proposing are psychologically valid. We need to see how well the program holds up under more detailed comparisons of its behavior with human behavior.

Designing and evaluating such comparisons present some difficulties, however. As has been pointed out, Copycat is not a model of how people solve letter-string analogy problems *per se*; rather, the letter strings are meant to be taken as tiny abstract models of real-world situations. Copycat's knowledge of letters and strings is very limited, and it does not involve many detailed aspects of human perception of letter strings, such as that English-speaking people read from left to right and know the alphabet better forward than backward.

These aspects of perception are specific to letter strings and are not relevant to the larger task of modeling recognition processes in general. Thus, since the program is not modeling the domain-specific aspects of how people solve letter-string analogy problems, direct comparisons between the details of how people solve these letter-string problems and how Copycat solves them (such as precise timing comparisons) are not useful for determining the program's psychological plausibility.

In spite of these difficulties, there are some comparisons that can be made. One reason the letter-string domain was chosen was because people *can* relate to it and can solve the problems. After a bit of practice, people generally have no trouble obeying the restrictions of the domain as far as producing and judging answers are concerned. Thus, there can be some useful comparisons between what people do and what the program does, as long as they are not too fine-grained with regard to the letter-string domain or the specific actions of the program.

As will be seen in chapter 3, Copycat is nondeterministic and thus produces different answers on different runs (e.g., on most runs on **abc** ⇒ **abd**, **ijk** ⇒ ? the answer **ijl** is given, but on some runs **ijd** is given, and other answers show up occasionally). Moreover, as will be seen, Copycat's *temperature* at the end of a run gives the program's assessment of the quality of the answer constructed in that run, so it is possible, by performing a large number of runs on the same problem, to determine both the relative frequencies of different answers to a given problem and Copycat's assessment of their relative quality (the most frequently given answer is not always the answer judged to be the best).

Many people have proposed seeing how well the frequencies of Copycat's different answers to a given problem match the frequencies given by a population of people, and how well Copycat's rankings of the quality of different answers match the average rankings given by people. However, these are not appropriate comparisons. Copycat has its own biases, and it is not meant to match the average behavior of a *population* of people; rather, it is meant to model something more akin to a single *individual*, who has his or her own individual biases. That is, Copycat is meant to be a plausible model of a single person with a certain set of biases and preferences. The frequencies of different answers are meant to model the degrees to which the competing pressures leading to those different answers are present in the mind of a single person solving the given problem.

What comparisons are useful, then? Since Copycat is meant to be a plausible model of an individual, it should not exhibit behavior that is unhumanlike. It should not do things that humans never do, and it should have the potential to do the things that humans actually do (given the limitations of the letter-string domain). For the purposes of this project, I chose two types of comparisons to help further evaluate the program's psychological plausibility in this regard:

> • For a given problem, the program should be able (on different runs) to get all the answers that people abiding by the constraints of the microworld get, and should never produce answers that people find completely un-justified. Since the letter-string domain reflects general issues in high-level

perception and analogy-making, the answers that people get are a function of how they respond to these general issues that are embedded in the letter-string problems. Thus, the program's response to these general issues should be similar to that of people, in terms of the range of answers that can be given.

• The difficulties experienced by people should also be experienced by the program. People find some problems more difficult than others, so the program should experience roughly the same relative difficulties (provided that the difficulties are not due to something outside the domain, such as a case where one of the strings spells a word). For example, people universally find problem 7 (**abc** $\Rightarrow$ **abd, xyz** $\Rightarrow$?) harder than problem 1 (**abc** $\Rightarrow$ **abd, ijk** $\Rightarrow$?); it would therefore be implausible if the program solved both with equal ease. One way to test this is to compare the relative times taken by people and by the program on these problems (and others). Also, if people reliably experience a particular difficulty in solving a problem, then the program should also experience that difficulty. For example, if people given **abc** $\Rightarrow$ **abd, xyz** $\Rightarrow$? always initially try to replace the **z** by its successor, and hit an impasse, it would be implausible if the program were able to avoid this difficulty. Or if people often have a hard time making sense of the target string in **abc** $\Rightarrow$ **abd, mrrjjj** $\Rightarrow$?, it would be implausible if the program easily noticed the relationships among the group lengths. When I say that the program should experience the same difficulties as people, I mean not that these difficulties should be "pre-programmed" in any sense, but that the behavior should emerge naturally from the mechanisms being proposed in the program's architecture—that is, from the mechanisms whose psychological plausibility is being evaluated.

Satisfying these various criteria will not prove that the program has psychologically valid mechanisms; it will only show, to the degree that the criteria are satisfied, that the mechanisms it has are not implausible. And although these specific psychological tests can help to lend more plausibility to the model, the most important criteria are more general: Does the program exhibit flexible and insightful behavior in its microworld? Does it act as if it had fluid concepts, as people do? Does it help us to better understand what concepts are?

Chapter 3

The Architecture of Copycat

3.1 Jumbo

Before embarking on the Copycat project (first described in Hofstadter 1984a), Hofstadter originated two other computer modeling projects—Jumbo and Seek-Whence—to investigate high-level perception and conceptual slippage. The Jumbo program was developed by Hofstadter (1983) and the Seek-Whence program by Meredith (1986). Jumbo was intended to be a short-term test of some ideas about high-level perception processes rather than a long-term project resulting in a sophisticated cognitive model. It was expressly designed as a "warmup" for the more ambitious Seek-Whence and Copycat projects. Because Jumbo contained precursors of many of the features of Copycat, it will be useful to briefly describe Jumbo's architecture before giving an overview of Copycat. (Seek-Whence will be discussed and compared with Copycat in chapter 9.)

Jumbo's task was the creation of plausible anagrams. (Its name comes from the "Jumble" anagram puzzles that appear in newspapers.) It was given a set of "jumbled" letters, and its job was to use those letters to create one or more English-like words. Jumbo had no dictionary; its knowledge consisted of how, in English, consonant and vowel clusters are formed out of letters, syllables out of clusters, and words out of syllables. Given a set of isolated letters (atomic units), it was able to gradually and hierarchically construct "gloms" (chunks at the level of letters, clusters, syllables, or words).

The point of the program was to model, in a very simple domain, "the unconscious composition of coherent wholes out of scattered parts"—the process of "constructing larger units out of smaller ones, with temporary structures at various levels and permanent mental categories trying to accommodate to each other" (Hofstadter 1983). The program needed to engage in a large amount of back-and-forth motion in constructing, destroying, and regrouping structures; it needed data structures that were "fluidly reconformable" in the process of coming up with a single structure that included all the letters and obeyed some formal rules of English words—a "pseudo-word." Of course, the solution of anagram puzzles could have been done more easily and quickly by a brute-force method in which all combinations were tried out and checked against a dictionary, but this would have defeated the purpose of the project, which was to construct a psychologically plausible model of some ideas for mechanisms underlying general perceptual processes.

The philosophy of the Jumbo project (as well as of the Seek-Whence and Copycat projects) is that high-level perception is not the result of using a set of serially applied, conscious mental rules, but rather that it emerges as a statistical outcome of large numbers of independent activities occurring in parallel, competing with and supporting one another, and influencing one another by creating and destroying temporary perceptual constructs. Such a system has no global executive deciding which processes to run next and what each should do. Rather, all processing is done locally by many simple, independent agents that make their decisions probabilistically. The system is self-organizing, and coherent and focused behavior is a statistically emergent property of the system as a whole. The presumption behind this philosophy is that the processes making up this "seething broth" of activity are below the level of consciousness, and thus cannot be examined introspectively, but that any computer model attaining a good degree of human-like flexibility will have to be implemented at this "subcognitive" level. These ideas have been discussed in detail by Hofstadter (1984a, 1985d); another argument for modeling at the subcognitive level has been given by Smolensky (1988).

The architecture of Jumbo (as well as that of Seek-Whence and Copycat) was inspired in part by the Hearsay-II speech-recognition program. Hearsay-II's input is a raw, unperceived waveform, and the program consists of a number of independent "knowledge sources" that interact both cooperatively and competitively to hierarchically build up a coherent interpretation of the utterance. Likewise, in Jumbo all processing is done by "codelets"—small special-purpose pieces of code that act independently to build up hierarchical gloms from an initially unconnected set of jumbled letters. As will be seen, Jumbo's (and Copycat's) codelets are much simpler and act more locally than Hearsay's knowledge sources, and many more of them run in the course of solving a problem.

In addition to the ideas from Hearsay-II, there were two metaphors that guided the development of Jumbo's architecture. The first metaphor involves biological cells—in particular, the way in which complex molecules are constructed in parallel and asynchronously by independent processes taking place throughout a cell's cytoplasm. For each type of molecule, there is a standard chemical pathway for assembling it, which may involve dozens of steps. The cell has no central executive coordinating these steps; rather, these construction activities rely on essentially random encounters between enzymes and substrates. The construction of complex molecules comes about as a result of wave after wave of enzymatic activity in which products of one set of enzymes become substrates for the next wave of enzymes, and in which enzymes are themselves produced in response to the current "needs" of the cell. In Jumbo, codelets play the role of enzymes, randomly encountering letters and gloms (molecules) in the program's "cytoplasm" and attempting to join them together to form ever-larger structures. Complex structures are built up gradually by chains of codelets.

For any given set of letters there are, of course, many possible "glomming" paths (i.e., ways of putting letters and gloms together) to explore, just as in real-world perception there are a huge number of possible ways in which unconnected raw sensations can be put together to form a global semantic interpretation. One of the purposes of the Jumbo project was to test ideas about a strategy for efficiently searching through this potential combinatorial explosion of possibilities and quickly zeroing in on a good and coherent interpretation (or "pseudo-word"). These ideas were inspired in part by a second metaphor: the parallel, probabilistic, and dynamically self-adjusting search strategy used by a person in looking for a mate. When searching for romance, you initially consider many people simultaneously—the people you happen by chance to meet (though this is not totally random, since you tend to look in places where you think you will be more likely to meet interesting people). Some people you can dismiss almost immediately as possible romantic partners; they are clearly just not your type for some reason or other. Others you consider a bit more seriously, though the amounts of consideration are not equal; the amount of time and interest put into each possibility depends on your initial attraction to the person. You get to know some of these people better, and on the basis of your further evaluation of them (and also on the basis of how much they like you) you decide whom to concentrate on. You spend more and more time with a smaller and smaller set of people, though all the while perhaps still giving some small amount of consideration to one or two people you initially didn't find very interesting or to new people that you happen to meet. Thus, you are constantly reallocating your time and interest among the possible candidates for your affections according to how promising each relationship seems, until finally a relationship seems so promising that you decide to "commit" and give the lion's share of your time to this one person. However, commitment is not necessarily the end of the story; even after marriage you are likely to meet other people, and you may engage in "harmless flirtations" with people who (depending on their attractiveness and the strength of your commitment) might receive some further consideration. Depending on its seeming promise and on the state of your marriage, the rival exploration might even come to threaten your original commitment.

Hofstadter termed this strategy, in which many possible courses of action are explored in parallel but not all are are given the same amount of consideration or explored at the same speed, a *parallel terraced scan*. (The exploration is "terraced" because it is carried out in stages of increasing depth, entry into each new stage being contingent upon the success of the previous stage.) Possible paths are explored at a speed and to a depth proportional to moment-to-moment evaluations of their promise: the speed of an exploration process is locally adjustable to reflect the current assessment of the promise of the path being explored. In most situations in the real world, there are too many possibilities to explore; given real-time pressures, it is impossible to check them all out fully, or even to give some time to each of them. Instead, there has to be parallel investigation of many possibilities to different levels of depth. The system can afford lots of quick forays, even into unlikely territory, but it cannot afford to explore all of them deeply, much less to act upon every one. No path of exploration should be excluded in principle, though many have to be excluded in fact, since time is limited (e.g., when searching for a mate, you can't meet everyone in the world, though you probably shouldn't absolutely exclude anyone or any group *a priori*; whom you *do* meet is probabilistic).

As time goes on and as progress is made, the mode of search gradually changes from highly parallel and random (with a large number of possibilities of different degrees of promise considered simultaneously) to highly serial and deterministic (with only the few most promising possibilities considered). The Jumbo project proposed this type of strategy as a general feature of intelligence.

In the following description of glom construction (or destruction, or regrouping) in Jumbo, the influences of the cell metaphor and the romance metaphor on the program's architecture can be clearly seen. In Jumbo, a glom (such as "sch," say, from the set of letters "c o s h n o g i l") is built only after a series of evaluations of its quality. The initial evaluations are quick and superficial, but the later ones are more elaborate. If at any time one of these evaluations is too negative (decided probabilistically), the process of evaluation is curtailed. The glom is built only if the evaluation process goes all the way to the end. Each evaluation step is carried out by a codelet, and if the codelet's verdict is favorable then that codelet posts a new codelet to carry out the next evaluation in the series. Thus, any given glom in Jumbo is built up by a series of codelet actions. An evaluation (made by a codelet) of a potential glom not only helps determine *whether* the evaluation process should continue; it also returns a numerical score, reflecting the codelet's estimate of *how promising* that particular glom is. That score is used to assign an *urgency* value to the next codelet in the series, which helps to decide how long that next codelet has to wait before it can run. (Similar multi-codelet chains also lead to the destruction or regrouping of gloms.)

Jumbo's parallelism arises from the interleaving of many different glom-building processes. This occurs as follows: All codelets waiting to run are placed in a data structure called the *Coderack*, and at each time step the system probabilistically chooses one codelet from the Coderack to run, the choice being based on the relative urgencies of all codelets in the Coderack at that time. The higher a codelet's urgency, the higher the probability that the codelet will be selected; this means that even low-urgency codelets have some chance of being selected. (As will be described below, the system's temperature affects these probabilities, with high temperature tending to level the effects of urgency and low temperature making them more pronounced.) When a codelet is chosen to run, it is removed from the Coderack. At the beginning of a run of the program, the Coderack contains a standard initial population of codelets. As codelets run and are removed from the Coderack, they often add new, followup codelets whose purpose is to continue pursuing seemingly promising tasks. Like the enzyme population in a cell, the Coderack's population changes, as processing proceeds, in response to the needs of the system as judged by previously run codelets.

Since all waiting codelets reside in the Coderack, and one codelet is chosen at a time from the entire Coderack population, a parallel terraced scan of possibilities results: in a given run, many competing or cooperating attempts at building various gloms are interleaved, the speed of each glom-building process being a statistical outcome of the urgencies of its component codelets. Thus, many interleaved processes proceed in parallel, each at a speed and to a depth proportional to its estimated promise as assessed from moment to moment. (The parallelism in Jumbo is asynchronous, in the sense that events do not depend on precise timing relationships with other events; there is no sense in which two processes can said to be "in phase" with respect to each other.)

In the Jumbo project, Hofstadter also first introduced his notion of a temperature variable, whose value reflects the overall "happiness" of the program at a given time—that is, how close the program estimates it is to creating a single high-quality coherent pseudo-word (the happier the program, the lower the temperature). This value, in turn, is used to control the amount of randomness with which decisions are made in the program. The temperature starts out high and falls as structures are built. Since the program uses probability to choose which codelet runs next, the idea is that, as the program gets closer to a solution, the temperature falls, causing a decrease in randomness, which results in a speedup of the rate at which promising possibilities are explored with respect to less promising ones. Thus, good paths of exploration tend to crowd out worse ones at an ever-increasing rate, and the system is "frozen" into a solution when the temperature gets low enough. (The differences between this notion of temperature and that used in the optimization process known as "simulated annealing" are discussed in the next section.)

In summary: The main ideas of the Jumbo program include a cell-inspired architecture in which structures are built up in a piecemeal fashion by competing and cooperating chains of simple, independently acting agents (codelets); a notion of fluid reconformability of structures built by the program (such as gloms); a parallel terraced scan of possible courses of action; and a temperature variable that dynamically adjusts the amount of randomness in response to how "happy" the program is with its existing structures. The result is that the program's overall behavior is not directly programmed; rather, it is a statistically emergent outcome of the interaction of many microscopic computational activities. All these ideas provide the basis for Copycat's architecture as well. Since the point of the Jumbo project was to test these ideas to some extent before using them in the Seek-Whence and Copycat projects, their implementation in Jumbo was by no means completely satisfactory. Many of the ideas, such as temperature, were only very sketchily implemented, and the program was rather limited. Copycat is a much fuller and more sophisticated implementation of these basic ideas. It has required (on the part of Hofstadter and myself) a great deal of further development and reworking of the basic ideas from Jumbo, as well as the addition of many mechanisms not present in Jumbo.

3.2 Broad Overview of Copycat

Copycat's task is to use the concepts it possesses to build perceptual structures—descriptions of objects, bonds between objects in the same string, groups of objects in a string, and correspondences between objects in different strings—on top of the three "raw," unprocessed strings given to it in each problem. The structures the program builds represent its understanding of the problem and allow it to formulate a solution. Since for every problem the program starts out from exactly the same state with exactly the same set of concepts, its concepts have to be adaptable, in terms of their relevance and their associations with one another, to different situations. In a given problem, as the representation of a situation is constructed, associations arise and are considered in a probabilistic fashion according to a parallel terraced scan (as in Jumbo) in which many routes toward understanding the situation are tested in parallel, each at a rate and to a depth reflecting ongoing evaluations of its promise.

Copycat's solution of letter-string analogy problems involves the interaction of the following mechanisms:

- concepts consisting of a central region surrounded by a halo of potential associations and slippages, in which the relevance of the concept and the proximity to other concepts change as the process of perception and analogy-making proceeds
- mechanisms for probabilistically bringing in concepts related to the current situation and conceptual slippages appropriate for creating an analogy
- a mechanism by which concepts' relevances decay over time unless they are reinforced
- agents that continually look for interesting properties and relationships among objects and structures in a working area and attempt, on the basis of their findings, to build new descriptions, bonds, groups, and correspondences
- mechanisms for applying top-down pressures from concepts already deemed to be relevant
- mechanisms allowing competition among pressures
- the parallel terraced scan, allowing rival views to develop at different speeds
- temperature, which measures the amount of perceptual organization in the system (low temperature meaning a high degree of organization) and which, on the basis of this value, controls the degree of randomness used in making decisions.

Figure 3.1 is a schematic diagram showing the four main elements of Copycat's architecture: the Slipnet, the Workspace, the Coderack, and a thermometer representing the temperature. These elements will be described below.

3.2.1 The Slipnet

Copycat's concepts reside in a network of nodes and links called the *Slipnet* (because it is the source of all slippages). A small part of it is illustrated in figure 3.2, which shows nodes, links (solid lines), and some labels on links (thick fuzzy lines).

A concept's central region is a node, and its associative halo potentially includes any of the nodes linked to the central node.

Activation in the Slipnet

A node (such as *successor* or *group*) is activated when instances of it are perceived (by codelets, as described below). During a run of the program on a given problem, the probability that a node (such as *successor*) will be brought in or be considered further by codelets at any given time as a possible organizing concept is a function of the node's current activation level. Thus, there is no black-and-white answer to the question of whether a given concept is consciously used at a given time; continuous activation levels and probabilities allow different concepts to be present—and thus to exert influence on the course of processing—to different degrees. All concepts have the potential to

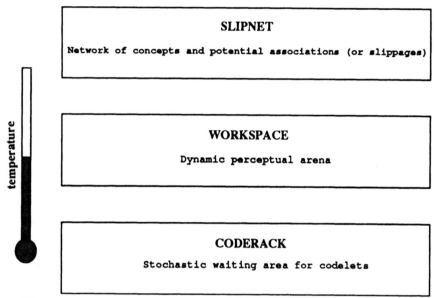

Figure 3.1
A schematic diagram of Copycat's architecture.

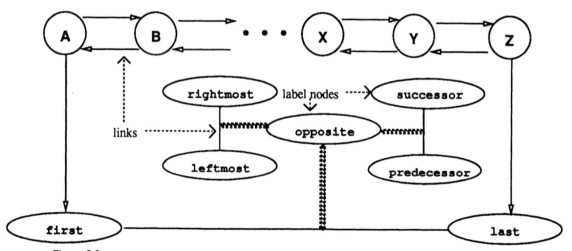

Figure 3.2
A small part of Copycat's Slipnet.

be brought in and used. Which ones become relevant, and to what degree, depends on the situation the program is facing.

A node spreads activation to nearby nodes as a function of their proximity; thus, conceptual neighbors of relevant nodes have the potential to be brought in. For example, the node *A*, when active, spreads some activation to *first* (since *A* is the first letter in the alphabet), giving the latter some probability of being used as a description. Nodes lose activation unless their instances continue to be perceived by codelets.

Conceptual Depth in the Slipnet

The rate of activation decay is not the same for all nodes, but is a function of the node's *conceptual depth* value. (Hofstadter [1984a] has called this measure *semanticity*.) The conceptual depth of a node is a static, pre-assigned number intended to capture the generality and abstractness of the concept. For example, the concept *opposite* is deeper than the concept *successor*, which is in turn deeper than the concept *A*. It could be said roughly that the depth of a concept is how far that concept is from being directly perceptible in situations. For example, in **abc ⇒ abd, kji ⇒** ? the presence of instances of *A* is trivially perceived, recognizing the presence of *successorship* takes a little bit of work, and recognition of the presence of the notion *opposite* is a subtle act of abstract perception. Deep notions such as *opposite*, which are far from direct perception, are more likely to be involved in what people consider to be the *essence* of a situation than more shallow, easily perceived notions such as the letter category of a particular object (e.g., *A*). Therefore, once aspects of greater depth are perceived, they should have more influence on the ongoing perception of the situation than aspects of lesser depth.

The idea is that a deep concept (such as *opposite*) is normally relatively hidden from the surface and cannot easily be brought into the perception of a situation, but once it has been perceived it should be regarded as highly significant. Thus, conceptually deeper nodes, once active, decay more slowly than conceptually shallower nodes, allowing deeper notions to persist longer (and thus have more influence on what structures are built) than shallower ones. This builds into the architecture a strong drive, if a deep aspect of a situation is perceived, to try to use this aspect in constructing an overall understanding of the situation.

The hierarchy defined by conceptual-depth values is quite distinct from abstraction hierarchies such as

poodle ⇒ *dog* ⇒ *mammal* ⇒ *animal* ⇒ *living-thing* ⇒ *thing*.

These terms are all potential descriptions of a particular object at different levels of abstraction. By contrast, the terms *A*, *successor*, and *opposite* are not descriptions of one particular object in **abc ⇒ abd, kji ⇒** ?; rather, they are descriptions of different aspects of the situation, at different levels of abstraction. Conceptual depth is also different from Gentner's (1983) "abstractness" measure; the differences will be discussed in subsection 9.1.1.

The conceptual-depth values in the Slipnet are fixed, and were pre-assigned by me mainly on the basis of intuition (as well as through trial and error). They are discussed in more detail later in this chapter and in appendix B.

Links and Slippages in the Slipnet

The length of a link between two nodes represents the conceptual proximity or degree of association between the nodes: the shorter the link, the greater the degree of association. (The apparent lengths of links in figure 3.2 are not meant to represent their actual relative lengths.) Like activation, link lengths are not constant; they can vary in response to what has been perceived. Many links have *labels* that are themselves nodes. For example, as shown in figure 3.2, the link between *rightmost* and *leftmost* is labeled by the node *opposite*, as is shown in figure 3.2. Likewise, the successor and predecessor links between letters are labeled by the nodes *successor* and *predecessor* (these labels are not shown in the figure). When a label node is active (indicating that the relationship it represents, e.g. *opposite*, is perceived to be relevant to the problem at hand), all the links labeled by that node shrink—that is, such relationships are perceived as being closer, or more slippable.

Decisions about whether or not a slippage is allowed from a given node (say, *rightmost*) to a neighboring node (say, *leftmost*) are made probabilistically, as a function of the conceptual proximity of the two nodes. (Such decisions are made by codelets.) For example, in the problem **abc ⇒ abd, kji ⇒ ?**, if the program notices that the initial and target strings are alphabetically in opposite directions, then *opposite* will be activated, thereby increasing the allowability of slippages between nodes connected by an *opposite* link, such as *rightmost ⇒ leftmost*. Thus, the plausibility of allowing a slippage between two nodes depends on context.

Concepts in the Slipnet

In this model, a *concept* (such as *rightmost*) is identified not with a single node but rather with a region in the Slipnet, centered on a particular node and having blurry rather than sharp boundaries: neighboring nodes (such as *leftmost*) can be seen as being included in the concept probabilistically, as a function of their proximity to the central node of the concept. Here "included in" means "slippable from," or, in other words, "equated for the purpose of the given analogy." Just as in quantum mechanics, where the spatial position of an electron is "decided" only at the time it is measured, the composition of a concept in semantic space is decided only when slippages are explicitly made. For instance, in the problem **abc ⇒ abd, iijjkk ⇒ ?**, is the group **kk** an instance of the concept *letter*? If one makes a correspondence from the **c** to the group **kk**, then one is effectively saying "in this context, yes"; that is what the slippage *letter ⇒ group* says. This is what we mean by "fluid concepts": people are able to take a rule like "Replace the rightmost letter by its successor" and allow the words in it (such as "letter") to be flexibly extended. In this context, one sees the rule as "Replace the rightmost 'letter' by its successor," where the scare quotes around the word "letter" signify that here it is being used loosely to refer to a *group* as well. The whole point of the Copycat project is to study how perception and concepts interact so that one knows which words in the rule to allow to slip, and how to let them slip, while still maintaining the spirit of the original rule.

One could metaphorically compare a concept in the Slipnet to the metropolitan area of a city. For example, the New York metropolitan area is not a well-defined area with exact boundaries, but rather a central region diffusing continuously into outlying suburbs, with rather blurry edges. One could say that the conceptual proximity of a given location to New York is the probability that a person who lives there will answer "New York" when asked where he or she is from. (For anyone from outside the strict city limits, this might entail a slippage, e.g., *Hoboken ⇒ New York*.) The conceptual proximity here is context-dependent; it depends not only on the physical distance of the given location from the center of Manhattan, but also on who is asking the question and why, how familiar that person is with New York, how interested he or she is in the answer, how much time there is to answer, how reluctant one might be to answer

"New Jersey," and so on. Likewise, in the Slipnet, the conceptual proximity from a given node and its neighbors is context-dependent. For example, in some situations (e.g., **abc** ⇒ **abd**, **kji** ⇒ ?) the node *leftmost* may be closely associated with the node *rightmost*, making a slippage from one to the other more permissible, whereas in other situations (e.g., **abc** ⇒ **abd**, **ijk** ⇒ ?) the conceptual proximity and the likelihood of allowing that slippage are much less.

Since the conceptual proximity between two nodes is context-dependent, concepts in the Slipnet are emergent rather than explicitly defined. In other words, it is not pre-ordained whether, say, *group* is part of the concept *letter*, or whether *leftmost* is part of the concept *rightmost*. As will be seen, the degree to which a given node is part of a given concept emerges from a large number of activities that take place as the program attempts to solve the problem it is faced with. Moreover, since the proximity between two nodes gives only the *probability* that a slippage will be possible, concepts are blurry and never explicitly defined.

In sum: Concepts are able to adapt (in terms of relevance and association to one another) to different situations. Copycat does not include learning in the usual sense; the program neither retains changes in the network from run to run nor creates new permanent concepts. However, this project does concern learning if that term is taken to include this notion of adaptation of one's concepts to novel contexts.

3.2.2 The Workspace

In addition to the Slipnet, where long-term concepts reside, Copycat has a *Workspace*, in which perceptual structures are built hierarchically on top of the "raw" input (the three strings of letters). The program builds six types of structures:

- *descriptions* of objects (e.g., *leftmost* as a description of the **a** in **abc**)
- *bonds* representing relations between objects in the same string (e.g., a successorship bond between the **a** and the **b** in **abc**)
- *groups* of objects in the same string (e.g, the **ii** group in **iijjkk**)
- *correspondences* between objects in different strings (e.g., a **c-kk** correspondence in **abc** ⇒ **abd**, **iijjkk** ⇒ ?)
- a *rule* describing the change from the the initial to the modified string (e.g., "Replace the rightmost letter by its successor")
- a *translated rule* describing how the target string should be modified to produce an answer string (e.g., "Replace the rightmost *group* by its successor").

Any structure has a time-varying *strength* value that is a function of a number of factors; these will be discussed in subsection 3.4.4.

Figure 3.3 displays a possible state of Copycat's Workspace illustrating many of these structures. Here a number of bonds (short arcs between letters within a string, representing various sameness and successorship relations) have been built. Note that each successor bond has a spatial direction (indicated by an arrow on the arc), whereas sameness bonds have no direction. In the current version of Copycat, only one bond can be built between two adjacent letters. This means that, for example, the **a** and the **b** in **abc** cannot be connected by

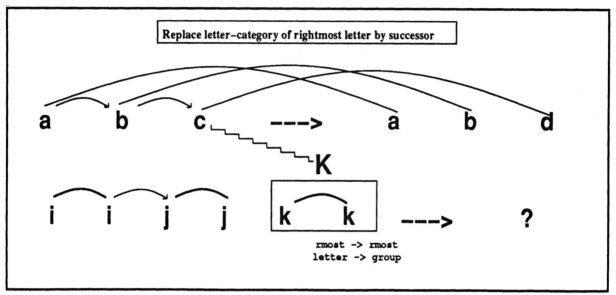

Figure 3.3
A possible state of Copycat's Workspace, with several types of structures shown.

both a right-going successor bond and a left-going predecessor bond; a choice has to be made about which direction the bond is to go in. The same is true for groupings of letters: for example, the string **abc** can be seen as either a right-going successor group or a left-going predecessor group, but not both simultaneously. Such choices often make a considerable difference in the ultimate analogy.

In figure 3.3, a group has also been built, indicated by the rectangle around the two **k**'s. It is marked on top by a single **K**, which gives the letter category of this group. Once built, a group acts as a unitary object much like a letter: it now can itself be an element in a bond, in a group, or in a correspondence. In addition, three initial-to-modified-string correspondences have been built. The rule "Replace letter category of rightmost letter by successor" (shown at the top of the figure) has been based on these correspondences. Here "letter category" makes explicit which aspect of the **c** has changed. The reason for spelling this out in the rule is that objects—letters and groups—in the Workspace can have more than one changeable aspect. For example, the group **jjj** in **mrrjjj** might be perceived to have letter category *J* and length 3. If both these aspects are perceived, either one can be a candidate for modification when making an analogy. This will be seen clearly in the run of the program on **abc** ⇒ **abd**, **mrrjjj** ⇒ ? that will be displayed in chapter 4. Finally, there is also a correspondence (represented by a jagged line) from the **c** to the group of **k**'s, and below it are displayed the concept mappings it is based on: *rightmost* ⇒ *rightmost* and *letter* ⇒ *group*. These reflect the view that the group **K** plays the same role in the target string as the **c** plays in the initial string: Each is rightmost in its string. However, that mapping requires a slippage from *letter* to *group*. (The letter categories of the two corresponding objects, *C* and *K*, are ignored in this correspondence, since in the Slipnet there is no close relation between these nodes.)

Descriptions attached to letters and groups are not displayed in figure 3.3; the set of descriptions the program starts out with will be displayed later on.

Copycat's Workspace is meant to correspond to the mental region in which representations of situations are dynamically constructed. (The counterpart of Copycat's Workspace in Jumbo was called the "Cytoplasm," reflecting the influence of the cell metaphor.) As in Jumbo, this construction process is carried out by large numbers of simple agents called *codelets*. A codelet is a piece of code that carries out some small, local task that is part of the process of building a structure. For example, in problem 5, one codelet might notice that the two r's in **mrrjjj** are instances of the same letter; another codelet might estimate how well that proposed bond fits in with already-existing bonds; another codelet might build the bond. *Bottom-up* codelets ("noticers") work toward building structures on the basis of whatever they happen to find, without being prompted to look for instances of specific concepts; *top-down* codelets ("seekers") look for instances of particular active nodes, such as *successor* or *sameness-group*. As in Jumbo, codelets waiting to run reside in a data structure called the *Coderack*, and are chosen one at a time to run (on the basis of the relative urgencies of all the currently waiting codelets).

Any structure is built by a series of codelets running in turn, each deciding probabilistically—on the basis of progressively deeper estimations of the structure's promise—whether to continue the evaluation process by generating one or more followup codelets or to abandon the effort at that point. If the decision is made to continue, the running codelet assigns an urgency value (on the basis of its estimation of the structure's promise) to each followup codelet, and posts the followup on the Coderack. This urgency helps to determine how long each followup codelet will have to wait before it can run and continue the evaluation of that particular structure—the higher the urgency, the shorter the wait is likely to be.

Once a structure has been built, it can indirectly influence the building of other structures, helping to accelerate the construction of structures that support it and working to suppress the construction of structures that rival it. Incompatible structures cannot exist simultaneously; fights between such structures are decided probabilistically on the basis of their strengths.

3.2.3 The Coderack

Codelets can be viewed as representing various pressures in a given problem. Bottom-up codelets represent pressures present in all situations (the desire to make descriptions, to find relationships, to find correspondences, and so on). Top-down codelets represent pressures evoked by the situation at hand (e.g., the desire, in the problem **abc** $\Rightarrow$ **abd**, **mrrjjj** $\Rightarrow$?, to construct more sameness groups in the target string once some have already been made).

Any run starts with a standard initial population of bottom-up codelets (with pre-set urgencies) on the Coderack. As was said before, at each time step one codelet is chosen to run and is removed from the current population on the Coderack. Since the choice is probabilistic, biased by relative urgencies in the current population, Copycat differs from an "agenda" system such as Hearsay-II, which, at each step, executes the waiting action with the highest estimated priority. The the urgency of a codelet does not represent an estimated *priority*;

rather, it represents the estimated relative speed at which the pressures represented by this codelet should be attended to. If the highest-urgency codelet were always chosen to run, the lower-urgency codelets would never be allowed to run, even though the pressures they represent have been judged to deserve some attention. Using probabilities to choose codelets allows each pressure, over time, to get the amount of consideration it is judged to deserve, even when the judgments change as processing proceeds. This allocation of resources is an emergent statistical result rather than a pre-programmed deterministic one.

Codelets that take part in building a structure send activation to nodes in the Slipnet that represent the concepts associated with that structure. These activations in turn affect the makeup of the codelet population, since active nodes (e.g., *successor*) are able to add codelets to the Coderack (e.g., top-down codelets that try to find successor relations between pairs of objects). Thus, as the run proceeds, new codelets are added to the Coderack population either as followups to previously run codelets or as top-down scouts for active nodes. (Also, new bottom-up codelets are continually added to the Coderack.) A new codelet's urgency is assigned by its creator as a function of the estimated promise of the task it is to work on. In particular, the urgency of a followup codelet is a function of the result of the evaluation done by the codelet that posted it, and the urgency of a top-down codelet is a function of the activation of the node that posted it. (The urgency of each type of bottom-up codelet is fixed.) Thus, the codelet population on the Coderack changes, as the run proceeds, in response to the system's needs as judged by previously run codelets and by activation patterns in the Slipnet, which themselves depend on what structures have been built.

The speed of a structure-building process emerges dynamically from the urgencies of its component codelets. Since those urgencies are determined by ongoing estimates of the promise of the structure being built, the result is that structures of greater promise will tend to be built more quickly than less promising ones. The upshot is a parallel terraced scan—more promising views tend (statistically) to be explored faster than less promising ones. There is no top-level executive directing the processing here; all processing is carried out by codelets. Although Copycat runs on a serial computer, and thus only one codelet runs at a time, the system is roughly equivalent to one in which many independent activities are taking place in parallel, since codelets work locally and to a large degree independently.

The fine-grained breakup of structure-building processes thus serves two purposes: it allows many such processes to be carried out in parallel, by having their components interleaved, and it allows the computational resources allocated to each such process to be dynamically regulated by continually updated estimates of the promise (reflected by codelet urgencies) of the pathway being followed.

It is important to understand that in this system the structure-building processes, each of which consists of many codelets running in a series, are themselves *emergent* entities. Any sequence of codelets that results in a coherent macroscopic act (e.g., the forming of a successor group out of the entire string **iijjkk**, which involves the building of several bonds and the formation of several groups within the string) can *a posteriori* be labeled a process but large-scale processes are not laid out in advance. That is, a process is not pre-determined and then broken up into small components; instead, processes are simply the pathways visible, after the fact, that lead to some coherent macroscopic act of construction or destruction of organizational structure. Only the codelets themselves are pre-determined; the macroscopic processes of the system are emergent.

For example, there is nothing in the program that says "See if the target string can be made into a successor group," with instructions on how to do so; there are only individual codelets that perform small, local actions. Thus, although one can look back at a run of the program and identify certain "processes" that were interleaved and that ran at different speeds, the way this actually comes about is very different from standard time-sharing systems in which each of a number of well-defined and separate processes is given a certain time slice as a function of its priority. At any given time during a run of Copycat, one cannot take the codelets currently in the Coderack and determine which ones belong to which large-scale process. Until the program has run to completion, it cannot be said what the various processes are; it is even unclear what should be dubbed a process. Each codelet's task is one step in a very large number of potential processes that may or may not unfold. To describe the program's large-scale actions in terms of "processes," as has been done here, is really just a convenient shorthand. (A general discussion of the necessity of randomness in intelligent systems and the notion of emergent rather than predetermined macroscopic *processes* is given by Hofstadter and Mitchell [in press].)

3.2.4 Temperature

A final mechanism, *temperature* (discussed above with respect to the Jumbo project), has two roles: it measures the degree of perceptual organization in the system (its value at any moment is a function of the amount and quality of structure built so far) and it controls the degree of randomness used in making decisions (e.g., which codelet should run next, which objects a codelet should choose to work on, which structure should win a fight). Higher temperatures reflect the fact that there is little information on which to base decisions; lower temperatures reflect the fact that there is greater certainty about the basis for decisions. Thus, decisions are made with more uniform randomness at higher temperatures than at lower temperatures. The program also uses temperature in deciding when to stop building perceptual structures and to construct an answer—stopping is more likely at low than at high temperatures. The final temperature at the end of a run can be taken as a rough indication of the program's satisfaction with the answer it has created (the lower the temperature, the higher the program's assessment of the final answer).

The role of temperature in Copycat (and Jumbo) differs from that in simulated annealing (Kirkpatrick et al. 1983), an optimization technique sometimes used in connectionist networks (see, e.g., Hinton and Sejnowski 1986 and Smolensky 1986). In simulated annealing, temperature is used exclusively as a top-down randomness-controlling factor, its value falling monotonically according to a pre-determined, rigid annealing schedule. By contrast, in Copycat, the value of temperature reflects the current quality of the system's understanding;

temperature thus acts as a feedback mechanism to determine the degree of randomness used by the system. A similar mechanism has been used by Wilson (1987) in the context of genetic algorithms, and by various neural network researchers (e.g., Lewenstein and Nowak [1989]).

Copycat's temperature-controlled nondeterminism allows the program to avoid an apparent paradox in perceiving situations: you can't explore every possibility, but you don't know which possibilities are worth exploring without first exploring them. You need to carry out *some* exploration in order to assess the promise of various possibilities, and even to get a clearer sense of what the possibilities are (e.g., the notion of *length* in **abc** $\Rightarrow$ **abd**, **mrrjjj** $\Rightarrow$?, which initially would in all likelihood not even be considered a possibility to explore). You must be open-minded, but the territory is so vast that you cannot explore all of it. In Copycat, the fact that codelets are chosen probabilistically rather than deterministically allows the exploration process to be a fair one, neither deterministically excluding any possibilities *a priori* nor being forced to give equal consideration to every possibility.

This is the role of nondeterminism in Copycat: it allows different pressures to be given the amounts of consideration they seem to deserve, with this allocation of resources shifting dynamically as new information is obtained. The possibility that seems best should never crowd out other possibilities entirely—especially early in a run, when the information about what is "best" tends to be unreliable. Temperature is, in effect, a measure of how reliable the current information is. And temperature, in turn, by controlling the degree of randomness, controls the degree to which the system is guided by the current information. The program's initial random explorations can be seen as a means toward gaining greater certainty about what to do next. Temperature-controlled nondeterminism is what allows the program to gain and use this increased certainty.

There is much redundancy at the level of individual codelets, especially among the codelets exploring the most promising possibilities, and the action of any one codelet does not make a difference in the program's overall behavior. Rather, all high-level effects, such as the parallel terraced scan, are statistical results of large numbers of codelet actions and probabilistic choices made by the program of which codelets to run. (A typical run of Copycat consists of hundreds—or sometimes, depending on the problem, thousands—of codelet steps.)

Copycat's distributed asynchronous parallelism, like Jumbo's, was inspired by the self-organizing activity that takes place in a biological cell (Hofstadter 1984a). As was outlined in the discussion of Jumbo, in a cell all activity is carried out by large numbers of widely distributed enzymes of various sorts. These enzymes depend on random motion in the cell's cytoplasm in order to encounter substrates (relatively simple molecules, such as amino acids) from which to build up larger structures (such as proteins). Complex structures are built up through long chains of enzymatic actions, and separate chains proceed independently and asynchronously in different spatial locations throughout the cytoplasm. Moreover, the enzyme population in the cell is itself regulated by the products of the enzymatic activity, and is thus sensitive to the moment-to-moment needs of the cell. In Copycat, as in Jumbo, codelets roughly act the part of enzymes. All of the activity is carried out by large numbers of codelets, which choose objects in a probabilistic, biased way for use in the building of structures. As in a cell, the processes by which complex structures are built are not explicitly programmed, but are emergent outcomes of chains of codelets working in asynchronous parallel throughout Copycat's Workspace (its "cytoplasm"). And just as in a cell, the population of codelets on the Coderack is self-regulating and sensitive to the moment-to-moment needs of the system. To carry this analogy further, the Slipnet could be said to play the role of DNA, with active nodes in the Slipnet corresponding to genes currently being expressed in the cell, controlling the production of enzymes.

Hofstadter's purpose in inventing this metaphor was to draw inspiration from the mechanisms of self-organization in a fairly well-understood natural system, and to use these ideas in thinking about the mechanisms of high-level perception. The mechanisms of enzymes and DNA in a cell are not to be taken literally as a model of perception. Rather, general principles can be abstracted and carried over from the workings of cells to the workings of perception. Distributed asynchronous parallelism, emergent processes, the building up of coherent complex structures from initially unconnected parts, self-organization, self-regulation, and sensitivity to the ongoing needs of the system are all central to our model of perception, and thinking about the workings of the cell has helped in devising mechanisms underlying these principles in Copycat.

3.3 The Slipnet in Detail

Figure 3.4, an expanded version of figure 3.2, shows all the nodes and links in the Slipnet. (The sizes of nodes and the lengths of links in this diagram are arbitrary, and do not indicate anything about the actual nodes and links.)

3.3.1 Slipnet Nodes

The network includes nodes representing the following possible descriptors for objects and structures:

- The 26 letters of the alphabet.
- The numbers 1 through 5. (The program does not know any numbers higher than 5, and currently the only way the program uses numbers is to describe the lengths of groups.)
- The nodes *leftmost*, *rightmost*, and *middle* (the various possible positions of an object in a string) and the nodes *whole* (which is used to describe a grouping of a whole string) and *single* (which is used to describe a letter that is the sole constituent of its string).
- The two possible spatial directions for bonds and groups, *left* and *right*.
- The two possible types of objects in strings, *letter* and *group*.
- The two distinguished positions in the alphabet, *first* and *last*.
- The three possible types of bonds that can be built between objects: *predecessor*, *successor*, and *sameness*. Note that *successor* and *predecessor* relations are labels ("s" and "p") on links between letters and numbers.
- The three types of groups that can be made out of related objects in a string: *predecessor-group*, *successor-group*, and *sameness-group*.

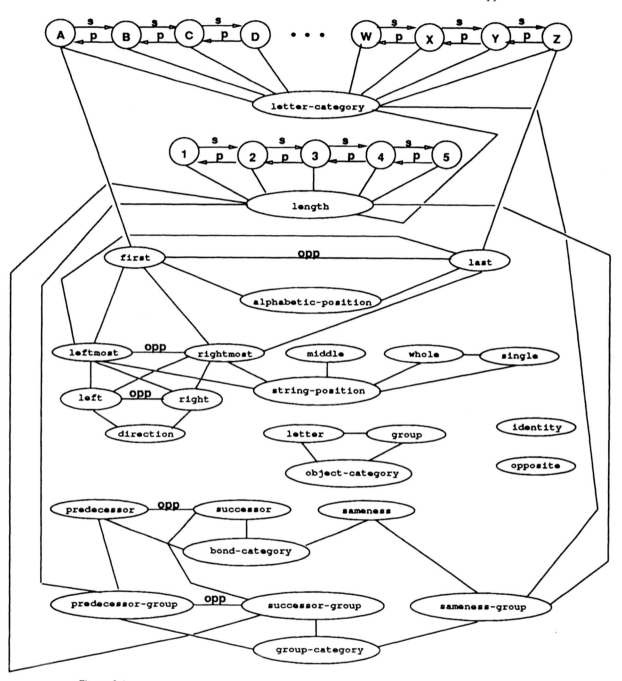

Figure 3.4
Copycat's Slipnet.

In addition, the network includes the following nodes representing the various *categories* of descriptions—that is, nodes corresponding to *types* of descriptions rather than descriptions themselves:

- *letter-category* (linked to the letter-category nodes, *A–Z*)
- *length* (linked to the number nodes, *1–5*)
- *string-position* (linked to the three string-position nodes, *leftmost, middle,* and *rightmost*)
- *direction* (linked to the two possible spatial directions, *left* and *right*)
- *object-category* (linked to the two types of objects, *letter* and *group*)
- *alphabetic-position* (linked to the two distinguished alphabetic positions, *first* and *last*)
- *bond-category* (linked to the three possible bond categories, *predecessor, successor,* and *sameness*)
- *group-category* (linked to the three possible group categories, *predecessor-group, successor-group,* and *sameness-group*).

When a node corresponding to a description category (e.g., *length* or *alphabetic-position*) is active above a certain threshold, this means that descriptions of that type (e.g., *1, 2, . . . ,* or *first* and *last*) are relevant, and attempts should be made (via top-down codelets) to use such descriptions in making sense of the given letter strings. The use of these nodes will be described in more detail later in this chapter, and will be illustrated in chapter 4.

Finally, there are the nodes *identity* and *opposite*, which label relationships in the Slipnet. In figure 3.4, *opposite* relations are labeled with "opp," and any node has an implicit identity relation to itself. Note that there is a distinction in the system between *sameness* and *identity*: the former is a type of relation between letters or groups, such as the two **r**'s in **mrrjjj** (actual objects in the Workspace) and the latter is a type of relation between nodes in the Slipnet. This distinction was made in the current version of Copycat in order to separate the relevance of *sameness relations* inside a string (e.g., between the two **r**'s in **mrrjjj**) from the relevance of *identity mappings* between strings (e.g., the *rightmost* ⇒ *rightmost* mapping between the **c** and the **k** in **abc** ⇒ **abd, ijk** ⇒ ?).

3.3.2 Activation in the Slipnet

Activation levels of Slipnet nodes are not binary but can vary continuously between 0 and 100% (at 100%, the node is said to be "fully active"). When a node's activation reaches a certain threshold (50% in the current version of the program), there is a probability (which is a function of the node's activation) that the node will discontinuously become fully active. In a very rough sense, a Slipnet node can be thought of as analogous to a cell assembly (Hebb 1949), with the node's activation level corresponding to the percentage of neurons active in the cell assembly. If enough neurons are active in a cell assembly, the entire assembly will tend to become active as a result of close connections among the cells. This is modeled by the probabilistic discontinuous jump in activation in a Slipnet node when the activation is above a certain threshold. (The 50% threshold in the current version of Copycat was chosen through trial and error.)

A node becomes fully activated when a codelet builds an instance of it in the Workspace, and activation spreads over links between neighboring nodes as a function of the length of the link. In addition, the activation of each node decays over time, with the decay rate depending on the node's conceptual depth. The higher the conceptual depth, the slower the decay. In the current version of the program, every time the Slipnet is updated each node loses a percentage of its activation equal to 100 minus that node's conceptual depth.

3.3.3 Conceptual-Depth Values of Slipnet Nodes

The following is a list of the nodes in order of increasing conceptual depth (nodes listed on the same line have equal conceptual-depth values):

- *A* through *Z*
- *letter*
- *letter-category*
- *1* through *5*
- *leftmost, rightmost, middle, whole, single, left, right*
- *predecessor, successor, predecessor-group, successor-group*
- *first, last*
- *length*
- *string-position, direction*
- *alphabetic-position, bond-category, group-category*
- *sameness, sameness-group*
- *object-category, identity, opposite.*

The conceptual-depth value for each node was assigned by me and is permanent (it does not vary during a run or from run to run). The actual values are given in appendix B. There was no formal method for assigning these rankings; they were reached through a combination of intuition, trial and error, and some arbitrariness, and are not necessarily optimally tuned in the current version of the program. An experiment on the program that involved modifying these values will be described in chapter 8.

3.3.4 Slipnet Links

There are five main classes of links in the Slipnet, some of which are similar to typical classes in semantic networks:

- *Category links*, which link the various possible descriptors of a given category node to that category node (e.g., linking the 26 letters to the node *letter-category*, or the three types of bonds to the node *bond-category*).
- *Instance links*, the inverse of Category links, which link the category nodes to their instances in the Slipnet (e.g., linking *letter-category* to the 26 letters).
- *Property links*, which link certain nodes with properties of the concept. In the current version of Copycat there are only two such links: the link from *A* to *first* and the link from *Z* to *last*.
- *Slip links*, which represent potential slippages. These include:

Opposite links (labeled "opp"): *leftmost* ↔ *rightmost*, *left* ↔ *right*, *first* ↔ *last*, *predecessor* ↔ *successor*, and *predecessor-group* ↔ *successor-group*.

Various unlabeled links encoding various associations: *letter-category* ↔ *length* (linked because both are potential descriptions of groups), *letter* ↔ *group*, and *single* ↔ *whole*.

• *Lateral links*, which represent various non-hierarchical semantic relationships among nodes. In the current version of Copycat these links are not potential slippages, though it is possible that some of them (e.g., the *successor* and *predecessor* links) should be added to the Slip-link category. The lateral links include:

Successor and *predecessor* links between letter and number nodes (labeled "s" and "p").

Links between nodes representing spatial directions and spatial positions in the string (e.g., *right* ↔ *rightmost*).

The links *first* ↔ *leftmost*, *first* ↔ *rightmost*, *last* ↔ *leftmost* and *last* ↔ *rightmost*. In each link, both nodes refer to extremities—one to a spatial extremity in a string, the other to an extreme position in the alphabet.

Links between the various types of bonds and the associated types of groups (e.g., *predecessor* ↔ *predecessor-group*).

The links *predecessor-group* ↔ *length*, *successor-group* → *length*, and *sameness-group* → *length*. These links encode the relatively weak associations between the three group categories and the notion of *length*. Thus, when groups are formed and the corresponding nodes are activated, a small amount of activation is spread to *length*, which creates some possibility that the lengths of groups will be perceived.

The link *sameness-group* → *letter-category*. In the current version of the program, sameness groups (e.g., the **ii** group in **iijjkk**) are the only kind of groups that can have letter-category descriptions (e.g., *I*) attached.

As was described in the previous section, the lengths of *labeled* links (namely, the *opposite*, *predecessor*, and *successor* links) decrease when the node corresponding to the label is activated. All other links have lengths that do not change over the course of a run. In the current version of Copycat, a simple method for shrinking links was used: a link shrinks—discontinuously, and by a fixed proportion—only when its label node is fully (100%) active. Recall that when the activation of a node reaches a certain threshold (50% in the current version of the program) there is a probability, depending on the node's activation, that the node will discontinuously become fully active. Therefore, when a label node begins to get highly activated, there is a good chance that it will jump to full activation, thus making all of its associated links shrink. In the current version of Copycat, when the label node is fully active the links shrink to 40% of their original length. It might be more realistic for a link to shrink continuously, in proportion to the degree of activation of its label node. This should be explored in future versions of the program.

As was noted above, the network does not retain any changes from run to run; all node activations and link lengths are reset to their initial values at the beginning of each new run. The initial lengths of labeled links and the fixed lengths of other links were (as were nodes' conceptual-depth values) assigned by me, on the basis of intuition and trial and error, and are not necessarily optimally tuned. These lengths are given in appendix B.

3.3.5 Slippages in the Slipnet

In the current version of Copycat, slippages can made only between nodes directly connected by some Slip link. This is the source of some rigidity in the current program. In principle, the program should be able to perceive relations and make slippages between nodes separated by any number of links, given sufficient pressure. For instance, to solve **abc** ⇒ **abd**, **ace** ⇒ ? the program would need to be able to perceive "double successor" relations between the letters in **ace** even though there are no explicit "double successor" links in the Slipnet—and so Copycat cannot currently solve this problem.

It might seem like a weakness of the Copycat program that all potential slippages are already present in its Slipnet. However, this is also true for people: a potential slippage is simply an association between two concepts that could, in principle, allow one to be substituted for the other with the right kind of pressure. For example, the association between *wife* and *husband* is potentially present in our minds, but it takes pressure (such as the challenge of finding the analogue of the American first lady in Great Britain) for a slippage between them to occur. Likewise, even though all potential slippages are present in the Slipnet, it takes pressure for the program to make them, as well as pressure for the concepts involved to become relevant. Many slippages are not plausible *a priori*. As will be seen in chapter 4, the program virtually never makes *opposite* slippages without pressure to do so. In fact, in the absence of pressure it barely even considers them. The point of the Copycat program is to model the processes by which such pressures, and thus such slippages, come about.

The fact that there are only a small number of possible slippages in the Slipnet may also seem unrealistic, but it should be emphasized that Copycat's small repertoire of relatively simple concepts is meant to stand for the large number of more complex concepts in a person's mind. Copycat's concepts are meant to capture in an idealized form some of what is interesting about real-world concepts. Thus, it is essential that the program avoid taking advantage of the fact that it has only a small number of concepts and the fact that each problem involves only a small number of elements. The program never searches explicitly through all the nodes and links in its network. Instead, codelets use nodes that become relevant, and make slippages that become plausible, in response to pressures arising both from structures that previously run codelets have built and from existing associations in the network. In short, the program does not exploit the smallness of its microworld.

3.3.6 Top-Down Codelets Posted by Nodes

Several nodes in the Slipnet (e.g., *successor*, *predecessor*, *successor-group*, and *predecessor-group*) are able, when 50% or more active, to post specific top-down codelets to the Coderack. The task of such a top-down codelet is to specifically seek instances of its parent node in the Workspace (e.g., to look for successor relations). The different types of top-down codelets are listed and described in subsection 3.5.2.

3.3.7 Concepts in the Slipnet

The combination of the mechanisms discussed here—dynamic, context-dependent activation (representing perceived relevance) and link lengths (representing perceived conceptual proximity) along with top-down pressure from activated nodes (in the form of codelets seeking instances of those nodes)—results in a model of concepts as "active symbols" (Hofstadter 1979, chapter 11; Hofstadter 1985d). Concepts in the Slipnet are active and dynamic, rather than passive and static: they are emergent rather than explicitly defined, they change in response to what is perceived in a given situation, and they adapt in appropriate ways to different situations. When activated, concepts (e.g., *successor*, or *group-length*) attempt to further instantiate themselves (via top-down codelets) in the current situation. In doing so, they have to compete against one another for the resources of the system. That is, nodes compete indirectly, via codelets, for running time and for locations to build structures corresponding to instances of themselves.

3.4 Perceptual Structures in Detail

3.4.1 What the Program Starts Out With

Although I call the structures described in this section "perceptual structures," the word "perceptual" here is meant to be taken in the same spirit as the phrase "high-level perception"—that is, to refer to the non-modality-specific perceptual processes that occur in the mind when it tries to form an interpretation of a situation, be it a visual scene, a spoken sentence, or an abstract situation such as "my family," "Great Britain," or the "Iran-Contra affair." Thus, the term "perceptual structure" is meant to be general: it can refer both to modality-specific mental structures (such as the structures constructed by Hearsay-II corresponding to phrases, words, syllables, and phonemes), and to abstract mental structures (such as the perceived chunk "the Watergate burglars" or a mental correspondence between Reagan and Nixon).

At the beginning of a run, Copycat is given the three strings of letters. Its initial knowledge about each component letter consists only of the letter's *letter-category* (e.g., **a** is an instance of category *A*), its *object-category* (e.g., **a** is a *letter*, as opposed to a *group*), its *string-position* (if it has a named one, e.g., *leftmost*), and which letters are adjacent to it in its string. Only the leftmost, the rightmost, and the middle letter (if there is one) have *string-position* descriptions. The descriptor *middle* is used to describe only the single middle object in a string of three objects: the **b** in **abc** and the group **jj** in **iijjkk** can both be seen as *middle* objects. The letter **b** in **abc** is initially described as *middle*, but the letters **j** and **j** are not. The *group* **jj**, once it is made, is described as *middle* only if a description-making codelet (see subsection 3.5.2) adds that description to it; this is possible only if the other two groups (**ii** and **kk**) have also been made, so the string is seen as consisting of three objects.

The three strings are presented to the program with no pre-attached bonds or pre-formed groups. It is thus left entirely to the program to build up perceptual structures constituting its understanding of the problem in terms of concepts it deems relevant.

Figure 3.5 displays the initial descriptions given to the letters in the problem **abc** ⇒ **abd, iijjkk** ⇒ ? before the beginning of a run. In the figure, the large boldface lower-case letters are objects in the Workspace, and the descriptions of each letter are listed above it. A description actually consists of two parts: a *descriptor* (e.g., *leftmost*) and a *description-type* (for *leftmost* this would be *string-position*) that names the specific facet being described. The structure of a description (e.g., "*string-position: leftmost*") is similar to that of a slot and a filler in a frame-based representation. However, the words "slot" and "filler" imply that there is a ready-made slot (e.g., *string-position*) attached to the object, waiting to be filled. In Copycat, this is not the case. When the program adds a new description to an object (e.g., adding *alphabetic-position: first* to the **a**), it is adding both the slot and the filler; the slot did not exist ahead of time (i.e., the notion of using *alphabetic-position* as a way to describe the *a* in **abc** is not an explicit possibility initially; this notion comes about only in response to pressure). Thus, new slots can be added to objects as new concepts (e.g., *alphabetic-position*) become relevant.

In figure 3.5, only the descriptors (and not the description types) are displayed. For example, the **a** in the initial string has three descriptions: "*letter-category: A,*" "*string-position: leftmost,*" and "*object-category: letter.*" For each description, both the descriptor and the description type are names of Slipnet nodes.

As can be seen, each letter in the string **abc** happens to have three descriptions; however, many letters in **iijjkk** do not have *string-position* descriptions.

In figure 3.5, a descriptor name in large boldface indicates that that description is *relevant* and thus visible to codelets. A description is relevant only when the Slipnet node corresponding to its description type is fully active (e.g., *left-*

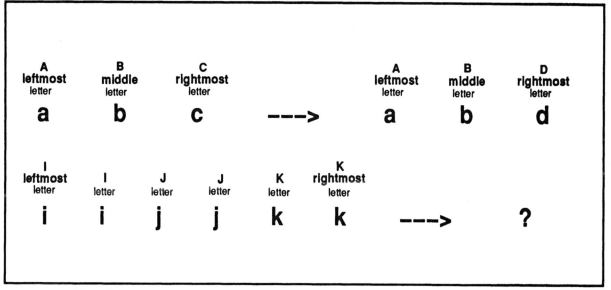

Figure 3.5
The initial descriptions given to the letters in **abc** ⇒ **abd, iijjkk** ⇒ ?.

most is relevant when *string-position* is 100% active). Thus, the relevance of a description in the Workspace depends on context: it depends on the activation of the description-type node, which depends on what has been perceived.

At the start of each run, the description-type nodes *letter-category* and *string-position* are initially set to be fully activated, and their activation is clamped (i.e., held constant) for a certain number of time steps. That is, descriptions of these two types are assumed to be relevant *a priori*, since the program's default assumption is that letter categories and string positions are what codelets should use in constructing bonds, correspondences, and other structures. This is shown in figure 3.5 by the use of large boldface for letter-category and string-position descriptors. (The descriptor *letter* is not initially relevant.) However, the relevance of descriptions can change over the course of a run: if descriptions of these types do not turn out to be useful in subsequent structure building, the activation of these description-type nodes will eventually decay, and the corresponding descriptions will no longer be perceived as relevant. Likewise, other descriptors (such as *letter*, or descriptors added during the course of the run) can become relevant as the run proceeds. The program is thus initially biased to assume that certain concepts are relevant, so that some aspects of the letters will be visible to early codelets. This reflects the notion that a given situation will have aspects that are *a priori* consciously part of one's perception of the situation (e.g., from the example in section 2.2, you are at least initially conscious of the fact that your friend Greg is driving). However, these biases shift in context-dependent ways as a run proceeds, as new structures are built, and as new information is uncovered about what should be considered relevant to the problem at hand. As will be seen, new descriptions can also be added to an object by description-making codelets long after the object has been created.

When a group (e.g., **ii**) is formed by the program, it becomes a new object in its own right, and it is automatically given the same default types of descriptions that a letter is initially given (e.g., a *string-position* description)—if they apply to it. Also, a probabilistic decision is made whether or not to add a *length* description; the longer the group, the less likely a description of its length will be explicitly attached to it. In other words, the length of a short group is more easily and immediately perceived than that of a longer group. The probability of adding a length description is generally low even for short groups—unless group lengths have already been deemed relevant (i.e., unless *length* is active in the Slipnet), in which case it goes up significantly. Just as for descriptions attached to letters, a group's descriptions lose relevance if they do not turn out to be useful.

In summary: Objects are given certain descriptions by default, other descriptions can be added later if they seem called for, and descriptions lose relevance if they turn out not to be of much use in subsequent structure building. This is similar to Barsalou's (1989) account of how people construct mental representations: every time a representation (e.g., "frog") is constructed in working memory, certain context-independent, highly accessible descriptions tend to be automatically activated (e.g., frogs are green, frogs move by hopping), though this information might later be inhibited if it turns out to be irrelevant in the current context (e.g., a French restaurant). Other, less immediate information is incorporated only because of its relevance in the current context (e.g., frogs' legs are edible).

Some descriptions are *distinguishing*—that is, they serve to distinguish an object from others in its string (e.g., in the string **abc**, the description *rightmost* distinguishes the **c**, since no other object has that description, but the description *letter* does not distinguish the **c**).

3.4.2 General Description of Structure Building

In order to formulate a solution, Copycat must use the concepts it has to make sense of each string as well as to find a set of correspondences between the initial string and the target string. To accomplish this, the program gradually builds various kinds of structures in the Workspace that represent its high-level perception of the problem, in a way similar to the way in which Hearsay-II builds layers of increasingly abstract perceptual structures on top of raw representations of sounds. These structures correspond to Slipnet concepts of various degrees of conceptual depth being brought to bear on the problem, and accordingly each such structure is built of parts copied from the Slipnet.

As was noted above, Copycat is able to build in its Workspace *descriptions* of objects (i.e., of letters or groups), *bonds* between objects within a string (the current version of Copycat can build bonds only between spatially adjacent objects), *groups* of objects within a string, *correspondences* between objects in different strings, a *rule* describing the change from the initial string to the modified string, and a *translated rule* describing how the target string should be modified to produce an answer string. Structures in the Workspace can be built and destroyed, although the more built-up, complex, and interrelated the structures become (causing the temperature to fall) the more the program hesitates to destroy them.

Figure 3.6 (identical to figure 3.3) displays a possible state of Copycat's Workspace in which several structures have been built. As was mentioned in

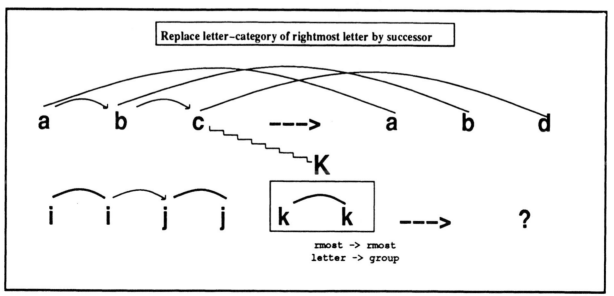

Figure 3.6
A possible state of Copycat's Workspace, with several types of structures shown.

chapter 2, the current version of Copycat assumes that the initial and the modified string (e.g., **abc** and **abd**) will be identical except for one letter. This is a simplification for the purposes of the current program, which cannot presently deal with more complex changes from the initial to the modified string. (Of course, the program can deal with more complex changes from the target to the answer string, as in **abc** ⇒ **abd**, **iijjkk** ⇒ ? or **abc** ⇒ **abd**, **mrrjjj** ⇒ ?.) This restriction on what type of change is allowed from the initial to the modified string limits the space of problems Copycat can currently deal with, but the space of interesting problems of this type is still so large that the current program barely scratches the surface. In the current version of Copycat, codelets do almost no examination of the modified string. The program instead concentrates on making sense of the initial and target strings and constructing a mapping between them. In the current version of Copycat, no bonds or groups are built in the modified string; the only analysis done of the modified string is to spell out the one-to-one letter correspondences between it and the initial string (represented by long horizontal arcs in figure 3.6) and to determine what relationship, if any, there is between the changed letter and its replacement. If there is any such relationship (as there is in **abc** ⇒ **abd**, namely successor-ship), then a description reflecting that relationship is added to the replacement letter's (here, **d**'s) list of descriptions.

The rule is formed by a codelet that fills in the template "Replace _____ by _____" with some descriptors of the changed letter and a descriptor of its replacement. These descriptors are chosen probabilistically, with a bias toward choosing descriptors of greater conceptual depth. Thus, although "Replace letter-category of rightmost letter by successor," "Replace letter-category of rightmost letter by *D*," and even "Replace *C* by *D*" are all possible, the first is more likely to be formed than the latter two, since the descriptors *rightmost* and *successor* are conceptually deeper than *C* and *D*. (There are some analogy problems in which one of the latter two rules would be preferable to the first, and thus the rule-preference function is actually not as straightforward as described above. It is described in detail in subsection 3.5.2, and it will be illustrated in some of the variant problems discussed in chapter 5.)

3.4.3 How Copycat Decides to Stop
Copycat decides probabilistically when to translate the rule and come up with an answer. This works as follows: The formation of a rule triggers the program to begin posting "rule translator" codelets to the Coderack. These continue to be posted at each time step until one of them runs and succeeds in constructing an answer, thus ending the run. The job of a rule-translator codelet is to translate the rule according to whatever slippages have been made, and to apply the translated rule to the target string and produce an answer. When a rule translator is chosen and runs, the first thing it does is decide probabilistically whether it really should go ahead and translate the rule, or whether it should "fizzle" instead. One might think at first that the decision should be based entirely on the temperature—reasoning that if the temperature is low then the program has a good sense of what is going on in the problem and should go ahead and try to produce the answer, and if the temperature is high then not enough structure has been built yet and the program should keep trying to improve

its understanding of what is going on. However, suppose this strategy were adopted and then the program were given the problem **abc** ⇒ **abd**, **wqlh** ⇒ ?, where no structures can be built in the target string. The temperature will never get very low on this problem, and if the decision to stop were based only on temperature the program might keep attempting to build structures for an inordinately long time before finally making the low-probability decision to quit. Instead, the program should be able to sense in some way that it has attempted for long enough to make sense of the problem and that it is unlikely to find any more structures. At this point the program should be more likely to give up at a high temperature than it would if the outlook were more promising.

In Copycat this works as follows: A rule translator's decision whether to translate the rule (thus stopping the program) depends both on the temperature and on the amount of structure that has already been built. Recall that the temperature is a function not only of the *amount* of structure that has been built but also of its *quality*. Thus it is possible for there to be a fair amount of structure and for temperature to still be high if the structure is weak. One example would be if in **abc** ⇒ **abd**, **ijk** ⇒ ? the program had, by chance, built the weak **a** ⇒ **k** and **c** ⇒ **i** correspondences. There would be a fair amount of structure in that case; however, it would be weak, so the temperature would still be relatively high.

There are three possibilities:

1. The temperature is low. This means that a reasonable amount of high-quality structure has been built, and that the program should go ahead and try to produce an answer at this point. In this case, the rule translator has a higher probability of deciding to go ahead and translate the rule.

2. The temperature is high, and not much structure has been built (this would be true for **abc** ⇒ **abd**, **wqlh** ⇒ ?). In this case, the rule translator again has a higher probability of deciding to go ahead and translate the rule. The idea here is that rule translators tend not to run until many other codelets have had a chance to run and build structure. (This is not deterministic; however, it is statistically true, since the posting of rule translators is triggered only when a rule has been formed, which tends to take place well after other structure-building codelets have had a chance to run.) Thus, if a rule translator is running and finds that very little structure has been built, then the assumption is that the program would have already had a chance to build structures if there were any to build, so there must not be much structure in the problem. The program should thus give up and go ahead with producing an answer given the current set of structures, since it is unlikely to find a better one.

3. The temperature is high, but a fair amount of structure does exist (as in the **abc** ⇒ **abd**, **ijk** ⇒ ? example given above, or as might be the case in **abc** ⇒ **abd**, **ijklmnopqrs** ⇒ ?, before the program finishes building all the bonds in the target string). Here Copycat assumes that there *is* structure to be found, but the program has not yet found all of it or perhaps the structure that it has found could be changed for the better. In this case, the rule translator is likely to decide to fizzle, allowing the program to continue exploring ways of building structures.

Even in cases 1 and 2, the probability of going ahead and translating the rule is fairly low, though it is higher than in case 3. And in general, many rule-translator codelets have to run before one succeeds in translating the rule. Thus, even in the first two cases, it takes pressure—in the form of many rule translators—in order for the program to stop. The desired behavior of the program in deciding when to stop emerges from the statistics of an ensemble of many codelets rather than from the individual action of a single codelet. This ensemble behavior is what is observed when statistics are taken over many runs of the program on the same problem. These will be displayed in chapter 4.

Once the rule has been translated, the program stops running codelets and creates its answer to the problem according to the translated rule. (There is a special-purpose function, not described in detail here, for applying a given translated rule to the target string and creating an answer.) If a rule translator succeeded, given the structures shown in figure 3.6, the rule would be translated as "Replace letter-category of rightmost *group* by successor" (using the slippage *letter* ⇒ *group*), yielding answer **iijjll**.

3.4.4 Strengths of Structures

As has been described, Copycat's Workspace contains *objects* (letters and groups) and *perceptual structures* (descriptions, bonds, groups, correspondences, and rules) that are built on top of objects. (Note that the word "group" is used to denote both the structure grouping together a set of components and the resulting object itself. In what follows, it should be clear from context which one is meant.) Each structure has a time-varying *strength* that measures its quality, and each object has a time-varying *happiness* that measures how well it fits into the current set of structures.

A structure's strength at a given time is used by codelets to make probabilistic decisions, such as whether to continue evaluating that particular structure, what urgencies should be assigned to codelets that will further evaluate it, and whether that structure should win a fight against an existing incompatible structure. The strength of a given structure can vary as processing proceeds in response to new structures being built, old structures being destroyed, and activations in the Slipnet changing. The strengths of all existing structures are thus continually being updated over the course of a run. Here I describe in general terms how the strength of each type of structure is calculated.

The strength of a structure is a function of both internal and external aspects—that is, a function both of intrinsic aspects of the structure and of the structure's relation to other structures that have been built. The internal and external aspects that contribute to the strength of each type of structure are listed below.

Descriptions   The strength of a description is a function of:

1. The conceptual depth of the descriptor.

2. The activation of the description type.

3. The "local support" of the description—i.e., the number of other descriptions of the same type in the same string. That is, relevant, deep descriptions are strong, and there is a bias toward building types of descriptions that have already been used in the problem. For example, if

a length description has already been attached to the **rr** group in **mrrjjj**, then a proposed length description of the **jjj** group will have some local support.

Bonds   The strength of a bond is a function of:

1. The type of bond it is. *Sameness* bonds are intrinsically stronger than *successor* or *predecessor* bonds, reflecting the realities of human perception. People are clearly quicker to recognize two neighboring objects as being identical than to recognize them as related in some abstract way.

2. The activation of the associated Slipnet node. For example, when the node *successor* is active, successor bonds become stronger.

3. The bond's local support: the number of other bonds of both the same category (e.g., *successor*) and the same spatial direction (e.g., *right*) that currently exist in the same string.

Groups   The strength of a group is a function of:

1. The type of group it is (e.g., sameness groups are intrinsically stronger than successor and predecessor groups).

2. The activation of the associated group category. For example, when *successor-group* is active, successor groups become stronger.

3. The group's length (the longer, the stronger).

4. The group's local support: the number of other groups of both the same category and spatial direction that currently exist in the same string.

Correspondences   A correspondence between two objects is based on a set of concept mappings between descriptors of the two objects, as in figure 3.6. Concept mappings are either *identities* (e.g., *rightmost* ⇒ *rightmost*) or *slippages* (e.g., *letter* ⇒ *group*). When a correspondence is made, some descriptors can be ignored (e.g., in the **c-k** correspondence in figure 3.6, the descriptors C and K are ignored since these nodes are not close enough in the Slipnet, and thus play no role in supporting the correspondence). In Copycat, the strength of a correspondence depends on many things, reflecting a number of desiderata. These are related to the mapping constraints given by Gentner (1983) and by Holyoak and Thagard (1989), which will be discussed in chapter 9.

The strength of a correspondence is a function of the following:

1. The number of concept mappings it is based on, reflecting the idea that the more similarities there are, the stronger the correspondence. For example, figure 3.7 displays two possible mutually supporting correspondences (jagged lines) and a possible competing proposed correspondence (dotted line) in the problem **abc** ⇒ **abd**, **xyz** ⇒ ?. (Concept mappings are displayed only for the diagonal correspondences.) The **a-z** correspondence is based on two concept mappings, whereas the **c-x** correspondence is based on only one, and thus the **a-z** correspondence is stronger in this regard.

2. The proximity of the two nodes in each concept mapping, reflecting the idea that the stronger the similarities, the stronger the correspondence. In figure 3.7, the proposed **c-z** correspondence is based on an identity mapping (*rightmost* ⇒ *rightmost*) whereas the existing **a-z** correspondence

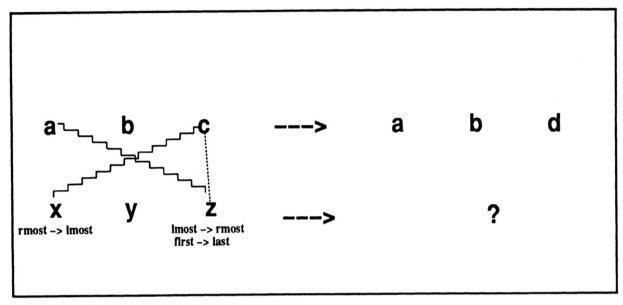

Figure 3.7
A possible set of correspondences (jagged lines) and a possible competing correspondence (dotted line) in the problem **abc** ⇒ **abd**, **xyz** ⇒ ?.

is based on two slippages, so the proposed **c-z** correspondence is stronger in this regard.

3. The conceptual depth of the two nodes in each concept mapping, reflecting the idea that the deeper the similarities, the stronger the correspondence. Even though the inclusion of deep similarities adds strength to a correspondence, there is also a pressure resisting *slippages* between descriptors with a high degree of conceptual depth (such as *first* and *last*), since better analogies are generally ones in which shallow aspects slip while deep aspects remain invariant. For example, the slippage *first* ⇒ *last* (shown in the figure) is between deep concepts and is thus hard to make; however, once it has been made it adds considerable strength to its correspondence, since it reflects a deep similarity between **a** and **z**. This conflict of pressures will be discussed and demonstrated in the run of Copycat on this problem, given in the next chapter.

4. The internal coherence of the correspondence—that is, the degree to which the underlying concept mappings support one another. Two concept mappings support each other (or, in other words, are *conceptually parallel*) if their corresponding descriptors are conceptually related (i.e., the nodes are linked in the Slipnet) and if the two concept mappings represent the same *relationship* (e.g., *opposite*). Thus, *leftmost* ⇒ *rightmost* and *first* ⇒ *last* support each other, since the pairs *leftmost* and *first*, and *rightmost* and *last*, are conceptually related (the nodes in each pair are linked in the Slipnet), and both concept mappings are *opposite* slippages. A correspondence including both these concept mappings is internally coherent. This is illustrated in figure 3.8. This internal coherence is one of the reasons the **a-z** correspondence in **abc** ⇒ **abd**, **xyz** ⇒ ? can come to be seen as strong.

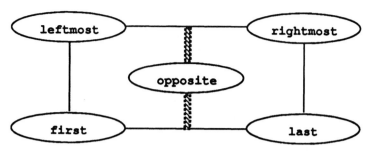

Figure 3.8
A small piece of the Slipnet, illustrating the source of the internal coherence of concept mappings *first ⇒ last* and *leftmost ⇒ rightmost*. (The links between *leftmost* and *last*, and *rightmost* and *first*, are not shown.)

5. The size of the objects involved in the correspondence. There is a bias toward correspondences that connect larger parts of the two strings (i.e., correspondences involving groups tend to be stronger than correspondences involving letters, and correspondences involving large groups—in particular, whole-string groups—tend to be stronger than correspondences involving small groups). This reflects a desire for mappings involving large, coherent parts of the two strings, which is similar to Gentner's (1983) notions of "structure-mapping" and "systematicity" (these will be discussed in detail in chapter 9).

6. The strengths of the other correspondences that support the given correspondence. Two correspondences support each other if a concept mapping in one supports (i.e., is conceptually parallel to) a concept mapping in the other. For example, in figure 3.7 the two diagonal correspondences support each other because they contain (respectively) the conceptually parallel concept mappings *leftmost ⇒ rightmost* and *rightmost ⇒ leftmost*. In contrast, the concept mappings *leftmost ⇒ rightmost* and *middle ⇒ middle* would not support each other but would not be incompatible with each other, while *rightmost ⇒ leftmost* and *rightmost ⇒ rightmost* (or *right ⇒ right*) would contradict each other and are thus incompatible (in Copycat, incompatible correspondences cannot exist simultaneously). A requisite for any strong analogy is a set of strong, mutually supporting correspondences.

These notions of internal coherence and mutual support between correspondences are related to some of the ideas put forth by Thagard (1989) about "conceptual coherence" in scientific theorizing. Many components of the definition of correspondence strength have counterparts in Gentner's (1983) structure-mapping theory and in Holyoak and Thagard's (1989) ACME program. These comparisons will be discussed further in chapter 9.

Rules   The strength of a rule is a function of:

1. The conceptual depth of the descriptors used in the rule. For example, "Replace letter-category of rightmost letter by successor" is stronger than "Replace *C* by *D*."

2. How the changed letter in the initial string has been mapped to the target string. For example, suppose that in the problem **abc** ⇒ **abd**, **cccc** ⇒ ? the **c** in **abc** is seen as corresponding to the entire group of four **c**'s in the target string. The rule "Replace *C* by *D*" is more compatible with this world view than is the normally stronger "Replace letter-category of rightmost letter by successor," since the descriptor *rightmost* plays no role in the **c-cccc** mapping. The strength formula takes such mappings into account in determining how compatible the rule in question is with the structures that have been built so far.

The strength calculations for structures often involve looking at *all* the other structures of that type in the same string. Such a complete search might be implausible in a complex, real-world situation, even though the number of mental structures a person imposes on a given situation is small relative to the number of objects in the situation. Another problem is that it is, in general, hard to define real situations in terms of discrete objects; what is or is not a single object is blurrier in the real world than in the more cut-and-dried letter-string microworld (or, for that matter, in almost all domains current AI programs work in). The role of the functions for calculating strengths of structures is therefore not to propose detailed psychological mechanisms for how strength values are computed, but rather to produce plausible numbers that can be used in the mechanisms that we *are* proposing, as well as to spell out the pressures that are involved in coming up with these numbers.

3.4.5 Importance, Happiness, and Salience of Objects

A notable facet of the Copycat project is that the program itself determines what is important or salient in a given situation, and can dynamically modify this assessment as it runs. It is an essential part of this project to deal with this issue, rather than leaving it aside, as is done by most other AI approaches to analogy (e.g., by assigning an *a priori* label of "important" to certain aspects of given situation). This is done as follows.

Each object (letter or group) in the initial and target strings has two time-varying values associated with it, *importance* and *happiness*, which are combined to determine the object's overall *salience*—its attractiveness to codelets. These values are functions of the structures that are attached to the object. As will be seen, these values are used in various ways by the program as it runs. Importance, happiness, and salience are calculated in the following way:

- The *importance* of an object is a function of (1) how many relevant descriptions it has (recall that a description—say, *string-position: leftmost*—is relevant if its description type—here *string-position*—is fully active) and (2) how active the corresponding descriptors (e.g., *leftmost*) are. For example, the leftmost **i** in **iijjkk** would usually have a higher importance than its right neighbor, since the former has a *string-position* description and the latter does not. (In general, objects on the edges of strings have higher importance than internal objects, though if *string-position* descriptions happened to become irrelevant this difference would vanish.) The intuition here is that the objects perceived to be important in a situation are the ones that are easiest to describe (i.e., have many relevant descriptions) and whose descriptors are most visible (i.e., highly activated). In addition, once the changed object in the initial string (e.g., the **c** in **abc** ⇒ **abd**) has been identified, its importance is raised, since it plays the leading role in defining the relationship between the initial string and the modified string. Also, the importance of any object inside a group (e.g., the individual **k**'s in the group **K**) is lowered, since when objects are grouped, they follow a utilitarian philosophy, partially relinquishing their individual interests for the good of the larger unit.

• The *happiness* of an object depends on how well it has been incorporated into the overall set of structures that have been built so far, and on the strength of the structures it is part of. Thus, an object's happiness is a function of the strengths of the structures (bonds, groups, and correspondences) attached to it. For example, in figure 3.6, the **c** in **abc** is happier than the **b** because it has a correspondence to something in the target string.

• The *salience* of an object—in effect, the object's attractiveness to codelets— is a function of the object's importance and its unhappiness (the inverse of its happiness). Increased importance leads to higher salience because important objects merit attention in their own right. Increased unhappiness leads to higher salience because unhappy objects need attention from codelets in order to increase their happiness. If an important object is very happy, it doesn't need much attention (e.g, the **c** in figure 3.6 doesn't need much attention). Likewise, if an unhappy object is not very important, it doesn't merit the same attention that should be given to an equally unhappy important object. For example, the rightmost **j** in figure 3.6 is not as important as the leftmost **i**, so the former would tend to get less attention, even though both are equally unhappy.

The *temperature* at any time is a weighted average of the unhappinesses of all objects, with each object's unhappiness being weighted by its importance. Thus, an important object has more of an effect on temperature than an unimportant one. The details of how temperature is calculated are given in appendix B.

3.5 Codelets and Structure Building in Detail

3.5.1 General Comments about Codelets and Structure Building

In Copycat, there is a distinction between codelet *types* and codelet *instances*. The program has a fixed number of codelet types, which are pre-written pieces of code, but it is *instances* of these platonic types that are placed on the Coderack (sometimes with specific arguments filled in) and that run. As will be seen, there are several different types of codelets, but, at a given time, the Coderack can contain a much larger number of instances waiting to run (and rarely are instances of all codelet types present at the same time), with various types being represented by various *densities* of instances, the densities being a result of what has happened in the run so far.

In general, each codelet type (with a few exceptions; see below) is associated with some aspect of evaluating or building a particular type of structure (a description, a bond, a group, a correspondence, or a rule). Because structure building in Copycat is broken up into small steps a parallel terraced scan of possibilities can be carried out. In the current version of the program, the evaluation and the building of any individual structure are carried out by a chain of three codelets: a *scout*, a *strength tester*, and a *builder*.

First, a scout codelet probabilistically chooses one or more objects on the basis of the relative saliences of the various objects in the Workspace. Thus, objects of high salience tend to be chosen more often (and thus paid more attention) than objects of lower salience. The scout then determines whether its particular type of structure can be attached to the chosen object(s). There are two types of scout codelets: a *bottom-up scout* is willing to consider any variety of the particular structure type it is looking for (e.g., the bottom-up bond scout codelet will consider bonds of any type), whereas a *top-down scout*, which is posted by some active Slipnet node (e.g., *successor*), sees if it can attach the specific structure associated with that node (e.g., a successor bond) to the chosen objects. In summary, a scout codelet "tests the waters" for a possible structure.

If the scout codelet discovers any reason for building its structure, it places a strength-tester codelet on the Coderack, giving it the proposed structure as an argument, and assigning it an urgency on the basis of certain somewhat superficial and quickly evaluated aspects of the structure. (If no reason is found to attach the structure to the chosen objects, then no strength-tester codelet is posted, and the chain fizzles at this point.) When the strength tester runs, it calculates the strength of the proposed structure, and, on the basis of this calculation, decides probabilistically whether to post a builder codelet. If the decision is "yes," a builder codelet is placed on the Coderack, its urgency being a function of the proposed structure's strength. If "no," the chain fizzles at this point.

When the builder codelet runs, it tries to build the structure, fighting against incompatible already-existing structures if necessary. For example, the proposed **c-z** correspondence in figure 3.7 would have to fight against the two existing correspondences, since it is not compatible with them. The outcome of a fight is decided probabilistically on the basis of the competing structures' strengths, and the new structure has to defeat *all* the existing incompatible structures before it can knock them down and be itself installed. Thus, when there is more than one strong rival, the odds are against a new structure. However, if the proposed structure wins all the fights, all the rival structures are destroyed and the new structure is built.

Thus, the three-codelet chain for building a given type of structure goes as follows:

> • A *scout* codelet probabilistically chooses an object or objects on which to build the structure, and asks "Is there any reason for building this type of structure with these objects?"
>
> • If yes, a *strength-tester* codelet asks "Is the proposed structure strong enough?"
>
> • If yes, a *builder* codelet tries to build the structure, fighting against competitors if necessary.

This three-codelet chain means that promising structures will tend to be explored and built more quickly than less-promising structures, since promising structures result in higher urgencies for the codelets in the chain. An experiment analyzing the effect of this scheme on Copycat's performance will be described in chapter 8.

This small pathway should not be identified with what was referred to above as a "path of exploration." A path of exploration does not involve just one structure; it involves an entire set of steps leading to an answer, in which a large number of codelets and structures participate. A path of exploration is defined as any of the ways in which the program could structure its perceptions of the problem in order to construct an analogy. Such paths are not laid out in advance for the program to search; rather, they are constructed by the program as its processing proceeds, just as in a game of chess paths through the tree of possible moves are constructed as the game is played. The evaluation of a given move in a game of chess blurs together the evaluations of many possible look-ahead paths that include that move. Similarly, any given action in building a structure by a codelet in Copycat is a step included in a large number of possible paths toward a solution, and an evaluation obtained by a codelet of a proposed structure blurs together the estimated promises of all these paths.

3.5.2 Codelet Types

Copycat has codelet types to scout out all types of structures—descriptions, bonds, groups, correspondences, and rules—as well codelets to evaluate the strength of a structure, to build a structure, to break structures that have been built, and to translate rules.

The different codelet types in Copycat are described below, with the arguments taken by each codelet indicated.

The description here is at a medium level of detail, leaving out some details for the sake of clarity. More detailed descriptions of the various codelet types are given in appendix C.

Often, a scout codelet chooses one or more objects to use in attempting to build a structure. The choice of what object or objects to use is probabilistic, and is in most cases based on the relative salience of objects in the Workspace (where more salient objects are more likely to be chosen). Unless stated otherwise, this is what "chooses an object" means in the descriptions given below.

Description-Scout Codelets

Bottom-up description scout (no arguments) A codelet of this type chooses an object (say, the **a** in **abc**) and a description already attached to that object (say "*letter-category: A*") and sees if any new description can be attached to the object on the basis of *property* links in the Slipnet. For example, if the letter **a** were chosen, this codelet might choose the descriptor *A* and look for any conceptually close properties it has in the Slipnet. If *first* were seen as close enough to *A* in the Slipnet (a probabilistic decision), the codelet would propose a new description, "*alphabetic-position: first*," and would post a strength-tester codelet to further evaluate this proposed description.

Top-down description scout (argument: a description-type node) A codelet of this type represents a pressure to build a specific *type* of description. It is placed on the Coderack by an active description-type node (such as *alphabetic-position*), which then becomes the argument. A codelet of this type chooses an object (say, the **a** in **abc**) and sees if a new description of the given type (say, *alphabetic-*

position) can be attached to the object. If the object is the **a**, then the codelet can propose the description *"alphabetic-position: first."* If the object is the **b**, then since no alphabetic-position description is possible, the codelet will fizzle. If such a description can be made, this codelet proposes it and posts a strength-tester codelet to continue the evaluation. The nodes that can post top-down descriptor-scout codelets are *string-position*, *alphabetic-position*, and *length* (which tries to describe groups in terms of their lengths).

Bond-Scout Codelets

Bottom-up bond scout (no arguments)   A codelet of this type chooses a pair of adjacent objects (e.g., the **b** and the **c** in **abc**) and sees if there is any bond that can be made between them (e.g., successorship). If so, this codelet proposes the bond and posts a strength-tester codelet to evaluate it.

Top-down bond scout (argument: a bond-category node or a direction-category node) Codelets of this type represent pressure to build bonds of a specific bond category or in a specific direction. They are placed on the Coderack by an active bond-category node (*predecessor*, *successor*, or *sameness*) or an active direction-category node (*left* or *right*), which then becomes the argument. A codelet of this type chooses a pair of adjacent objects and sees if a bond of the given bond category or direction can be made between them. If so, this codelet proposes the bond and posts a strength-tester codelet to evaluate it.

Group-Scout Codelets

A group is based on a set of bonds between adjacent objects, all of the same bond category and the same direction (e.g., two right-going successor bonds in **abc**). The building of groups is triggered only when bonds have already been built. Thus, there is no bottom-up group scout that is willing to look for any kind of group whatsoever. Instead, when a bond (e.g., successor) is built, the corresponding bond-category node (e.g., *successor*) is activated; it spreads activation to the node representing the associated group category (e.g., *successor-group*), which posts top-down group-scout codelets to seek instances of groups of that category.

Top-down group scout (argument: a group-category node or a direction-category node) Codelets of this type represent pressure to build groups of a specific group category or in a specific direction. They are placed on the Coderack by an active group-category node (such as *successor-group*) or an active direction-category node (such as *left*), which then becomes the argument. A codelet of this type with a group-category argument chooses a number of adjacent bonds and sees if they are the right kind for the given group category (e.g., *successor*), not caring which direction they are in as long as they are all in the same direction. A codelet of this type with a direction-category argument chooses a number of adjacent bonds all having the given *direction*, not caring which bond category they have as long as they have the same bond category (e.g., *successor*).

If the chosen bonds have this desired form, the codelet proposes a group based on these bonds and posts a strength-tester codelet to evaluate it. (If the codelet has a group-category argument and there is enough local support for this group category, this codelet can even propose a group consisting of just a single letter, though in most circumstances this is unlikely. How single-letter groups get proposed and built will be described in chapter 4, where a sample run of the program's solution **abc** $\Rightarrow$ **abd**, **mrrjjj** $\Rightarrow$ **mrrjjjj** is presented.)

Group-string scout (no arguments) Codelets of this type represent pressure to construct a group out of the entire string (not caring which category or direction the group has). The construction of groupings of both initial and target strings as wholes is so desirable for the program that an entire codelet type is dedicated to attempting this task. The codelet sees if there are bonds of the same category and direction that span the string. If so, it proposes a group based on these bonds, and posts a strength-tester codelet to evaluate it.

Correspondence-Scout Codelets

Bottom-up correspondence scout (no arguments) This codelet chooses two objects, one from the initial string and one from the target string. It sees if there are any possible concept mappings that can be made between descriptors of the two objects. A concept mapping can be made between two descriptors if they are both relevant (i.e., the description type of each is fully active), of the same description type (e.g., *string-position*), and sufficiently close in the Slipnet. For example, the correspondence between the **c** and the group **K**, pictured in figure 3.6, has two concept mappings: *rightmost* ⇒ *rightmost* (both string-position descriptors) and *letter* ⇒ *group* (both object-category descriptors). The two letter-category descriptors, *C* and *K*, although relevant at the time, were not sufficiently close to each other in the Slipnet for a concept mapping to be made between them.

If there is at least one such concept mapping between *distinguishing* descriptors (e.g., the *rightmost* ⇒ *rightmost* mapping shown in figure 3.6), then the codelet proposes a correspondence between the two objects including *all* the qualifying concept mappings (non-distinguishing ones such as *letter* ⇒ *group* come along for the ride) and posts a strength-tester codelet to evaluate the proposed correspondence. (If the correspondence is built, any slippages that were made as part of it are added to a global list of slippages that is visible to all codelets in the workspace. This list is used by the rule-translator codelet, discussed below.)

Important-object correspondence scout (no arguments) The task of codelets of this type is to find the target-string counterparts of *important* objects in the initial string. The idea here is to model the way people, when making an analogy, focus on important objects and roles in one situation (e.g., you focus on Ronald Reagan as "the president" in the Iran-Contra situation) and actively try to retrieve the object filling the corresponding role in the other situation (e.g., you actively try to figure out who is "the president" in the Watergate situation).

To accomplish its task, a codelet of this type chooses an object from the initial string probabilistically, using importance rather than salience as its bias. It then chooses one of the object's descriptions and sees if there is any object in the target string that has the "same" description, taking into account any slippages that have already been made. For example, in the problem **abc** ⇒ **abd**, **kji** ⇒ ? this codelet might choose the **a** in **abc**, choose its description *leftmost*, and try to make a correspondence with the leftmost object in **kji**. But if a correspondence has already been made between the **c** and the **k** with the slippage *rightmost* ⇒ *leftmost*, then this codelet will take that into account and consider a correspondence between the **a** and the *rightmost* object in the target string. If the desired target-string counterpart is found, then this codelet proposes a correspondence between the two objects in the same manner as would a bottom-up correspondence-scout codelet.

Rule-Scout Codelets

Rule scout (no arguments)   This codelet fills in the rule template (as was mentioned above, the current version of Copycat has only one rule template: "Replace _____ by _____"). To do this, it probabilistically chooses a descriptor of the changed letter in the initial string and a descriptor of the letter in the modified string that replaces it, with a bias toward descriptors with greater conceptual depth. After proposing this rule, this codelet posts a strength-tester codelet to evaluate it.

Strength-Tester and Builder Codelets

The strength-tester and builder codelets work in basically the same way for all types of structures:

Strength tester (argument: a proposed structure)   This codelet calculates the proposed structure's strength and probabilistically decides, on the basis of the result, whether to post a builder codelet. If it posts such a codelet, the urgency of the builder codelet is a function of the strength.

Builder (argument: a proposed structure)   This codelet builds the proposed structure (if it hasn't already been built by a previous codelet chain), fighting against already-existing incompatible structures if necessary.

Strength testers and builders also activate nodes in the Slipnet that are related to the particular structure being evaluated or built. This is described in detail in appendix C.

Other Codelets

Replacement finder (no arguments)   As was mentioned above, the current version of Copycat assumes that the initial and modified strings will be identical except for one letter (as in **abc** ⇒ **abd**). This codelet chooses a letter at random in the initial string and builds a "replacement" correspondence between the chosen letter and its counterpart (at the same position) in the modified string. (Replacements from the letters in **abc** to the letters in **abd** were represented as horizontal arcs in figure 3.6.) If the replacement involves a change (as for the **c**-to-**d** replacement in **abc** ⇒ **abd**), this codelet marks the initial-string letter as "changed" and gives the corresponding modified-string letter a description describing the change relation (e.g., successorship), if there is one. (For example, if the **c** changed to a **q**, there would be no change relation, so no description would be given.) The process of finding replacements in the modified string for initial-string letters does not follow the usual three-codelet building process: since the program assumes a one-to-one letter-to-letter mapping between the initial and modified strings, the initial-string-to-modified-string mapping is trivial to determine. Of course, this assumption severely limits the range of problems that Copycat as it now stands can solve, and this stage will have to be much more general if the program is to be extended to solve problems with more complex initial-string-to-modified-string changes. Some examples of such problems are discussed in appendix A.

Breaker (no arguments)   This codelet's task is to try to break some structure. But the first thing it does is decide probabilistically, on the basis of the current temperature, whether it should instantly fizzle (the lower the temperature, the more likely a breaker codelet is to fizzle). If it decides to proceed, it chooses a structure at random and decides probabilistically, as an inverse function of the structure's strength, whether to break the structure.

Rule translator (no arguments)   This codelet first decides probabilistically, on the basis of temperature and how much structure has been built already, whether to fizzle without doing anything. If it decides to proceed, it translates the rule according to the translation instructions given in the slippages in the Workspace. Once the rule has been translated, the program proceeds to construct an answer according to the directions in the translated rule, and then halts.

Codelets, for the most part, are biased to choose salient objects to work on. Recall that the salience of an object is a function of both its importance and its unhappiness. This is related to the "romance" metaphor discussed in section 3.1. Before any bonds, groups, or correspondences are formed, all objects are equally unhappy, so the relative salience of the various objects is determined wholly by their relative importance. But as structures are built, the objects that are "hitched up" become happier, depending on the strength of their ties to other objects; thus, their salience goes down, which means they are chosen less often by codelets. In terms of the metaphor, the happier the romance (i.e., the happier the objects in a given structure) the less the "outside flirting" done by the romantic partners (the less the codelets trying to build other structures look at the already "involved" objects, since higher happiness causes lower salience). However, the more desirable a person (the more important an object) the more flirting is done (the more codelets look at that object, since higher importance leads to higher salience).

Thus, the dynamic salience values are used as a form of self-monitoring in order to help the system properly allocate its cognitive resources. Once an object is happily "hitched up" (well integrated into a good interpretation of the situation), the system should not waste a lot of additional cognitive resources on that object. Likewise, unhappy objects should be given more attention by the system. Important objects should continue to receive attention even if they have been well integrated (and what is seen as "important" can vary over the course of a run). Moreover, these resource-allocation decisions should not be all-or-nothing: any object should always have a chance of getting some attention from the system. This general resource-allocation strategy is captured by the use of salience to guide codelets' probabilistic choices of what to work on. Temperature, described in detail below, is another kind of self-watching mechanism. The issue of self-watching, and some problems with it in Copycat, will be discussed further in chapter 7.

3.6 Temperature in Detail

Copycat's temperature variable measures the current disorganization in the system's understanding of the problem: the value of the temperature at a given time is a function of the unhappiness of the objects in the problem, which is in turn a function of the amount and quality of perceptual or organizing structure that has been built so far. Thus, temperature starts high, falls as structures are built, and rises again if structures are destroyed, or if their strengths decrease, or if new objects (i.e., groups) are formed and need to be incorporated into a coherent structuring of the problem. In turn, the value of temperature controls the degree of randomness used in probabilistic decision making in the system. There are two related ideas here. The first is that when there is little perceptual organization (and thus high temperature) the information on which decisions are based (such as the urgency of a codelet or the strength of a particular structure) is not very reliable, and decisions should be more random than would seem to be indicated by this information. When a large amount of structure deemed to be good has been built (and thus temperature is low), the information is considered to be more reliable, and decisions based on this information should be more deterministic.

The second idea is that early on, when not much is known about the situation to be understood, the system should pursue a large number of parallel explorations, so that enough information can be obtained in order to make *intelligent* decisions later on about what possibilities to focus on. Thus, early exploration should be parallel and fairly random (i.e., stochastic with a fairly uniform distribution), and exploration should gradually become more and more focused, serial, and deterministic as more comes to be understood about the situation at hand. Temperature, by implementing feedback between the quality of the program's understanding and the degree of randomness at a given time, provides a mechanism for achieving this continuous transition. This mechanism will be illustrated in detail in the sample runs of Copycat given in the next chapter.

The solution to the well-known "two-armed bandit" problem (Given a slot machine with two arms, each with an unknown payoff rate, what strategy of dividing one's play between the two arms is optimal for making a profit?) is an elegant mathematical verification of these ideas (an excellent discussion of this solution and its implications is given in Holland 1975). The solution states that the optimal strategy is to be at all times *willing* to sample either arm, but with probabilities whose ratio diverges increasingly fast as time progresses. In particular, as more and more information is gained through sampling, the optimal strategy is to exponentially increase the probability of sampling the better-seeming arm relative to the probability of sampling the worse-seeming arm. (One never knows with absolute certainty which of the two actually *is* the better arm, since all information gained is merely statistical evidence.)

Copycat's parallel terraced scan can be likened to such a strategy extrapolated to a many-armed bandit—in fact, a bandit with a dynamically changing number of arms, each arm representing a potential path of exploration toward an answer. (This is similar in some ways to the search through schemata in a genetic algorithm; see Holland 1988.) There are far too many possible paths for an exhaustive search, so in order to guarantee that in principle every path has a nonzero chance of being explored, paths have to be chosen and explored probabilistically. Each step in exploring a path (e.g., a choice of a codelet to run next, a decision whether or not to build a particular structure, or a competition between two structures) is like sampling an arm, in that information is obtained that can be used to decide the rate at which that path should be further sampled in the near future. The role of temperature is to cause the exponential increase in the relative speed at which promising paths are explored. As temperature decreases, the degree of randomness with which decisions are made decreases exponentially, so the speed at which good paths crowd out bad ones increases exponentially as more information is obtained.

The claim made here is that this type of strategy, in which information is used as it is obtained to bias probabilistic choices and thus to speed up convergence toward some resolution, but never to absolutely rule out any path of exploration, is essential for flexibility in understanding and dealing with situations in the real world, in which there is a limited amount of time to explore an intractable number of possibilities.

Temperature affects the following decisions:

- The program's choice of which codelet to run next, based on relative urgencies in the Coderack. At very high temperatures, this choice is fairly unbiased, meaning that every codelet on the Coderack has approximately an equal chance of being selected. As temperature falls this choice becomes more and more biased, and at very low temperatures the program is almost certain to choose one of the highest-urgency codelets next.

- A scout codelet's choice of which objects to use in scouting out a structure, based on salience. At high temperatures all objects have roughly equal chance; at low temperatures the most salient objects are chosen almost all the time.

- A strength-tester codelet's decision whether to fizzle or to post a builder codelet, based on its calculation of the strength of the structure being considered. At high temperatures strength is less strongly weighted in the decision (i.e., the decision is more random).

- A builder codelet's decision whether to break already-existing incompatible structures, based on the competing structures' relative strengths. Again, at high temperatures strength is less strongly weighted.

- A breaker codelet's decision whether to break a chosen structure, based on the structure's strength. Again, at high temperatures strength is less strongly weighted.

- A codelet's decision of whether two nodes in the Slipnet are sufficiently close for the purpose of adding a new description to an object (such as adding the descriptor *first* to the **a** in **abc**) or making a slippage (such as *first* ⇒ *last*). At higher temperatures the decision is made more randomly, and riskier (more distant or deeper) slippages have a better chance of being allowed.

- A rule-scout codelet's decision of which descriptors to choose for filling in the rule template, based on the descriptors' conceptual depth. At higher temperatures, conceptual depth is weighted less strongly.

- A group-scout codelet's decision whether or not to propose a single-letter group or to add a length description to a proposed group. At higher temperatures this decision is made more randomly, making the construction of single-letter groups and length descriptions—normally very low-probability events—somewhat more likely (though the probability is still fairly low).

The precise formulas for how temperature affects probabilistic biases are given in appendix B.

Temperature allows Copycat to close in on a good solution quickly once parts of it have been discovered. In addition, since high temperature means more randomness, temporarily raising the temperature gives Copycat a way to get out of ruts or to deal with snags; it can allow old structures to break, and it can allow restructuring to occur, so that a better solution can be found. That is, when the system runs into an impasse, the temperature can go up in spite of the fact that seemingly good organizing structures exist. Such a use of temperature is illustrated in the run of the program on **abc** $\Rightarrow$ **abd, xyz** $\Rightarrow$? given in chapter 4.

Temperature in Copycat has some similarities to the notion of inhibitory control. Kaplan and Kaplan (1982) note that when you are stuck in solving a problem your inhibitory control is lowered, which makes it easier for representations to emerge that were previously activated only below the level of consciousness. This makes it possible for you to come up with connections you did not even know were there. However, when your inhibitory control is lowered you run the risk of coming up with crazy, nonsensical ideas as well as useful new insights. High temperature corresponds to lowered inhibitory control. It allows structures that at low temperature would have been squelched immediately to be considered more seriously, and sometimes to be built. As will be seen in the next chapter, Copycat's use of temperature allows the program to come up with both insightful and bizarre solutions to certain problems (in particular, to problems 5 and 7 given in the previous chapter). The interesting thing is that the program has mechanisms that allow it to get reasonable and insightful solutions most of the time, while avoiding bad or crazy solutions quite reliably (though it does produce some from time to time).

The results of some experiments involving temperature will be given in chapter 8. These results demonstrate the necessity of nondeterminism for flexibility in analogy-making in Copycat, but they also demonstrate some problems with the effectiveness of the temperature mechanism in the current version of the program.

3.7 Main Loop of the Program

At the beginning of a run of the program, the Coderack contains a standard initial population of codelets: an equal number of bottom-up bond scouts, bottom-up replacement finders, and bottom-up correspondence scouts. The program initially assumes that these types of structures will be relevant in every problem. It may be wrong (for example, in the problem **hjpb** $\Rightarrow$ **hjpx, wlqzs** $\Rightarrow$? the letters were chosen randomly and there are no bonds to be found), but this fact will become clear only after some codelets have run.

The main loop of the program is as follows.

> Until a rule has been built and translated, do the following:
>> Choose a codelet and remove it from the Coderack.
>> Run the chosen codelet.
>> If N codelets have run, then:
>>> update the Slipnet;
>>> post bottom-up codelets;
>>> post top-down codelets.
> Finally, build the answer according to the translated rule.

Every N codelet runs (where N is a parameter, currently set to 15), the Slipnet is updated: for each node, any activation from instances discovered during the preceding N steps is added in, activation is spread between neighboring nodes, each node's activation decays at a rate determined by the node's conceptual depth, and, for each node more than 50% active, a probabilistic decision is made as to whether the node should discontinuously become fully active. The formulas used in these various steps are given in appendix B. (Of course, this discrete updating process—every N steps—is meant to model the continuous activation, spreading of activation, and decay of activation that go on in the mind. It could be made more continuous in the program by setting N to 1, for instance, but that would be computationally too expensive for the small gain in continuity.)

In addition, various bottom-up and top-down codelets are placed on the Coderack. Top-down codelets are posted by active Slipnet nodes, but new bottom-up codelets are needed as well—not only because the initial set of bottom-up codelets might have missed certain possible structures, but also because new structures are being built and new objects (groups) are being created all the time, and very often these need to be themselves incorporated into higher-level structures. Relying solely on top-down codelets would often prevent the program from finding certain structures that did not happen to correspond to previously active Slipnet nodes. Thus, every N steps, not only top-down codelets but also bottom-up codelets of all the various types have some chance of being posted. (Some difficulties with determining the necessary number of codelets to post, and how these difficulties were dealt with in the current version of Copycat, will be discussed in chapter 7.)

Chapter 4

Copycat's Performance on the Five Target Problems

4.1 Introduction

In this chapter I present the results of Copycat's performance on the five target problems discussed in chapter 2. As was noted in that chapter, these problems were chosen because they illustrate, in an idealized and thus very clear form, some of the essential abilities required for high-level perception and analogy-making in general. In previous chapters I discussed a number of these abilities and described the way in which the Copycat program models the mental mechanisms underlying these abilities. Here I will present statistics summarizing what the program does on each of the five problems, and for each problem I will give a set of annotated screen dumps from one run (in one case, two runs) which show how the mechanisms described in the previous chapter work together to produce the flexibility needed for the program to deal with a range of different situations in its microworld.

Since the program is permeated with nondeterminism, different answers arise on different runs. However, the nondeterministic decisions the program makes (which codelet to run next, which objects a codelet should choose, etc.) are all at a microscopic level, relative to the macroscopic level of what answer the program gets on a given run. Every run is different at the microscopic level, but statistics lead to far more deterministic behavior at the macroscopic level. For example, there are a huge number of possible routes (at the microscopic level of individual codelets and their actions) that the program can take to arrive at the solution **abc** ⇒ **abd**, **ijk** ⇒ **ijl**, and a large number of micro-biases tend to push the program down one of those routes rather than down one of the huge number of possible routes to **abc** ⇒ **abd**, **ijk** ⇒ **ijd**. Thus, at a macroscopic level, the program is fairly deterministic: it gets the answer **ijl** almost every time.

This notion of microscopic nondeterminism resulting in macroscopic determinism is often demonstrated in science museums using a contraption in which several thousand small steel balls tumble down, one after another, through a dense grid of pins, each ball eventually landing in one of many adjacent bins. Though each ball takes a unique path at the micro level, as more and more balls fall the pattern of balls in the bins gradually becomes a perfect gaussian curve, with most of the balls falling into the central bins and fewer falling into the edge bins. In Copycat, the set of bins corresponds to the set of different possible answers, and the precise micro path an individual ball takes corresponds to the actions of the Copycat program (at the level of individual codelets) during a single run. With enough runs, a reliably repeatable pattern of answer frequencies will emerge.

I present these patterns in the form of bar graphs, one for each problem, giving the frequency of occurrence and the average end-of-run temperature for each different answer. Each bar graph summarizes 1000 runs of Copycat. The number 1000 is somewhat arbitrary; after about 100–200 runs on each problem, the basic statistics do not change much. The only difference is that as more and more runs are done on a given problem, certain bizarre and improbable "fringe" answers, such as **hjk** or **ijj** for **abc ⇒ abd, ijk ⇒ ?**, begin to appear very occasionally. So even though 200 or so runs usually gives reliable statistics for the main range of answers to a given problem, I wanted to display at least a few of the fringe answers to each problem; thus, I ran the program on each problem 1000 times. This allows the bar graphs to make a very important point about Copycat: even though the program has the potential to get strange and crazy-seeming answers the mechanisms it has allow it to steer clear of them almost always.

Along with each bar graph, I give the results of a survey given to a number of undergraduate and graduate students at Indiana University and the University of Michigan for the purpose of determining the range of answers people give on these problems. As was discussed in chapter 2, ideally Copycat should be able to get all the answers that people get to a given problem—as long as those answers do not use knowledge that is not in the microworld—and it should never get answers that people find completely unjustified. This would indicate that the program is responding to the same pressures and perceiving the same things about the problems that people do (at least, people adhering to the restrictions of the microworld). The frequencies and temperatures given here are not meant to be compared precisely with frequencies and preferences of answers given by people, since the program is not meant to model people at such a fine grain. A summary of how Copycat's overall range of answers compares with that of human subjects surveyed will be given in chapter 6.

4.2 Frequency and Average Final Temperature of Answers for the Five Target Problems

The bar graph for abc ⇒ abd, ijk ⇒ ?[1]

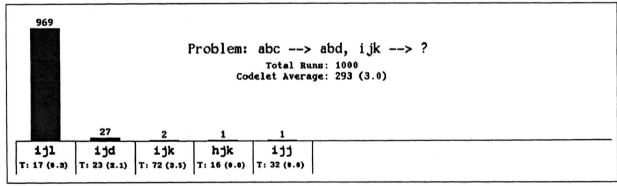

Each bar's height gives the relative frequency of the answer it corresponds to, and printed above each bar is the actual number of times that answer was given. The average final temperature appears below each bar, with the standard error given in parentheses. The standard error is equal to the standard deviation divided by the square root of the answer's frequency; it is a better error measure than standard deviation for this purpose, since it also takes into account the number of runs on which this answer was given. The average number of codelets per run is given in the center of the bar graph, also with the standard error in parentheses.

The frequency of an answer roughly corresponds to how obvious or immediate it is, given the biases of the program. For example, **ijl**, produced 969 times, is much more immediate to the program than **ijd**, produced 27 times, which is in turn much more obvious than **ijk**, produced twice, or the stranger answers **hjk** and **ijj**, each produced only once.

To get the answer **ijk**, the program used the rule "Replace C by D" and, since there are no C's in **ijk**, left the target string alone. To get **hjk**, the program mapped **abc** and **ijk** onto each other in opposite directions and replaced **ijk**'s *leftmost* letter by its *predecessor*. To get the answer **ijj**, the program replaced the rightmost letter by its *predecessor*. These last two analogies are always possible in principle, since the required slippages are between nodes that are linked in the Slipnet. However, as can be seen by the infrequency of these answers, such slippages are extremely unlikely in this problem.

As was noted above, the relative frequencies of different answers in each bar graph are not meant to predict the relative frequencies of different answers given by a population of experimental subjects. Copycat has its individual preferences and biases, which might not match those of the average of a population; Copycat is meant to model something more akin to a single individual. The frequency of different answers is meant to model the degree to which an individual person, solving the given problem, considers (consciously or unconsciously) different ways in which to make sense of the problem and to construct an analogy. The different frequencies represent, in some sense, the degree to which different potential pathways (leading to different answers) tug at the heartstrings (or mindstrings) of the analogy-maker in the process of solving a problem. For example, in solving **abc** ⇒ **abd**, **ijk** ⇒ ? there is always a tug (however unconscious) to describe the initial change as "Replace the rightmost letter by D," even if this description never reaches the surface to give the answer **ijd**. These various tugs are invisible when we look only at the final answer of a given run, but by running the program many times and collecting statistics we gain a view of the statistical effects of these various pressures.

The average final temperature corresponds roughly to how good that answer seems to the program; the program assesses **ijl** (average temperature 17) to be somewhat better than **ijd** (average temperature 20), and much better than **ijk** (temperature 69) and **ijj** (temperature 32). However, the final temperature for the run with the strange answer **hjk** was only 16, indicating that the program assessed this backward mapping to be quite good. The reasons for this will be discussed in the next section, in which several detailed runs of the program are illustrated.

One can get a sense of what the actual temperature values mean in terms of the quality of an answer by seeing how various sets of perceptual structures built by the program affect the temperature. This will be illustrated in detail in the next section. Roughly, an average final temperature below 30 indicates that the program was able to build a fairly strong, coherent set of structures—in other words, that the program in some sense had a reasonable "understanding" of what was going on in the problem. Higher final temperatures usually indicate that some structures were weak, or that there was no coherent way of mapping the initial string onto the target string. The program decides probabilistically when to stop and produce an answer. Though it is much more likely to stop when the temperature is low, it sometimes stops before it has had an opportunity to build all possible structures. For example, there are runs on **abc ⇒ abd, ijk ⇒ ?** on which the program stops before the target string has been grouped as a whole; the answer is still often **ijl**, but the final temperature is higher than it would have been if the program had continued. This kind of run increases the average final temperature for this answer. The lowest possible temperature for **ijl** is about 7, which is about as low as the temperature ever gets.

There are clearly some flaws in the way temperature is calculated in the program as it now stands. For example, the answer **ijd** has an average final temperature almost equal to that of **ijl** (even though it is much less frequent), whereas most people feel it is a far worse answer. The only difference in the structures Copycat builds for these two answers is the rule: **ijd** results from the rule "Replace the rightmost letter by *D*," and **ijl** from the rule "Replace the rightmost letter by its successor." The latter rule is much more likely to be proposed (hence the higher frequency of **ijl**) and is also considerably stronger, but the current formula for calculating the temperature (given in appendix B) is not really tuned correctly; answers resulting from weak rules have lower final temperatures than they really deserve. This should be addressed in future work on this project.

Thirty-eight human subjects answered this problem after reading a description of the letter-string domain and its limitations (they were asked to abide by the limitations). On all the problems, subjects were allowed to give multiple answers if they felt that there was more than one reasonable answer, and not all the subjects answered every problem, so the total number of answers for each problem is often not equal to the number of subjects. Many of the answers reflect the subjects' second, third, fourth, etc., choices (though on most problems most people gave only one or two answers). The purpose of this survey was to collect all the different answers people give, not just their preferred answers. All the responses I received are listed below. The frequency of each answer is given in parentheses, though (as I have said) the purpose of the survey was to compare Copycat's and people's *ranges* of answers rather than the *frequencies* of different answers. The subjects were not asked to give justifications for their answers, but when reporting the results here I give what I presume the justification was if it does not seem obvious. Answers that Copycat cannot currently get (or that Copycat gets for a different reason than human subjects) are starred.

For this problem, human subjects gave the following answers (the number giving each answer is shown in parentheses):

ijl (37)

ijd (2)

ijk (2).

The bar graph for abc ⇒ abd, iijjkk ⇒ ?

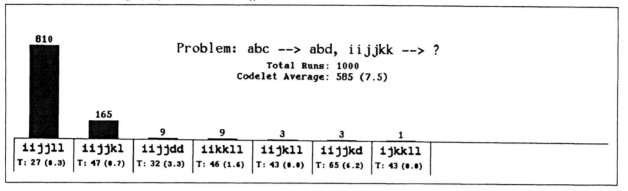

Here the most frequent (and lowest-temperature) answer by far is **iijjll**. The second most frequent answer is **iijjkl**, which ignores the letter groups in **iijjkk** and rigidly sticks to the rule of replacing the rightmost letter by its successor. After these two, all the other answers are very much on the fringes in terms of frequency, and none are considered by the program to be of high quality. ("On the fringe" is a qualitative description of an answer, but it can be defined roughly as an answer that is produced on less than about 1 or 2 percent of the runs.) To get the answer **iijjdd**, the program describes the original change as "Replace the rightmost letter by *D*," and replaces the rightmost group by **d**'s. The next two answers reflect various bizarre ways of viewing the target string. For **iikkll**, the program groups together the two rightmost groups (parsing the string as **ii-jjkk**), calls that larger group "the rightmost group," and replaces all the letters in it by their successors. (This method of replacing a group by its "successor" is built into the function that constructs the answer from the translated rule.) The answer **iijkll** reflects a similar strange view, except the two **k**'s in **iijjkk** are grouped with only the rightmost **j** (**iij-jkk**), and these three letters are seen as "the rightmost group." The next answer, **iijjkd**, reflects the same rule as in **iijjdd**, but this time it is followed "to the letter" (and since groups were not noticed here, the temperature is accordingly higher than for **iijjdd**). The final answer, **ijkkll**, is the result of another strange grouping of the target string: all letters except the leftmost **i** are grouped together, seen as the "rightmost group," and replaced by their successors.

The reasons Copycat came up with some of these strange answers will be analyzed further in chapter 7, which discusses some problems with the program. Happily, these last five answers account for only 2.5% of the total; perhaps more significantly, none but **iijjdd** has a final temperature lower than 43, which in Copycat's terms is fairly high. The program considers **iijjll**, with an average final temperature of 27, to be much more reasonable.

The answers given by the human subjects were the following (again, answers Copycat cannot get are starred):

iijjll (26)

iijjkl (12)

iikjkl* (5) (Replace the rightmost letter of each group of three by its successor.)

iikjkk* (3) (Replace the third letter by its successor.)

iikkll* (3) (Replace the third and the following letters by their successors. Copycat gets this same answer, but for a different reason.)

iijjkd (3)

iijjdd (1)

iijjkk (1)

ijjkkl* (1) (Replace the rightmost letter of each group of two by its successor.)

iijjkh* (1) (justification uncertain).

The bar graph for abc ⇒ abd, kji ⇒ ?

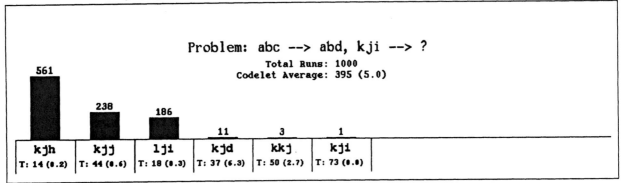

Three answers predominate here, **kjh** being the most common (and having the lowest average final temperature), **kjj** second, and **lji** a close third (the latter being somewhat less common, but having a much lower average final temperature). The answer **kjd** comes in a very distant fourth, and there are two "fringe" answers, with only one instance of each: **kkj**, which resulted from a grouping of the rightmost two letters, and **kji**, reflecting the literal-minded rule "Replace C by D." This last answer has a very high temperature of 73, indicating that on this run almost no structures were built before the program decided to stop.

In the survey, 26 subjects answered this problem. The answers were:

kjj (17)

lji (8)

kjh (6)

kjd (2)

kji (1)

kjl* (1) (This is either a confusion of answers **lji** and **kjh** or an insistence on changing the rightmost letter, even though the subject thought it should be changed to the successor of *K* rather than of *I*.)

The bar graph for abc ⇒ abd, mrrjjj ⇒ ?[2]

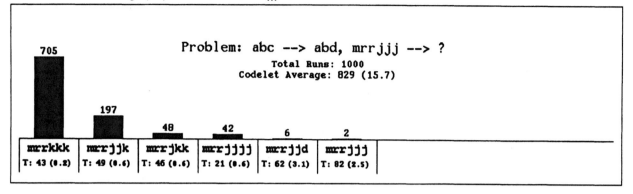

Here the most common answer by far is the straightforward **mrrkkk**, with **mrrjjk** a fairly distant second. For Copycat, these are the two most immediate answers; however, the average final temperatures associated with them are fairly high, because of the lack of any coherent structure tying together the target string as a whole. Next there are two answers with roughly equal frequencies: **mrrjkk**, a strange answer that comes from grouping only the rightmost two *j*'s in **mrrjjj** and viewing this group as the object to be replaced, and **mrrjjjj**, which was discussed in chapter 2. The average final temperature associated with this answer is much lower than those of the other answers, which shows that the program assesses it to be the most satisfying answer, though far from the most immediate. As in many aspects of real life, the immediacy of a solution is by no means always perfectly correlated with its quality. The other two answers are on the fringe: **mrrjjd** comes from replacing the rightmost letter with a *D*, and **mrrjjj** comes from the rule "Replace *C* by *D*."

In the survey, 50 subjects answered this problem. The answers were:

mrrkkk (28)

mrrjjk (19)

mrsjjj* (5) (Replace the third letter by its successor.)

mrsjjk* (4) (Parse the string as **mrr-jjj**, and replace the third letter of each group by its successor.)

mrrjkk* (4) (Parse the string as **mr-rj-jj** to correspond to **a-b-c**, and replace the rightmost group by its successor.)

mrrjjjj (2)

mrskkk* (2) (Replace each letter following the leftmost two letters by its successor.)

mrrjjj (2)

mrrjjd (1)

mssjjj* (1) (Replace each instance of the third letter by its successor.)

The bar graph for abc ⇒ abd, xyz ⇒?

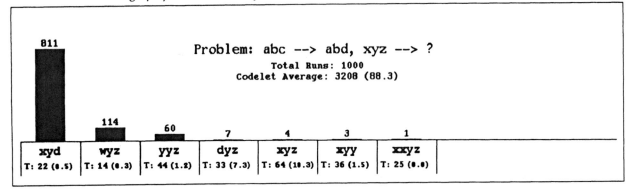

As was discussed above, the answer **xya** is not available to the program; by design, Z has no successor. A more detailed statistic (not displayed here) shows that on 97% of the runs the program tries to take the successor of Z and fails, which then forces it to do some restructuring. On the other 3% of the runs, Copycat gets answers such as **xyd**, **xyz**, and (on one run in 1000) **wyz** directly, without hitting the **z** snag first. These answers are analogous to **ijd**, **ijk**, and **hjk** for problem 1, and these similarly make up 3% of the total on problem 1.

As will be seen in the screen dumps later in this chapter, Copycat often hits the same snag again and again in the same run—on average nine times per run—before it succeeds in finding a way of solving the problem. The most common answer by far is **xyd**, for which the program decides that if it cannot replace the rightmost letter by its successor then the next best thing is to replace it by a **d**. A distant second in frequency, but the answer with the lowest average temperature, is **wyz**, which many people (including myself) consider to be the most elegant solution. To get this answer, the program has to restructure its perceptions of what corresponds to what, noticing that *A* and *Z* are at opposite ends of the alphabet, so there is a plausible correspondence between them if the spatial *and* alphabetic directions of the two strings (**abc** and **xyz**) are also seen as opposite. The next answer, **yyz**, reflects a view that neglects the opposite alphabetic directions of the two strings. Although it allows the *leftmost* letter to be replaced, it insists on holding fast to the notion of replacing it by its *successor*, since the rightmost letter of **abc** was replaced by *its* successor.

The other four answers are on the fringes as far as frequency goes. The answer **dyz** is a comical blend of intelligence and rigidity; it exhibits a good deal of flexibility in the willingness to slip *rightmost* to *leftmost*, but it holds a rigid view of the **abc** ⇒ **abd** change, insisting on replacing the leftmost letter by *D*. (This contradictory mixture of intelligence and rigidity is very much akin to the notion of frame blends described in chapter 2. Many people find this answer funny, and indeed frame blends are central to certain kinds of humor. Some connections between such answers in the letter-string domain with frame blends and jokes are discussed in Hofstadter and Gabora 1990.) The answer **xyz** comes from interpreting (or reinterpreting, after hitting the impasse) the **abc** ⇒ **abd** change as "Replace *C* by *D*." The answer **xyy** allows that the two strings are to be perceived in opposite alphabetic directions (thus a *successor* ⇒ *predecessor* slippage), but refuses to give up the idea that the strings have the same spatial direction, and thus insists on changing the rightmost letter, as was done in **abc**. The answer **xxyz** was arrived at by very strange reasoning that resulted from continuing high temperature: the program parsed the target string as **x-yz**, where **yz** was seen as a group of length 2 and **x** was seen as a group of length 1. Copycat noticed the successor relation between the group lengths and, as was done for **mrrjjjj**, decided to replace the group **yz** by its length-successor—namely the successor group of length 3, **xyz**. The final answer was thus **x-xyz**. This is one of the strangest analogies Copycat ever made, but, like other fringe answers, it shows very clearly that extremely farfetched routes are in principle available to the program, especially at high temperatures.

In the survey, 50 subjects answered this problem. The subjects were allowed to answer **xya** (and almost all of them did so) but were then informed that, since Copycat does not have the concept of circularity, it cannot produce this answer. They were then asked to come up with one or more different answers. There were a large number of different answers given. Many of the answers that Copycat also got were probably given for different reasons. These are starred along with the answers that Copycat cannot get.

> **xyz*** (14) (If the **z** can't be changed, then just leave it alone. Copycat can get this answer, but for a different reason.)
>
> **xyy*** (13) (If the **z** can't be moved forward in the alphabet, then the next best thing is to move it backward. Again, Copycat can get this answer, but for a different reason.)
>
> **xy*** (9) (If **z** has no successor, then it just falls off the end of the string.)
>
> **xyd** (9)
>
> **wxz*** (4) (This is based on the desire to imitate the alphabetic space between the two rightmost letters in **abd**, which can be done by moving the leftmost two letters back in the alphabet.)
>
> **wyz** (2)
>
> **xyzz*** (1) (Doubling the **z** is a tricky way of taking its "successor.")
>
> **xzz*** (1) (If you can't take the successor of the **z**, the next best thing is to take the successor of its neighbor, the **y**.)
>
> **xyw*** (1) (This results from reasoning similar to that which yields **wyz**, but here the subject insists that the rightmost letter be the one that is replaced.)
>
> **zxw*** (1) (The subject specified that he or she wanted to change the rightmost letter and at the same time imitate the relationships in **abd**; by reversing the string and then replacing the rightmost letter by its predecessor, this was possible.)
>
> **xyx*** (1) (The subject specified the desire to answer **xyy**; however, he or she did not like the fact of the double **y**, so instead the letter before *Y* was used.)
>
> **abd*** (1) (Replace the whole string by **abd**.)
>
> **wxx*** (1) (Justification uncertain).

4.3 Screen Dumps from Runs on the Five Target Problems

In this section, annotated screen dumps of Copycat's graphics are given for runs on each of the five problems. These screen dumps are meant to clarify how the program actually solves these problems. A numbered series of screen dumps is displayed for each run, showing how the Workspace (and for some frames, the Slipnet) evolves over time.

Screen dumps from a run on abc ⇒ *abd,ijk* ⇒ *?*
The following is a set of screen dumps from a fairly typical run of Copycat on this problem.

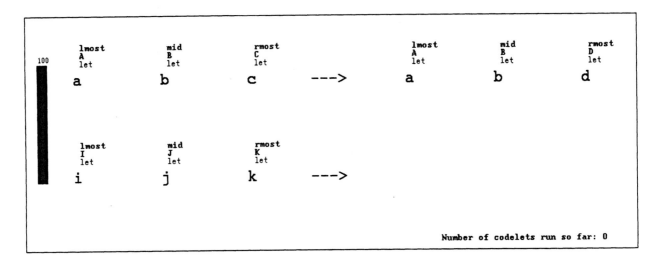

1. Workspace: The program is presented with the three strings in the Workspace. Each letter has a list of initial descriptions, including string-position, letter-category, and object-category descriptions. (The first two description types are initially relevant by default; relevant descriptions appear in boldface.) The temperature, represented by a "thermometer" at the left, is at its maximum value of 100 degrees (0 is the minimum), so initial decisions are made fairly randomly, though there are still some biases, even at the highest temperature. This screen dump was made before the run began; as is indicated at the bottom right of the Workspace, no codelets have run so far.

100 ■ A	100 ■ B	100 ■ C	D	E	F	G	H	100 ■ I	100 ■ J	100 ■ K	L	M
N	O	P	Q	R	S	T	100 ■ U	100 ■ V	100 ■ W	X	Y	Z
1	2	3	4	5	left	right	lmost	rmost	middle	pred	100 ■ succ	same
pred group	succ group	same group	first	last	100 ■ letter	group	iden	opp	whole	single	100 ■ letter cat	length
alpha pos	100 ■ string pos	direction	object cat	bond cat	group cat							

Slipnet: The initial state of the Slipnet is displayed above (nodes only; no links are shown). The black square inside any node's rectangle represents its activation: the size of the square is proportional to the level of activation, and the actual numerical level, ranging from 0 to 100%, is displayed above each square. The nodes are (in the order displayed) *A-Z, 1-5, left, right, leftmost, rightmost, middle, predecessor, successor, sameness, predecessor group, successor group, sameness group, first, last, letter, group, identity, opposite, whole, single, letter-category, length, alphabetic-position, string-position, direction, object-category, bond-category,* and *group-category.* The nodes corresponding to the default initial descriptions given to each letter are activated, each at 100%.

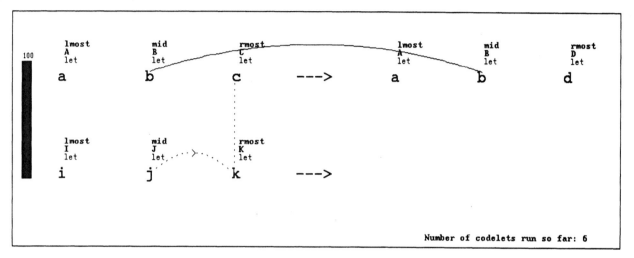

2. Workspace: Six codelets have run, and a few have had some success. The modified-string replacement for the **b** in **abc** has been found (solid arc across the arrow), a bond has been proposed in the target string from the **j** to the **k** (dotted arc), and a correspondence has been proposed between the **c** and the **k** (dotted vertical line). In general, structures that have been *proposed* are represented by dotted or dashed arcs and lines, and structures that have been *built* are represented by solid arcs and lines. Since no initial-string or target-string structures have been actually built yet, the temperature remains at 100. (In the current version of Copycat, the arcs between letters in the initial and modified strings do not affect the temperature.)

100	100	100						100	100	100		
■	■	■						■	■	■		
A	B	C	D	E	F	G	H	I	J	K	L	M
N	O	P	Q	R	S	T	U	V	W	X	Y	Z
							100	100	100			
							■	■	■			
1	2	3	4	5	left	right	lmost	rmost	middle	pred	succ	same
					100						100	
					■						■	
pred group	succ group	same group	first	last	letter	group	iden	opp	whole	single	letter cat	length
	100											
	■											
alpha pos	string pos	direction	object cat	bond cat	group cat							

Slipnet: Activation in the Slipnet has not changed yet, since it is updated only every 15 codelets.

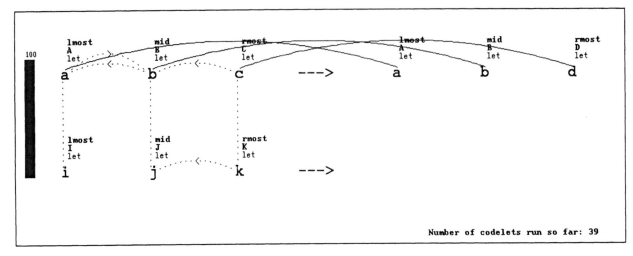

Number of codelets run so far: 39

3. Workspace: Now 39 codelets have run. All three replacement arcs between letters in **abc** and **abd** have been built. (Since determining these is trivial, they are almost always constructed quite early on.) Several possible bonds and correspondences are being considered, but since none has been built yet the temperature remains at 100.

100	100	100	47	3	3	3	47	53	100	100	47	3
■	■	■	■	.	.	.	■	■	■	■	■	.
A	B	C	D	E	F	G	H	I	J	K	L	M
3	3	3	3	3	3	3	3	3	3	3	3	3
.	.	.	.	.	.	.	.	.	.	.	.	.
N	O	P	Q	R	S	T	U	V	W	X	Y	Z
					4	14	100	100	100			
						.	■	■	■			
1	2	3	4	5	left	right	lmost	rmost	middle	pred	succ	same
			15		4	8					100	8
			.			.					■	
pred group	succ group	same group	first	last	letter	group	iden	opp	whole	single	letter cat	length
	100		27									
	■		.									
alpha pos	string pos	direction	object cat	bond cat	group cat							

Slipnet: The initial activations have decayed and spread in various ways (e.g., the activation of the node *letter* has decayed, each of the 26 letter-category nodes has received a tiny bit of activation from the node *letter-category*, and *letter-category* has also spread some activation to *object-category* and *length*), and additional activation has come from codelet actions in the Workspace (e.g., the letter categories involved in the proposed bonds were reactivated by the codelets proposing the bonds).

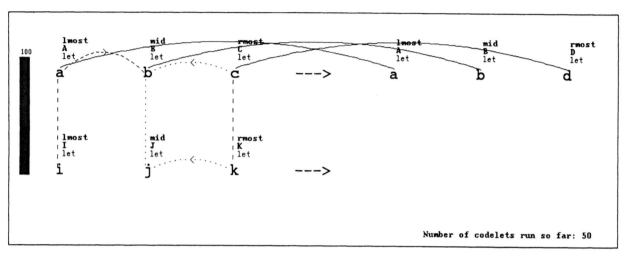

4. Workspace: Now 50 codelets have run, and various proposed structures can be seen at various stages of consideration. The dotted arcs and lines (the proposed **c-b** and **k-j** predecessor bonds and the proposed **b-j** correspondence) are structures that have been proposed by a scout codelet and are waiting to be examined by a strength-tester codelet. The dashed arcs and lines (the proposed **a-b** successor bond and the proposed **a-i** and **c-k** correspondences) are structures that have passed their respective strength testers' evaluations and are waiting to be built by a builder codelet. Note that there are many actions not shown in these screen dumps—for example, the actions of scout codelets that fizzle without proposing anything (as would happen if, say, a correspondence-scout codelet examined the **c** and the **j** to see if there were any grounds for a correspondence between the two; there would not be any).

100	100	53	48	3	3	3	8	48	53	53	48	3
■	■	■	■	.	.	.	■	■	■	■	■	.
A	B	C	D	E	F	G	H	I	J	K	L	M
3	3	3	3	3	3	3	3	3	3	3	3	3
.	.	.	.	.	.	.	.	.	.	.	.	.
N	O	P	Q	R	S	T	U	V	W	X	Y	Z
					12	16	100	100	100			
					.	.	■	■	■			
1	2	3	4	5	left	right	lmost	rmost	middle	pred	succ	same
			34		1	6					100	10
			■		.	.					■	.
pred group	succ group	same group	first	last	letter	group	iden	opp	whole	single	letter cat	length
	100		24									
	■		■									
alpha pos	string pos	direction	object cat	bond cat	group cat							

Slipnet: Further spreading of activation and further decay have occurred (e.g., *first* has received some activation from *A*), and nodes whose instances have been recently examined by codelets (e.g., *A* and *B*) have received additional activation.

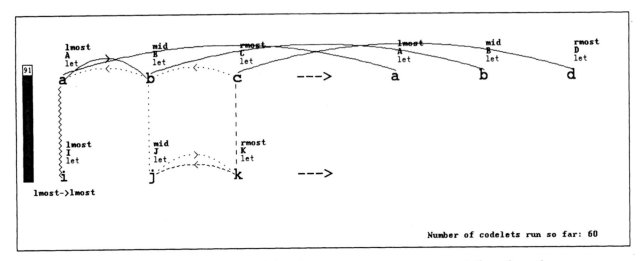

Number of codelets run so far: 60

5. Workspace: After 60 codelets have run, some structures (other than the trivially determined arcs between **abc** and **abd**) have finally been built, and appear as *solid* arcs or jagged lines: the **a-b** successor bond and the **a-i** correspondence. Beneath the correspondence is its single concept mapping: *leftmost* ⇒ *leftmost*. In response to these structures, the temperature has fallen to 91. Other proposed structures are still being explored at different spatial locations and at different speeds.

100	100	48	8	3	3	3	4	8	100	100	8	3
■	■	■	.	.	.	.	.	.	■	■	.	.
A	B	C	D	E	F	G	H	I	J	K	L	M
3	3	3	3	3	3	3	3	3	3	3	3	3
.	.	.	.	.	.	.	.	.	.	.	.	.
N	O	P	Q	R	S	T	U	V	W	X	Y	Z
					15	100	100	100	40		100	
					.	■	■	■	■		■	
1	2	3	4	5	left	right	lmost	rmost	middle	pred	succ	same
			45			5	100				100	11
			■			.	■				■	.
pred group	succ group	same group	first	last	letter	group	iden	opp	whole	single	letter cat	length
	100		22									
	■		.									
alpha pos	string pos	direction	object cat	bond cat	group cat							

Slipnet: The newly built structures have affected the Slipnet: the nodes *successor* and *right* (corresponding to the category and direction of the **a-b** bond) are activated, as is the node *identity* (corresponding to the type of concept mapping underlying the **a-i** correspondence—that is, *lmost* ⇒ *lmost* is an *identity* mapping).

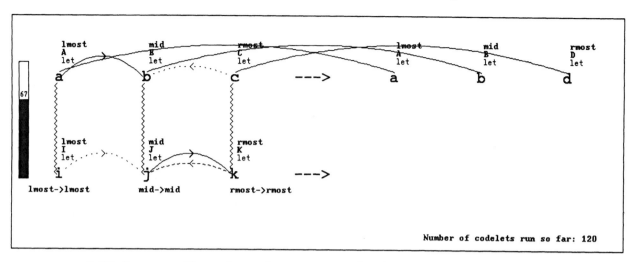

6. Workspace: The active nodes *successor* and *right* have begun to exert a top-down influence in two ways: by increasing the strengths of proposed successor bonds (the activation of *successor* causes successor links in the Slipnet to shrink, making the proposed bond between, say, the **i** and the **j** stronger) and by causing codelets to be posted expressly to look for *successor* bonds and *right*-going bonds. The existence of right-going successor bonds in the Workspace also increases the strength of proposed bonds of this type. Another such bond has been built between the **j** and the **k**, and an **i-j** bond is being considered. Also, correspondences have been built from all three letters in the initial string to letters in the target string, based on their string-position descriptions. In response to these structures, the temperature has fallen to 67.

8	100	100	3	3	3	3	47	53	100	53	48	3
·	■	■	·	·	·	·	■	■	■	■	■	·
A	B	C	D	E	F	G	H	I	J	K	L	M
3	3	3	3	3	3	3	3	3	3	3	3	3
·	·	·	·	·	·	·	·	·	·	·	·	·
N	O	P	Q	R	S	T	U	V	W	X	Y	Z
					10	100	100	100	100	13	100	
					·	■	■	■	■	·	■	
1	2	3	4	5	left	right	lmost	rmost	middle	pred	succ	same
	25		60	20		2	100				100	12
	■		■	■		·	■				■	·
pred group	succ group	same group	first	last	letter	group	iden	opp	whole	single	letter cat	length
80	100	70	14	80								
■	■	■	·	■								
alpha pos	string pos	direction	object cat	bond cat	group cat							

Slipnet: The node *first* is becoming active, owing to continuing activation of *A*. The node *first* has also spread activation to *last* as well as to *alphabetic position*, which will post codelets to try to make such descriptions. (As will be seen, *alphabetic-position* will decay, and will not have much effect in this problem.) Likewise, *successor* and *right* have spread small amounts of activation (respectively) to *predecessor* and *left*, but not enough for these to have any influence yet. *Successor* and *right* have also spread activation (respectively) to the superordinate nodes *bond-category* and *direction*. *Successor* has also spread some activation to *successor group*.

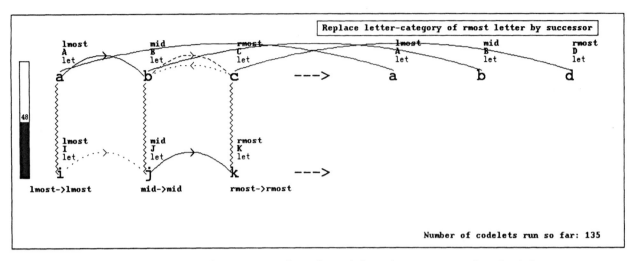

7. Workspace: A coherent view, based on right-going successor bonds, is beginning to emerge, enforced by the presence of such bonds in the two strings as well as by the top-down influence from the active nodes in the Slipnet. Some of the explorations along different lines, seen in the previous screen dumps, are proceeding relatively slowly (e.g., the proposed **c-b** predecessor bond, which is still waiting for its strength tester to run) or have fizzled entirely (e.g., the previously displayed proposed **k-j** predecessor bond) in response to these pressures. A rule ("Replace letter-category of rightmost letter by successor") has been constructed to describe the **abc-abd** change; it appears in a box above the modified string. The temperature has fallen to 48 in response to the building of this strong rule.

44	100	100	43	3	3	3	8	48	100	100	8	3
■	■	■	■	.	.	.	.	■	■	■	.	.
A	B	C	D	E	F	G	H	I	J	K	L	M
3	3	3	3	3	3	3	3	3	3	3	3	3
.	.	.	.	.	.	.	.	.	.	.	.	.
N	O	P	Q	R	S	T	U	V	W	X	Y	Z

					34	50	60	100	100	27	100	
					■	■	■	■	■	.	■	
1	2	3	4	5	left	right	lmost	rmost	middle	pred	succ	same

	53		36	12		2	100				100	12
	■		■	.		.	■				■	.
pred group	succ group	same group	first	last	letter	group	iden	opp	whole	single	letter cat	length

64	100	100	13	100	
■	■	■	.	■	
alpha pos	string pos	direction	object cat	bond cat	group cat

Slipnet: *Successor* continues to spread activation to *successor-group*, which is now active enough to begin posting codelets to look for such groups. The nodes *first* and *alphabetic-position* have lost some activation through decay.

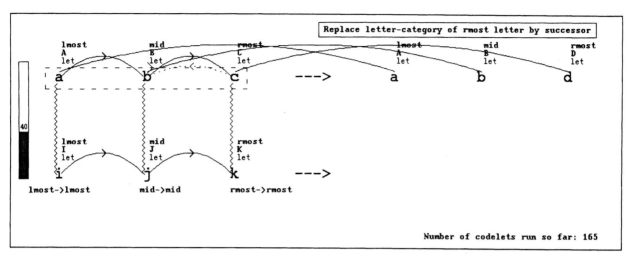

8. Workspace: Now, 165 codelets into the run, the notion of right-going successor bonds has taken over almost completely though other possibilities are still being explored, albeit much more slowly—e.g., the proposed **c-b** predecessor bond), and a grouping of the initial string as a whole is being considered (dashed rectangle). The temperature has fallen to 40, reflecting the program's assessment of the promise of the structures it has built so far. As the temperature gets lower and lower, the program's decisions become more and more deterministic, its behavior more and more serial (i.e., a small number of high-urgency codelets overwhelm a larger number of low-urgency ones, so fewer and fewer other possibilities are being considered), and its actions more and more dominated by top-down forces (as top-down codelets crowd out bottom-up ones). A single dominating point of view begins to be "frozen" into place.

53	93	53	48	3	3	3	43	100	100	100	47	3
A	B	C	D	E	F	G	H	I	J	K	L	M
3	3	3	3	3	3	3	3	3	3	3	3	3
N	O	P	Q	R	S	T	U	V	W	X	Y	Z
					36	100	100	100	16	37	100	
1	2	3	4	5	left	right	lmost	rmost	middle	pred	succ	same
	73		38	4		2	100				100	12
pred group	succ group	same group	first	last	letter	group	iden	opp	whole	single	letter cat	length
41	100	100	11	100								
alpha pos	string pos	direction	object cat	bond cat	group cat							

Slipnet: *Successor-group* continues to gain activation, increasing the pressure (via the posting of top-down codelets) to find and build successor groups.

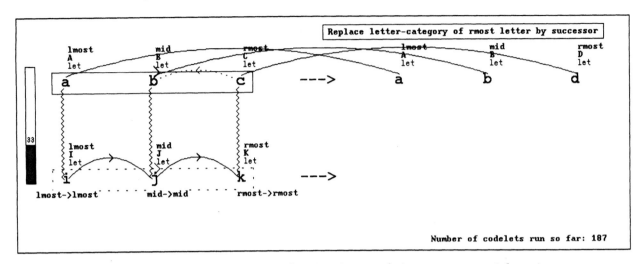

9. Workspace: The entire initial string is now being seen as a right-going successor group. (The direction is represented by a right-going arrow at the top of the solid rectangle; the bonds inside the group still exist, but their display has been suppressed.) This creates pressure (via top-down codelets, and increased strength of right-going successor bonds and groups) to view the target string in the same way, and indeed a similar grouping is being considered there (dotted rectangle).

8	12	8	8	3	3	3	47	100	100	100	48	3
·	·	·	·	·	·	·	■	■	■	■	■	·
A	B	C	D	E	F	G	H	I	J	K	L	M
3	3	3	3	3	3	3	3	3	3	3	3	3
·	·	·	·	·	·	·	·	·	·	·	·	·
N	O	P	Q	R	S	T	U	V	W	X	Y	Z

1	2	3	4	5	left	right	lmost	rmost	middle	pred	succ	same
			44			100	60	70	6	39	100	
			■			■	■	■	·	■	■	

pred group	succ group	same group	first	last	letter	group	iden	opp	whole	single	letter cat	length
	100		23	2		100	100		100		100	12
	■		·	·		■	■		■		■	·

alpha pos	string pos	direction	object cat	bond cat	group cat
33	100	100	10	100	
■	■	■	·	■	

Slipnet: The building of a whole-string successor group in the initial string has activated *whole*, and has sent *successor-group* and *group* into full activation.

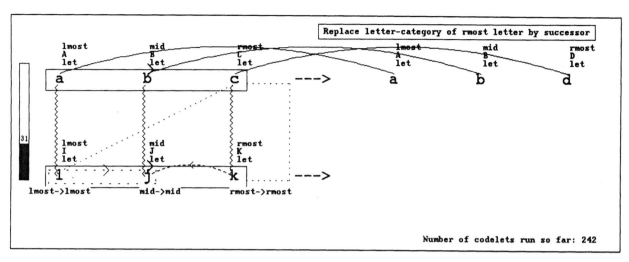

10. Workspace: Both strings have now been grouped as wholes, and a correspondence is being considered between the two groups (dotted bent line to the right of the two groups). The temperature has fallen to 31, but even at this relatively late stage a few rival possibilities are still being explored (though with very low urgency): a left-going **k-j** predecessor bond, a group in the target string containing only the **i** and the **j**, and a correspondence between the **c** and the **i**, based on the (here) fairly weak link between *rightmost* and *leftmost* in the Slipnet. None of these proposed structures (especially the last) is very strong, and in view of the strong and coherent set of structures that have been built these rivals have very little chance of getting anywhere at this point.

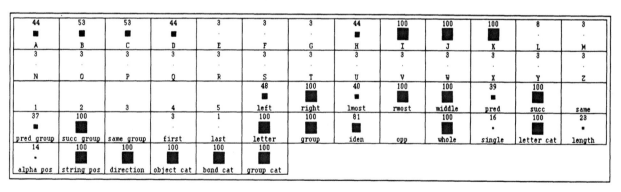

Slipnet: *Successor group* has spread small amounts of activation to *predecessor group* and to *length*. *Group* has spread activation to its superordinate node *object-category*, which is now fully active.

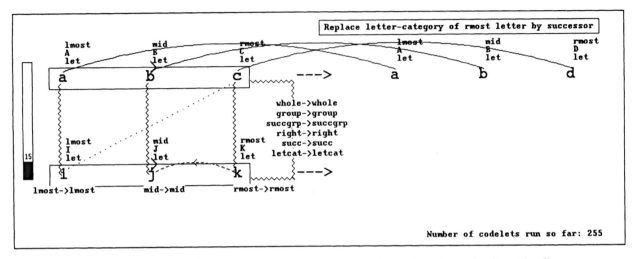

11. Workspace: The group-to-group correspondence has been built with all its concept mappings listed alongside it (*letcat* ⇒ *letcat* means that both groups are based on bonds between letter categories). The temperature has fallen to 15, indicating the program's assessment that it is very close to a good answer.

100	100	8	7	3	3	3	47	100	100	53	44	3
■	■	.	.	.	.	.	■	■	■	■	■	.
A	B	C	D	E	F	G	H	I	J	K	L	M
3	3	3	3	3	3	3	3	3	3	3	3	3
.	.	.	.	.	.	.	.	.	.	.	.	.
N	O	P	Q	R	S	T	U	V	W	X	Y	Z
					39	100	36	50	40	39	100	
					■	■	■	■	■	■	■	
1	2	3	4	5	left	right	lmost	rmost	middle	pred	succ	same
39	100		2	1	30	100	100		100	16	100	24
■	■				■	■	■		■	.	■	■
pred group	succ group	same group	first	last	letter	group	iden	opp	whole	single	letter cat	length
11	100	100	100	100	100							
.	■	■	■	■	■							
alpha pos	string pos	direction	object cat	bond cat	group cat							

Slipnet: The state of the Slipnet is similar to that in the previous frame, with some nodes (e.g., *rightmost, middle, letter*) decaying in activation.

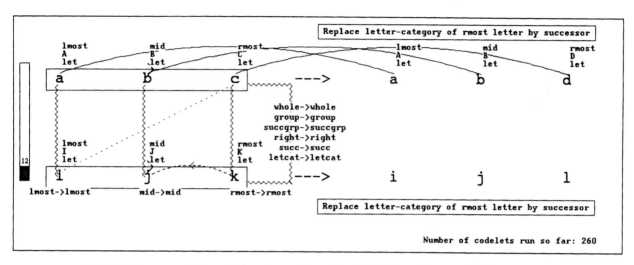

12. Workspace: The rule has been "translated" (although since all the concept mappings are identities, no changes were needed), and the answer **ijl** has been constructed according to the translated rule (the answer, with the translated rule beneath it, appears at the right-hand side of the screen). The low final temperature of 12 indicates that the program is very satisfied with this answer. This run consisted of 260 codelets (the average number of codelet steps for this problem is about 290).

53	53	44	4	3	3	3	48	53	53	48	7	3
■	■	■	.	.	.	.	■	■	■	■	.	.
A	B	C	D	E	F	G	H	I	J	K	L	M
3	3	3	3	3	3	3	3	3	3	3	3	3
.	.	.	.	.	.	.	.	.	.	.	.	.
N	O	P	Q	R	S	T	U	V	W	X	Y	Z
					36	100	14	30	16	39	100	
					■	■■	.	■	.	■	■■	
1	2	3	4	5	left	right	lmost	rmost	middle	pred	succ	same
39	90		26	1	16	80	100		40	16	100	24
■	■■		■	.	.	■	■■		■	.	■■	■
pred group	succ group	same group	first	last	letter	group	iden	opp	whole	single	letter cat	length
9	100	100	100	100	100							
.	■■	■■	■■	■■	■■							
alpha pos	string pos	direction	object cat	bond cat	group cat							

Slipnet: The final configuration of the Slipnet indicates what concepts were found to be relevant in this problem: the individual letter categories' activations have decayed, and the notions of *right, successor, successor-group, group,* and *identity* are activated, along with nodes corresponding to various categories (e.g., *bond-category*).

Screen dumps from a run on abc ⇒ abd, iijjkk ⇒ ?
The following is a set of screen dumps from a fairly typical run of Copycat on
this problem.

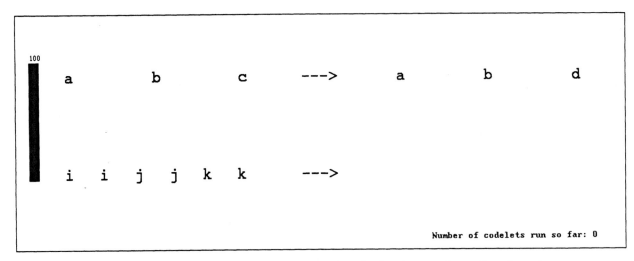

1. Workspace: The program is presented with the three strings. For the sake
of clarity, the descriptions of each letter are not displayed here; they are as given
in figure 3.5.

100	100	100						100	100	100			
■	■	■						■	■	■			
A	B	C	D	E	F	G	H	I	J	K	L	M
N	O	P	Q	R	S	T	U	V	W	X	Y	Z
								100	100	100			
								■	■	■			
1	2	3	4	5	left	right	lmost	rmost	middle	pred	succ	same
					100						100	
					■						■	
pred group	succ group	same group	first	last	letter	group	iden	opp	whole	single	letter cat	length
	100											
	■											
alpha pos	string pos	direction	object cat	bond cat	group cat							

Slipnet: The Slipnet starts out in the same initial state as in the last problem.

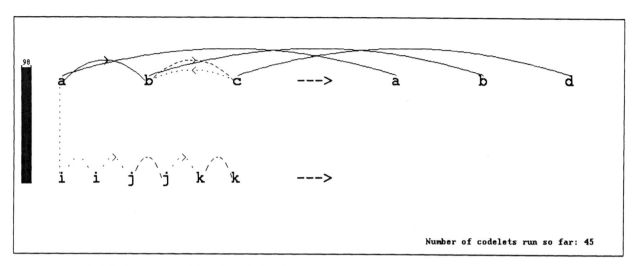

Number of codelets run so far: 45

2. Workspace: After 45 codelets have run, an **a-b** successor bond has been built and several possible structures are being considered. Sameness bonds (e.g., between the two **k**'s) are intrinsically stronger than successor and predecessor bonds, so they tend to be evaluated and built more quickly (their codelets receive higher urgencies).

100	100	53	44	3	3	3	48	53	100	53	48	3
A	B	C	D	E	F	G	H	I	J	K	L	M
3	3	3	3	3	3	3	3	3	3	3	3	3
N	O	P	Q	R	S	T	U	V	W	X	Y	Z
					16	100	100	38	6		100	
1	2	3	4	5	left	right	lmost	rmost	middle	pred	succ	same
			34		1	6					100	10
pred group	succ group	same group	first	last	letter	group	iden	opp	whole	single	letter cat	length
	100		24									
alpha pos	string pos	direction	object cat	bond cat	group cat							

Slipnet: Activation has spread and decayed from the initially active nodes, and *successor* and *right* have been activated in response to the bond that was built.

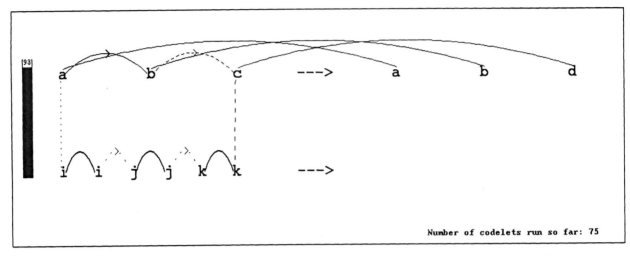

Number of codelets run so far: 75

3. Workspace: Three sameness bonds have been built in the target string, and other structures continue to be considered.

100	100	48	4	3	3	3	44	53	53	48	4	3
■	■	■	.	.	.	.	■	■	■	■	.	.
A	B	C	D	E	F	G	H	I	J	K	L	M
3	3	3	3	3	3	3	3	3	3	3	3	3
.	.	.	.	.	.	.	.	.	.	.	.	.
N	O	P	Q	R	S	T	U	V	W	X	Y	Z
					14	100	36	100	1	10	100	100
					.	■	■	■	.	.	■	■
1	2	3	4	5	left	right	lmost	rmost	middle	pred	succ	same
	20	70	85	20		4					100	12
	■	■	■	■							■	.
pred group	succ group	same group	first	last	letter	group	iden	opp	whole	single	letter cat	length
100	100	49	20	100								
■	■	■	.	■								
alpha pos	string pos	direction	object cat	bond cat	group cat							

Slipnet: The activation of the nodes *successor* and *sameness* has caused top-down bond scouts to be posted to look for more relationships of these types. These nodes have begun to spread activation to *successor-group* and *sameness-group* ("same group"), which will in turn post codelets to look for groups of these categories. The activation of the node *right* (the direction of the **a-b** successor bond) has caused top-down bond scouts and top-down group scouts to be posted to look for bonds and groups in this direction.

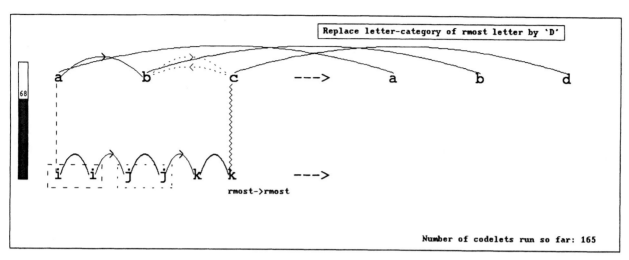

Replace letter-category of rmost letter by 'D'

Number of codelets run so far: 165

4. Workspace: After 165 codelets have run, some sameness groups are being considered (made up of the i's and the j's) and a correspondence between the c and the rightmost k has been built. Also, a rule, "Replace letter-category of rightmost letter by D," has been built. If the program were to stop right now, its answer would be **iijjkd** (which the program sometimes gets, as can be seen from the bar graph for this problem in the previous section). This rule is relatively weak, though, and will soon face competition from a stronger rule.

47	100	100	100	3	3	3	44	100	100	44	3	3
A	B	C	D	E	F	G	H	I	J	K	L	M
3	3	3	3	3	3	3	3	3	3	3	3	3
N	O	P	Q	R	S	T	U	V	W	X	Y	Z
					24	30	100	100		13	25	100
1	2	3	4	5	left	right	lmost	rmost	middle	pred	succ	same
	27	100	100	35		2	100				100	24
pred group	succ group	same group	first	last	letter	group	iden	opp	whole	single	letter cat	length
100	100	70	11	100	100							
alpha pos	string pos	direction	object cat	bond cat	group cat							

Slipnet: The nodes *successor* and *right* have decayed, but the nodes *sameness* and *sameness group*, being of greater conceptual depth, remain highly active. For the time being, the program is concentrating more on finding and evaluating sameness bonds and sameness groups.

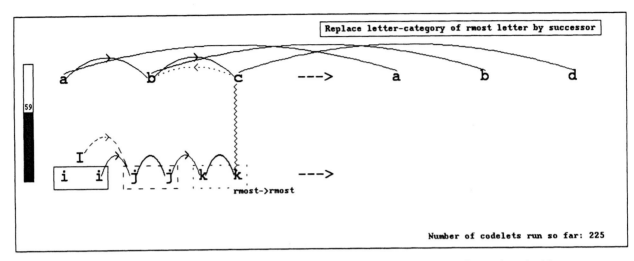

5. Workspace: Here, 225 codelets into the run, successorship has taken hold as the fabric of the initial string. In the target string, a sameness group has been built out of the two **i**'s, and two other such groups are being considered. A successor bond is being considered between the group **I** and its right neighbor, the letter **j** (perhaps owing to top-down pressure from the activation of *successor* and *right*). The previous weak rule has been replaced by the stronger rule "Replace letter-category of rightmost letter by successor"; thus, if the program were to stop now, it would answer **iijjkl**. The temperature continues to fall.

100	100	100	44	3	3	3	47	100	100	100	43	3
■	■	■	■	.	.	.	■	■	■	■	■	.
A	B	C	D	E	F	G	H	I	J	K	L	M
3	3	3	3	3	3	3	3	3	3	3	3	3
.	.	.	.	.	.	.	.	.	.	.	.	.
N	O	P	Q	R	S	T	U	V	W	X	Y	Z
					40	100	60	100	100	35	100	90
					■	■	■	■	■	■	■	■
1	2	3	4	5	left	right	lmost	rmost	middle	pred	succ	same
	71	100	38	9	12	100	100				100	24
	■	■	■	.	■	■	■				■	.
pred group	succ group	same group	first	last	letter	group	iden	opp	whole	single	letter cat	length
51	100	100	100	100	100							
■	■	■	■	■	■							
alpha pos	string pos	direction	object cat	bond cat	group cat							

Slipnet: *Successor* and *right* have been activated, in response to the new bonds that have been built. These are now posting top-down codelets to search for more bonds of this type. *Successor* has also spread activation to *successor-group*. In addition, *group* has been activated in response to the **ii** group that was built.

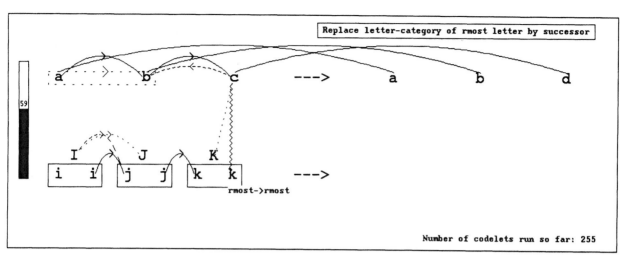

6. Workspace: All three sameness groups have been built in the target string, and a successor bond is being considered between the group **I** and the group **J** (which will compete with the proposed successor bond between the group **I** and the letter **j**). There is also a competition unfolding between the **c-k** correspondence and the proposed **c-K** correspondence. The latter correspondence has a better chance, even though it involves a slippage (*letter ⇒ group*) whereas the former does not. There are two reasons for this: (1) As was discussed in subsection 3.4.4, there is a bias toward correspondences that connect larger parts of the two strings (e.g., correspondences involving groups tend to be stronger than correspondences involving letters), and (2) the group **K** is now much more salient than either of its component letters, so there will be many more attempts to build the latter correspondence than the former, and statistics will tend to work in its favor.

53	100	100	48	3	3	3	48	100	100	53	48	3
■	■	■	■	.	.	.	■	■	■	■	■	.
A	B	C	D	E	F	G	H	I	J	K	L	M
3	3	3	3	3	3	3	3	3	3	3	3	3
.	.	.	.	.	.	.	.	.	.	.	.	.
N	O	P	Q	R	S	T	U	V	W	X	Y	Z
					34	100	38	100	40	39	100	100
					■	■	■	■	■	■	■	■
1	2	3	4	5	left	right	lmost	rmost	middle	pred	succ	same
	77	100	100	3	100	100	100				100	24
	■	■	■	.	■	■	■				■	.
pred group	succ group	same group	first	last	letter	group	iden	opp	whole	single	letter cat	length
33	100	100	100	100	100							
■	■	■	■	■	■							
alpha pos	string pos	direction	object cat	bond cat	group cat							

Slipnet: The state of the Slipnet is similar to that in the last frame.

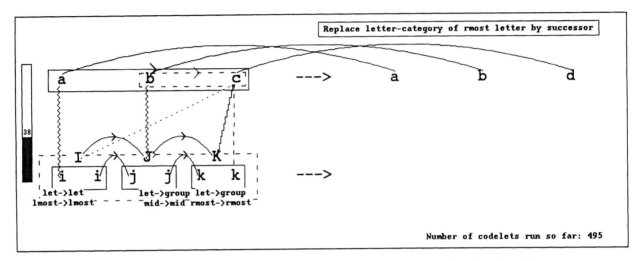

7. Workspace: Now, 495 codelets into the run, the initial string has been grouped as a right-going successor group. Strong top-down pressures from *successor* and *successor-group* have helped to accelerate a similar view of the target string, but at the level of groups rather than individual letters. The **c-K** correspondence has won over the **c-k** correspondence (though the latter is once again being considered). Also, a **b-J** correspondence has been built. (This means that a description-building codelet has at some point described the J group as "middle.") There is still a correspondence between the **a** and the leftmost letter **i** rather than the group **I**. The temperature has gone down to 38, reflecting the assessed promise of the structures that have been built so far. A "diagonal" **c-I** correspondence has been proposed, but it is very weak (it is based only on the weak concept mapping *rightmost* ⇒ *leftmost*). And, though a codelet for testing the strength of the **c-I** correspondence has been posted, its urgency is very low, and is suppressed even further by the low temperature.

44	100	100	44	3	3	3	8	8	100	100	4	3
■	■	■	■	.	.	.	.	.	■	■	.	.
A	B	C	D	E	F	G	H	I	J	K	L	M
3	3	3	3	3	3	3	3	3	3	3	3	3
.	.	.	.	.	.	.	.	.	.	.	.	.
N	O	P	Q	R	S	T	U	V	W	X	Y	Z
					33	100	100	100	16	29	100	90
					■	■	■	■	.	■	■	■
1	2	3	4	5	left	right	lmost	rmost	middle	pred	succ	same
19	65	100	1	1	100	100	59		16	6	100	30
.	■	■	.	.	■	■	■		.	.	■	■
pred group	succ group	same group	first	last	letter	group	iden	opp	whole	single	letter cat	length
5	100	100	100	100	100							
.	■	■	■	■	■							
alpha pos	string pos	direction	object cat	bond cat	group cat							

Slipnet: Again, the state of the Slipnet is similar to that in the previous frame, as the activity in the program begins to coalesce on a single set of structures.

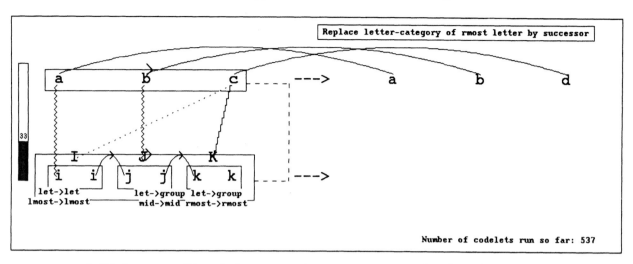

8. Workspace: The whole-target-string successor group has been built, and a correspondence is being considered between the two whole-string groups.

53	53	48	8	3	3	3	43	100	100	53	47	3
■	■	■	.	.	.	.	■	■	■	■	■	.
A	B	C	D	E	F	G	H	I	J	K	L	M
3	3	3	3	3	3	3	3	3	3	3	3	3
.	.	.	.	.	.	.	.	.	.	.	.	.
N	O	P	Q	R	S	T	U	V	W	X	Y	Z
					37	100	44	100	2	37	100	100
					■	■	■	■	.	■	■	■
1	2	3	4	5	left	right	lmost	rmost	middle	pred	succ	same
25	100	100	26	1	30	100	100		100	11	100	32
.	■	■	■	.	■	■	■		■	.	■	■
pred group	succ group	same group	first	last	letter	group	iden	opp	whole	single	letter cat	length
3	100	100	100	100	100							
.	■	■	■	■	■							
alpha pos	string pos	direction	object cat	bond cat	group cat							

Slipnet: The Slipnet continues to remain in basically the same state. The nodes *predecessor, predecessor-group,* and *length* are activated at a low level because of the spreading of activation from *successor, successor group,* and *sameness group.* The node *whole* has become fully active in response to the whole-string groups that have been built.

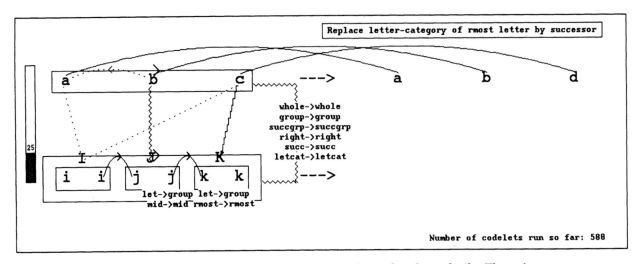

9. Workspace: The whole-string correspondence has been built. The **a-i** correspondence has been broken, and an **a-I** correspondence is being considered in its place. The temperature has fallen to 25.

100	100	48	8	3	3	3	3	4	3	4	3	3
■	■	■	.	.	.	.	.		.		.	.
A	B	C	D	E	F	G	H	I	J	K	L	M
3	3	3	3	3	3	3	3	3	3	3	3	3
.	.	.	.	.	.	.	.	.	.	.	.	.
N	O	P	Q	R	S	T	U	V	W	X	Y	Z
					34	100	34	100		19	100	100
					■	■	■	■		.	■	■
1	2	3	4	5	left	right	lmost	rmost	middle	pred	succ	same
39	100	100	19	1	100	100	100		100	16	100	37
■	■	■	.		■	■	■		■	.	■	■
pred group	succ group	same group	first	last	letter	group	iden	opp	whole	single	letter cat	length
2	100	100	100	100	100							
	■	■	■	■	■							
alpha pos	string pos	direction	object cat	bond cat	group cat							

Slipnet: The Slipnet remains in basically the same state, with minor variations. This stability shows the degree to which the program is devoting its resources to a single set of organizing themes.

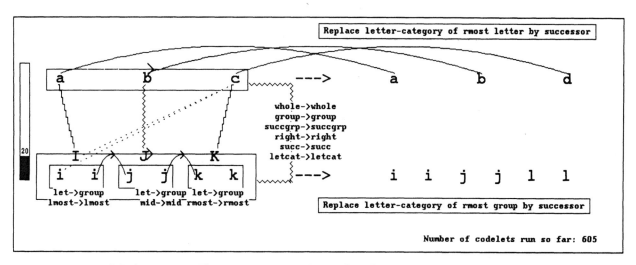

10. Workspace: The **a-I** correspondence has been built, the rule has been translated (according to the slippage *letter ⇒ group*), and the answer **iijjll** has been given. The low temperature of 20 reflects the program's satisfaction with this answer (though of course it is not as low as it was for **ijk ⇒ ijl**, since there is a slippage here—namely, *letter ⇒ group*—that did not have to be made in that problem).

8	8	8	3	3	3	3	3	3	3	3	3	3
.	.	.	.	.	.	.	.	.	.	.	.	.
A	B	C	D	E	F	G	H	I	J	K	L	M
3	3	3	3	3	3	3	3	3	3	3	3	3
.	.	.	.	.	.	.	.	.	.	.	.	.
N	O	P	Q	R	S	T	U	V	W	X	Y	Z
					44	50	60	100		35	100	100
					■	■	■	■		■	■	■
1	2	3	4	5	left	right	lmost	rmost	middle	pred	succ	same
39	90	100	22	1	30	100	100		40	16	100	37
■	■	■	.	.	■	■	■		■	.	■	■
pred group	succ group	same group	first	last	letter	group	iden	opp	whole	single	letter cat	length
2	100	100	100	100	100							
.	■	■	■	■	■							
alpha pos	string pos	direction	object cat	bond cat	group cat							

Slipnet: The final configuration of the Slipnet reflects what was important in this problem: not any particular letter category, but rather the notions of *rightmost, successorship, sameness, successor group, sameness group,* and so on. *Length* is more highly activated here than it was in the previous problem, owing to the spreading of activation from *successor-group* and *sameness-group*. However, it still remains in the background.

Screen dumps from a run on abc ⇒ abd, kji ⇒ ?
Two runs, leading to different answers, will be displayed for this problem. The first set of screen dumps is from a fairly typical run of Copycat on this problem. The Slipnet is not shown on this run, though relevant aspects of its state will be described in the accompanying text.

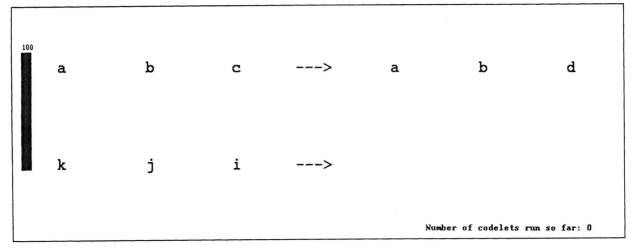

1. The program is presented with the three strings. Again, descriptions are not displayed; they are the same as in the problem **abc** ⇒ **abd, ijk** ⇒?.

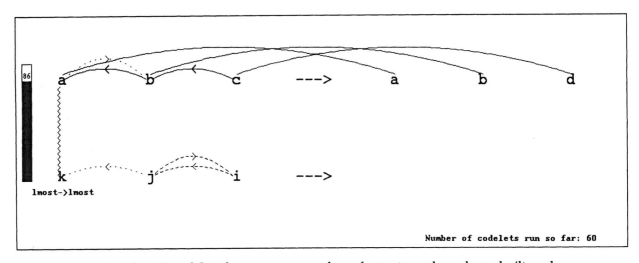

2. After 60 codelets have run, a number of structures have been built and the temperature has fallen to 86. The activation of *predecessor* and *left* resulting from the left-going predecessor bonds creates pressures for the program to build predecessor bonds and left-going bonds in **kji**. However, in contrast with the previous two problems, these two pressures cannot be satisfied simultaneously in the target string, since the target string runs in an opposite alphabetic direction from the initial string. There is thus competition between these pressures in the target string. The pressure to see predecessor bonds is stronger than the pressure to see left-going bonds, since the former has greater conceptual depth. But there is another set of very strong pressures that rivals this: *leftmost* ⇒ *leftmost* and *rightmost* ⇒ *rightmost* correspondences attempt to enforce a view in which bonds in the two strings have the same direction, since these correspondences are incompatible with the *left* ⇒ *right* and *right* ⇒ *left* slippages that would result from a view in which bonds in the two strings were in opposite directions.

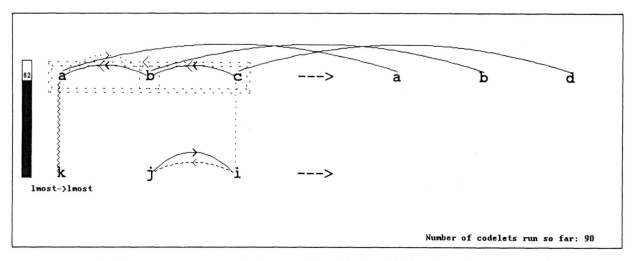

3. Here some groups are being considered in the initial string, the strongest of which is the whole-string predecessor group. A **j-i** predecessor bond has been built in the target string, in response to top-down pressure from *predecessor*. But the proposed vertical **c-i** correspondence will fight against it, since the concept mapping *rightmost* ⇒ *rightmost* is incompatible with the existence of bonds on the two sides of the correspondence going in opposite directions. A correspondence linking these bonds would require the slippage *left* ⇒ *right*, but this is incompatible with *rightmost* ⇒ *rightmost*.

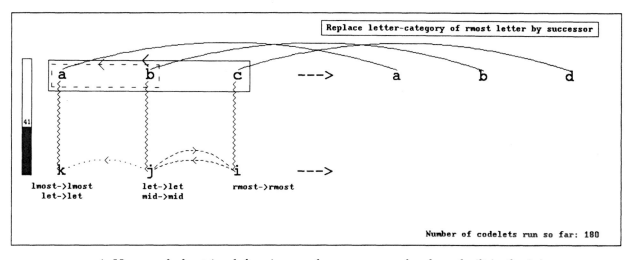

4. Here a whole-string left-going predecessor group has been built in the initial string. The *rightmost* ⇒ *rightmost* correspondence has won, breaking the **j-i** bond. This "vertical" (i.e., *leftmost* ⇒ *leftmost*, *rightmost* ⇒ *rightmost*) correspondence viewpoint is working hard to force the program to build bonds all in the same direction, in spite of the strong pressure from *predecessor*, which remains active in the Slipnet and which lobbies for the building of predecessor bonds going in one spatial direction in the initial string and in the opposite direction in the target string.

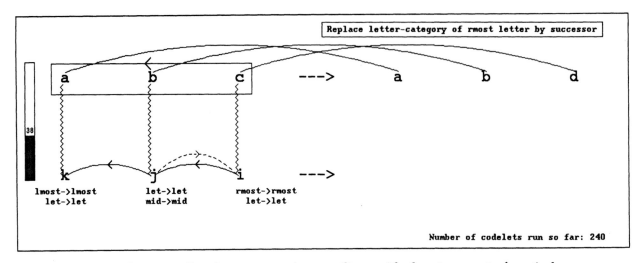

5. The same-direction pressure is prevailing, with the strong set of vertical correspondences remaining intact and with left-going successor bonds being built in the target string. The temperature is already fairly low, making it unlikely that this viewpoint will be destroyed at this point, even though there are still attempts being made to build predecessor bonds in the target string.

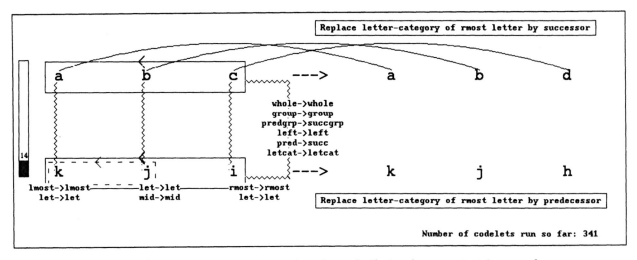

6. A left-going successor-group has been built in the target string, and a correspondence involving the slippages *predecessor-group ⇒ successor-group* and *predecessor ⇒ successor* has been built between the two whole-string groups. The rule has been translated using the latter slippage ("Replace letter-category of rightmost letter by *predecessor*"), and the answer **kjh** has been given.

Screen dumps from another run on abc ⇒ abd, kji ⇒ ?
The following is a set of screen dumps from a less typical run of Copycat on the same problem, which led to a different answer.

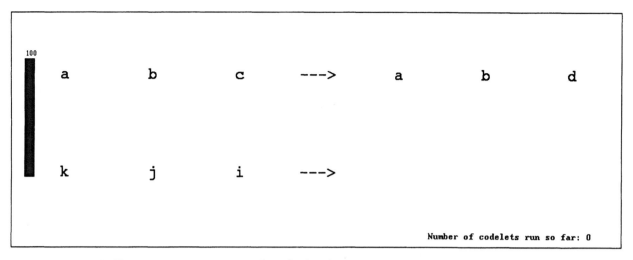

1. The program is presented with the three strings.

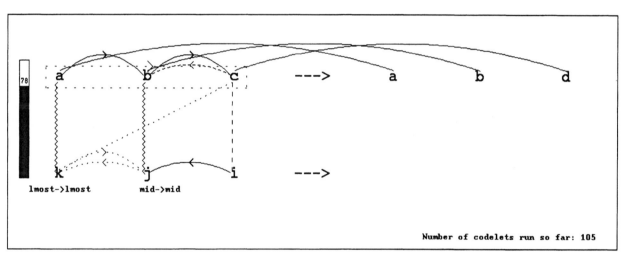

2. Now we skip ahead 105 codelets into the run. Right-going successor bonds have been built in the initial string. As in the previous run, this sets up two opposing top-down pressures for the target string: a pressure to see successor bonds (which in the target string are *left-going*) and a pressure to see right-going bonds (which in the target string are *predecessor* bonds). Various proposed bonds are being considered, and a left-going **i-j** successor bond has been built. As in the previous run, the vertical correspondences lobby for building target-string bonds in the same direction as those of the initial string. Some fights are in store—in particular, between the strong proposed **c-i** correspondence (which is supported by the already-built **a-k** correspondence) and the **i-j** bond (which is supported by the activation of the node *successor*).

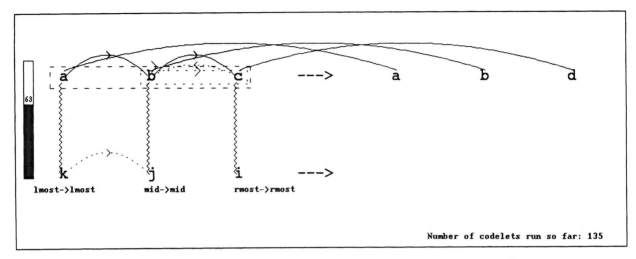

3. The **c-i** correspondence has been built, destroying the **i-j** bond in the process. At this point it looks as if the same-direction view is going to win out, as it did in the previous run.

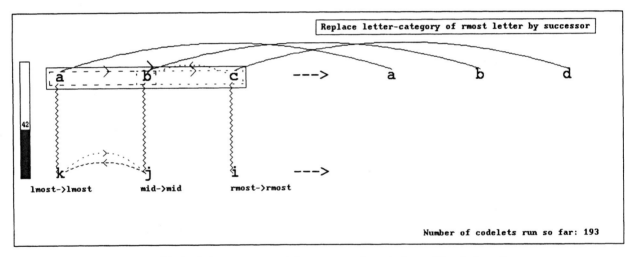

4. But trouble isn't far away, as a **j-k** successor bond vies with a **k-j** predecessor bond to be built.

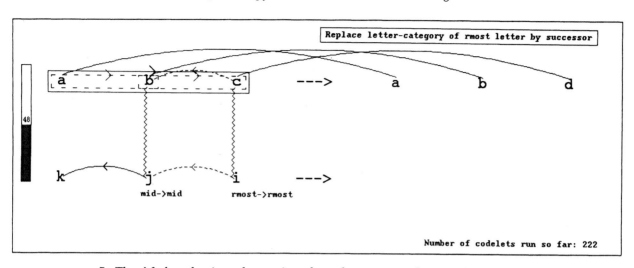

5. The **j-k** bond wins, destroying the **a-k** correspondence. This causes the temperature to go up slightly. Also, a left-going **i-j** successor bond is now waiting to be built.

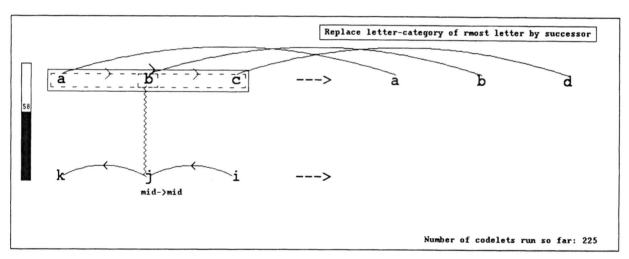

6. The **i-j** bond has been built, also destroying a correspondence, and now it looks as if the successorship viewpoint is going to win the day. The temperature has gone up again, because the **c-i** correspondence has been broken.

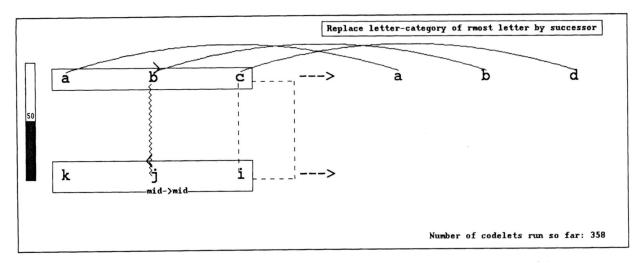

7. The successorship viewpoint is becoming more entrenched, for the following reasons: (1) the target string has been perceived as a successor group; (2) a correspondence is being considered between the two groups as wholes; and (3) the temperature is falling (it is now 50). Even so, a *rightmost* ⇒ *rightmost* correspondence (which would contradict the opposite-direction correspondence between the two groups as wholes) is being considered.

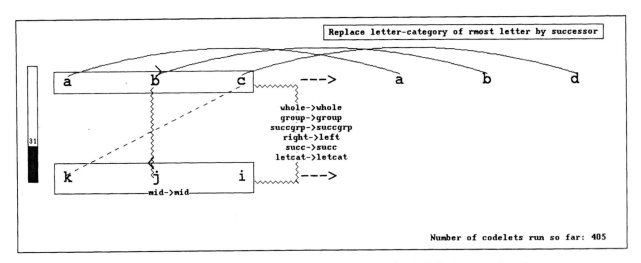

8. A whole-string correspondence involving a *right* ⇒ *left* slippage has been built between the two successor groups. This activates *opposite*, and the combination of that slippage and the activation of *opposite* gives a great deal of support to a proposed diagonal **c-k** correspondence, with the slippage *rightmost* ⇒ *leftmost*.

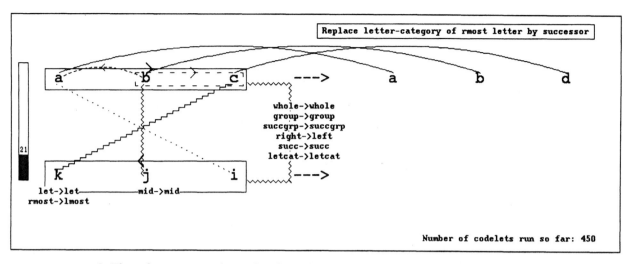

9. The **c-k** correspondence has been built, and this (along with the continuing activation of *opposite*) creates further support for an **a-i**, *leftmost ⇒ rightmost* correspondence. A **bc** group has been proposed, challenging the much stronger **abc** group, but the low temperature makes it very unlikely that this proposed group will get anywhere at this point. The same is true for the proposed **b-a** predecessor bond.

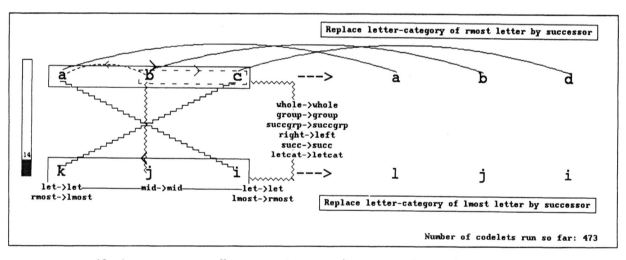

10. A strong, mutually supporting set of correspondences has been built, resulting in a low temperature of 14. The rule has been translated, according to the instructions in the concept mappings, as "Replace letter-category of *leftmost* letter by successor", yielding the answer **lji**.

Screen dumps from a run on abc ⇒ abd, mrrjjj ⇒?
The set of screen dumps given below shows one way in which Copycat arrives at the answer **mrrjjjj** (and thus they are from a not-so-typical run on this problem; this answer is given only about 4% of the time). This problem is different from the problem **abc ⇒ abd, xyz ⇒?** (shown in the next set of screen dumps) in that

there is no obvious "snag" (such as the fact that *Z* has no successor) blocking a good answer. Rather, the straightforward answer **mrrkkk** just does not seem very strong, since there are no bonds tying together the target string as a whole. In particular, the strong successorship structure in **abc** is completely lacking in **mrrjjj** when only the letter categories are considered. Copycat usually simply gives up and produces one of the two more obvious answers, even though the temperature remains fairly high. (Most people also give one of these two answers.) But on some more interesting runs (such as the one shown here), Copycat does manage to see the relations between the lengths of the groups in the target string, and to produce **mrrjjjj**.

The point here is to illustrate how a number of pressures interact to allow the notion of *group length*, which in most problems remains essentially dormant, to come to be seen as relevant in this problem. On most runs, the groups **rr** and **jjj** are constructed. As happened in **iijjkk**, each group's letter category (*R* and *J* respectively) is explicitly noted, since letter category is relevant by default. By contrast, although there is some probability that lengths will be noticed at the time the groups are made, it is low, since *length* is not normally strongly associated with the concept of *group*. Once the groups **rr** and **jjj** have been made, the concept *sameness-group* becomes very relevant. This creates top-down pressure for the system to describe other objects—especially in the same string—as sameness groups if that is possible. The only way to do this here is to describe the single **m** as a "sameness group" with just one letter. This is strongly resisted by an opposing pressure: a single-letter group is an intrinsically weak and farfetched construct. It would be disastrous for the program if it were willing to bring in unlikely notions such as single-letter groups without strong pressure: the program would then waste huge amounts of time exploring unlikely possibilities in every problem. As was discussed in chapter 2, under the limitations of time and cognitive resources one has in real life, it is crucial to resist looking at situations in nonstandard ways unless there is strong pressure to do so.

Copycat resists farfetched notions such as single-letter groups. But in this problem the existence of two other groups in the string, coupled with the lone **m**'s unhappiness at its failure to be incorporated into any large, coherent structure, pushes against this resistance. These opposing pressures fight, and the outcome is decided probabilistically. If the **m** winds up being perceived as a single-letter group, its length will very likely be noticed (single-letter groups are noteworthy precisely because of their abnormal length), making *length* more relevant in general and thus increasing the probability of noticing the other two groups' lengths. Moreover, *length*, once brought into the picture, has a good chance of staying relevant, since descriptions based on it turn out to be useful. (Had the target string been **mrrrrjj**, length might be brought in; however, it would not turn out to be useful, so it would likely fade back into obscurity.) In **mrrjjj**, once lengths are noticed, the successor (or predecessor) bonds among them can then be constructed by bond scouts that are continually present as a kind of background process, always seeking new bonds. In particular, the chance of spotting successor relations among the group lengths is enhanced by the presence on the coderack of top-down successor scouts resulting from the already-seen successor bonds in **abc**. Thus, the crux of discovering this solution lies in the triggering of the concept of *length*.

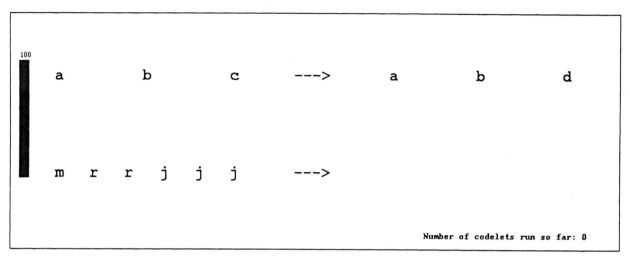

1. The program is presented with the three strings. (Again, the Slipnet will not be displayed on this run, though aspects of its state will be described from time to time.)

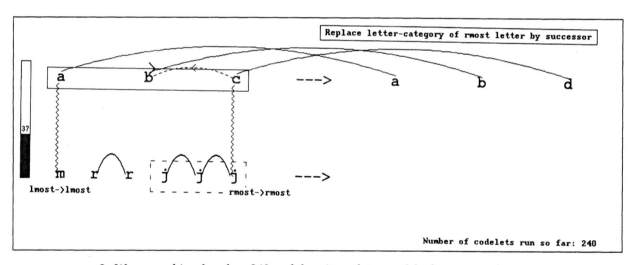

2. We now skip ahead to 240 codelets into the run. Much progress has been made: a whole-string successor group has been built in the initial string, sameness bonds have been built in the target string, a **jjj** sameness group is being considered, correspondences have been built between the two leftmost letters and between the two rightmost letters in each string, and a rule has been built. The temperature has fallen to 37. If the program were to stop at this point, the answer would be **mrrjjk**.

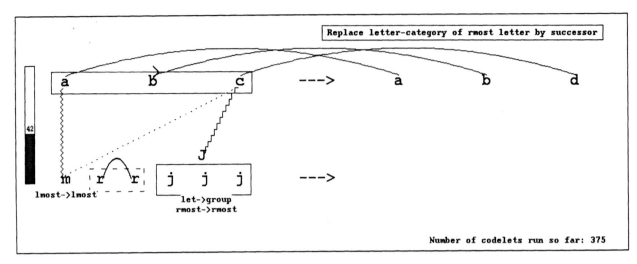

3. The group J has been built, creating more top-down pressure to see same-ness groups in the string, and a correspondence has been made between the c and the J. (If the program were to stop at this point, the answer would be **mrrkkk**.) A grouping of the two r's is being considered, as is a weak diagonal correspondence between the c and the m. The temperature has gone up a bit as a result of the creation of a new object (here, the group J). New groups cause the temperature to go up; this is because temperature is a function of the happiness of all the objects, and while the existence of the group increases the happiness of its members, it itself starts out unhappy (e.g., the group J has no bonds to anything else in its string). The result can add up to an increase in total unhappiness. This initial unhappiness is a necessary thing: it serves to quickly attract codelets to the new group.

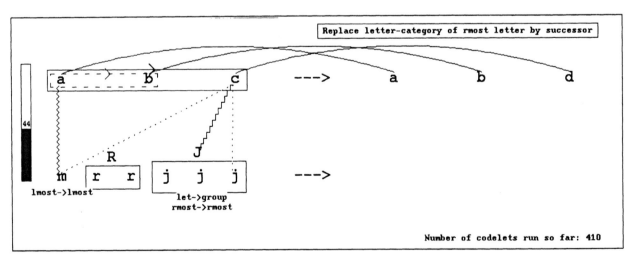

4. The group of r's has been built. A few additional competing structures (an **ab** group; a **c-j** correspondence) are being considered. The new group **R** causes a slight increase in temperature, much as the group J did in the previous screen dump.

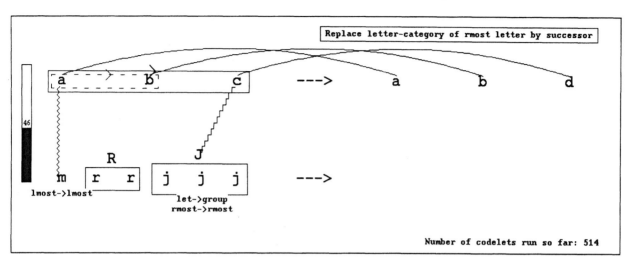

5. About 100 codelets have run since the previous screen dump, but no new structures have been built. There are several pressures at work at this point. First, the single **m** remains unhappy, since it is not integrated into any structures in its string. Second, the groups **R** and **J** remain unhappy, because—in spite of many tries by various bond scouts, especially top-down bond scouts trying to make successor bonds—no bonds can be made between them. This continuing unhappiness keeps the temperature relatively high. Finally, the presence of two sameness groups in the target string and the high activation of the node *sameness-group* create strong pressure to look for more such groups in the target string.

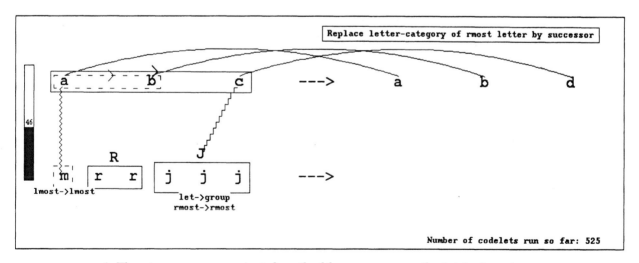

6. The strong pressures just described have overcome the intrinsic resistance to proposing a sameness group consisting of a single letter; indeed, such a group, consisting of the single **m**, has been proposed (dashed rectangle around **m**). Top-down group category scouts can in principle propose such groups at any time, but such a proposal is intrinsically very unlikely and almost never

happens unless there are strong pressures that make it more likely. The probability of proposing a single-letter group is a function both of the amount of local support in the string (the number of other groups of the same type) and of the activation of *length*—i.e., if group lengths have already been deemed to be important, then it is more likely that single-letter groups can be proposed. Here, with group lengths not yet in the picture, the proposal of such an oddball group is a result of a combination of factors: unhappiness of the lonely single letter (which makes it salient, causing lots of codelets to concentrate on it, so that after many tries one may succeed), strong local support for such a group in the string, and relatively high temperature (making intrinsically unlikely events a bit more likely).

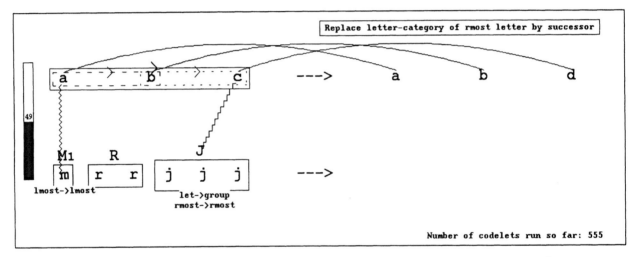

7. The single-letter group has been built, and its length has been noticed (displayed as a "1" next to the **M**). There are two ways in which group lengths can be noticed in Copycat:

> • A group-builder codelet can attach a length description at the time the group is built. A group-builder codelet always has some probability of doing this, the probability being a function of both the length of the group (the shorter the more probable, with probability dropping off very quickly with increasing length) and the activation of *length* (when it is relevant, noticing length is much more likely). Thus, *a priori*, there is not much likelihood that a group builder will notice the lengths of two-element groups, less for three-element groups, and so on. But it is rather likely that a group builder will notice the length of single-letter groups, since it is precisely their short length that makes them noteworthy.

> • Length descriptions can also be attached to already-formed groups (e.g., the **rr** group here) by top-down description codelets. These are posted by *length* once it becomes activated (as it is now, as a result of the spreading of activation from the node *1*).

The probability of creating a length description in either of these two ways is, of course, also dependent on temperature.

The activation of *length* means that *length* is now a relevant notion, which creates pressure on the program (in the form of top-down description scouts) to continue to use *length* as an organizing theme. If *length* does not turn out to be a useful notion, its activation will decay and this pressure will subside.

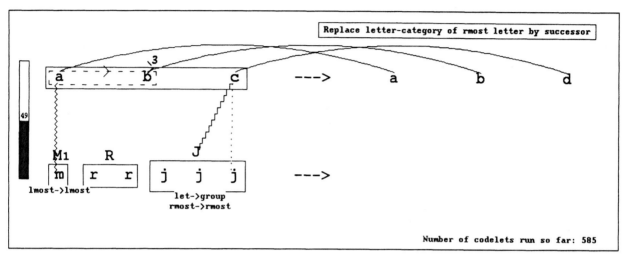

8. A length description of *3* has been attached to the **abc** group by a chain of top-down description codelets triggered by *length*, which remains active.

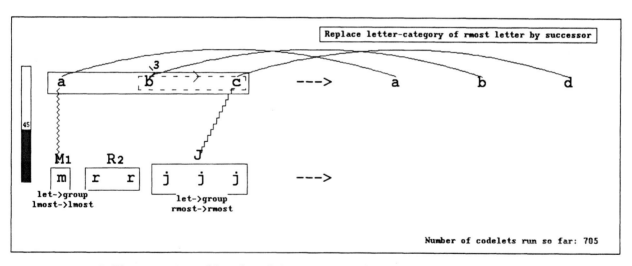

9. The activation of *length* and the existence of the description *1* created pressure for length descriptions in the target string. (The existence of the *1* provides local support for other length descriptions.) As a result, a length description has been attached to the group of **r**'s. Also, a correspondence has now been built from the **a** to the group **M** (a subtle change from the previous **a**-to-letter-**m** correspondence).

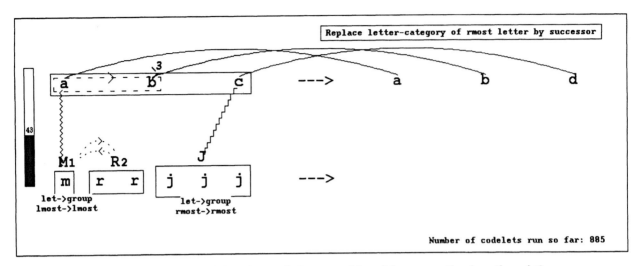

10. Some proposed bonds are being considered between the lengths of the M and R groups. There is some resistance to building these bonds. Bonds between lengths, being less standard, are not as strong as bonds between letter categories (an *a priori* bias given to the program), and the lack of other length bonds in the target string increases the resistance to them.

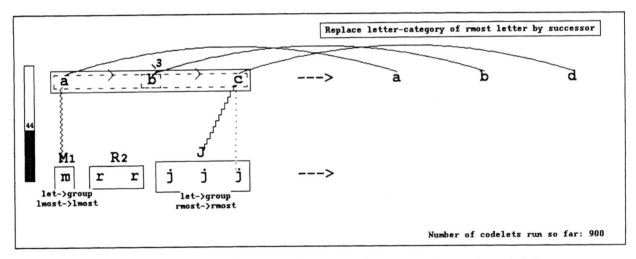

11. The proposed length bonds did not pass their strength tests (a probabilistic decision) and have fizzled. In the meantime, a number of other proposed structures are being considered.

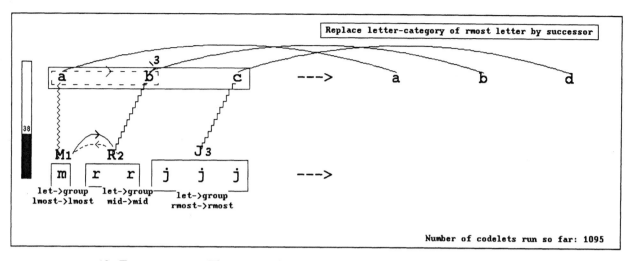

12. Try, try again. This time, the relatively high temperature, the top-down pressure from *successor*, and many repeated attempts at building bonds have combined for success: a successor bond has finally been built between the group **M** and the group **J** on the basis of length. In addition, the group **J** has now been given the length description 3.

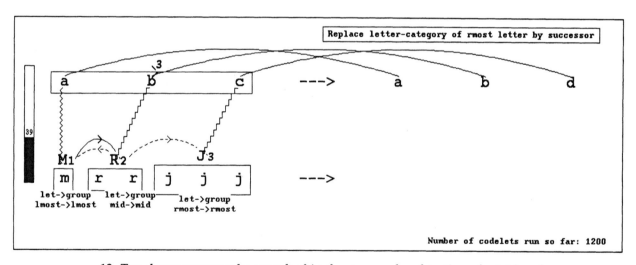

13. Top-down pressure has resulted in the proposal and testing of a 2-3 bond, now waiting to be built. This time, building the bond will be much easier, since another one already exists in the same string, giving local support to the new proposed bond.

Notice that over 100 codelets have run since the previous screen dump. The temperature is still relatively high, and the program is still exploring a number of different possibilities (e.g., codelets are still attempting to build successor bonds among the letter categories of the target-string groups, or to use the notion of *alphabetic-position*; these attempts are not displayed in the screen dumps). None of these possibilities is panning out.

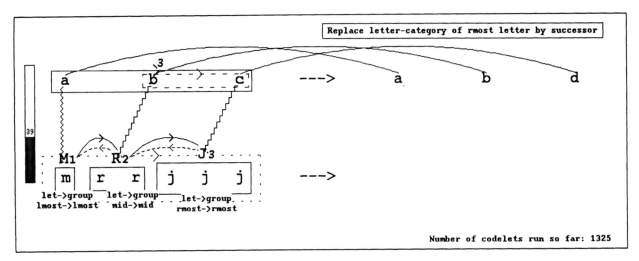

14. The *2-3 length* bond has now been built in the target string, and a grouping of the whole target string, based on the successorship bonds, is being considered. In the Slipnet, the activations of the nodes *sameness* and *sameness-group* have faded, since these concepts have served their purpose and are now no longer very relevant to what is going on. Instead, *successor*, *successor-group*, and *length* have taken over as the main organizing themes.

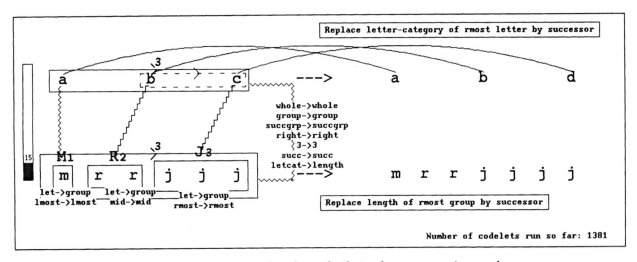

15. The whole-string group has been built in the target string and a correspondence has been made between the two strings as wholes, with the slippage *letter-category* ⇒ *length* (the respective description types on which the groups' bonds were based). The temperature has fallen to the low value of 15, indicating the program's satisfaction with this way of structuring the problem. The rule has been translated according to the slippages *letter-category* ⇒ *length* and *letter* ⇒ *group* to yield "Replace *length* of rightmost *group* by successor," which produces the answer **mrrjjjj**.

Although this run may have looked quite smooth, there were many struggles involved in coming up with this answer. It was hard not only to make a single-letter group, but also to bring the notion of group length into the picture and to build bonds between group lengths. The program, like people, usually gives up before all these hurdles can be overcome, and gives one of the more obvious answers.

The moral of all this is that in a complex world (even one with the limited complexity of Copycat's microworld) one never knows in advance what concepts may turn out to be relevant in a given situation. It is thus imperative not only to avoid dogmatically open-minded search strategies, which entertain all possibilities equally seriously, but also to avoid dogmatically closed-minded search strategies, which absolutely rule out certain possibilities *a priori*. Copycat opts for a middle way, which of course leaves open the potential for disaster (as can be seen in the occasional bizarre answers it gets). This is the price that must be paid for flexibility. People, too, occasionally explore and even favor peculiar routes. The program, like people, has to have the potential to concoct crazy and farfetched solutions in order to be able to discover subtle and elegant ones, such as **mrrjjjj**. To rigidly close off any routes *a priori* would necessarily remove critical aspects of Copycat's flexibility. On the other hand, the fact that Copycat so rarely produces really farfetched answers demonstrates that its mechanisms manage to strike a pretty effective balance between open-mindedness and closed-mindedness, imbuing it with both flexibility and robustness.

The screen dumps above show one way in which Copycat can arrive at **mrrjjjj**, but there are other ways. For example, it could first notice the relationship between the lengths of the **R** and **J** groups, which would then create very strong pressure for creating a single-letter group. Part of Copycat's flexibility rests in the fact that there are a number of different ways in which it can arrive at each of the different answers to any problem. Not only are there a huge number of *microscopic* pathways to a given answer; there are also a number of different *macroscopic* pathways.

Screen dumps from a run on abc ⇒ abd, xyz ⇒ ?

The set of screen dumps given below shows one way in which Copycat arrives at the answer **wyz** after hitting the impasse brought on by its inability to take the successor of Z. The two main mechanisms for resolving the impasse are (1) raising the temperature, thus allowing structures to be broken more easily (by breaker codelets and by rival structures) and allowing less obvious pathways to have a better chance of being explored, and (2) focusing attention on the apparent *cause* of the impasse: the **z** in **xyz**. Part of this focusing of attention involves high activation of the node Z, which in turn spreads activation to the node *last* (Z being the last letter in the alphabet). The activation of *last* increases the probability that it will be attached to the **z** as a description. The node *last* also spreads activation to its neighbor *first*, and this, combined with the fact that *alphabetic-position* is now seen as a relevant way of describing objects, gives *first* a good chance of being attached to the **a**. When this has taken place, a correspondence between the **a** and the **z** (via a *first* ⇒ *last* concept mapping) is more plausible, since the notions of *first* and *last* have been brought into the program's perception of the problem. As was mentioned above, concept mappings that take into account deep similarities (e.g., between *first* and *last*) are seen as strong, but this pressure conflicts with a resistance to making slippages between deep aspects of the two situations. The idea is that there should be a desire to avoid slippage as much as possible, since a perfect analogy is one in which no slippages are needed (e.g., **abc** ⇒ **abd, ijk** ⇒ **ijl**). If one is forced to make slippages, then the shallower the descriptions that slip the better, since in making an analogy one wants to preserve the *essence* of the two situations, which means that deep aspects should remain invariant. However, a good analogy should *expose* deep aspects of the two situations that might not have been recognized before, in the way that the *first* ⇒ *last* concept mapping exposes a deep similarity between **abc** and **xyz**. Thus, in analogy-making there is a fundamental conflict between a resistance to deep slippages and a desire for deep concept mappings.

The upshot is that in Copycat it takes strong pressures (including high temperature, which increases the chances of low-probability, risky slippages) to force the *first* ⇒ *last* slippage, but once that slippage has been made, it is seen as quite strong, and its strength increases even more when a resolution to the impasse begins to fall into place as a result of it.

The **a-z** correspondence has to fight against much of the currently existing structure, but if it can prevail (and this is more likely at high temperature) it can trigger a complete restructuring of the program's previous perception of the strings: the strings **abc** and **xyz** can be seen as opposites in both spatial and alphabetic directions, with the **c** corresponding to the **x**. This view leads to the slippages *rightmost* ⇒ *leftmost* and *successor* ⇒ *predecessor*, causing the program to translate the original rule as "Replace *leftmost* letter by *predecessor*," which yields the answer **wyz**.

1. The program is presented with the three strings. (Descriptions are displayed again here because there will be important additions to them in the course of the run. The Slipnet is also displayed in some of the frames.)

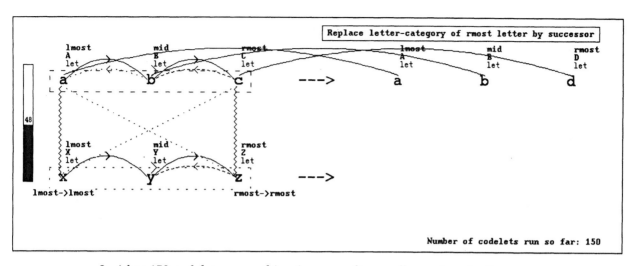

2. After 150 codelets, everything is proceeding well, much as in the run on **abc** ⇒ **abd, ijk** ⇒?. There are two strong vertical correspondences (*leftmost* ⇒ *leftmost* and *rightmost* ⇒ *rightmost*). Diagonal correspondences (*leftmost* ⇒ *rightmost* and *rightmost* ⇒ *leftmost*) are being examined fleetingly; however, as in **abc** ⇒ **abd, ijk** ⇒?, they are very weak and of very low priority for further examination.

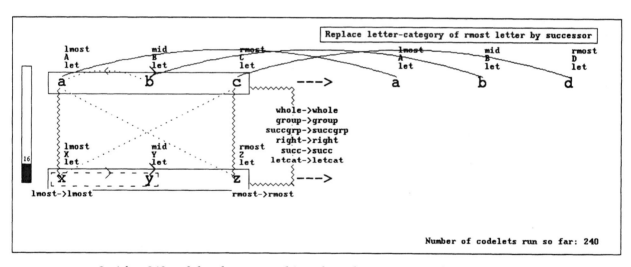

3. After 240 codelets have run, things have been structured just as in the run on **abc** ⇒ **abd, ijk**?. The temperature is very low, and the program is almost ready to try to construct its answer.

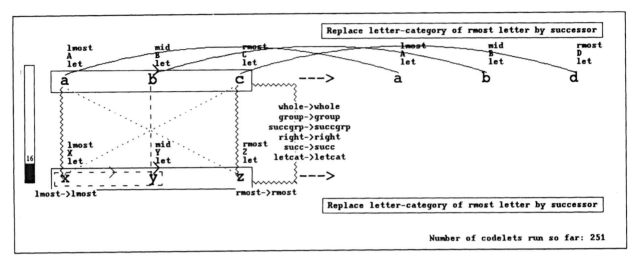

4. Since no slippages are involved in the correspondences between **abc** and **xyz**, the rule needs no translation. As it did for **ijk**, the program attempts to follow the rule "Replace letter-category of rightmost letter by successor." Here, however, it hits a snag: Z has no successor.

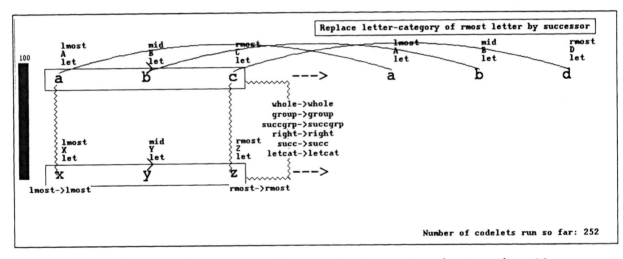

5. **Workspace:**   In response to the snag, the temperature shoots up from 16 to 100, reflecting the fact that the program is now at an impasse and that it has gone from being very certain about the quality of the structures it has built to being quite uncertain and far away from an answer. The temperature is clamped at 100, reflecting a "state of emergency" which will not be revoked until the program judges that progress (in the form of new structures) has been made. At this high temperature, actions that normally have a low probability of occurring (e.g., breaker codelets succeeding in breaking structures) are more likely to take place. But even at this maximum temperature, decisions are not totally random; the same kinds of biases exist at high and low temperatures. The biases just become more and more pronounced as the temperature falls.

53	53	48	7	3	3	3	3	3	3	3	3	3
■	■	■	.	.	.	.	.	.	.	.	.	.
A	B	C	D	E	F	G	H	I	J	K	L	M
3	3	3	3	3	3	3	3	3	7	8	8	100
.	.	.	.	.	.	.	.	.	.	.	.	■
N	O	P	Q	R	S	T	U	V	W	X	Y	Z
					38	100	8	100	100	41	100	
					■	■	.	■	■	■	■	
1	2	3	4	5	left	right	lmost	rmost	middle	pred	succ	same
39	100		50	8	100	100	100		100	16	100	24
■	■		■	.	■	■	■		■	.	■	.
pred group	succ group	same group	first	last	letter	group	iden	opp	whole	single	letter cat	length
100	100	100	100	100								
■	■	■	■	■								
alpha pos	string pos	direction	object cat	bond cat	group cat							

Slipnet: The program's other response to the impasse is to focus on its apparent cause: the **z**. It does this by clamping the activation of all the **z's** descriptors at 100, thus making the **z** very salient and making these descriptors strong foci of attention. Notice in the Slipnet that the nodes *Z, rightmost,* and *letter* are all fully activated. As with temperature, these clamps will not be released until the program determines that a sufficient amount of progress has been made toward getting out of this impasse. The way this works is that every time the Slipnet is updated, the program checks to see if any new structures have been built; if some have, it decides probabilistically, on the basis of their strength, whether to rescind the "state of emergency."

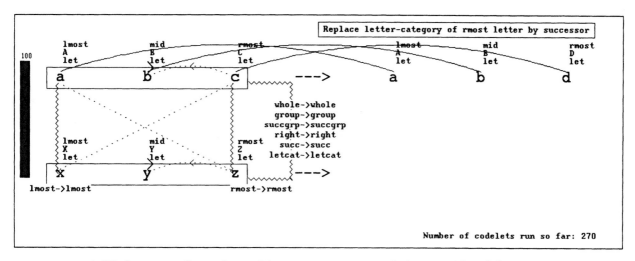

6. Workspace: Several possible new structures are being considered, but none have yet gotten very far, and the original structures remain intact.

A	B	C	D	E	F	G	H	I	J	K	L	M
4	100	100	3	3	3	3	3	3	3	3	3	3

N	O	P	Q	R	S	T	U	V	W	X	Y	Z
3	3	3	3	3	3	3	3	3	3	3	100	100

1	2	3	4	5	left	right	lmost	rmost	middle	pred	succ	same
					14	30	100	100	16	21	40	

pred group	succ group	same group	first	last	letter	group	iden	opp	whole	single	letter cat	length
39	50		18	43	100	100	81		16	6	100	24

alpha pos	string pos	direction	object cat	bond cat	group cat
100	100	100	100	100	

Slipnet: The node Z remains active and is spreading activation to the node *last*, which is beginning to become activated.

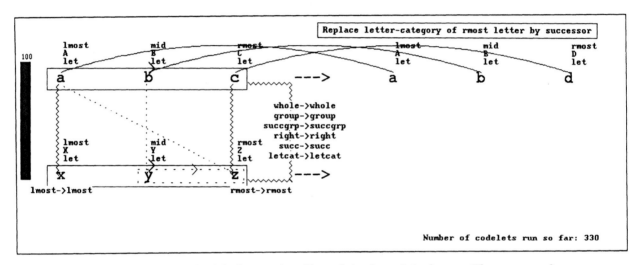

7. Workspace: The Workspace is still stuck in the original state. The proposed **a-z** correspondence, here lacking the *first* ⇒ *last* concept mapping (since these descriptors have not yet even been attached to the letters) is too weak to have much chance of going anywhere, even at this high temperature.

A	B	C	D	E	F	G	H	I	J	K	L	M
8	8	8	8	3	3	3	3	3	3	3	3	3

N	O	P	Q	R	S	T	U	V	W	X	Y	Z
3	3	3	3	3	3	3	3	3	48	53	100	100

1	2	3	4	5	left	right	lmost	rmost	middle	pred	succ	same
					32	100	100	100	40	37	100	

pred group	succ group	same group	first	last	letter	group	iden	opp	whole	single	letter cat	length
33	100		22	100	100	100	100		100	12	100	22

alpha pos	string pos	direction	object cat	bond cat	group cat
100	100	100	100	100	100

Slipnet: The node *last* is now fully active, and has spread activation to *first* and to *alphabetic-position*. The latter is also now fully active and is posting top-down description scouts to try to make descriptions of this type.

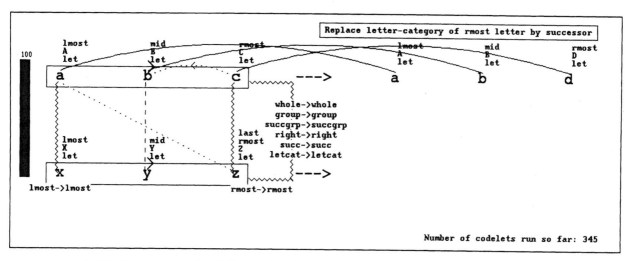

8. Workspace: After 345 codelets have run, *last* has been added to the **z**'s list of descriptions as a result of top-down pressures from the activation of *last* and *alphabetic-position*.

100	100	100	4	3	3	3	3	3	3	3	3	3
■	■	■	.	.	.	.	.	.	.	.	.	.
A	B	C	D	E	F	G	H	I	J	K	L	M
3	3	3	3	3	3	3	3	3	8	48	53	100
.	.	.	.	.	.	.	.	.		■	■	■
N	O	P	Q	R	S	T	U	V	W	X	Y	Z
					43	100	100	100	100	39	100	
					■	■	■	■	■	■	■	
1	2	3	4	5	left	right	lmost	rmost	middle	pred	succ	same
37	100	3	33	100	100	100	100		40	15	100	23
■	■		■	■	■	■	■		■	.	■	■
pred group	succ group	same group	first	last	letter	group	iden	opp	whole	single	letter cat	length
100	100	100	100	100	100							
■	■	■	■	■	■							
alpha pos	string pos	direction	object cat	bond cat	group cat							

Slipnet: In the Slipnet, the node *first* continues to gain activation from *last*.

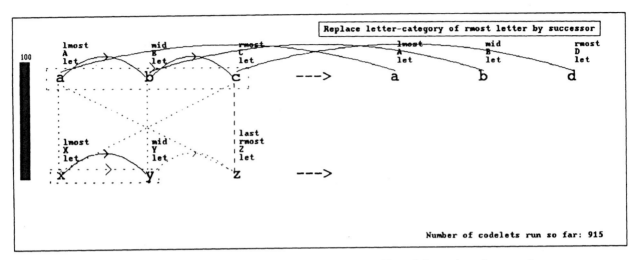

9. Workspace: Now, 915 codelets into the run (570 codelets after the previous screen dump), after much thrashing by the program and little progress, several breaker codelets have succeeded in breaking some structures, though the skeleton of the original successorship structure is still intact. (Breaker codelets have a good chance of running and breaking structures only at high temperatures.) As was detailed in chapter 3, both bottom-up and top-down codelets continue to be posted to the Coderack as the program runs. What have they all been doing? Most of the codelets that run are redundantly working on building the same structures that already exist. This redundancy is an essential part of the program—it allows *statistics*, rather than any single codelet or small set of codelets, to control what happens on a large scale. Other codelets are trying (and, so far, failing) to build new structures, and yet others are attempting (and occasionally succeeding) to break existing structures. A large number of the codelets are focusing again and again on the **z**, which is very salient, now having *four* fully active descriptors. Often at this point in other runs what happens is that the rule is broken and the weaker rule "Replace letter-category of rightmost letter by *D*" is built (this is more likely than usual, owing to the high temperature and the lack of progress on other fronts) and is used by the program to get the answer **xyd**.

53	100	100	3	3	3	3	3	3	3	3	3	3
■	■	■	·	·	·	·	·	·	·	·	·	·
A	B	C	D	E	F	G	H	I	J	K	L	M
3	3	3	3	3	3	3	3	3	8	48	100	100
·	·	·	·	·	·	·	·	·		■	■	■
N	O	P	Q	R	S	T	U	V	W	X	Y	Z
					14	100	100	100	40	100	100	
					·	■	■	■	■	■	■	
1	2	3	4	5	left	right	lmost	rmost	middle	pred	succ	same
100	100		100	100	100	90	100				100	35
■	■		■	■	■	■	■				■	■
pred group	succ group	same group	first	last	letter	group	iden	opp	whole	single	letter cat	length
100	100	100	100	100	100							
■	■	■	■	■	■							
alpha pos	string pos	direction	object cat	bond cat	group cat							

Slipnet: The node *last* has continued to spread activation to *first*, which is now fully activated.

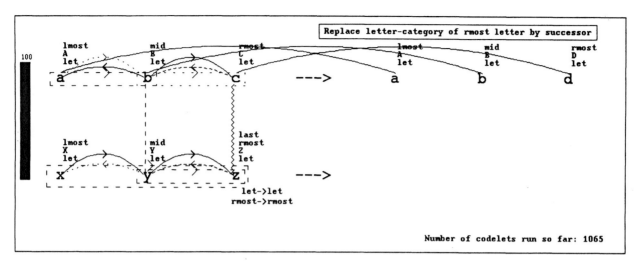

10. At codelet step 1065, a bit of restructuring is being tried out: a **b-a** predecessor bond has broken the **a-b** successor bond.

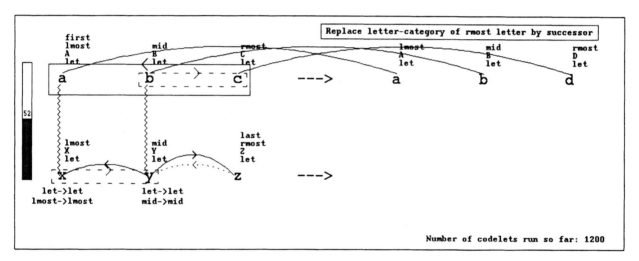

11. The program's view of both strings is in the midst of being restructured, gradually changing from right-going successorship to left-going predecessorship. In the hope that this is a promising new course, the program has released the clamp on the temperature. No longer forced to stay at 100, it is now being computed in the normal way, and it has fallen to 52. Meanwhile, the descriptor *first* has been added to the **a**'s list of descriptions. This addition came about as a result of the spreading of activation from *last* to *first*, and as a result of the fact that *alphabetic position* is now viewed as relevant and has thus become the source of top-down codelets that attempt to construct *alphabetic position* descriptions.

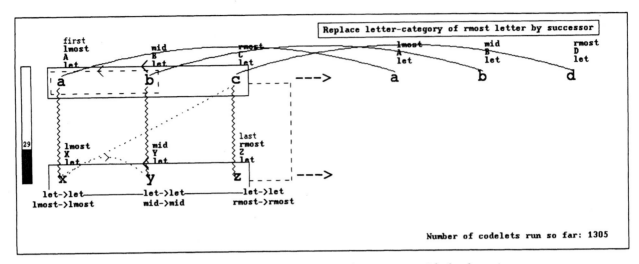

12. Workspace: A new viewpoint has taken over, with both strings now grouped as left-going predecessor groups and with the low temperature reflecting the program's high assessment of this new way of structuring things.

13	48	8	4	3	3	3	3	3	3	3	3	3
·	■	·	·	·	·	·	·	·	·	·	·	·
A	B	C	D	E	F	G	H	I	J	K	L	M
3	3	3	3	3	3	3	3	3	43	53	53	44
·	·	·	·	·	·	·	·	·	■	■	■	■
N	O	P	Q	R	S	T	U	V	W	X	Y	Z
					100	50	70	100	6	100	41	
					■	■	■	■	·	■	■	
1	2	3	4	5	left	right	lmost	rmost	middle	pred	succ	same
100	41		53	22	100	100	100		100	16	100	26
■	■		■	·	■	■	■		■	·	■	·
pred group	succ group	same group	first	last	letter	group	iden	opp	whole	single	letter cat	length
64	100	100	100	100	100							
■	■	■	■	■	■							
alpha pos	string pos	direction	object cat	bond cat	group cat							

Slipnet: The nodes *first*, *last*, and *alphabetic-position* have decayed considerably, and these descriptors are thus no longer relevant (indicated in the Workspace by the fact that the descriptors are no longer in boldface), and are now being ignored.

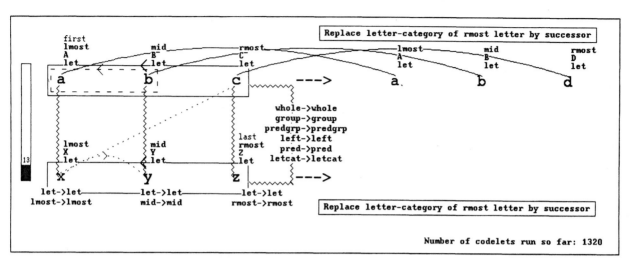

13. The program has used this new, seemingly good set of structures to attempt once again to get an answer, but the same snag appears again. It could certainly be said that the program shows a lack of common sense for having expected that this trivial form of restructuring could resolve the impasse. But it could also be said that people often get pulled into mental dead-end paths whose futility should have been obvious in the first place. Once one gets started along a certain mental pathway, it is sometimes hard to get off it. Obvious ways of viewing situations (such as trying to take the successor of Z here) act like attractors; it is hard to avoid them. In general, this is a useful feature of perception. In real life, the most obvious view is usually the right view, so it is good to be quickly drawn into it. However, in some situations this results in behavior like that of the program on this problem, where one is drawn again and again into the same wrong way of looking at things, perhaps with slight variations. Unfortunately, this happens to the program far too often. During an average run on this problem, Copycat continually gets into states that cause it to hit the same snag over and over again (on average nine times before getting an answer), because it lacks some essential mechanisms for remembering and watching its own behavior. The need for such "self-watching" mechanisms will be discussed further in chapter 7.

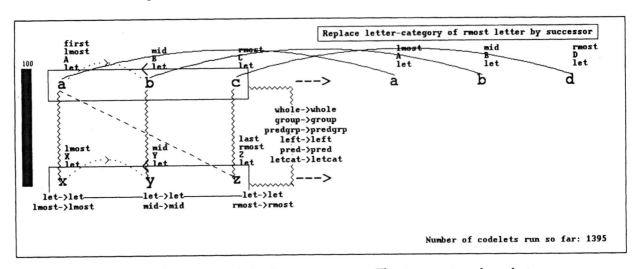

14. Now the program is back at square one. The temperature has shot up again, and the z's descriptors have again been clamped in response to the snag. The **a** and the **z** are now both quite salient (since each has four fully active descriptors), and are thus being chosen very often by codelets. Now a correspondence between them is more plausible, because of the possibility of the concept mapping *first* ⇒ *last*. As was pointed out above, it is initially difficult to make this slippage because of the conceptual depth of the descriptors involved (deep slippages are harder to make than shallow ones), but once it has been made it is seen as fairly strong (deep concept mappings are stronger than shallow ones). An **a-z** correspondence has been proposed and has passed its strength test (thanks in part to the high temperature, which makes intrinsically unlikely events more likely), but it still faces a lot of competition from the still quite strong currently existing structures. Even at high temperature and in this desperate condition, it is still essential for the program to resist unusual notions—they should be allowed to be considered seriously only under strong pressures. Otherwise the program would be wasting all its time exploring unmotivated crazy possibilities.

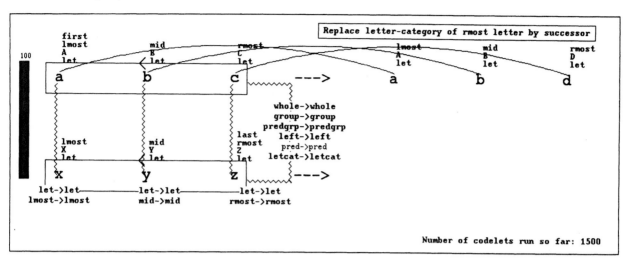

15. The **a-z** correspondence did not manage to defeat the existing rival structures, and it has fizzled.

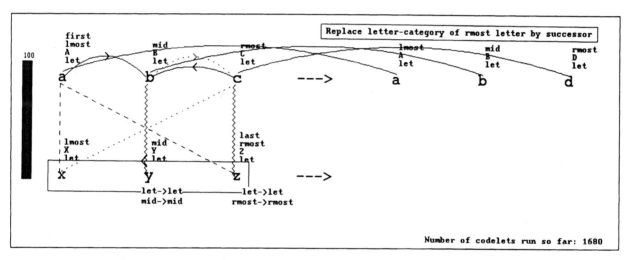

16. Some structures have been broken, and a bit of restructuring is being tried again: this time an **a-b** successor bond defeated the **b-a** predecessor bond. Another attempt is being made to build the **a-z** correspondence (the **a** and the **z** remain quite salient, so many attempts are being made to use them in structures), but it still faces strong competition from the existing **c-z** correspondence.

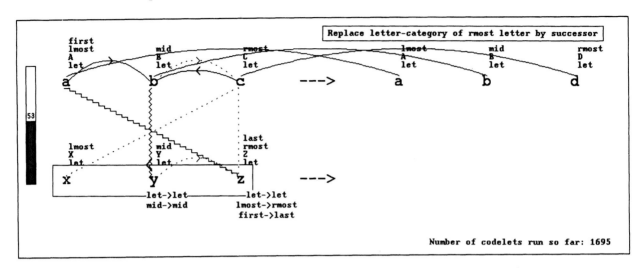

17. Thanks to the strength of the *first* ⇒ *last* concept mapping, the high temperature, and the large number of tries, the **a-z** correspondence has beaten the normally far stronger **c-z** correspondence (though the latter is being considered again). The creation of this fairly strong new structure has caused the temperature to be unclamped, and it has fallen to 53. The new correspondence has two slippages, *leftmost* ⇒ *rightmost* and *first* ⇒ *last*, and in response to these slippages, the node *opposite* has suddenly jumped into prominence. The existence of the **a-z** correspondence and the activation of *opposite* will make the proposed **c-x** correspondence (before, too weak to have much of a chance at all) much more plausible.

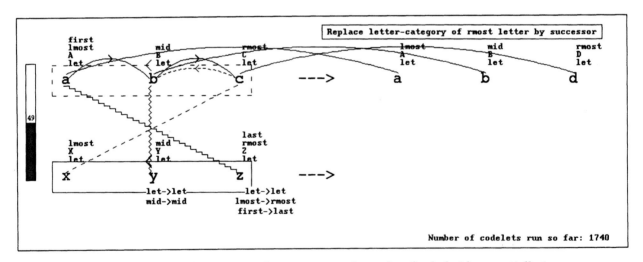

18. The competing proposed **c-z** correspondence has fizzled. Also, partially in response to the new diagonal correspondence, the initial string is being viewed as consisting of right-going successor bonds—the opposite of the bonds in the target string. However, there is still some competition lurking. A proposed group is threatening to turn the whole initial string around so that it is in the

same direction as the target string (as indicated by the left-pointing arrow on top of the dashed rectangle). The **c-x** correspondence has passed its strength test and is waiting to be built.

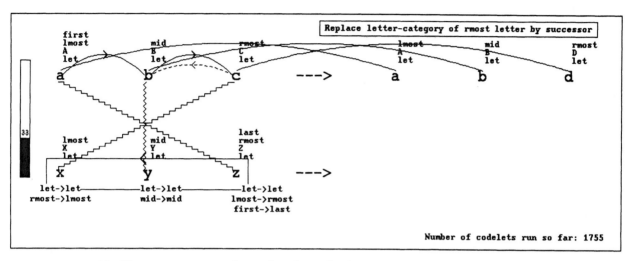

19. The **c-x** correspondence has been built, and the proposed predecessor group in the initial string has fizzled. The temperature has fallen to 33, reflecting the estimated promise of these new structures.

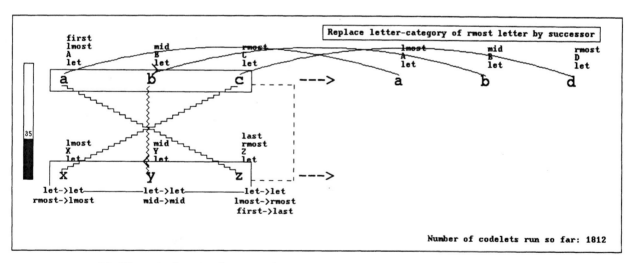

20. The initial string has now been grouped as a right-going successor group, opposite to the target string. This turnaround was made possible by the diagonal correspondences. A whole-string group-to-group correspondence is now being considered.

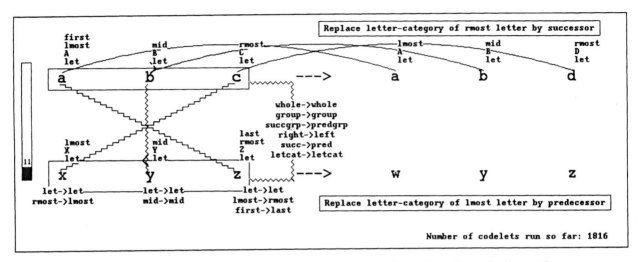

21. The whole-string group-to-group correspondence has been built, with slippages *successor-group* ⇒ *predecessor-group, right* ⇒ *left*, and *successor* ⇒ *predecessor*. The last, along with the slippage *rightmost* ⇒ *leftmost*, is used to construct a sweeping translation of the rule to "Replace letter-category of *leftmost* letter by *predecessor*," which yields the answer **wyz**.

It is interesting to compare the analogy **abc** ⇒ **abd**, **xyz** ⇒ **wyz** with the analogy **abc** ⇒ **abd**, **ijk** ⇒ **hjk**. The latter analogy appeared once in 1000 runs on that problem. The former analogy is much more strongly justified, since not only does Z have no successor, but the **a** and the **z** can be seen as corresponding extremities of the alphabet. Lacking this justification, the latter analogy is much more farfetched, and indeed Copycat hardly ever constructs it. However, once it has been made, Copycat views it as a strong answer. (Recall that the final temperature on the run that produced it was 16.) This is because once the improbable *opposite* slippage is made, *opposite* becomes activated, which allows additional *opposite* slippages to be made and to be seen as strong. This feedback effect is very important to the working of the program—the key challenge is to make sure that the feedback is due to *justified* rather than unjustified slippages, or else the program will dig itself into a hole, ending up with a bizarre answer such as **hjk**.

4.4 Summary

The various series of screen dumps presented above show how all the mechanisms described in chapter 3 work together to produce a system that can flexibly adapt its concepts to new situations. As can be seen, Copycat starts from a standard initial state on each new problem, but as it runs, it discovers unique aspects of the problem, bringing out certain associations, downplaying others, and usually homing in on a suitable set of relevant concepts and avenues of approach. In addition, when the system's original approach leads it to an impasse, it is able to fluidly restructure its perceptions to find a better way of looking at things.

The screen dumps also clarify the fundamental roles of nondeterminism, parallelism, and non-centralized and simple perceptual agents (i.e., codelets), the interaction of bottom-up and top-down pressures, and the reliance on statistically emergent (rather than explicitly programmed) high-level behavior in achieving these abilities. The claim being made for this model is that these are also fundamental features of high-level perception in general.

The result of all these features is an emergent parallel terraced scan of possibilities, in which a fight for cognitive resources takes place, and in which one point of view gradually (or sometimes rapidly) comes to dominate. Nondeterminism pervades this process. Large, global, deterministic decisions are never made (except perhaps toward the end of a run). The system relies instead on the accumulation of small, local, nondeterministic decisions, none of which alone is particularly important for the final outcome of the run. As can be seen in the screen dumps, large-scale effects occur only through the statistics of the lower levels: the ubiquitous notion of a "pressure" in the system is really a shorthand for the statistical effects over time of a large number of codelets and of activation patterns of nodes in the Slipnet.

The program starts out exploring possible structures with a high degree of randomness, and lets both *a priori* biases and information accumulated along the way guide the evolving search. The idea of the parallel terraced scan is to try to allocate time to different paths of exploration in proportion to their estimated promise. As the "two-armed bandit" problem illustrates, it is a bad idea to devote all of one's resources to what currently seems to be the best path if one has very little information on which to base one's estimate of quality. It would also defeat the purpose of the parallel terraced scan if the promise of every single possibility had to be evaluated before any further exploration could be done—there are too many possibilities to be evaluated. The best strategy is to explore many different possibilities (without excluding any *a priori*), continuously adjusting the speed of exploration of each possibility as a function both of ongoing estimates of its promise as it unfolds and of the global sense of how reliable those estimates are. In Copycat this effect is an emergent one, achieved statistically though a large number of temperature-controlled nondeterministic choices.

As structures are formed and a global interpretation coalesces, the system gradually makes a transition from being quite parallel, random, and dominated by bottom-up forces to being more deterministic, serial, and dominated by top-down forces. The claim being made here is that such a transition is characteristic of high-level perception in general.

Chapter 5

Copycat's Performance on Variants of the Five Target Problems

---

5.1 Introduction

In this chapter I present the performance of the program on 24 variants of the five target problems. As will be seen, the variants given here constitute families of analogy problems that explore in greater detail certain of the issues in perception and analogy-making that have been discussed above. Copycat's behavior on these problems demonstrates how, starting from exactly the same state on each new problem, it deals with these issues, how it responds to variations in pressures, and how it is able to fluidly adapt to a range of situations.

There are a huge number of ways in which the original five problems can be varied. For example, consider **aabc ⇒ aabd, ijkk ⇒?**, a variant of **abc ⇒ abd, ijk ⇒?** in which the doubling of letters is meant to alter the "stresses" on various locations in the strings **abc** and **ijk**. One effect this might have is to make the double **a** and the double **k** stand out and in some sense "attract" each other, thus pushing toward a diagonal mapping in which the two double letters are seen to correspond. Another variation would be to triple the letters instead of doubling them, which would again slightly alter the pressures, perhaps increasing the salience of the sameness groups. Many other variations in this vein could be made as well.

Another way of manipulating pressures is to include distinguished letters— **a** and **z**—in strategic spots, since it is possible that they will be seen as more salient than other letters and thus attract more attention, changing the pressures in the problem.

Another technique is to alter the relational fabric of a string or of a segment of a string—specifically, to use successor relations where sameness relations existed, or vice versa. A variant of this technique is to get rid of a fabric altogether, or to introduce a fabric where there originally was none. Yet another technique is to experiment with strings of different lengths.

Another very important technique is to manipulate pressures by introducing or deleting same-category letters. These kinds of variations were illustrated in problems 1a–1d in chapter 2. For example, given the change **abc ⇒ abd**, the target **cde** is similar to the target **ijk** except that it contains a **c**, which might attract special attention because of its identity with the **c** of **abc**. By including more or fewer such letters, or by manipulating their positions inside the strings, one can create a spectrum of differing pressures.

Each of these pressures taken singly can provide a wealth of variants on a given problem, but by using several of them in conjunction one can create a huge family of problems related to an original problem. This chapter surveys a small sampling of such variants on the five target problems, revealing how the variations in pressures affect the program's behavior.

Each variant highlights and tests some aspect of the program's behavior, and the sum total of all these results gives a clear picture of the program's abilities. The results in this chapter also give a sense of what kinds of answers Copycat tends to prefer. A bit anthropomorphically, these results can be said to illustrate the program's "personality."

The variants in this chapter are divided into five sets, corresponding to the five target problems. (In many cases this division is somewhat arbitrary, since many of the problems could be considered variants of more than one of the five original problems.) The results are presented in the form of bar graphs similar to the ones given in the previous chapter. The bar graph from the previous chapter for the appropriate one of the original five target problems is displayed again at the beginning of each section, so that it can be referred to more easily.

5.2 Variants of abc ⇒ abd, ijk ⇒?

The bar graph for the original problem: abc ⇒ abd, ijk ⇒?

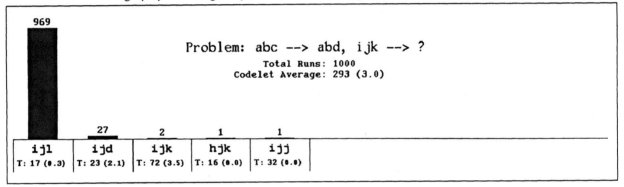

Variant 1: abc ⇒ abd, ijklmnop ⇒?

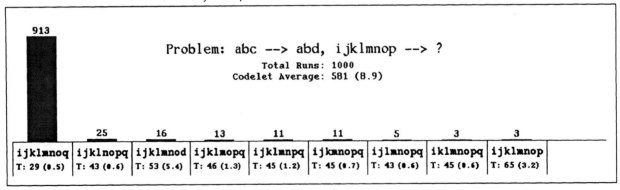

Here the length of the target string is extended. In principle, this should not affect Copycat's performance very much: when successor bonds begin to be built in the target string, top-down forces should cause the program to quickly see the entire string as a successor group, just as in the original problem (which I will abbreviate as **ijk**). Here the proportion of instances of the "Replace the rightmost letter by its successor" answer (**ijklmnoq**) is almost as high as in **ijk**, but the average time taken to find a solution is significantly higher here (581 codelets versus 293 codelets), which indicates that the top-down forces are not as strong as they should be. This problem with Copycat's performance will be discussed in chapter 7. The average temperature for this answer is somewhat higher than that for **ijl** for two reasons: (1) Here there are many letters in the target string that do not correspond to anything in the initial string. (2) Since the target string is longer, the program does not manage to group the whole string here as often as it did in **ijk**.

Copycat also gets a variety of low-frequency fringe answers, reflecting various parts of the target string that were grouped and seen as corresponding to the "rightmost letter". All the fringe answers except **ijklmnod** and **ijklmnop** have this property. This is one of the program's shortcomings: when given long strings, it occasionally makes several small groups and does not merge them together into larger groups. People also do this on occasion, but usually there is some justification for making the smaller groups.

In the survey of human subjects, 26 answered this problem. As was discussed in chapter 4, subjects were allowed to give multiple answers if they felt that there was more than one reasonable answer, and not all the subjects answered every problem, so the total number of answers for each problem is often not equal to the number of subjects. Many of the answers reflect the subjects' second, third, fourth, etc., choices (though on most problems, most people gave only one or two answers).

The frequency of each answer is given in parentheses, though, again, the purpose of the survey was to compare Copycat's range of answers against that of the human subjects rather than to compare the frequencies of different answers. (A summary of how Copycat's performance compares with peoples' in terms of range of answers will be given in the next chapter.) As in chapter 4, the answers that Copycat cannot presently get are starred. Also, I give the presumed justification for an answer whenever I think that it is not obvious.

The subjects' answers were the following:

ijklmnoq (21)

ijlllmnop* (4) (Replace the third letter by its successor.)

ijlmnopq* (4) (Replace the third and all following letters by their successors.)

ijklmnod (3)

ijlllmoop* (3) (Replace the rightmost letter of each group of three by its successor—the rightmost two letters do not form a group of three, so don't change them.)

ijklmnqr* (2) (Group the string as **ijk-lmn-op** and replace **op** by its "successor," **qr**.)

ijdlmnop* (1) (Replace the third letter by **d**.)

ijklqrst* (1) (Group the string as **ijkl-mnop** and replace the rightmost group by its "successor," **qrst**.)

ijklmnop (1)

ijlmnpqr* (1) (justification uncertain).

Variant 2: abc ⇒ abd, xlg ⇒?

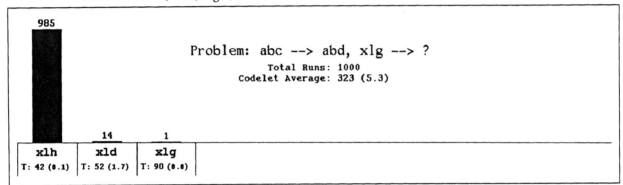

Here there is no relational structure in the target string. This results in higher average temperatures for all the answers. The answer **xlh** ("Replace the rightmost letter by its successor") still wins by a landslide, since this rule is much stronger than "Replace the rightmost letter by *D*" or "Replace *C* by *D*" (the rules responsible for the other two answers), even at these relatively high temperatures.

Even though the average temperatures are higher, there is not a large difference between the time taken by Copycat to get an answer to this problem and to **ijk**: 323 versus 293. This is because (as was described in subsection 3.4.3), when the program "senses" that there is probably no structure to be found, as in the target string here, it is more willing to give up and to produce an answer even though the temperature is high.

In the survey, 26 of the subjects answered this problem; their answers follow:

xlh (24)

xld (3)

xlg (1)

ymh* (1) (Replace all letters alphabetically after *B* by their successors.)

ylg* (1) (Replace the latest letter in the alphabet—here, *X*—by its successor.)

xsm* (1) (justification uncertain)

xxlg* (1) (justification uncertain).

Variant 3: abc ⇒ abd, xcg ⇒?

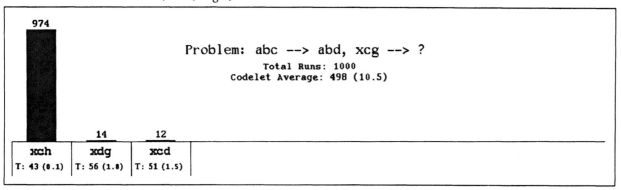

This variant is similar to the previous one, but here the target string contains a **c**, so there should be more pressure than in the original problem to describe the **abc ⇒ abd** change as "Replace C by D." This pressure did cause the program to construct this rule and to get the answer **xdg** on 14 out of 1000 runs. (This rule was used only twice in 1000 runs on **ijk** and once in the previous variant.) Here the presence of a **c** in the target string makes the rule "Replace C by D" stronger than the rule "Replace the rightmost letter by D," even though the former rule contains descriptors of lesser conceptual depth (i.e., C versus *rightmost*). There are three reasons why the answer **xdg** does not show up even more often: (1) The C ⇒ C correspondence, though fairly strong, is still quite a bit weaker than the *rightmost* ⇒ *rightmost* correspondence, since the latter has greater conceptual depth and is supported by *leftmost* ⇒ *leftmost*. (2) In addition, the C ⇒ C correspondence has to fight against the strong "Replace the rightmost letter by its successor" rule, which creates pressure for the **c** in **abc** to correspond to the rightmost letter of **xcg** rather than to the **c** in **xcg**. (3) The C ⇒ C correspondence prevents the **b** from mapping onto anything in the target string, whereas the *rightmost* ⇒ *rightmost* view allows a correspondence between the two strings' respective middle letters.

In the survey, 49 of the subjects answered this problem; their answers follow.

> **xch** (43)
> **xdg** (6)
> **xcd** (4)
> **xdh*** (1) (Replace C by D *and* the rightmost letter by its successor.)
> **ycg*** (1) (Replace the latest letter in the alphabet by its successor.)
> **xcg*** (1) (justification uncertain)
> **bdg*** (1) (justification uncertain).

Variant 4: abc ⇒ abd, abcd ⇒?

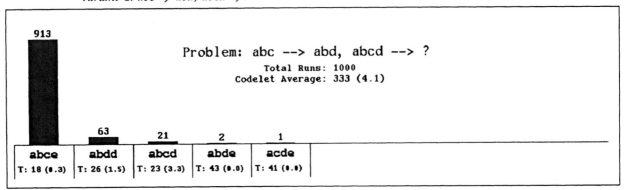

Here there is a stronger conflict—the very same three letters appear in the initial and target strings, so it is tempting to map **a** to **a**, **b** to **b**, and **c** to **c**, and to answer **abdd**. This additional pressure for the "Replace *C* by *D*" answer is reflected in the bar graph: it was given 63 out of 1000 times, considerably more often than in the previous two variants. But the same pressures discussed for those variants also come up here, as well as the strong pressure to see the initial string and target string map on to each other as wholes, since both can be perceived as successor (or predecessor) groups. The result is a still overwhelming predominance of **abce** ("Replace the rightmost letter by its successor"). There are also 21 instances of **abcd**, obtained by the rule "Replace the rightmost letter by *D*." Copycat does not notice that this answer is identical to the original target string. The last two answers, **abde** and **acde**, result from partial groupings of the target string.

In the survey, 34 subjects answered this problem. Their answers follow:

abce (26)

abdd (12)

abde* (7) (Replace the third and the following letters by their successors. Copycat also gives this answer, but for a different reason.)

abcd (3)

abd* (1) (Replace the target string by **abd**.)

abef* (1) (Group the target string as **ab-cd** and replace the group **cd** by its "successor" **ef**.)

abdc* (1) (Swap *D*'s and *C*'s.)

Variant 5: abc ⇒ abd, cde ⇒?

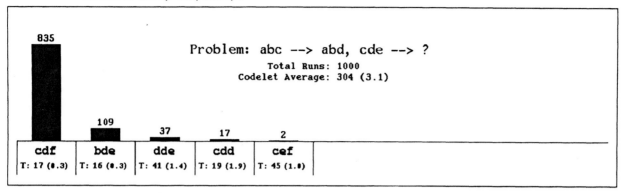

Here the target string can be perceived as a successor (or predecessor) group, but there is a *C* on the left, which generates a bit more pressure than in the previous variant for the program to make a **c-c** correspondence, with concept mappings *C* ⇒ *C* and *rightmost* ⇒ *leftmost*. If this correspondence is made, then there is considerable pressure to map the initial string to the target string as a whole, but in opposite spatial and alphabetic directions, yielding answer **bde**. This pressure is reflected in the bar graph: although most of the time the program answers **cdf** ("Replace the rightmost letter by its successor"), there are also a fair number of **bde** answers. The average temperature for these is roughly the same as for **cdf**: the opposite slippages are hard to make but once they are made, the opposite-direction mapping is seen as strong.

There are also some instances of **dde**, which came either from the rule "Replace *C* by *D*" or from the translated rule "Replace the *leftmost* letter by its successor" (i.e., the **c-c** correspondence was made, but not the whole-string correspondence and therefore not the *successor* ⇒ *predecessor* slippage). Also there were 17 instances of **cdd**, which came from the rule "Replace the rightmost letter by *D*," and one "bad grouping" answer (**cef**, where only the rightmost two letters were grouped).

The 26 subjects who answered this problem gave these answers:

cdf (25)
cdd (3)
dde (2)
ddf* (1) (Replace *C* by *D and* the rightmost letter by its successor.)
cde* (1) (justification uncertain)
dce* (1) (Swap *D*'s and *C*'s.)

Variant 6: abc ⇒ abd, cab ⇒?

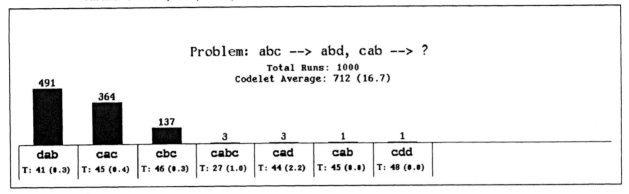

Problem: abc --> abd, cab --> ?
Total Runs: 1000
Codelet Average: 712 (16.7)

dab	cac	cbc	cabc	cad	cab	cdd
491	364	137	3	3	1	1
T: 41 (0.3)	T: 45 (0.4)	T: 46 (0.3)	T: 27 (1.0)	T: 44 (2.2)	T: 45 (0.0)	T: 48 (0.0)

The target string here has a **c** on the left, and as in the **abcd** variant, it also contains the same letters as the initial string, so there is some pressure to map **a** to **a**, **b** to **b**, and **c** to **c**, and the pressure is increased by the additional *rightmost* ⇒ *leftmost* concept mapping. The target string is not in alphabetical order (in either spatial direction), so no whole-group mapping can be made. The results of these different pressures can be seen in the bar graph: there are many more instances of the *C* ⇒ *C* answer (**dab**) than were seen in the previous variants. However, in spite of these pressures, there are overall still slightly more *rightmost* ⇒ *rightmost* answers than *C* ⇒ *C* answers when the two runners-up are taken together: the straightforward **cac** together with **cbc**, for which the program grouped the **a** and **b** in the target string and saw this group as the string's "rightmost letter" (this is the only group that Copycat can find in the target string, which is why this answer appeared relatively often). This shows the strength of the more abstract rule "Replace the rightmost letter by its successor" over "Replace C by D," even in the face of much pressure for the latter.

Among the fringe answers, there are three instances of a strange answer, **cabc**, which came from a view in which the target string was grouped as **c-ab**, the **c** being seen as a group of length 1 and the **ab** as a group of length 2. As in **mrrjjj**, the program replaced the *length* of the rightmost group by its successor, yielding **cabc**, even though the pressures here do not seem to be sufficient to warrant building a single-letter group and bringing in the notion of group length. This happened only three times in 1000 runs, but I think even that is too often; the program is a bit too willing to perceive single-letter groups. There are three instances of the usual "Replace the rightmost letter by *D*" answer (**cad**) and one instance of **cdd**, which comes from grouping the rightmost two letters and replacing the group with **dd**.

The strange answer **cab** (very puzzling to me before I looked in detail at what the program had done) resulted from what most people would consider to be very confused reasoning. The final configuration of the Workspace from this run is shown in figure 5.1. The program parsed the target string as **c-ab** and built a *rightmost* ⇒ *leftmost* correspondence from the **c** to the **c** and a *leftmost* ⇒ *rightmost*, *letter* ⇒ *group* correspondence from the **a** to the group **ab**. The

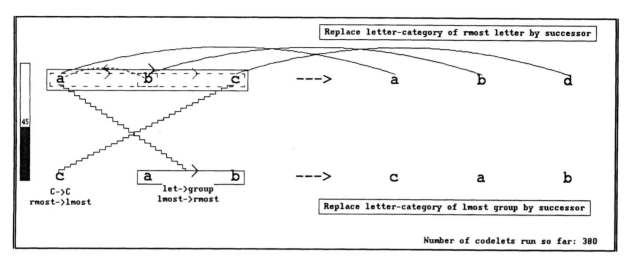

Figure 5.1
The final configuration of the Workspace on a run leading to the solution abc ⇒ abd, cab ⇒ cab.

slippages *rightmost ⇒ leftmost* and *letter ⇒ group* caused the rule to be translated as "Replace the *leftmost group* by its successor." However, there was no leftmost group (that is, no group with the description *leftmost*), so the program left the target string alone. This type of reasoning highlights ways in which Copycat can be very unhumanlike. Fortunately, this particular answer was produced by only 1 in 1000 runs.

In the survey, 26 subjects answered this problem:

> **cac** (16)
>
> **dab** (10)
>
> **cad** (3)
>
> **dac*** (2) (Replace *C* by *D and* the rightmost letter by its successor.)
>
> **cab*** (1) (justification uncertain)
>
> **bda*** (1) (justification uncertain).

Variant 7: abc ⇒ abd, cmg ⇒?

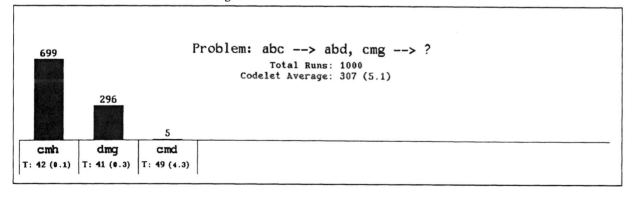

Here there is a **c** on the left in the target string; however, in contrast with **cab**, there are no exact letter-category matches for the **a** and the **b**. This increases the pressure to make the *rightmost ⇒ rightmost* mapping rather than the $C ⇒ C$ mapping. This can be seen in the bar graph, where the $C ⇒ C$ answer (**dmg**) is less frequent than in the previous variant.

In the survey, 27 subjects answered this problem:

  cmh (24)

  dmg (3)

  cmd (2)

  dmh* (2) (Replace C by D *and* the rightmost letter by its successor.)

  cng* (1) (Replace the latest letter in the alphabet by its successor.)

  cmg* (1) (justification uncertain).

Variant 8: abc ⇒ qbc, ijk ⇒?

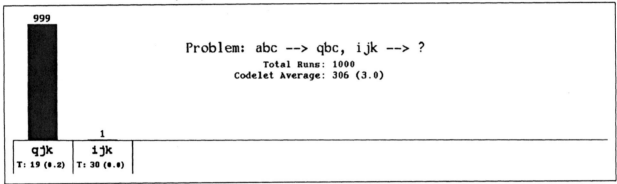

Since *A* and *Q* have no relation in the Slipnet, the three possible rules here are the following: (1) "Replace the leftmost letter by *Q*," which yields answer **qjk**. (2) "Replace the first letter [of the alphabet] by *Q*," which would yield **ijk**. (The single instance of **ijk** in these 1000 runs resulted from this rule.) This rule is possible only if the **a** is given the description *first*. (3) "Replace *A* by *Q*," which would also yield **ijk**. (This rule was never used in the 1000 runs.)

In the survey, 26 subjects answered this problem. Several gave illegal answers—either answers that involved counting long distances in the alphabet (even though subjects had been instructed not to do so) or answers using the rule "Replace the leftmost letter by any letter." These are not included in the list of answers below:

  qjk (15)

  ijk (2).

Variant 9: aabc ⇒ aabd, ijkk ⇒?

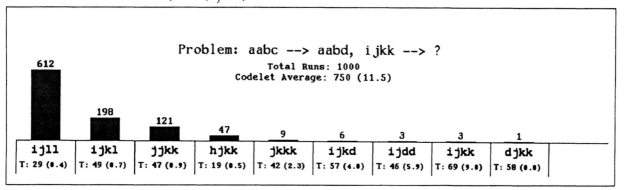

Problem: aabc --> aabd, ijkk --> ?

Total Runs: 1000
Codelet Average: 750 (11.5)

612	198	121	47	9	6	3	3	1
ijll	**ijkl**	**jjkk**	**hjkk**	**jkkk**	**ijkd**	**ijdd**	**ijkk**	**djkk**
T: 29 (0.4)	T: 49 (0.7)	T: 47 (0.9)	T: 19 (0.5)	T: 42 (2.3)	T: 57 (4.0)	T: 46 (5.9)	T: 69 (9.0)	T: 58 (0.0)

Here there is a double **a** on the left of one string and a double **k** on the right of the other, creating some pressure for the program to see a mapping between the two double letters and, on the basis of that mapping to change the leftmost letter (**i**) instead of the rightmost group (**kk**) or the rightmost letter (**k**). The **i** could be changed either by replacing it by its successor (**jjkk**) or, on the basis of the diagonal (*leftmost ⇒ rightmost*) correspondence, seeing the two strings as going in opposite alphabetic directions and thus replacing the **i** by its *predecessor* (**hjkk**).

Even with this pressure to change the **i**, the answer **ijll** ("Replace the rightmost group by its successor") is still the most common answer, and **ijkl** ("Replace the rightmost letter by its successor") is second, indicating the strength of the *leftmost ⇒ leftmost, rightmost ⇒ rightmost* view. However, the pressure is felt to some extent: **jjkk** makes a good showing, and **hjkk** has some representatives as well (and also has by far the lowest average temperature). This is to be contrasted with the results on **ijk**: in 1000 runs, the program only once gave an answer involving a replacement of the leftmost letter.

The answers on the fringe here include **jkkk** (which is similar to **jjkk**, but which results from grouping the *two* leftmost letters), the usual "Replace the rightmost letter (or group) by *D*" answers (**ijkd** and **ijdd**), **ijkk** ("Replace *C* by *D*"), and **djkk** (replacing the **i**, but by a **d** instead of by its successor or predecessor).

In the survey, 26 subjects answered this problem:

ijkl (19)

ikkk* (4) (The justification for this answer is very likely the following: make the diagonal mapping from **aa** to **kk**, and the opposite diagonal mapping from **bc** to **ij**. Then map the rightmost letter of **bc** (the **c**) to the rightmost letter of **ij** (the **j**), and replace it by its successor; this yields the answer **ikkk**. The current version of Copycat could not get this answer, because it is not able to make descriptions such as "rightmost letter of leftmost group.")

ijkd (3)

hjkk (3)

jjkk (3)

ijll (2)

ijlk* (1) (Replace the third letter by its successor.)

ijkk (1)

ijkh* (1) (The subject most likely saw the idea **ijkk** ⇒ **hjkk**, but still could not let go of changing the *rightmost* letter.)

Variant 10: abcm ⇒ abcn, rijk ⇒?

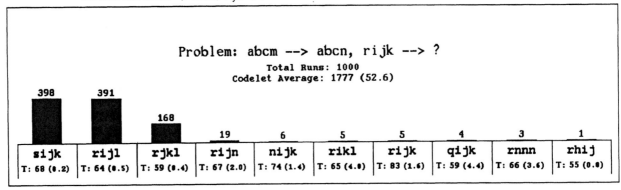

Here an extra, unrelated letter is added at opposite ends of the initial and target strings. This creates pressure for the program to map the leftmost successor (or predecessor) group **abc** onto the rightmost group **ijk**, generating a *leftmost* ⇒ *rightmost* slippage, which in turn generates a *rightmost* ⇒ *leftmost* slippage, lobbying for the answer **sijk**. Copycat gave that answer slightly more often than it gave **rijl**, which is based on the straightforward "Replace the rightmost letter by its successor." It also answered **rjkl** a fair amount of the time, on the basis of seeing the group **ijk** as the "rightmost element" of the target string and replacing it by its "successor." I don't think many people would give this answer; no one gave it in the survey.

There are also several fringe answers. Several were unexpected, and one of these—**qijk**—actually seems to me quite reasonable and even clever (even though no human subject ever gave it): the diagonal *group* ⇒ *group*, *leftmost* ⇒ *rightmost* correspondence caused the two groups to be seen as going in opposite directions, generating a *successor* ⇒ *predecessor* slippage; thus, the leftmost letter was replaced by its predecessor. The answer **rnnn** comes from replacing the rightmost group **ijk** by *N*'s.

The answer **rhij** is another example of bizarre reasoning on the part of Copycat. The final configuration of the workspace from this run is shown in figure 5.2. The program grouped **ijk** as a left-going predecessor group, and top-down pressure from that group caused the **r** to be seen as a single-letter left-going predecessor group (note the left-going arrow on top of the box around **r**). The mapping from the successor group **abc** to the predecessor group **r** caused the slippage *successor* ⇒ *predecessor*, and the mapping from the **m** to the group **ijk** caused the slippage *letter* ⇒ *group*. These together resulted in the translated rule "Replace letter-category of rightmost *group* by *predecessor*."

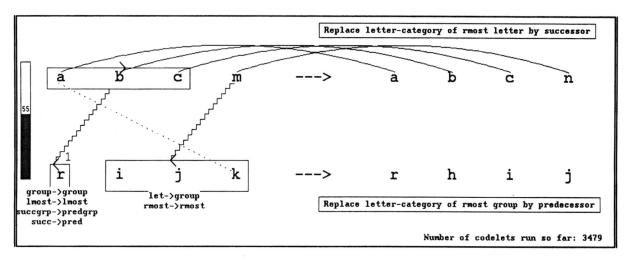

Figure 5.2
The final configuration of the Workspace on a run leading to the solution **abcm** ⇒ **abcn**, **rijk** ⇒
rhij. Note the right-going arrow on the group **abc**, indicating that it is a *successor* group, and the
left-going arrows on the groups **r** and **ijk**, indicating that they are *predecessor* groups.

In the survey, 16 subjects answered this problem:

rijl (14)

sijk (4)

rijn (2)

rijk (1)

rijh* (1) (justification uncertain).

In this problem, a person might describe the **abcm** ⇒ **abcn** change as something like "Replace the only letter not in a group by its successor." This, I think,
is a quite intelligent way to see the change, but Copycat is not currently able to
make such a description.

5.3 Variants of abc ⇒ abd, iijjkk ⇒?

The bar graph for the original problem: abc ⇒ abd, iijjkk ⇒?

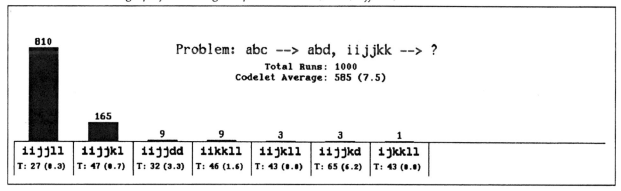

Variant 11: abc ⇒ abd, hhwwqq ⇒?

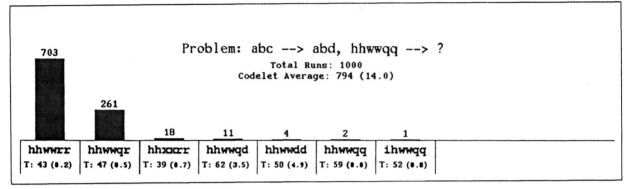

Here there is no successor structure unifying the groups in the target string, so, in contrast with **abd ⇒ abd, iijjkk ⇒?**, the initial and target strings cannot be mapped onto each other as wholes. This difference is reflected in the results on this variant: the ratio of **hhwwrr** ("Replace the rightmost *group* by its successor") to **hhwwqr** ("Replace the rightmost *letter* by its successor") is less than 3:1, versus the almost 5:1 ratio of **iijjll**'s to **iijjkl**'s in the original problem. This shows that even though the *letter ⇒ group* mapping is stronger than the *letter ⇒ letter* mapping in both problems, the whole-string mapping in the original problem serves to further support the *letter ⇒ group* view.

Here there are also the usual "Replace the rightmost group [or letter] by *D*" answers (**hhwwdd** and **hhwwqd**), and also a ridiculously farfetched answer, **hhxxrr**. The final configuration of the Workspace on one of these runs is shown in figure 5.3. This answer is based on assigning lengths of 2 to the groups in the target string, grouping the **ww** and **qq** groups into a single

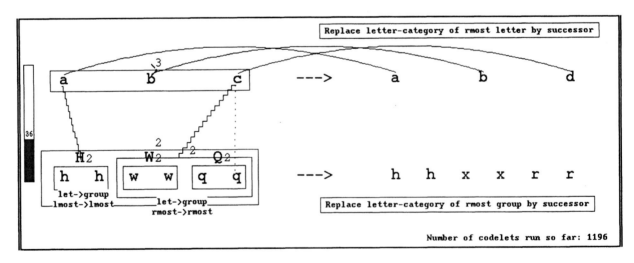

Figure 5.3
The final configuration of the Workspace on a run leading to the solution **abc ⇒ abd, hhwwqq ⇒ hhxxrr**.

group (solely on the very flimsy ground that they have the same length), viewing that single group as the object corresponding to the rightmost letter in **abc**, and replacing it by its "successor." Since there is no whole-string mapping, the slippage *letter-category* $\Rightarrow$ *length* was not made, so the group is replaced by its letter-category "successor". Note the three levels of grouping in the target string—the **hh** group length (2) has a sameness bond to the **ww-qq** group length (2)—and the mapping of the **c** onto the "group" **WQ**.

The fact that such an answer could be constructed 18 times out of 1000 demonstrates some problems with Copycat: perceiving a sameness relation between two groups of the same length (not to mention building a higher-level group *based* on that sameness relation) is very strange and unhumanlike, and such behavior should be suppressed in the program. It would have been easy to explicitly prohibit this behavior (e.g., by explicitly forbidding sameness bonds between groups), but such an *ad hoc* prohibition would run totally against the spirit of this project. Rather, the prevention of such behavior should arise naturally from more general perceptual mechanisms in Copycat. An *ad hoc* solution would only serve to cover up an interesting and unexpected way in which the program went wrong. Instead, displaying the farfetched answers Copycat occasionally gets is much more instructive and interesting for two reasons. First, these answers point out ways in which the program is inaccurate as a model of human perception; second, since these answers are so unexpected, they often bring up deep issues about perception that we might not have thought of otherwise. For example, it is unlikely that a person would ever perceive **hhwwqq** in the way Copycat did in figure 5.3. Why not? And how do people manage to avoid such bizarre ways of looking at situations? Unexpected behavior like this on the part of the program helps make it clearer just how difficult it is to understand the mental mechanisms that we are investigating.

In the survey, 33 subjects answered this problem:

hhwwrr (20)

hhwwqr (11)

hhxwqq* (4) (Replace the third letter by its successor.)

hhxxrr* (3) (Replace the third and the following letters by their successors.)

hhxwqr* (3) (Replace the third letter of each group of three by its successor.)

hhxxqq* (2) (Replace each instance of the third letter by its successor?)

hhwwqd (1)

hhwwqq (1)

hhwwr* (1) (Replace the rightmost group by its one-letter successor.)

hhwwrs* (1) (justification uncertain).

Variant 12: abc ⇒ abd, lmfgop ⇒?

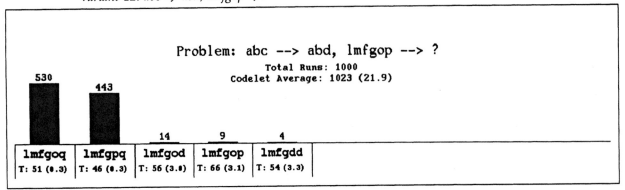

Here we have three successor groups (or predecessor groups) rather than three sameness groups making up the target string. The former are considerably weaker than the latter, since successor and predecessor bonds are intrinsically weaker than sameness bonds. Again, this intrinsic difference is meant to reflect the psychologically real difference (in the real world) between the strength of sameness relations—as well as the speed at which they are perceived—and any other kind of relations. Thus, the program is less likely to build the three target-string groups here than it was in **iijjkk**. The bar graph shows that this is indeed the case: here the "letter" answer (**lmfgoq**) is more frequent than the "group" answer (**lmfgpq**), though the frequencies and average final temperatures are close. There are also some instances of "Replace the rightmost letter [or group] by *D*" (**lmfgod** and **lmfgdd**) and "Replace *C* by *D*" (**lmfgop**).

In the survey, 37 subjects answered this problem:

lmfgoq (24)

lmfgpq (5)

lmggop* (4) (Replace the third letter by its successor.)

lmfgqr* (4) (**qr** is seen as the successor of **op**.)

lmggoq* (2) (Replace the rightmost letter of each group of three by its successor.)

lmfgop (2)

lmg* (1) (Drop all but the first three letters, and replace the rightmost by its successor.)

lmfgod (1)

lmghpq* (1) (Replace the third and the following letters by their successors.)

lmfgoo* (1) (justification uncertain).

Variant 13: abc ⇒ abd, lmnfghopq ⇒?

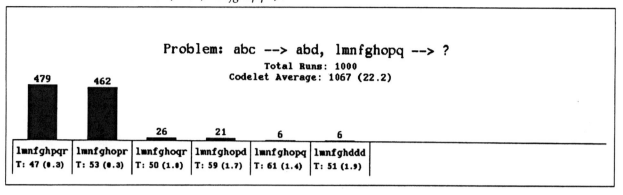

Problem: abc --> abd, lmnfghopq --> ?

Total Runs: 1000
Codelet Average: 1067 (22.2)

479	462	26	21	6	6
lmnfghpqr	lmnfghopr	lmnfghoqr	lmnfghopd	lmnfghopq	lmnfghddd
T: 47 (0.3)	T: 53 (0.3)	T: 50 (1.0)	T: 59 (1.7)	T: 61 (1.4)	T: 51 (1.9)

This variant is the same as the previous one except that the groups in the target string are each longer by 1. Since the strength of a group is a function in part of its length, it is more likely that the groups will be built here than in the previous variant. This is reflected in the bar graph: here, the "group" answer **lmnfghpqr** is more frequent than the "letter" answer **lmnfghopr**, though again they are fairly close. One of the other answers here, **lmnfghoqr**, reflects Copycat's perennial grouping problems: only the two rightmost letters of **opq** were grouped. Finally, two answers come from replacing the rightmost letter or group by **d**'s, and the answer **lmnfghopq** resulted from the rule "Replace C by D."

In the survey, 26 subjects answered this problem:

> **lmnfghopr** (15) (Replace the rightmost letter by its successor.)
> **lmofgiopr*** (10) (Replace the rightmost letter of each group by its successor.)
> **lmnfghpqr** (5) (Replace the rightmost group by its successor.)
> **lmofghopq*** (5) (Replace the third letter by its successor.)
> **lmoghipqr*** (3) (Replace the third and the following letters by their successors.)
> **lmnfghrst*** (2) (Here **rst** is seen as the successor of **opq**.)
> **lmnfghopd** (1) (Replace the rightmost letter by **d**.)
> **lmnfghopq** (1)
> **lmngghopq*** (1) (justification uncertain)
> **lmofgiopq*** (1) (justification uncertain).

Variant 14: aabbcc ⇒ aabbcd, iijjkk ⇒?

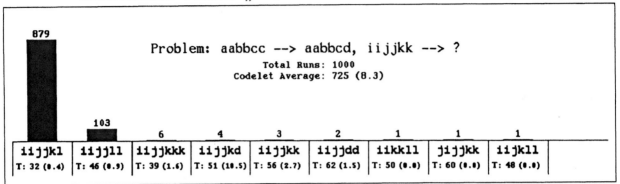

Here the groups in **aabbcc** tend to map to the groups in **iijjkk**, and, since both strings form successor (or predecessor) groups at the group level, the two strings tend to map onto each other as wholes. All this serves to prevent the rightmost *letter* in **aabbcc** from mapping onto the rightmost *group* in **iijjkk**, which prevents answer **iijjll** from being given very often. Thus **iijjkl** predominates.

There are also a number of fringe answers; the only one of a new type (again displaying bizarre reasoning) is **iijjkkk**. Here **jj** and **kk** were grouped on the basis of a sameness bond between their lengths (each group has length 2) rather than a successor bond between their letter categories. Then the group **cc** was mapped to the group **jjkk** (both are rightmost sameness groups) with the slippage *letter-category* to *length*. The rightmost **c** was mapped to the group **kk**. The result was the translated rule "Replace the length of the rightmost group (here **kk**) by its successor."

In the survey, 26 subjects answered this problem:

iijjkl (26)
iijjkd (2)
iijjll (1)

5.4 Variants of abc ⇒ abd, kji ⇒?

The bar graph for the original problem: abc ⇒ abd, kji ⇒?

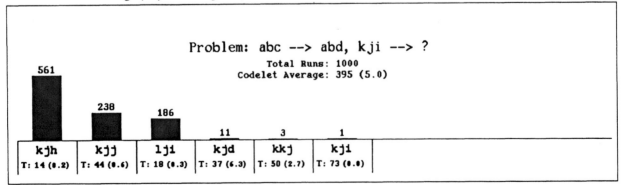

Variant 15: abc ⇒ abd, edc ⇒?

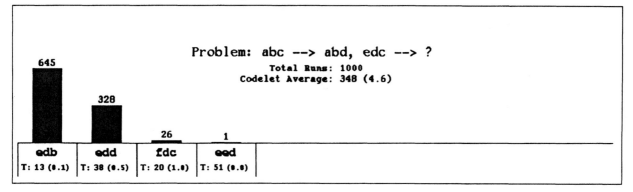

This variant is similar to the original, except now there is a **c** on the right, increasing the pressure to make a vertical (*rightmost* ⇒ *rightmost*) rather than a diagonal (*rightmost* ⇒ *leftmost*) mapping. (This problem also fits in with variants 3–7 given above.) This pressure is reflected by the high frequencies of answers **edb** and **edd** (representing vertical mappings) relative to **fdc** (representing a diagonal mapping). (The answer **eed** of course results from one of the bad groupings Copycat is plagued with: **e-dc**.) In fact, in this variant, vertical mappings make up 97% of the total, versus 81% in **kji**. The answer **edb** is the analogue of answer **kjh** (**fdc** is the analogue of **lji**), and it has the lowest temperature here.

In the survey, 34 subjects answered this problem:

> **edd** (21)
> **edb** (10)
> **fdc** (7)
> **eec*** (1) (justification uncertain).

Variant 16: abc ⇒ abd, cba ⇒?

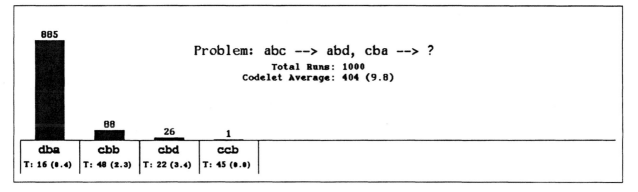

This is a variant of **abc ⇒ abd, kji ⇒?**; however, it also has some elements of **abc ⇒ abd, xyz ⇒?**, because trying to answer the analogue of **kjh** leads to a snag here (*A* has no predecessor). The bar graph shows that **dba** is by far the most frequent answer. Strong pressures lobby for this diagonal mapping: not only are the *A* ⇒ *A*, *B* ⇒ *B*, and *C* ⇒ *C* mappings very compelling, but also a vertical (*rightmost* ⇒ *rightmost*) mapping could lead to the slippage *successor* ⇒ *predecessor*, and then a snag. Thus **dba** by far predominates. The answer **cbb** corresponds to the answer **kjj** in the original problem, but **cbb** is much less frequent here than **kjj**, because of the strong forces described above. The answer **cbd** comes from the usual "Replace the rightmost letter by *D*" rule. Interestingly, every instance of this answer but one was the result of the program trying to take the predecessor of *A*, failing, and having to restructure its initial interpretation of the problem. (Its low average temperature is due to the fact that a strong whole-string mapping was made on these runs.) Even though hitting a snag is possible in this problem, the identical letter-category mappings help the program to avoid doing so most of the time. In **xyz** the program hit the "*Z* has no successor" snag at least once on 97% of the runs, but here the program hit the "*A* has no predecessor" snag only 20% of the time.

In the survey, 26 subjects answered this problem:

dba (15)

cbb (15)

cbd (4)

cba* (1) (justification uncertain)

cb* (1) (analogous to answer **xy** for **xyz**)

cbaa* (1) (analogous to answer **xyzz** for **xyz**).

5.5 Variants of abc ⇒ abd, mrrjjj ⇒?

The bar graph for the original problem: abc ⇒ abd, mrrjjj ⇒?

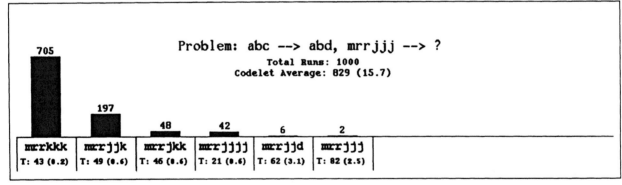

Variant 17: abc ⇒ abd, mrr ⇒?

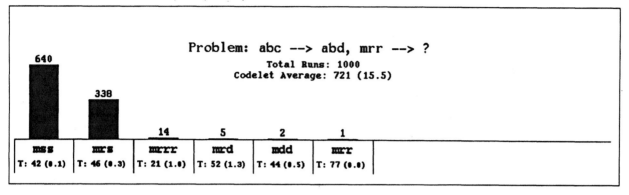

Here the string is shortened to one **m** and two **r**'s. There should be almost no pressure here for Copycat to perceive the **m** as a single-letter sameness group, since there is only one other possible sameness group in the target string, as opposed to two in **mrrjjj**. The answer **mrrr** (viewing **mrr** as a string whose groups increase in length, and replacing the two **r**'s by three **r**'s) seems to me almost completely unjustified here. As can be seen in the bar graph, the top two answers by far are **mss** and **mrs**, though here Copycat answers **mrs** significantly more often than it answered **mrrjjk** in the original problem (mostly because here, given that both strings consist of three letters, there is a strong set of leftmost, middle, and rightmost letter-to-letter correspondences between **abc** and **mrr**, which was not possible in **mrrjjj**). This view lobbies against grouping the string as **m-rr** and having the **c** correspond to the group **rr**, which is necessary for the answer **mss**.

Copycat answered **mrrr** 14 out of 1000 times, as compared with 42 out of 1000 times for **mrrjjjj** (thus, the latter occurred three times more often). But 14 out of 1000 is, I believe, still too high. It would be hard to find a person who would ever give this answer seriously; it is certainly not as justified here as **mrrjjjj** was in the original problem. As can be seen here and in some of the fringe answers to other problems, the current version of Copycat is somewhat too willing to make single-letter groups and to perceive relations among group lengths. However, a more detailed statistic (not displayed in the bar graph) shows a dramatic difference between Copycat's behavior on this variant and on the original problem: on **abc ⇒ abd, mrrjjj ⇒?**, the **m** was made into a single-letter group on 41% of the runs (only a fraction of those runs resulted in answer **mrrjjjj**), whereas in this variant this single-letter group was made on only 4% of the runs. Since **mrr** is so much shorter than **mrrjjj**, once this single-letter group is made, it is easier in this variant than in the original problem for the program to build the other structures (length descriptions given to groups, bonds between the groups based on length relationships, etc.) that are necessary to come up with an answer in which group length (rather than letter category) is replaced. Of course there is more top-down support in **mrrjjj** for all these structures, but there are more of them to make. Thus, once the single-letter group is made in **mrr**, there is a much better chance (*too* much better) that the "length" answer will be given than if the same event happens in **mrrjjj**.

In the survey, 26 subjects answered this problem:

mrs (24)

mrd (3)

mrr (2).

It is interesting that none of the human subjects gave Copycat's most frequent answer, **mss**. The subjects were evidently strongly affected by the fact that **abc** and **mrr** are the same length, which makes the one-to-one *letter* ⇒ *letter* mappings very strong.

Variant 18: abc ⇒ abd, mmrrrjjjj ⇒?

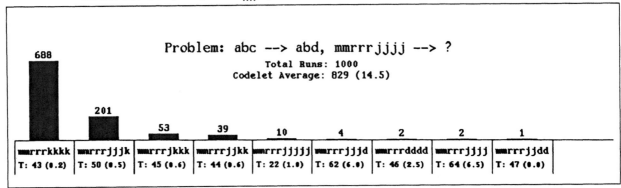

Here the target string can be parsed as 2–3–4 rather than 1–2–3. As can be seen from the bar graph, the 2–3–5 answer (**mmrrrjjjjj**) was given much less frequently than in the original problem (10 times here versus 42 times in the original). This is because the parsing based on group lengths is less likely to occur here than in the original problem: there, the building of a single-letter group made it more likely that group lengths would be noticed in the target string; here, since there is no single-letter group, group lengths are noticed less often.

In the survey, 23 subjects answered this problem:

mmrrrkkkk (17)

mmrrrjjjk (8)

mmrrrkkkkk* (3) (Replace the rightmost group by its length successor *and* its letter-category successor. This is analogous to the answer **mrrkkkk** in the original problem, which was discussed in section 2.1.)

mmrrrjkkk* (2) (Parse the target string into three groups of three letters each.)

mmrrrjjjd (2)

mmsrrjjjj* (2) (Replace the third letter by its successor.)

mmssskkkk* (2) (Replace the third and the following letters by their successors.)

mmrrrjjjj (1).

None of the subjects gave the 2–3–5 answer **mmrrrjjjjj**.

Variant 19: abc ⇒ abd, rssttt ⇒?

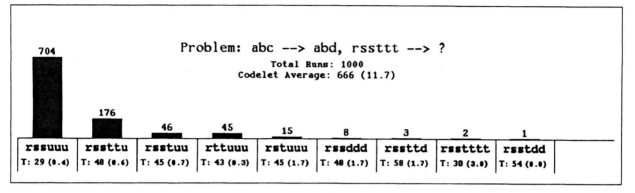

Here there are possible successor bonds both between letter categories and between group lengths. This means that the program is able to get a good letter-category answer (**rssuuu**) without resorting to the notion of group lengths; the pressure resulting from the lack of letter-level successor bonds in **mrrjjj** is missing here. This is indeed what happened, as can be seen: the program got **rssttt** only twice in the 1000 runs, versus 42 instances of **mrrjjjj** in the original problem. In addition, the average final temperature on **rssttt** here is roughly the same as the average final temperature on **rssuuu**. The other answers are similar to the answers given in the original problem (plus a few additional answers based on strange groupings of the target string).

In the survey, 23 subjects answered this problem:

rssuuu (16)

rssttu (9)

rstttt* (3) (Replace the third letter by its successor.)

rssuuuu*(2) (Replace the rightmost group by both letter and length successors. Here this answer is much better justified than **mrrkkkk** was for the original problem, since here there are successorship relations between both letter values and group lengths. As will be discussed in the next chapter, Copycat is currently unable to get this answer.)

rssttd (2)

rsstuu* (2) (Parse the string as **rs-st-tt**.)

rttttt* (1) (Replace each instance of the third letter—i.e., **s**—by its successor.)

rstuuu* (1) (Replace the third and the following letters by their successors.)

rsdttt* (1) (Replace the third letter by *D*.)

rssttt (1).

None of the subjects answered **rssttt**.

Variant 20: abc ⇒ abd, xpqdef ⇒?

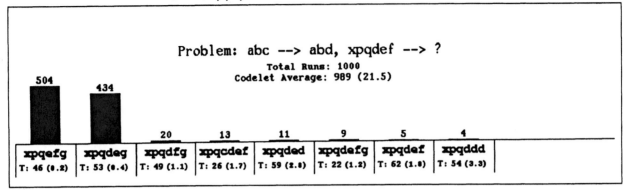

Here the target string consists of successor (or predecessor) groups that increase in length. As was pointed out in the discussion of variant 12 above (**abc ⇒ abd, lmfgop ⇒?**), successor and predecessor groups are weaker than sameness groups and are not built as readily. This is reflected in the bar graph, which shows that the answer **xpqefg** ("Replace the rightmost *group* by its successor") is quite close in frequency to **xpqdeg** ("Replace the rightmost *letter* by its successor"), indicating that on a fair number of the runs the program did not build the three target-string groups. When Copycat does build the groups and notices the relations among their lengths, there are two possible answers that can be given here: if the groups are seen as right-going successor groups, then the program answers **xpqdefg**, increasing the group length to the *right*; if the groups are seen as left-going predecessor groups, then the program answers **xpqcdef**, increasing the group length to the *left*. (Most people would opt for the former, but the program does not have the same left-to-right bias that people have.) The combination of these two answers is 2% of the total versus 4% of the total for **mrrjjjj** in **abc ⇒ abd, mrrjjj ⇒?**.

In the survey, 16 people answered this problem:

xpqdeg (6)
xpqdfg* (3) (Parse the string as **xp-qd-ef**.)
xprdef* (3) (Replace the third letter by its successor.)
xpqded (2)
xpqdee* (2) (justification uncertain)
xpqdgh* (1) (Parse the string as **xp-qd-ef**, and replace **ef** by its successor **gh**.)
yprdeg* (1) (Replace the rightmost letter of each group by its successor.)
xpqghi* (1) (**ghi** is seen as the successor of **def**.)
xprefg* (1) (Replace the third and the following letters by their successors.)
xpqefg (1)
xprdeg* (1) (Replace the rightmost letter of each group by its successor, where **x** is not a group.)
yqrdeg* (1) (justification uncertain)
ypqdef* (1) (justification uncertain).

None of the subjects gave either of the *length* answers.

Only 3 of 16 subjects gave answers in which the target string was parsed as **x-pq-def**, whereas most of Copycat's answers were based on this parsing. This indicates that Copycat is much more strongly tuned to perceive successor (and predecessor) groups than is the average human subject.

5.6 Variants of abc ⇒ abd, xyz ⇒?

The bar graph for the original problem: abc ⇒ abd, xyz ⇒?

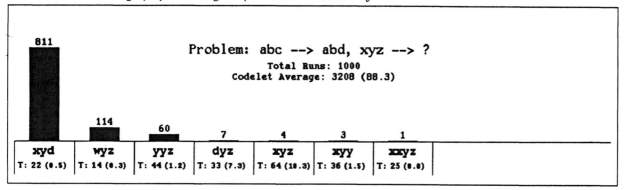

Variant 21: abc ⇒ qbc, xyz ⇒?

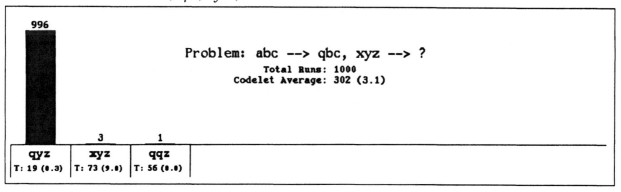

The purpose of this variant was to demonstrate that it is not easy for the program to make an **a-z** diagonal mapping based on *first* ⇒ *last*. As in variant 8 (**abc** ⇒ **qbc, ijk** ⇒?), the possible rules here are "Replace the leftmost letter by *Q*," "Replace the first letter [of the alphabet] by *Q*" (possible only if the **a** is given the description *first*), and "Replace *A* by *Q*." If either the first or the second rule were constructed, and if a *first* ⇒ *last, leftmost* ⇒ *rightmost* mapping were made from the **a** to the **z**, then the answer would be **xyq**. But in 1000 runs, Copycat never made this mapping: it answered **qyz** 996 times out of 1000, it answered **xyz** ("Replace *A* by *Q*") 3 times out of 1000, and it answered **qqz** once (**x** and **y** were grouped together to form the "leftmost group," which was replaced by instances of *Q*). This shows that it takes strong pressure to make the **a-z** diagonal mapping—pressure that is present in the original problem but not here.

In the survey, 26 subjects answered this problem. As was the case for variant 8 (**abc** $\Rightarrow$ **qbc, ijk** $\Rightarrow$?), several people gave illegal answers—either answers that involved counting long distances in the alphabet (even though subjects had been instructed not to do so) or answers using the rule "Replace the leftmost letter by any letter." These are not included in the list of answers below:

qyz (16)

xyz (4)

yz* (2) (justification uncertain—replace X by letter 16 steps away, which doesn't exist?)

qbc* (1) (Replace anything by **qbc**.)

yyz* (1) (justification uncertain).

Variant 22: rst $\Rightarrow$ *rsu, xyz* $\Rightarrow$?

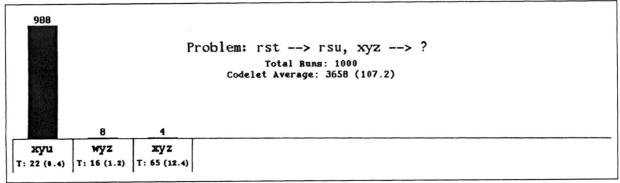

In this variant, because of the lack of an **a** there is no *first* $\Rightarrow$ *last* mapping possible to create pressure for a diagonal mapping between the initial and target strings. Accordingly, the program gave the answer **wyz** on only 8 of the runs, versus 114 times on the original problem. Here the answer **wyz** comes about solely on the basis of an unlikely *rightmost* $\Rightarrow$ *leftmost* slippage (more likely here than in most problems, owing to the high temperature resulting from the "Z has no successor" snag, but still quite unlikely). This illustrates the crucial role played by the *first* $\Rightarrow$ *last* mapping in Copycat's **wyz** solution to the original problem.

In the survey, 27 subjects answered this problem:

xyy* (8)

xy* (8)

xyz (8)

xyu (5)

xzz* (1)

xz* (1) (justification uncertain)

xyzz* (1)

wyz (1).

The subjects' answers to this problem are likely to have been influenced by their answers to **abc ⇒ abd, xyz ⇒?**, which they solved first. Copycat, of course, does not retain any memory of previous runs; thus, the order in which problems are presented has no effect on the program's behavior.

Variant 23: abc ⇒ abd, glz ⇒?

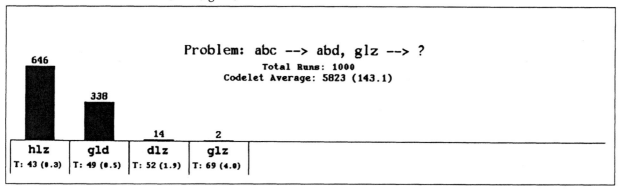

Here there *is* a possible *first ⇒ last* mapping between the **a** and the **z**; however, since the target string is not a successor group, there is no possible whole-string mapping between it and the initial string. If the **a** and the **z** are seen to correspond here, and the *leftmost* letter is changed, Copycat can only change it to its successor. (Thus, Copycat cannot get the answer **flz**.) Here the frequency of the "Replace the leftmost letter by its successor" answer (**hlz**) exceeds that of the "Replace the rightmost letter by *D*" answer (**gld**) by a considerable amount—a dramatic difference between the results here and on the previous variant, as well as between these results and those on the original problem. The reason **hlz** predominates here is that the *first ⇒ last* mapping makes the diagonal **a-z** correspondence strong, and, in contrast to the original problem, this correspondence does not face much competition from vertical correspondences, since no whole-string same-direction mapping supports them. So in this case, given the high temperature due to the Z snag and the intrinsic weakness of the "Replace the rightmost letter by *D*" rule, the *first ⇒ last* correspondence gets built more easily, and does not face strong competition from incompatible bonds, groups, and correspondences.

In the survey, 16 subjects answered this problem:

gld (5)
glz (4)
gl* (4)
flz* (2)
hlz (1)
glzz* (1)
gll* (1) (justification uncertain)
gly* (1).

Again, the subjects' answers to this problem are likely to have been influenced by their answers to **abc ⇒ abd, xyz ⇒?**, which they solved first.

Variant 24: abc ⇒ abd, cmz ⇒?

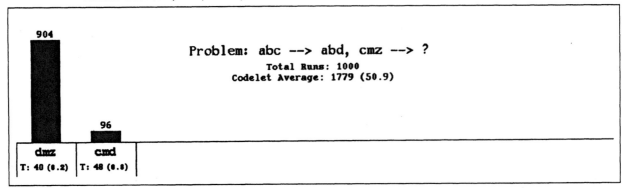

This variant gives Copycat the possibility of an easy out from the impasse: if it cannot take the successor of Z, it can resort to changing the **c** in the target string instead. As can be seen in the bar graph, on most of its runs the program either took advantage of this escape route or avoided the snag altogether, answering **dmz** 90% of the time. This can be compared with the previous variant (**abc ⇒ abd, glz ⇒?**, which has no **c** in the target string), in which leftmost-letter-change answers were given 79% of the time, and with the original problem, in which leftmost-letter-change answers were given only 18% of the time. It is also interesting to compare this with variant 7 (**abc ⇒ abd, cmg ⇒?**), which is the same as this variant except that there the rightmost letter was *G*, which has a successor. There, a leftmost-letter-change answer was given only 30% of the time. So here, given the snag and the resulting high temperature, mapping the **c**'s becomes more compelling, even though a *rightmost ⇒ leftmost* slippage has to be made.

As would be expected from the results on variant 7, the presence here of the **c** in the target string allowed the program to sidestep the *Z* snag entirely on 25% of the runs and go straight to the answer **dmz**, whereas on the original problem Copycat sidestepped the snag and went straight to a leftmost-letter-change answer (in that case **wyz**) on only 1 out of 1000 runs. (These statistics are not displayed in the bar graphs.)

In the survey, 26 people answered this problem:

cmd (7)
cmz* (5)
cmy* (5)
cm* (5)
dmz (4)
bmz* (2)
cmzz* (1)
cmm* (1) (justification uncertain)
abd* (1).

Once more, the subjects' answers to this problem are likely to have been influenced by their answers to **abc ⇒ abd, xyz ⇒?**, which they solved first.

5.7 Summary

The 24 variants discussed in this chapter demonstrate the range of Copycat's abilities and show how different constellations of pressures affect its behavior. Of course, many more variants could have been included, but the ones given are enough to convey a good sense of the program's behavior and "personality."

The program's behavior on these variants is the best argument for the model's plausibility: it is flexible enough to adapt to all these different situations and, for the most part, to act in appropriate ways. In some cases, Copycat is also able to make analogies that are not at all obvious and that demonstrate what many people would consider a fair degree of cleverness or insight.

The other side of the coin, of course, is represented by the bad analogies that the program makes, which reveal its internal flaws and weaknesses. But they also demonstrate that Copycat has the *potential* to get farfetched answers—a potential that is essential for flexibility—and yet manages to *avoid* them almost all the time, which demonstrates its robustness.

This chapter, in demonstrating the range of Copycat's intelligence (as well as the ways in which it lacks intelligence), has expanded on chapter 4 in addressing the criteria for judging this project. Copycat's performance on the variants of the original five problems demonstrates the program's abilities as it is "stretched"; it shows how well the program continues to perform as it is pulled away, little by little, from the most central problems that it was deliberately designed to solve. The program was not designed to work specifically on these variants; in fact, in almost every case, the program was not tested on the variants until after it had been completed. Copycat's performance on these variants thus gives evidence for the program's generality.

Chapter 6

Summary of the Comparisons between Copycat and Human Subjects

This chapter summarizes the results of comparing Copycat's behavior with that of human subjects. The comparisons made are those described in chapter 2: comparisons of the range of answers that Copycat and humans get and comparisons of the relative difficulties that Copycat and humans experience on various problems.

6.1 Comparing Ranges of Answers

The previous two chapters detailed the results of a survey given to a number of undergraduate and graduate students at Indiana University and the University of Michigan, for the purpose of determining the range of answers these subjects give on the five target problems and the 24 variants. The survey produced a fairly comprehensive list of the answers given by people to most of these letter-string problems. Copycat is able to get a large number of these answers; it gets almost half of the answers people give overall, and it gets two-thirds of the answers given by three or more people. (These numbers would be increased if the answers labeled "justification uncertain" were not included.)

6.1.1 Answers beyond Copycat's abilities
Most of the answers Copycat misses fall into the three following classes:

Answers involving descriptions of the numerical position of letters in the initial and target strings (e.g., "third letter," "leftmost two letters") Some subjects gave answers such as **abc ⇒ abd, iijjkk ⇒ iikjkk** ("Replace the third letter by its successor") or **abc ⇒ abd, iijjkk ⇒ iikkll** ("Replace the third and following letters by their successors"). Copycat is currently unable to make such descriptions; it does not have concepts such as "third" or "following". It was said in chapter 2 that Copycat's microworld excludes "complex" mathematical knowledge (such as noticing that the distance from *A* to *E* is twice as large as the distance from *M* to *O*), since we are trying to model subconscious recognition processes rather than highly conscious "expert" activities such as mathematics. However, descriptions such as "third" or "leftmost two" probably should not fall into the class of "highly conscious" mathematics. Such simple numerical concepts would be worthwhile additions to Copycat's repertoire. A related notion that people sometimes use is "alphabetically after" some letter, as in **abc ⇒ abd, xlg ⇒ ymh**, where the rule might be "Replace all letters alphabetically after *B* by their successors." Copycat does not currently have this concept.

Answers involving groupings not based on bonds between letters   For example, several people answered **abc ⇒ abd, mrrjjj ⇒ mrrjkk**, parsing the target string as **mr-rj-jj** on the basis of pressure to see three equal-length elements, as in **abc**. Copycat is currently unable to group letters unless there is a bond (indicating some kind of intrinsic relation) between them.

Answers involving descriptions of letters with respect to groups   For example, several people gave the answer **abc ⇒ abd, lmnfghopq ⇒ lmofgiopr**, using the rule "Replace the rightmost letter of each successor group by its successor." Copycat is currently unable to make descriptions such as "rightmost letter of successor group."

These classes do not include the answers labeled "justification uncertain." These answers were, with only two exceptions, given by only one person. The two exceptions were given by two people each. Some of these may be due to mistakes (e.g., getting the successor of a particular letter wrong) or due to the use of notions not included in the letter-string domain (e.g., using the shape of letters, or counting long distances between letters in the alphabet), even though the subjects were instructed ahead of time which types of concepts were to be excluded.

Some answers fall into more than one of the above classes. For example, the answer **abc ⇒ abd, mrrjjj ⇒ mrsjjk**, based on parsing the string as **mrr-jjj** and replacing the third letter of each group by its successor, falls into the second and third classes, since the two groups are not based on bonds between letters, and the answer involves the description "rightmost letter of group."

All these discrepancies point to abilities that Copycat lacks. Giving Copycat these abilities would involve extending the description-making and grouping mechanisms that the program already has—a worthwhile direction for future work on this project.

Other answers given by people but not by Copycat are harder to classify. In particular, some of the answers given by people to the problem **abc ⇒ abd, xyz ⇒?** involve concepts and intelligence far beyond Copycat's. For example, a very common answer is **xy**, for which people use imagery such as "the **z** falls off the edge of the alphabet," making an analogy between the edges of the linear alphabet and the edges of a cliff. Copycat, of course, has no such imagery (it has no imagery at all, unless knowledge such as "letter sequences are similar to number sequences" or "left-going is similar to right-going" could be be counted as a primitive form of imagery). People also sometimes answer **xzz**, reasoning that if you can't change the *rightmost* letter then the next best thing is to change the *next-to-rightmost* letter; or **xyy**, reasoning that if you can't take the *successor* of the rightmost letter, then the next best thing is to replace it by its *predecessor*. Such slippages do not come from correspondences with anything in **abc**; they are made only because the analogy-maker cannot do the desired thing and thus does something close to it. Copycat currently cannot make slippages that are not based on correspondences between the initial and target strings. Making such slippages under pressure is a very important ability for general intelligence, and giving such an ability to Copycat would make it a much more flexible program. This is another topic for future research. A third answer people occasionally give is **abd**—that is, "Replace the entire string, whatever it is, by **abd**." Even though this answer is given only in jest, the fact that it is given at all shows that people are able to describe the **abc** ⇒ **abd** change in that way. Copycat ideally should be able to come up with such a rule in principle, though in practice its construction should be extremely unlikely.

People also give answers that demonstrate more flexible views of the notion of successorship than Copycat has. For example, four people in the survey answered **abc** ⇒ **abd, lmfgop** ⇒ **lmfgqr**, seeing **qr** as the "successor" of the group **op**. Copycat currently can only give **pq** as the successor of **op**. Another flexible use of successorship is **abc** ⇒ **abd, xyz** ⇒ **xyzz**, in which the **zz** is seen as a possible "successor" of **z**.

Another set of answers results from doing two things at once, as in **abc** ⇒ **abd, rssttt** ⇒ **rssuuuu** ("Replace the rightmost group by its letter *and* length successor"). Many people feel this is the best answer to this problem, since **rssttt** has both alphabetical and numerical successorship relations. However, Copycat is currently able to construct only one bond between two given objects in a string; it cannot build both length and letter-category successor bonds simultaneously. The answer **abc** ⇒ **abd, mrrjjj** ⇒ **mrrkkkk**, discussed in chapter 2, is a less-justified example of this (and, in fact, is an example of what in chapter 2 was called a "frame blend"). Extending Copycat's bond-building capabilities in order to allow such analogies is another topic for future research. A related example is **abc** ⇒ **abd, xcg** ⇒ **xdh** ("Replace *C* by *D* and the rightmost letter by its successor"). Copycat is not currently able to construct conjunctive rules of this kind. It might be argued that this is not a very good analogy. But we want to give Copycat the ability to make *human-like* analogies, both good and bad—and that includes "multiple rule" analogies such as these.

Appendix A further illustrates the limitations of the current version of Copycat by giving a set of problems that the program is currently unable to solve.

6.1.2 Copycat's "unhumanlike" answers

Copycat also gives a number of answers that people almost never give. These fall into three main classes:

- *Bad-grouping answers*, such as **abc** ⇒ **abd, iijjkk** ⇒ **iijkll**, where the "rightmost group" was **jkk**. People occasionally give answers like this, but the groupings always are motivated in some way, such as dividing the string into two groups of length 3. Copycat's bad groupings have no such motivation.

- *Answers involving unmotivated slippages*, such as **abc** ⇒ **abd, ijk** ⇒ **ijj**, in which a correspondence involving the slippage *successor* ⇒ *predecessor* was made without sufficient reason.

- *Answers based on unmotivated uses of group lengths*. These include (among others) **abc** ⇒ **abd, xyz** ⇒ **xxyz; abc** ⇒ **abd, hhwwqq** ⇒ **hhxxrr** (variant 11); **abc** ⇒ **abd, cab** ⇒ **cabc** (variant 6); and **abc** ⇒ **abd, mrr** ⇒ **mrrr** (variant 17).

These are the classes of unrealistic answers that came out of Copycat's performance on the letter-string problems discussed in chapters 4 and 5. If more problems were added, other such classes would likely become apparent. The answers that Copycat gets but that people never get illustrate certain problems with the model (some of which will be discussed in the next chapter). It is encouraging, though, that these are always fringe answers, produced very rarely by the program.

I did not include "frame blend" answers, such as **abc ⇒ abd, xyz ⇒ dyz**, in the three classes of Copycat's unhumanlike answers given above. It is true that no one in the survey gave this particular answer, but people did give answers that involved similar (though perhaps less farfetched) frame blends, such as **xyz ⇒ xyw** or **ijkk ⇒ ijkh**. Moreover, people have proposed **dyz** and other such answers in jest, which means that they do actually come to mind. Thus, it is desirable that Copycat have the ability to get such answers, though, just as with the other fringe answers, it is also desirable that it not get them very often.

6.2 Comparing Relative Difficulties of Problems

For this comparison, 14 subjects were each given a verbal description of the letter-string domain and its limitations. They were then asked to solve eight problems that appeared one by one on a computer screen. The first three problems were for training purposes, so that the subjects could get used to the experimental setup; the next five were the five target problems (or slight variants) in random order (different orderings for different subjects). The subjects were timed on how long it took them to give an answer to each problem (though I did not tell them they were being timed, because I did not want them to feel any time pressure). The purpose here was to see if the order of difficulty of the five problems (judged by the amount of time taken to solve them) was the same for the program as for people. After solving each problem, each subject gave a short verbal report on solving it.

Unfortunately, a number of factors make it very difficult to compare the results here with those of the program. First, the time taken by Copycat to solve a given problem depends very much on what the final answer is. For example, on the problem **abc ⇒ abd, mrrjjj ⇒ ?** the program takes an average of 875 codelet steps to reach answer **mrrkkk**, versus 1126 for answer **mrrjjjj**; the latter is a harder answer to reach. Thus, any useful comparison with people would have to involve an answer-by-answer time comparison. But the number of subjects here was too small to get the range of answers and number of samples needed for such a comparison (e.g., only one subject answered **mrrjjjj**, and on some of the problems a number of subjects gave answers that Copycat cannot get). Another difficulty is noise in the data: even despite the three training problems, a few of the subjects still had trouble using the keyboard correctly, which increased the time recorded for various answers. Again, the number of subjects was too small to avoid noisy data. My conclusion is that in order to be useful this experiment would require many more subjects than were used in this study, and certain design flaws would have to be corrected (e.g., more training problems should be used in order for subjects to get used to the experimental setup). Therefore, the results given here should be considered to be those of a pilot study rather than those of a full-fledged experiment.

The comparisons of average overall time for each problem are given below, with the caveat that these results may not be very meaningful owing to experimental-design flaws. What is to be compared here is the time-ranked order of the five problems, and any significant differences in time between different problems. The times for the human subjects are given in average number of seconds, and the times for Copycat are given in average number of codelets run; these numbers cannot be directly compared in any way.

The times for the five problems solved by the 14 subjects were as follows:

abc $\Rightarrow$ **abd, ijkl** $\Rightarrow$**?**
average time: 24 seconds
standard error: 3 seconds

abc $\Rightarrow$ **abd, eeffgghh** $\Rightarrow$**?**
average time: 37 seconds
standard error: 8 seconds

abc $\Rightarrow$ **abd, srqp** $\Rightarrow$**?**
average time: 54 seconds
standard error: 12 seconds

abc $\Rightarrow$ **abd, mrrjjj** $\Rightarrow$**?**
average time: 55 seconds
standard error: 18 seconds

abc $\Rightarrow$ **abd, xyz** $\Rightarrow$**?**
average time: 59 seconds
standard error: 9 seconds

The times for these five problems when solved by Copycat are (with averages over 1000 runs):

abc $\Rightarrow$ **abd, ijkl** $\Rightarrow$**?**
average number of codelets run: 345
standard error: 4.0

abc $\Rightarrow$ **abd, eeffgghh** $\Rightarrow$**?**
average number of codelets run: 721
standard error: 9.9

abc $\Rightarrow$ **abd, srqp** $\Rightarrow$**?**
average number of codelets run: 467
standard error: 6.8

abc $\Rightarrow$ **abd, mrrjjj** $\Rightarrow$**?**
average number of codelets run: 829
standard error: 15.7

abc $\Rightarrow$ **abd, xyz** $\Rightarrow$**?**
average number of codelets run: 3208
standard error: 88.3

In spite of the caveat given above, a few interesting points can be made here. As common sense would tell us, the problem **abc** $\Rightarrow$ **abd, ijkl** $\Rightarrow$ **?** seems to be the easiest for both people and Copycat (and, of course, almost everyone answered **ijkm**), and the problems **abc ⇒ abd, mrrjjj ⇒ ?** and **abc ⇒ abd, xyz ⇒ ?** seem significantly more difficult for both the subjects and Copycat. On **abc ⇒ abd, mrrjjj ⇒ ?**, one subject gave a report expressing a sense of pressures similar to those pushing Copycat: "I was pretty lost with this one, since I didn't see any patterns resembling the given example; the letters in the string I was given [i.e., **mrrjjj**] didn't relate to each other in the same way that the others in the given example [i.e., **abc ⇒ abd**] did. The given letters weren't successors in the alphabet." On **abc ⇒ abd, xyz ⇒ ?**, all 14 subjects reported "hitting the snag"—that is, trying to take the successor of Z and failing. Thus, it would be implausible if Copycat easily bypassed this snag and went directly to another answer—and in fact, the program hit this snag on all but 3% of its runs. After hitting the snag, all but one of the subjects proposed the answer **xya** (the other one reported thinking of it but assumed that it would not be allowed). They were told that this answer, while very reasonable, was not possible under the restrictions of the domain, and were then asked to come up with another answer. (The time taken to give these instructions was not included in the recorded solution time.)

Some shortcomings of the model that will be discussed in the next chapter have an effect on the timing differences here. The problem **abc ⇒ abd, eeffgghh ⇒ ?** takes Copycat significantly longer than **abc ⇒ abd, ijkl ⇒ ?**, whereas the difference for people is not that great. As will be discussed in the next chapter, one reason for this seems to be that once people start to perceive groups in the string they get the idea very quickly, whereas such top-down forces in Copycat, although they exist, are still too weak; they don't sufficiently accelerate this view once it begins to be perceived. Likewise, the problem **abc ⇒ abd, xyz ⇒ ?** takes Copycat far longer than any other problem, whereas the difference for people is not that great. This is in part due to the fact that people tend to give up fairly quickly when faced with an impasse and give an answer that they may not find totally satisfying. But the large amount of time taken by Copycat on this problem is also due to its rather unhumanlike loopish behavior: since it lacks appropriate self-watching mechanisms, it gets trapped in the same state again and again, trying to take the successor of Z and failing.

Chapter 7

Some Shortcomings of the Model

The bar graphs and screen dumps in chapters 4 and 5 have demonstrated most of the mechanisms in Copycat, and in doing so have not only shown off the program's strengths but also revealed many of its weaknesses. In this chapter I will discuss some of these weaknesses and their general implications for models of high-level perception. The point of the chapter is not to detail wholly new abilities the program would need in order to solve a wider range of problems (e.g., the ability to construct more complex rules, the ability to build bonds between non-adjacent objects in a string, or the ability to form new concepts, such as "double successor," from existing Slipnet nodes), but rather to discuss some shortcomings of the mechanisms the program currently has. For the purposes of this chapter I will discuss two of the more salient and serious shortcomings of the program: shortcomings with respect to top-down forces and focus of attention, and shortcomings in self-watching.

7.1 Top-Down Forces and Focus of Attention

Top-down (expectation-driven) forces are an essential part of perception in general. This point is brought home very clearly by looking at some of the difficulties Copycat has in solving analogy problems in its microworld. One of the major weaknesses of the program as it now stands is that top-down pressures in the system are often not strong enough. This can be seen in Copycat's performance on problems involving long strings. For example, consider the problem **abc ⇒ abd, ijklmnop ⇒ ?** (variant 1 from chapter 5). Here, once the notion of successorship (or, equivalently, predecessorship) is deemed highly relevant, top-down forces should take over almost completely and should very quickly build successor bonds throughout the target string. As has been demonstrated, such forces exist in Copycat, but at present they are not strong enough. Sometimes successor bonds are built too slowly, and groups are formed out of chains of bonds that cover only part of the string. Figure 7.1, which shows the final configuration of the Workspace from a run on this problem, illustrates a case where this happened.

As can be seen in the figure, the target string has been divided into two separate successor groups (**ijklmn-op**) instead of one successor group comprising the entire string. What happened here was that successor bonds along the edges of the string were built fairly quickly, and the **op** group was built very early on, even before bonds were built between the middle letters. Only later were bonds in the middle, and then the left-hand group of six letters, built. In many cases, a single whole-string group will successfully compete against smaller groups such

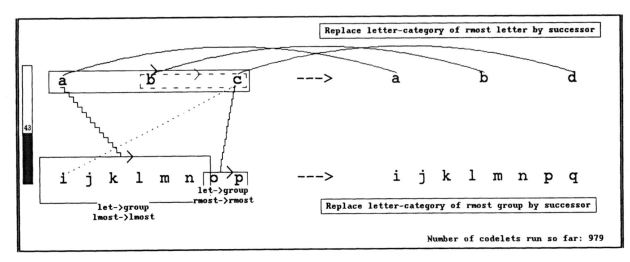

Figure 7.1
A "bad-grouping" answer.

as these; however, in this case that did not happen, and the program answered **ijklmnpq**, replacing the rightmost group of two by its "successor."

The results of similar bad groupings were seen in many of the bar graphs presented in chapters 4 and 5. For example, on the problem **abc ⇒ abd, iijjkk ⇒ ?** the program came up with several bad-grouping answers. Screen dumps showing the final Workspace configuration for two of these answers are given in figures 7.2 and 7.3. In figure 7.2, the program never grouped the two **j**'s, and instead built successor bonds from the group **I** to the leftmost **j** and from the rightmost **j** to the group **K**. This led to a parsing of the target string as two higher-level successor groups: **Ij** and **jK**. The **c** was then mapped onto the rightmost of these two groups, all of whose letters were replaced by their successors in the answer.

In figure 7.3, the program never grouped the two **i**'s, and instead parsed the string as **i-iJK**. Thus, at the top level the string was seen as consisting of two elements: the leftmost letter **i** and the successor group **iJK**. The **c** was seen as corresponding to the rightmost element, the group **iJK**, all of whose letters were therefore replaced by their successors in the answer. This answer, even more than the previous two, is extremely farfetched and unhumanlike.

One flaw seems to be that Copycat's top-down codelets are too global; they are not targeted specifically enough. A top-down successor-bond codelet will attempt to build a successor bond anywhere, but it seems that what is needed here is codelets that try to build specific types of bonds in specific places. For example, in the problem above, once a sameness bond has been built between the two **j**'s, there should be top-down pressure to try to build the same type of bond in the adjacent position, between the **i**'s. There should be similar pressure in the problem **abc ⇒ abd, ijklmnop ⇒ ?**: once the building of successor bonds has begun, top-down forces should try to build successor bonds adjacent to the already-existing ones.

A mechanism for implementing these kinds of specific top-down pressures would enable the program to follow what might be a more plausible route to the solution **abc ⇒ abd, mrrjjj ⇒ mrrjjjj**. If the **R** and **J** groups have been

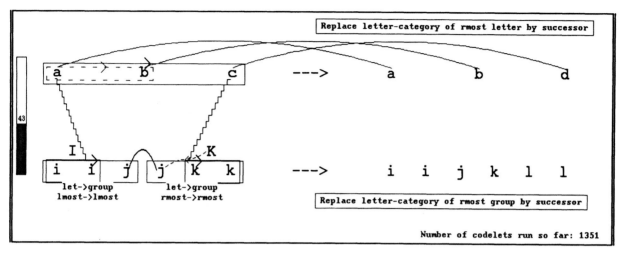

Figure 7.2
Another bad-grouping answer.

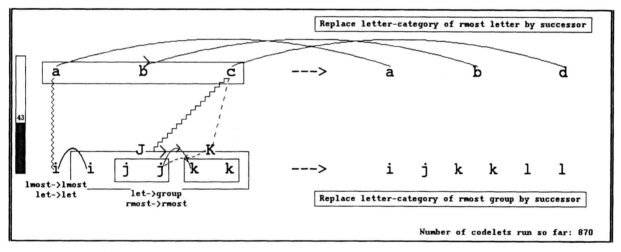

Figure 7.3
A third bad-grouping answer.

given length descriptions and a successor bond has been created between their lengths, then there should be top-down pressure to build the same type of bond in an adjacent position—namely, between the **m** and the **R** group. This specific goal would create pressure to perceive the **m** as a group of length 1, so that a successor bond could be built with the group of length 2. As was seen in some of the variants in chapter 5, the program is currently somewhat too willing to build single-letter groups without sufficient pressure. It seems more plausible that such an unusual group should be constructed in response to a strong *location-specific* top-down pressure, such as the one described above, rather than (as is currently the case) in response to more general pressure from other groups in the string.

In general, Copycat needs a kind of "planning" mechanism: a mechanism for conceiving of a specific desired structure (e.g., a successor bond between the group lengths of specific objects) in response to top-down pressure, and trying to build the necessary prior structures (e.g., a single-letter group) whose existence would make it possible to build the desired specific structure. All this is still meant to model subconscious perceptual activities in humans. AI researchers usually consider planning to be a highly conscious operation, but a subconscious version of it may play an important role in high-level perception.

Part of Copycat's difficulty in interpreting long strings such as **ijklmnop** has to do with the program's focus of attention. One flaw is that not enough attention (in the form of codelets) is directed to parts of the string that need attention (i.e., unhappy objects, such as the middle letters of **ijklmnop** early on in the run when no bonds involving them have been built). In the current version of Copycat, codelets are indeed biased to choose unhappy objects to work on (since salience depends in part on unhappiness), but it seems that this mechanism is not working well enough to avoid occasional bad groupings such as the examples shown here.

Finally, Copycat has no mechanisms for either extending already existing groups (though a proposed large group can fight against existing smaller sub-groups inside it) or merging two adjacent disjoint groups. The ability to fluidly extend, merge, split, and, more generally, change the boundaries of groups seems very important in high-level perception (Hofstadter 1983), and such mechanisms would certainly help Copycat in cases like the ones shown above.

The answers displayed in the screen dumps above (and other strange answers, some displayed in figures in chapter 5) are Copycat's "misspun tales," corresponding to the strange and humorously nonsensical stories occasionally generated by the story-generating program Talespin (Meehan 1976), which contrasted with the more coherent, meaningful stories that it was meant to generate. As was the case for Talespin, Copycat's misspun tales are often windows onto the program's internal deficiencies, such as those discussed in this chapter. It must be said, however, that not all instances of strange answers should be considered evidence for problems with the program. As has been pointed out, the *potential* availability of *all* paths of exploration is essential for the program's flexibility (and the current program's flexibility is limited by the fact that it cannot follow all the possible paths that people could follow). Contrary to what one might initially suppose, it should be considered positive evidence for the program's strength that strange answers (such as those above, or frame-blend answers such as **abc ⇒ abd, xyz ⇒ dyz**) do appear occasionally, since their existence proves that the program is indeed capable of following bad pathways and yet manages to steer clear of them almost all the time. This is precisely the kind of behavior that we want to see in Copycat. On the other hand, bad-grouping answers (and some other types of bad answers) tend to show up too often in the current version of the program, which indicates flaws of the kind discussed above in the way the program is working right now.

7.2 Self-Watching

An absolutely essential feature of cognition, whose necessity is shown quite clearly by some of Copycat's weaknesses, is *self-watching* (sometimes called "metacognition"): an ability to perceive patterns in one's own mental activities.

In Copycat, temperature acts as a primitive self-watching mechanism in which information about the state of the program's progress toward an answer feeds back into the program's behavior, determining the amount of randomness that should be used in making decisions. However, Copycat's performance on certain problems makes it clear that more sophisticated self-watching mechanisms are needed. A salient defect of Copycat is its mindlessly loopish behavior when solving the problem **abc ⇒ abd, xyz ⇒ ?**. As can be seen in the screen dumps for that problem, the program returns again and again to the same state of trying to take the successor of Z and failing. People too are prone to some loopish behavior, but not to the extent that it occurs in Copycat, which hits the same impasse, on average, nine times per run on this problem. A normal human would never do this; after two or three times one would notice a pattern, and would be able to break it. But Copycat lacks mechanisms for forming or remembering any kind of high-level description of its behavior, or of states that it has been in before. Copycat does save the exact state of the Workspace each time an impasse is hit, and the temperature remains clamped until the program decides (probabilistically) that new structures of sufficiently high quality have been built, but this is a very unsophisticated mechanism relative to the kind of high-level pattern recognition the program needs to apply to its own behavior in order to avoid being stuck in a loop. Such high-level pattern-recognition mechanisms are, in effect, analogy-making mechanisms—for example, the program would need to recognize that it was doing essentially "the same thing" each time it got stuck, even though the events leading up to the impasse might be very different each time. Thus, some of the same mechanisms that Copycat uses for making analogies between letter strings should apply to the problem of watching and responding to its own behavior. Giving Copycat such an ability would be an excellent topic for future research on this project. (The relations among self-watching, high-level pattern recognition, mechanisms for breaking out of loops, and creativity are discussed in Hofstadter 1985c.)

Another serious self-watching problem in Copycat is the need for the densities of various types of codelets on the Coderack at a given time (representing the various types of structures—descriptions, bonds, groups, correspondences, rules) to correspond at least roughly to the kinds of structures the program currently *needs* to build. For example, at a given time, the program might need more bonds in order to make more progress.

An example of this balancing problem is the following: Suppose that the node *successor* is active and thus posts a number of top-down bond scout codelets looking for successorship. But suppose that every object in the initial and target strings is already happily bonded. The newly posted successor-bond scouts will largely waste the program's time, since there is no strong need to scout for bonds. There should be some mechanism to inhibit bond-scout codelets when there seem to be enough bonds already. The same kind of inhibition is necessary for the other types of structures (groups, correspondences, etc.). But this kind of inhibition must be carried out carefully. Having too *few* codelets of a given type means that the program will often miss essential structures, and having too *many* of a given type (e.g., codelets looking for bonds) causes the program to waste much of its time again and again fruitlessly exploring structures that already exist. Maintaining a proper balance in the population of codelets has emerged as an absolutely central issue in this project.

This issue for Copycat corresponds to a general question that is central to high-level perception: How much time should one spend looking for new kinds of structures (and how should one allocate this time among the various types of structures), and how much time should one spend concentrating on concepts that have already been identified as relevant? This is the "exploration versus exploitation" tradeoff again. As can be seen in the screen dumps, the proper balance of bottom-up and top-down pressures changes as processing proceeds: the program starts out being dominated by bottom-up forces, but as structures are built and information is gained, processing gradually shifts toward being dominated more and more by top-down pressures. The reason for this is that as more structures are built and more nodes are activated, more and more top-down scout codelets are posted. Top-down scouts tend to have higher urgencies than bottom-up scouts, and thus gradually come to dominate on the Coderack in terms of number and urgency.

There are actually two balances in question here: the balance between bottom-up and top-down forces and the balance among codelets looking for the various types of structures. The method just described for achieving a good bottom-up-versus-top-down balance in Copycat works fairly well, and emerges naturally from other mechanisms in the system. However, it proved more difficult to develop ways of maintaining a reasonable balance among codelets looking for various types of structures (e.g., at a given time, should the program spend more time looking for groups than for bonds?). In order to achieve such a balance, the system requires self-watching mechanisms to determine what specific types of codelets it currently needs. Temperature is a kind of self-watching mechanism, but in the current version of Copycat temperature was not enough to solve this problem of codelet balance; more detailed self-watching mechanisms seem to be needed. (Some additional flaws in Copycat's current temperature mechanism are discussed in section 8.7.) In the current program, I have added a somewhat imperfect mechanism to help achieve a reasonable balance: when an attempt is made to post codelets (bottom-up or top-down) corresponding to a particular type of structure (e.g., bonds), the program first makes a rough assessment of the current need for that type of structure in the problem by looking more specifically (i.e., more specifically than is done when calculating temperature) at the causes of the unhappiness of objects in the problem (e.g., do many objects lack bonds to their neighbors?). The program then decides probabilistically, on the basis of this assessment, whether such codelets should be allowed to be posted (e.g., if many objects lack bonds, then it is likely that bond scouts will be allowed to be posted). This filtering mechanism works fairly well, but it is unsatisfactory. It is too global and centralized, and thus it goes against the philosophy of local and distributed processing that underlies Copycat. Self-watching is essential, but it should be done in a less centralized way than in the current version of the program.

The shortcomings discussed in this chapter are by no means the only weaknesses of the program; many more exist at various levels of detail. But the deficiencies concerning top-down forces, focus of attention, and self-watching are currently the most salient and interesting of the program's shortcomings, and are, I think, the issues most relevant to modeling high-level perception in general. They are the issues that should probably have highest priority in near-term future work on this project.

Chapter 8
Results of Selected "Lesions" of Copycat

In this chapter I give the results of seven experiments designed to elucidate the roles played by various aspects of the program's architecture. The purpose of doing these experiments was to further illustrate how the program works and to determine the necessity for the presence of certain architectural features by showing what happens when they are "lesioned" (i.e., removed or altered). In each experiment, the program was altered in some way and was then run 1000 times on one or more of the five target problems. (As was the case for the bar graphs in chapters 4 and 5, the bar graphs given in this chapter are not the same ones given in Mitchell 1990; a set of new runs was performed here in order to collect more detailed statistics.) For ease of reference, the original bar graph for the given problem is displayed along with the results of each experiment.

8.1 Experiment 1: Suppression of Terraced Scanning

Recall that in Copycat a structure is built by a chain of three codelets,

scout ⇒ strength tester ⇒ builder,

rather than by a single codelet. The purpose of this experiment was to examine the role played by this breakup of the process of structure building. For this experiment, the usual chain was compressed into a single codelet: the program was modified so that a single codelet carried out all three tasks (scouting out a possible structure, testing its strength, and, if the structure was found to be strong enough, building it). The same types of scout codelets as in the original program were present here; the difference was that, rather than posting follow-up codelets, each scout carried out all three tasks.

I ran this experiment on two problems: **abc ⇒ abd, iijjkk ⇒ ?** and **abc ⇒ abd, mrrjjj ⇒ ?**.

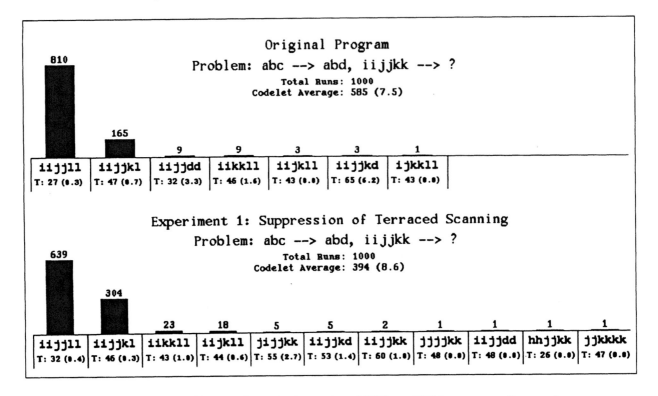

One striking difference here is the ratio of **iijjll** to **iijjkl** answers; the modified program produces a much larger proportion of the latter. In addition, the average final temperature for the answer **iijjll** is higher in the modified program. Another difference is the larger number of instances of badly justified fringe answers produced by the modified program. These fringe answers also have a slightly different character than in the original program: there are a number of answers based on the weak slippage *rightmost ⇒ leftmost*. These differences come about because structures are built more quickly in the modified program: a structure is built in one monolithic step rather than having to wait after each separate step for the next codelet in the chain to be chosen to run. Exploration of structures becomes all-or-nothing: if a structure is explored at all, it is fully evaluated all at once. This is different from the original program, in which the further exploration of promising structures is given high urgency and tends to proceed quickly whereas the further exploration of weak structures is given low urgency and tends to proceed slowly. Thus, in the modified program, the parallel terraced scan of possibilities loses some of its parallel and terraced nature. However, it is not lost entirely: even though *individual* structures are no longer considered and built in a parallel terraced manner, the program still carries out a parallel terraced scan of coherent *collections* of structures. Once certain structures are built (e.g., a new successor bond or a new correspondence), the resulting changes in the state of the Slipnet and the Workspace lead to top-down codelets and new structure-strength values that increase the likelihood and speed of exploring compatible and supporting structures.

In the modified program, most weak structures still fail to pass the strength test and are not built, but some (such as correspondences based on weak slippages), whose exploration would ordinarily be crowded out by other, higher-urgency explorations, are built here, and they then affect the building of subsequent structures. The effects on the program's behavior are statistical, but show that strong structures are not being built as often and that weak structures (including those leading to the fringe answers) are being built and are surviving more often than in the original program.

The same experiment was run on **abc⇒ abd, mrrjjj⇒ ?.**

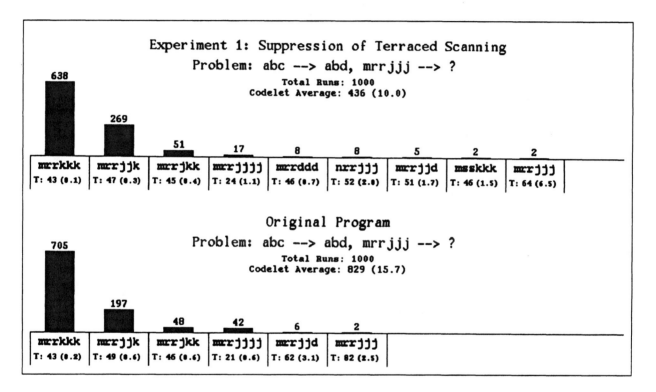

The results here are similar to those for **iijjkk**. There are about 1.3 times as many instances of **mrrjjk** as in the original, showing that strong structures (such as the **c-jjj** correspondence) were not built as often. There are also about 3 times as many instances of fringe answers here than in the original. And perhaps most significantly, the modified program produced **mrrjjjj** only about a third as often as the original program. As could be seen in the screen dumps in chapter 4 , a careful, terraced exploration of possible structures is important for arriving at this answer, and the results here back this up.

8.2 Experiment 2: Suppression of Breaker Codelets

Recall that breaker codelets tend to run only at high temperatures. If a breaker codelet decides to run, it chooses a structure at random and decides probabilistically, as an inverse function of the structure's strength, whether to break the structure. The purpose of this experiment was to determine the role played by these codelets. Breaker codelets were taken out of the program; everything else remained the same.

I ran this experiment on two problems: abc ⇒ abd, iijjkk ⇒ ? and abc ⇒ abd, xyz ⇒ ?.

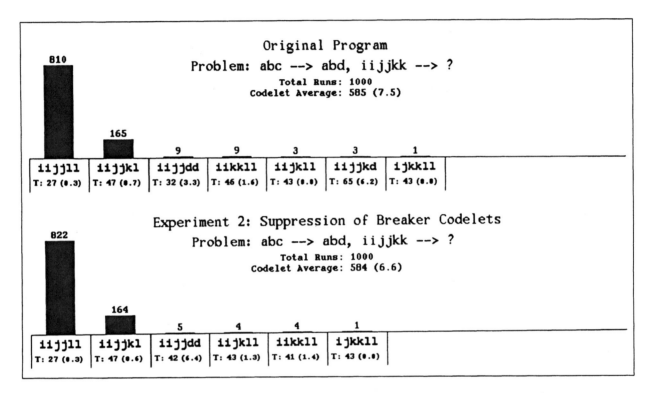

As can be seen by comparing the bar graphs, the absence of breaker codelets had virtually no effect on the program's performance here. The frequencies of the main two answers are roughly the same, and there are only small differences in the distribution of fringe answers. This is not surprising, since breaker codelets, which tend to run only at high temperatures, do not play much of a role in a problem in which the temperature falls rather quickly. The average time to produce an answer was almost the same in the two cases (584 codelet steps in the modified program versus 585 in the original).

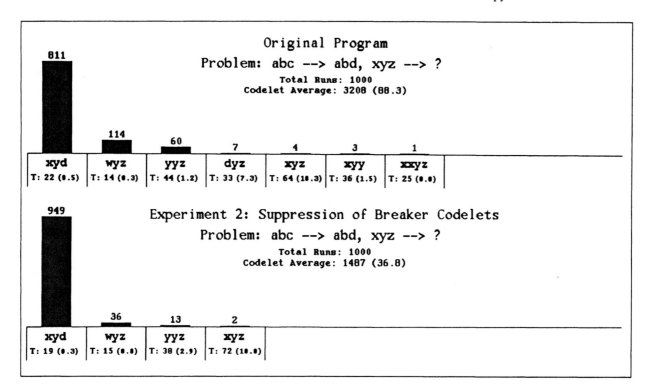

Here there is a significant difference in performance, illustrating the role of breaker codelets in this problem. There are roughly one-third as many instances of **wyz** and one-fifth as many instances of **yyz** in the modified version as in the original version.

Without codelets to break structures at high temperature, it is very difficult to escape from the impasse of trying to take the successor of Z, since the **c-z** correspondence is very strong and is supported by other strong structures. This is the case even though decisions are more random at high temperatures. This demonstrates the importance of structure-breaking codelets as a mechanism for escaping from impasses. Without them, the program's only escape from the snag is, in most cases, to restructure the rule from "Replace the rightmost letter by its successor" to "Replace the rightmost letter by *D*" and to answer **xyd**.

Interestingly, the program without breaker codelets tends to arrive at an answer much more quickly than the original program (1487 codelets on average, versus 3208 in the original). This is because when breaker codelets are suppressed, the program does not have to spend time building new structures to replace structures that have been broken; all that has to happen to produce **xyd** is for a new rule to defeat the existing one.

8.3 Experiment 3: Suppression of Different Conceptual-Depth Values

As was described in chapter 3, the conceptual-depth values in the Slipnet play a number of roles. The conceptual-depth value of a given node affects the node's rate of activation decay, the urgencies of top-down codelets posted by that node, the strengths of descriptions involving that node, the probability of a slippage involving that node, the strengths of concept mappings involving that node, and the probability of a rule-building codelet choosing that node as part of a rule. For this experiment, all nodes in the Slipnet were given equal conceptual-depth values (each was given a value of 50 on a scale from 0 to 100—see appendix 2 for the original values). Everything else remained the same.

I ran this experiment on abc ⇒ abd, iijjkk ⇒ ? and abc ⇒ abd, mrrjjj ⇒ ?.

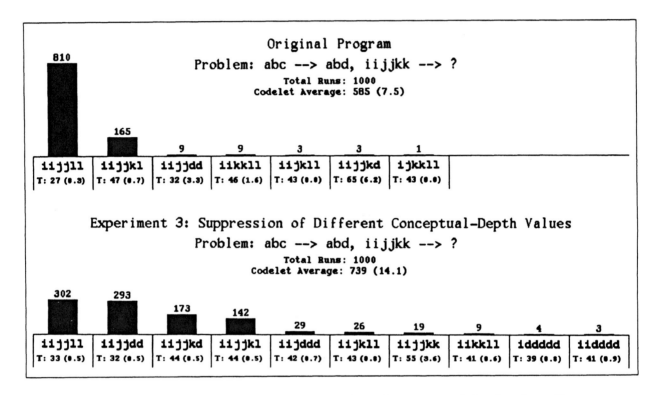

As can be seen from these bar graphs, making the conceptual-depth values all equal had a dramatic effect on the program's performance. The most striking difference here is the increase in answers derived from the rule "Replace the rightmost letter by D." This is to be expected, since the "D" rule is now just as strong as the "rightmost letter" rule. There are also a small number of instances of iijjkk, based on "Replace C by D." This rule is now just as strong as the other two rules, but the fact that the c is usually seen as corresponding to the rightmost letter or group in the target string prevents "Replace C by D" from being built very often. A rightmost ⇒ rightmost correspondence is asserting, in effect, that the c should be viewed as "the rightmost letter", whereas the "Replace C by D" rule is asserting that the c should be viewed as "a C." These views are incompatible, so in order to be built this rule would have to fight with and defeat the rightmost ⇒ rightmost correspondence. This puts it at a disadvantage with respect to the other possible rules.

Another difference is that here there are almost twice as many instances of answers for which the rightmost letter, rather than the rightmost group, is replaced. This is because the urgencies of most top-down codelets are not as high as in the original, so mutually supporting sameness groups are not explored or built as often or as quickly.

In general, there is less pressure from top-down codelets not only because their urgency is lower, but also because nodes (such as *sameness* and *sameness-group*) that originally had greater conceptual depth now tend to decay much more quickly, so not as many top-down codelets are posted. Thus, good structures do not get built as fast, and the temperature stays higher longer. This helps to increase the number of bad-grouping answers (many of which now involve replacing the letters in the bad group by **d**'s rather than by their successors, as in the frighteningly blockheaded answer **iddddd**).

The reduced force (in terms of both urgency and number) of top-down codelets, along with the fact that the temperature stays higher longer, means that on average it takes the program longer to get to an answer. The total average number of codelets run in the modified program is 739, versus 585 in the original.

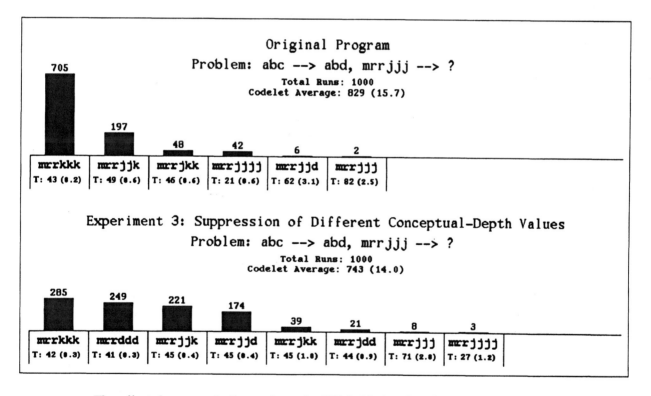

The effects here are similar to those for **iijjkk**. Notice that the modified program produced **mrrjjjj** only three times during the 1000 runs, whereas it was produced 42 times in the original program's 1000 runs. This shows the importance of strong top-down forces for arriving at this answer. (Strong top-down forces are needed to create a single-letter group and to notice and build bonds among group lengths.) Such top-down forces are significantly reduced in the modified program.

8.4 Experiment 4: Suppression of Dynamic Link Lengths

Recall that in Copycat links in the Slipnet shrink in length when the node labeling them is active. For example, when *opposite* is active, all *opposite* links (e.g., the link between *leftmost* and *rightmost*) shrink. For this experiment, the program was modified so that link lengths were no longer dynamic; links always remained at their original lengths.

I ran this experiment on three problems: **abc ⇒ abd, ijk ⇒ ?**, **abc ⇒ abd, kji ⇒ ?**, and **abc ⇒ abd, xyz ⇒ ?**.

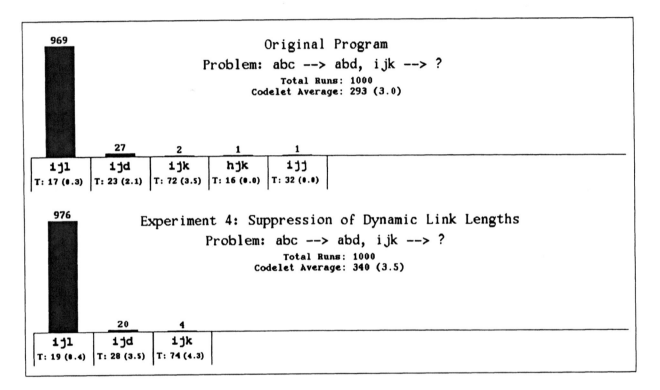

As can be seen, the modification had almost no effect on the relative frequencies of answers to this problem. The fringe answers **hjk** and **ijj** from the original program do not appear in the modified version; they each result from an (unlikely) *opposite* slippage that activates the node *opposite*, which, via shrunk link lengths, reinforces and allows other opposite slippages to take place. The suppression of dynamic link lengths serves to suppress such answers.

There is another difference here as well: the modified program took slightly longer to arrive at an answer (340 versus 293 codelets run, on average). It is slower because dynamic link lengths can act as a top-down force: when the concept *successor*, say, becomes active, this causes successor links (e.g., between *A* and *B* or *I* and *J*) to shrink, so that these relationships are seen as closer. This speeds up the building of successor bonds, since the bonds are judged to be stronger.

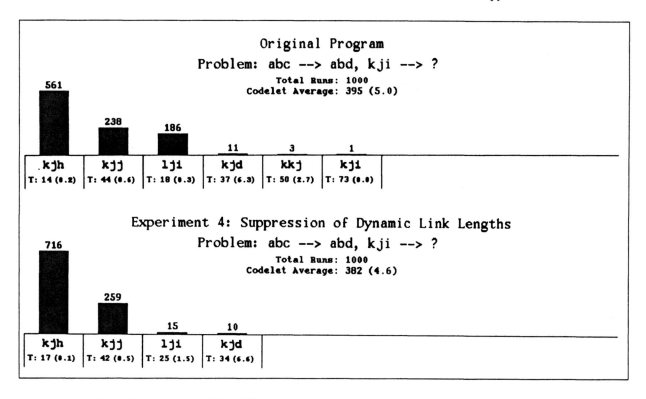

Original Program
Problem: abc --> abd, kji --> ?
Total Runs: 1000
Codelet Average: 395 (5.0)

kjh	kjj	lji	kjd	kkj	kji
561	238	186	11	3	1
T: 14 (0.2)	T: 44 (0.6)	T: 18 (0.3)	T: 37 (6.3)	T: 50 (2.7)	T: 73 (0.0)

Experiment 4: Suppression of Dynamic Link Lengths
Problem: abc --> abd, kji --> ?
Total Runs: 1000
Codelet Average: 382 (4.6)

kjh	kjj	lji	kjd
716	259	15	10
T: 17 (0.1)	T: 42 (0.5)	T: 25 (1.5)	T: 34 (6.6)

Here there is a visible difference in the two bar graphs: the number of **kjh** instances goes up significantly and the number of **lji** instances plummets in the modified version. The reason for this is as follows. The program answers **kjh** when it has made *vertical* correspondences (*leftmost* ⇒ *leftmost* and *rightmost* ⇒ *rightmost*) between **abc** and **kji**. As was shown in the screen dumps in chapter 4, these correspondences force a view in which one string is seen as a successor group and the other as a predecessor group. In this case, when a whole-string mapping is made between **abc** and **kji**, the slippage *successor* ⇒ *predecessor* is made automatically—the slippage is forced by the whole-string mapping, and *opposite* is activated only after the slippage is made. On the other hand, the answer **lji** is harder for the program (even the original version) to get. As was seen in chapter 4, it is produced when the program views **abc** and **kji** as moving in the same alphabetic direction but in different spatial directions. This view produces a whole-string mapping with the slippage *right* ⇒ *left*, which activates *opposite*. Only then, with links between *opposite* nodes being shrunk, is it likely that *diagonal* correspondences with slippages *leftmost* ⇒ *rightmost* and *rightmost* ⇒ *leftmost* will be built. These two slippages, although closely related to *left* ⇒ *right* and *right* ⇒ *left*, do not come about automatically when the latter two have been made. They must be made independently, although their construction is strongly facilitated by the shrinking of opposite links caused by the latter two slippages.

In short, the answer **lji** relies on dynamic link lengths, whereas **kjh** does not. The difference is that the slippage needed for the latter (*successor* ⇒ *predecessor*) is made automatically when **abc** and **kji** (viewed in opposite alphabetic directions) are mapped as wholes, whereas the slippage needed for the former (*rightmost* ⇒ *leftmost*) can be easily made only after a succession of events: the whole-string slippage (*right* ⇒ *left*) has been made, *opposite* has been activated, and links between *opposite* nodes have been shrunk.

It is possible that this asymmetry in the routes to the two answers is not psychologically realistic. It seems plausible that once the slippage *right* ⇒ *left* is made, the closely related slippage *rightmost* ⇒ *leftmost* should come immediately on its coattails, not merely as a result of the activation of *opposite*. The current version of Copycat has no mechanism implementing such a "coattails" effect, but it would be a desirable extension of the program. In general, such a coattails effect would allow certain slippages to be pulled along on the coattails of conceptually related slippages that have already been made. This would, for example, enable the program to produce additional answers to problems such as variant 23 in chapter 5: **abc ⇒ abd, glz ⇒ ?**. The current program cannot answer **flz**: there is no possibility of a *successor* ⇒ *predecessor* slippage, since the target string cannot be seen as a successor or predecessor group. The coattails effect would allow the slippage *successor* ⇒ *predecessor* to be brought in on the coattails of the conceptually related slippages *first* ⇒ *last* and *leftmost* ⇒ *rightmost*, even though *successor* ⇒ *predecessor* is not explicitly a part of any correspondence.

For this problem, the average time taken to arrive at an answer was not very different in the modified version and the original version: 382 codelets run on average in the modified version, versus 395 in the original. The reason for this was that, even though the modified version is intrinsically slower (as was seen on **ijk** above), it takes longer for the program to come up with the answer **lji** than **kjh**, so in the modified version the intrinsic slowness was balanced by the reduction in instances of answer **lji**.

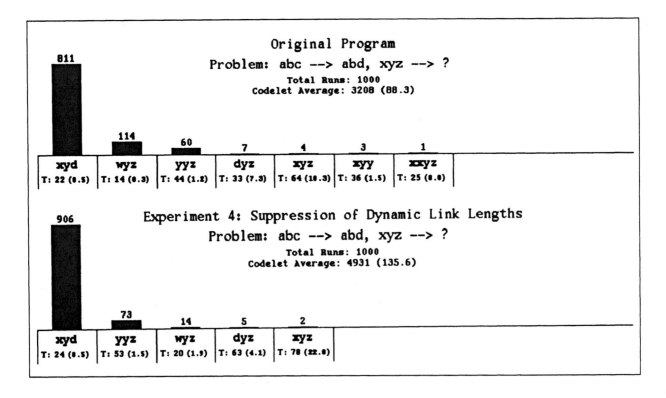

Original Program
Problem: abc --> abd, xyz --> ?
Total Runs: 1000
Codelet Average: 3208 (88.3)

xyd	wyz	yyz	dyz	xyz	xyy	xxyz
811	114	60	7	4	3	1
T: 22 (0.5)	T: 14 (0.3)	T: 44 (1.2)	T: 33 (7.3)	T: 64 (10.3)	T: 36 (1.5)	T: 25 (0.0)

Experiment 4: Suppression of Dynamic Link Lengths
Problem: abc --> abd, xyz --> ?
Total Runs: 1000
Codelet Average: 4931 (135.6)

xyd	yyz	wyz	dyz	xyz
906	73	14	5	2
T: 24 (0.5)	T: 53 (1.5)	T: 20 (1.9)	T: 63 (4.1)	T: 78 (22.0)

Here the number of instances of **wyz** goes way down, and the number of instances of **xyd** goes up. The answer **wyz** is very hard to make without dynamic link lengths. In the original program, once the **a-z** correspondence—with concept mappings *first* $\Rightarrow$ *last* and *leftmost* $\Rightarrow$ *rightmost*—has been built, *opposite* becomes active, making all *opposite* links shorter and hence making it more likely for the **c-x** correspondence to be built and for **abc** and **xyz** to be seen as going in opposite spatial and alphabetic directions. Without dynamic link lengths it is much harder for all these mutually supporting structures to be built, which means that the unreinforced **a-z** correspondence is so weak that it tends to be broken quickly. This is why the answer **xyd** is overwhelmingly prevalent in the modified program. There are still many instances of the answer **yyz**; this answer comes from building only the **a-z** correspondence (with slippage *leftmost* $\Rightarrow$ *rightmost*) without making a whole-string mapping with a *successor* $\Rightarrow$ *predecessor* slippage. Dynamic link lengths are thus not very important for the answer **yyz**. As was the case for **ijk**, the modified program takes longer to come up with an answer: on average, 4931 codelets ran here, versus 3208 in the original.

8.5 Experiment 5: Clamping Temperature at 100

Experiments 5, 6, and 7 all involve clamping the temperature at different values (high, low, and medium); the point is to better understand the roles of nondeterminism and of a time-varying temperature in the program's performance. In this experiment, temperature was clamped at its maximum value of 100. Recall that at a temperature of 100, although probabilistic decisions (such as whether to build a particular structure) are made with a high degree of randomness, they are still not *uniformly* random. Thus, there is still a bias toward high-urgency codelets: at a temperature of 100, the different possible urgencies are on a linear scale, with the highest possible urgency four times the lowest. (The actual formulas used for determining urgencies and probabilities as a function of temperature are given in appendix B.)

One difficulty with carrying out such an experiment is that, if the temperature is always 100, rule-translator codelets will essentially never decide that enough good structure has been built that the rule can be translated and an answer constructed. To take care of this difficulty, a separate value for temperature was maintained, calculated the same way as in the original program, as a function of the happinesses of the objects in the Workspace. This "real" temperature was visible only to rule-translator codelets. For all other purposes, the temperature was clamped at 100. (The "real" average final temperatures are displayed in the following bar graphs.)

For experiments 5, 6, and 7, I give the results of the modified programs on the problem **abc** $\Rightarrow$ **abd**, **mrrjjj** $\Rightarrow$. This problem was chosen because of the presumed role of temperature in the construction of the answer **mrrjjjj**.

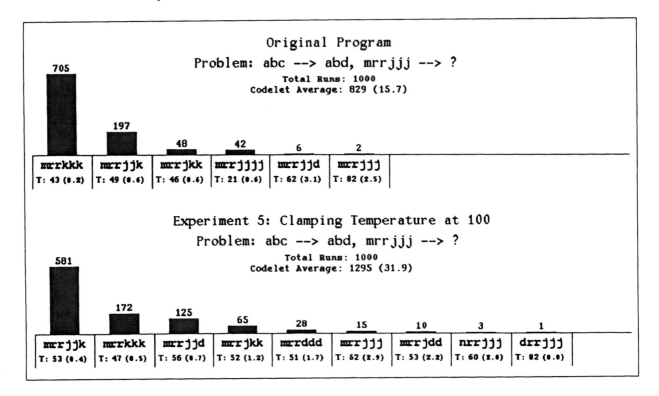

As can be seen, the modified program's performance is considerably different from that of the original program. As was discussed in chapter 3 and illustrated in chapter 4, temperature affects almost every aspect of the program, and it can be seen from the bar graph above that a persisting high temperature tends to prevent the building of a coherent set of structures. The answer mrrjjk dominates here, and the more structured mrrkkk is much less likely to be given. Answers that were on the fringes for the original program (e.g., mrrjjd and mrrjjj) are much more likely to be given here, and there are some additional fringe answers that were not produced by the original version. The answer mrrjjjj was not produced even once during the 1000 runs; since the temperature stays high, the necessary top-down forces never get the chance they need to construct the subtler structures required for this answer. Even if the program stumbles onto a good pathway, the high amount of randomness here makes it impossible for the program's resources to shift to exploring that pathway.

It can be seen that the average final temperatures for the modified program (corresponding to the real temperature values, as described above) tend to be higher than the corresponding temperatures for the original program—reflecting the fact that, on average, not as much strong structure was constructed here.

Since the persisting high temperature makes it hard to build a coherent set of structures, the modified program is much slower at coming up with answers than the original: on average, 1295 codelets ran, versus 829 in the original.

8.6 Experiment 6: Clamping Temperature at 0

Here the temperature was clamped at its minimum value of 0 for all purposes except deciding when to translate the rule. (As in experiment 5, temperature was calculated as usual for use by rule-translator codelets. The average final values of these real temperatures are displayed in the bar graph.) At a temperature of 0, the different possible urgencies are on an exponential scale, with the highest possible urgency on the order of 10^6 times the lowest. Thus, decisions about which codelet to run next are virtually deterministic—here the codelet-selection mechanism resembles an agenda system, with the highest-urgency codelet virtually certain to be chosen. Decisions made by codelets, such as whether to build a particular structure, are still probabilistic, though the probability distribution is much less uniform than for high temperatures. The probability of deciding to build a structure is a function of the program's estimation of the structure's strength. At low temperatures this estimation is believed to be reliable. For example, with a temperature of 0, if a structure's strength is estimated to be 75 (on a scale from 0 to 100), the probability that it will be built is 0.75. As the temperature increases, this probability gets closer and closer to 0.5.

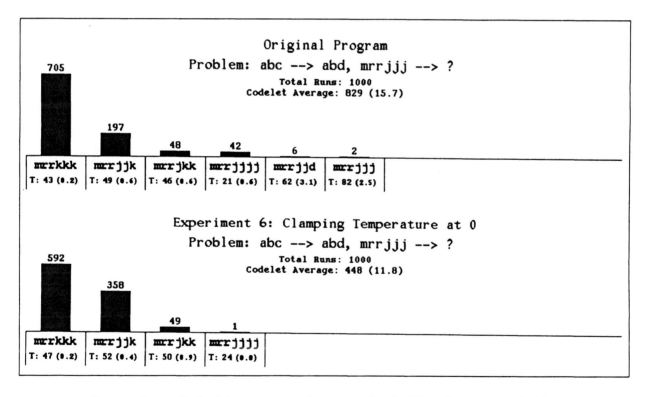

In experiment 5, decisions were made too randomly. Here the opposite holds: the low temperature means that decisions are made much more deterministically (e.g., at any time, the highest-urgency codelet is almost certain to be chosen next, the strongest structure in a competition is more certain to win, etc.), even when very little structure has been built. Again, this has striking effects on the program's performance. In contrast with the previous experiment, here the answer **mrrkkk** dominates, but even so there are still more instances of **mrrjjk** here than in the original. The most striking difference is the lack of fringe answers here (though there are several instances of **mrrjkk**—due, as usual, to the program's occasional grouping problems). Since the modified program is now quite deterministic, weaker rules (e.g, "Replace the rightmost letter by *D*" or "Replace *C* by *D*") never prevail. This modification makes the program quite conservative; thus, it does not produce as many fringe answers, but it also hardly ever comes up with **mrrjjjj** (just once in 1000 runs), which requires the exploration of some riskier routes. The high degree of determinism means that what appears to be the best possibility gets almost all of the program's attention at any given time, so less obvious structures (such as single-letter groups, length descriptions, and bonds between group lengths) are much less likely to be considered in any depth. The program's tendency, at any given time, to focus almost all of its resources on what it sees as the most promising avenue turns out to be a waste of time, since the program tends to explore the same strong structures again and again. This is why there are more instances of **mrrjjk** than in the original program: the program might, for example, spend a great deal of time exploring again and again the possibility of building the very strong **abc** whole-string group even after it has already been built, and never get around to building the **jjj** group before it decides to produce an answer. This is also the reason for the slightly higher average final temperature values in the modified version. These higher temperatures indicate that, in general, not as much strong structure was constructed.

In contrast with experiment 5, the modified program is much faster than the original at reaching an answer (448 codelets on average, versus 829 in the original). One reason is that the high degree of determinism results in a quite serial form of exploration, in which seemingly good structures are explored and built very quickly while seemingly weaker structures are hardly explored at all, even at very early stages. (This is similar to the effect seen in experiment 1.) Thus, the program does not spend time exploring many possibilities, and can come to an answer much more quickly. But again, the tradeoff is that certain possibilities (such as building single-letter groups or noticing group lengths) are in effect almost completely excluded from the start, and the program is thus liable to miss interesting but not immediately obvious ways of interpreting the situations. This shows the necessity for a balance between exploitation and exploration. In experiment 5, the program erred on the exploration side, and here it errs on the exploitation side. A belief underlying this model is that not only is a balance needed, but there must be a smooth and gradual transition from a more random and parallel *exploration* mode in early stages, to a more deterministic and serial *exploitation* mode in later stages when the system has more information upon which to base decisions. However, the results of the next experiment bring up some questions about the actual necessity for such a transition.

8.7 Experiment 7: Clamping Temperature at 50

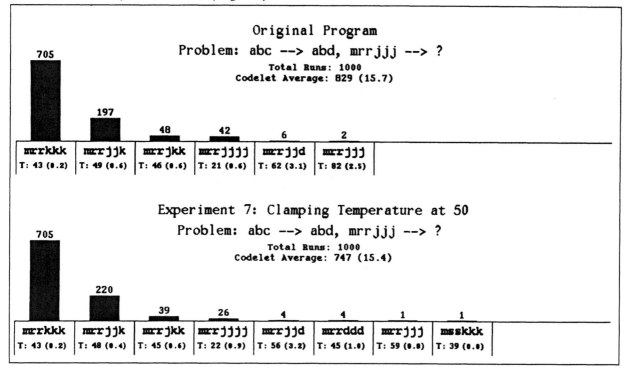

In contrast to the results of the two previous experiments, in which the answer **mrrjjjj** almost never appeared, here it appears with some frequency, although significantly less often than for the original program (26 times versus 42 times in 1000 runs). The total average number of codelets run is slightly less for the modified program, but the more detailed statistics are of interest here: the codelet averages for each answer are given in table 8.1.

As can be seen, the modified program is somewhat faster at getting the two most frequent answers (**mrrkkk** and **mrrjjk**). There are two reasons for this: (1) In order to get these answers, the original program spends a lot of time at high temperatures trying out a number of dead ends before it settles on its final set of structures, so in the early part of a run it tends to be slower than the modified program. (2) For runs resulting in these two answers, the temperature

Table 8.1

Average number of codelets run for the four main answers to **abc** ⇒ **abd**, **mrrjjj** ⇒?
in the original and modified programs (experiment 7). The numbers in the parentheses are standard errors.

	Original program	Modified program
mrrkkk	875 (18)	796 (17)
mrrjjk	656 (41)	529 (32)
mrrjkk	710 (51)	724 (81)
mrrjjjj	1126 (56)	1286 (86)

in the original program never gets very much below 50 anyway, so there is no speedup effect from falling temperature in the late part of a run.

However, the modified program is somewhat slower at getting **mrrjjjj**. The reason for this is that on runs leading to this answer there is a speedup in the original program in the late part of a run, due to falling temperature. As was discussed above, Copycat needs a certain degree of nondeterminism to discover the structures needed to get this answer; however, once it builds these structures, falling temperature helps to preserve them by "freezing them in." In experiment 5, with temperature clamped at 100, the program could much more easily build single-letter groups and length descriptions, but because of the continuing high temperature it could not hold onto them and tie them together. In experiment 6, with temperature clamped at 0, the necessary "risky" structures were very unlikely to be considered. In this experiment, with temperature clamped at 50, the program can build the necessary structures, but it is harder than in the original program to hold onto them. Once they are built, the modified program is more likely to lose them because of the persisting high temperature. This effect is responsible for the decrease in speed and frequency for **mrrjjjj** in the modified program.

These last three experiments have demonstrated to some extent the roles of nondeterminism and temperature in Copycat. The results of the experiments clearly demonstrate the necessity of nondeterminism, but leave some questions about the necessity for a varying temperature based on feedback. The lack of this mechanism made some difference in the results of experiment 7, but the difference was not large enough in that experiment to make a convincing argument for the necessity of such a mechanism. Two main questions need to be answered in future work on this project: (1) In what situations does a varying temperature have a significant effect? My intuition is that the most significant effects will be seen on complex problems in which a set of good, though initially hard-to-discover structures must be built and then quickly "frozen." (2) Precisely how should this mechanism be implemented? The current implementation of temperature in Copycat is imperfect; one flaw (concerning the contribution from weak rules such as "Replace the rightmost letter by *D*") was discussed in chapter 4. It also seems likely that the current implementation of temperature results in too much randomness in the program at all temperature values, which slows things down unnecessarily in early stages of a run and which prevents the program from moving quickly enough in later stages of the run. The results of experiment 7 support this conjecture; they indicate that it is not necessary for the temperature to start out at very high values (i.e., higher than 50) in order for the program to perform well, and that there is not enough of a speedup at lower temperatures. This conjecture needs to be investigated for other problems as well.

8.8 Summary

The experiments described in this chapter have further illustrated the roles played by certain architectural features of Copycat: the role of splitting up the task of building structures into chains of codelets (i.e., the terraced scan), the role of structure-breaking codelets, the role of conceptual-depth values in the Slipnet, the role of dynamic link lengths in the Slipnet, and the roles of nondeterminism and temperature. There are many more such experiments that could be done (removing all bottom-up or all top-down codelet types, running the program with no spreading activation in the Slipnet, limiting the Coderack to various different sizes, and so on), and in general it would be very interesting to systematically vary the parameters and formulas in the system and to observe the effects on Copycat's behavior. The experiments described in this chapter represent a first step in this longer-term process of exploring the effects of such variations on the model.

Chapter 9

Comparisons with Related Work

9.1 Comparisons with Other Research on Analogy-Making

A fair amount of research has been done in artificial intelligence and cognitive science on constructing computer models of analogy-making, almost all of it concentrating on the use of analogical reasoning in problem-solving. Most of these models concentrate on how a mapping is made from a source problem whose solution is known to a target problem whose solution is desired, with some kind of representation of the various objects, descriptions, and relations in the source and target problems given to the program at the outset. Very few computer models focus (as Copycat does) on how the *construction* of representations for the source and target situations interacts with the mapping process, and on how new, previously unincluded concepts can be brought in and can come to be seen as relevant in response to pressures that emerge as processing proceeds. In short, very few computer models of analogy-making attempt to model high-level perception, concepts, and conceptual slippage in the way Copycat does.

In this section, rather than giving a complete survey of computer models of analogy-making, I will discuss (and compare with Copycat) three different projects, chosen for their prominence in artificial intelligence and for their relevance to the Copycat project. This leaves out a discussion of many other models of analogy-making that are less related to Copycat. A good number of these are described by Hall (1989) and by Kedar-Cabelli (1988a).

9.1.1 Gentner et al.
Dedre Gentner's research is perhaps the best-known work in cognitive science on analogy. She has formulated a theory of analogical mapping, called the "structure-mapping" theory (Gentner 1983), and she and her colleagues have constructed a computer model of this theory: the Structure-Mapping Engine, or SME (Falkenhainer, Forbus, and Gentner 1989). The structure-mapping theory describes how mapping is carried out from a source situation to a (sometimes less familiar) target situation. The theory gives two principles for analogical mapping: (1) *relations* between objects rather than *attributes* of objects are mapped, and (2) relations that are part of a coherent interconnected system are preferentially mapped over relatively isolated relations (the "systematicity" principle). In effect, Gentner's definition of analogy presupposes these mapping principles. According to her, there is a continuum of kinds of comparison: an "analogy" is a comparison in which only systematic relations are mapped,

whereas a comparison in which both attributes and relations are mapped is a "literal similarity" rather than an analogy. I do not make such a sharp distinction, as can be seen from the spectrum of examples of analogy-making given in chapter 1.

One of Gentner's examples of an analogy is illustrated in figure 9.1 (from Falkenhainer, Forbus, and Gentner 1989). The idea "heat flow is like water flow" is illustrated by mapping one situation, in which water flows from a beaker to a vial through a pipe, onto a second situation, in which heat flows from coffee in a cup to an ice cube through a metal bar. The predicate-logic representations given for these two situations are displayed in figure 9.2. The idea is that the causal-relation tree on the left (representing the fact that greater pressure in the beaker causes water to flow from the beaker to the vial through the pipe) is a systematic structure and should thus be mapped to the heat-flow situation, whereas the other facts ("the diameter of the beaker is greater than the diameter of the vial," "water is a liquid," "water has a flat top," etc.) are irrelevant and should be ignored. Ideally, mappings should be made between *pressure* and *temperature*, *coffee* and *beaker*, *vial* and *ice cube*, *water* and *heat*, *pipe* and *bar*, and (more obviously) *flow* and *flow*. Once these mappings are made, a conjecture about the cause of heat flow in the situation on the right can be made by analogy with the causal structure in the situation on the left. Gentner claims that if people recognize that this causal structure is the deepest and most interconnected system for this analogy, then they will favor it for mapping.

Gentner gives the following (possibly conflicting) criteria for judging the quality of an analogy:

- *Clarity*—a measure of how clear it is which things map onto which other things.

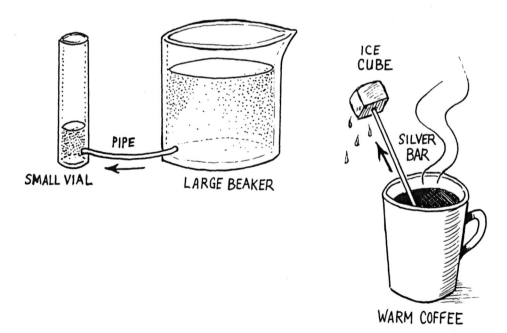

Figure 9.1
Water-flow and heat-flow situations (adapted from Falkenhainer, Forbus, and Gentner 1989).

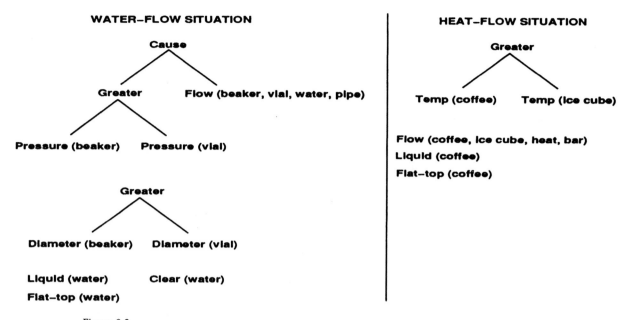

Figure 9.2
The predicate-logic representations for the water-flow and heat-flow situations (from Falkenhainer, Forbus, and Gentner 1989).

· *Richness*—a measure of how many things in the source are mapped to the target.

· *Abstractness*—a measure of how abstract the things mapped are, where the degree of "abstractness" of an attribute or relation is its "order". Attributes (e.g., "flat-top" in the example above) are of the lowest order, relations whose arguments are objects or attributes (e.g., "flow") are of higher order, and relations whose arguments are relations (e.g., "cause") are of even higher order.

· *Systematicity*—the degree to which the things mapped belong to a coherent interconnected system.

The computer model of this theory (SME) takes a predicate-logic representation of two situations, such as the representation given in figure 9.2, makes mappings between objects, between attributes, and between relations in the two situations, and then makes inferences from this mapping (such as "the greater temperature of the coffee causes heat to flow from the coffee to the ice cube"). The only knowledge the program has of the two situations is their syntactic structures (e.g., the tree structures given for the water-flow and heat-flow situations given above); it has no knowledge of any kind of semantic similarity between various descriptions and relations in the two situations. All processing is based on syntactic structural features of the two given representations.

SME first uses a set of "match rules" (provided to the program ahead of time) to make all "plausible" pairings between objects (e.g., *water* and *heat*) and between relations (e.g., *flow* in the case of water and *flow* in the case of heat). Examples of such rules are "If two relations have the same name, then pair them," "If two objects play the same role in two already paired relations (i.e., are arguments in the same position), then pair them," and "Pair any two functional predicates" (e.g., *pressure* and *temperature*). SME then gives a score to each of these pairings, based on factors such as: Do the two things paired have the same name? What kind of things are they (objects, relations, functional predicates, etc.)? Are they part of systematic structures? The kinds of pairings allowed and the scores given to them depend on the set of match rules given to the program; different sets can be supplied.

Once all plausible pairings have been made, the program makes all possible sets of consistent combinations of these pairings, making each set (or "global match") as large as possible. "Consistency" here means that each element can match only one other element, and a pair (e.g., *pressure* and *temperature*) is allowed to be in the global match only if all the arguments of each element are also paired up in the global match. For example, if *pressure* and *temperature* are paired, then *beaker* and *coffee* must be paired as well. Consistency ensures clarity of the analogy, and the fact that the sets are maximal shows a preference for richness. After all possible global matches have been formed, each is given a score based on the individual pairings it is made up of, the inferences it suggests, and its degree of systematicity. Gentner and her colleagues have compared the relative scores assigned by the program with the scores people give to the various analogies (Skorstad, Falkenhainer, and Gentner 1987).

Analogy-making as modeled in the Copycat program is in agreement with several aspects of Gentner's theory, including the main idea of systematicity: in general, the essence of a situation—the part that should be mapped—is a high-level coherent whole, not a collection of isolated low-level similarities. In Copycat, there is a pressure toward systematicity, which is an emergent result of several other pressures:

- The pressure, coming from codelets, to perceive relations and groupings within strings.
- The pressure to see things abstractly (which itself emerges from the preference for using descriptions of greater conceptual depth, and from the tendency of deeper concepts to stay active longer).
- The pressure to describe the change from the initial to the modified string in terms of relationships and roles, since these tend to be deeper than attributes (e.g., in formulating a rule for the change **abc** ⇒ **abd**, it is in general better to describe the **d** as "the successor of the rightmost letter" than as "an instance of *D*").
- The greater salience of larger relational structures (e.g., a whole-string group), which makes them more likely to be paid attention to and hence mapped.
- The high strength of correspondences between large relational structures (such as whole-string groups). Such correspondences are strong not only because they involve large structures, but also because they are based on many concept mappings.
- The pressure toward forming a set of compatible correspondences that, taken together, form a coherent world view.
- The system's overall drive to achieve as low a temperature as possible, which pushes for the building up of deep hierarchical perceptual structures and thus for an abstract, conceptually deep view of the situations to be produced.

Gentner captures several important notions in her characterization of a good analogy, and the same pressures exist in Copycat: the pressure toward "clarity" is enforced by Copycat's prohibition of many-to-one or one-to-many mappings without first making the "many" into a grouped unit; the pressure toward "richness" corresponds to Copycat's preference for having many correspondences and many concept mappings underlying a correspondence; and Copycat's drives toward abstraction and systematicity are described above. But note that Gentner's definition of "abstraction" (order of a relation) is not the same as the notion in Copycat of "conceptual depth" (which was described in section 3.2). In Copycat, there is no logic-based definition for conceptual depth; rather, these values are assigned by hand, with quite high values sometimes going to concepts that Gentner might call "attributes" (such as *first*, which could be seen as an attribute of an **a**).

Although there are points of agreement, there are also some fundamental issues on which our approach and Gentner's disagree, and some of the most important aspects of analogy-making addressed in the Copycat project are not dealt with in Gentner's theory and model.

Gentner's abstractness and systematicity principles capture something important about analogy-making, but there are often other pressures in an analogy—both superficial and abstract similarities that may not be parts of systematic wholes but are still strong contenders in a competition. An example of this in the Copycat domain can be illustrated by variant 9 in chapter 5:

aabc ⇒ aabd
ijkk ⇒?

Gentner's abstractness and systematicity principles would, I think, argue for the answer **ijll**, since the attribute *sameness-group* describing the group of **a**'s and the group of **k**'s is merely an attribute and is not related to the systematic set of successor relations in each string. According to the systematicity principle, it should thus not be mapped; it should be ignored. However, many people feel that the two groups should map onto each other nonetheless, and that the best answer is **hjkk**, in spite of what I think would be an *a priori* dismissal by the structure-mapping theory. Making any analogy involves a competition between rival views, and one cannot be certain ahead of time that the mapping with the highest degree of systematicity (in Gentner's sense) will be the most appealing.

Another weak point of Gentner's theory is that for any complex situation there are many possible sets of relations that exhibit systematicity, and the theory does not explain how it is decided that—on syntactic grounds alone—certain ones should be considered for mapping and not others. For example, suppose the heat-flow domain had contained the following relation:

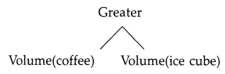

Greater

Volume(coffee)   Volume(ice cube)

There would be no reason, based on syntax alone, to prefer the structure concerning temperature over this structure for mapping. However, if this structure were chosen, the analogy-maker would mistakenly learn that, just as the pressure differential causes the water flow, the volume differential causes the heat flow. There is not even a semantic connection given between *temperature* and *heat* that might guide one to suspect the implication of temperature in understanding how heat flow occurs. In short, which facts are part of a relevant systematic whole and which are isolated and irrelevant depends on the situations at hand and cannot be determined by syntactic structure alone.

By contrast, in Copycat the mechanisms for deciding what things to concentrate on and which mappings to make involve semantics: they involve activation of concepts in the Slipnet in response to perception of instances of those concepts (or of associated concepts) in the letter strings, competition among objects clamoring to be noticed and among various descriptions of objects and relationships between objects, and certain *a priori* notions of salience. For the Structure-Mapping Engine, not only are the attributes and relations in each situation laid out in advance, but there is no notion of differential relevance among them: which ones get used in an analogy is entirely a function of the syntactic structure connecting them. In Copycat, the notions of differential relevance and graded inclusion of concepts in a situation—and of the program itself bringing in the concepts to be used to describe the situation—are fundamental, since Copycat is a model of how situations are interpreted as well as how mappings are made between them, and of how the two processes interact. The philosophy of Gentner and her colleagues is that the interpretation stage and the mapping stage can be modeled independently—that there are, in effect, separate "modules" for each. In contrast, a philosophy underlying the Copycat project is that the two are inextricably intertwined: the way in which the two situations are understood is affected by how they are mapped onto each other, as well as vice versa. Such an interaction could be seen in the screen dumps given in chapter 4. For example, in **abc ⇒ abd, kji ⇒ ?**, how **abc** was mapped to **kji** had a profound influence on how the latter was interpreted, and vice versa. The necessity of integrating these two processes is discussed further in Chalmers, French, and Hofstadter 1992.

Another fundamental difference between Copycat and Gentner's approach is that her theory does not include any notion of conceptual similarity or of slippage, notions absolutely central to Copycat. In the water-flow–heat-flow example given above, the representations of the two situations are sufficiently abstract to make the analogy a virtual isomorphism. For example, the concepts of *water flow* and *heat flow* have both been abstracted in advance into a general notion of *flow*. Likewise, in another analogy that Gentner describes, in which the hydrogen atom is mapped onto the solar system, all the important predicates in both situations have the same labels (e.g., *attracts, revolves around, mass*). This is necessary because of the theory's reliance on syntax alone. If this "identicality" constraint were to be relaxed, semantics and context dependence (i.e., some knowledge of conceptual proximity and how it is affected by context) would have to be brought in. (SME does allow for nonidentical functional predicates, such as *pressure* or *temperature*, to match; however, no consideration of semantics is involved in such matches.) At present, since the concepts contained in SME's pre-constructed representations are always in a sufficiently abstract form, there is no need for a Slipnet-like structure in which various concepts flexibly become more or less similar to one another in response to context. The analogy is already effectively given in the representations.

Another problem with Gentner's theory is that it relies on a precise and un-ambiguous representation of situations in the language of predicate logic. The structure-mapping theory's reliance on syntax alone requires that situations be broken up very clearly into objects, attributes, functions, first-order relations, second-order relations, and so on. For example, the water-flow–heat-flow analogy includes the following correspondences:

> *water* ⇒ *heat* (both are objects)
>
> *coffee* ⇒ *beaker* (both are objects)
>
> *flow (beaker, vial, water, pipe)* ⇒ *flow (coffee, ice cube, heat, bar)*
>   (both are four-place relations).

But suppose that, in the heat-flow situation, *heat* had been described not as an object but as an attribute of coffee, as in *emits-heat (coffee)*, or that *flow* had been given as a three-place rather than as a four-place relation: *flow (coffee, ice cube, heat)*, where the means of heat flow is considered to be irrelevant. Or suppose that, in the water-flow situation, *water flow* had been given as a five-place re-lation: *flow (beaker, vial, water, pipe, 10 cc per second)*, where the rate of flow is included. Any of these quite plausible changes would prevent a successful ap-plication of the structure-mapping theory. The problem is that in the real world the categories "object," "attribute," and "relation" are very blurry, and people, if they assign such categories at all, have to use them very flexibly, allowing initial classifications to slide if necessary at the drop of a hat. And to do this, one must take semantics into account (this point is also made by Johnson-Laird [1989]). In the water-flow–heat-flow representation *heat* is presented as an *ob-ject*, but in the solar-system–atom representations it could plausibly be given as an *attribute* of the sun (e.g., *generates-heat (sun)*). The classification of *heat* as an object is necessary for the water-flow–heat-flow analogy to work, but it is not necessarily a classification that the analogy-maker would make *before* figuring out what the mappings were. It seems likely that any two people (or even one person, at different times) would produce very different predicate-logic repre-sentations of, say, the water-flow situation, no doubt differing on which things were considered to be objects, which were attributes, which were relations, how many arguments a given relation has, and so on. Thus, a serious weakness of the structure-mapping theory is its inability to deal with any flexibility in the representation of situations.

To be sure, Copycat also breaks up a situation's representation too cleanly into object-attributes (descriptions) and relations between objects (bonds), where many people would not do so. For example, in the string **aaabcd**, should the fact that the **b** is the alphabetic successor of the group of **a**'s be represented as a bond between the two objects, or as a description belonging exclusively to the **b**? It depends on the context. If the problem were

> **aaabcd** ⇒ **aaaxcd**
> **pqqqrs** ⇒ ?,

one could plausibly use that fact as a description, viewing the **b** and the **r** as corresponding because they are both "successor of the sameness group", and answer **pqqqxs**. However, such a description might not be applied to the **b** in **aaabcd** if the problem were

aaabcd $\Rightarrow$ aaabce
pqqqrs $\Rightarrow$?.

In the latter, to get the answer **pqqqrt**, one would use the **A-b** successor relation only as one of the relations tying together the initial string. Copycat is currently unable to make descriptions such as "successor of the sameness group," but I believe that its architecture would allow one to fairly straightforwardly give it the ability to make and use such descriptions appropriately. The possibility for such real-time representational flexibility is lacking in a program like SME, which relies solely on the syntax of predicate-logic representations that are supplied to it before the fact. For such a program to work, the representations have to be tailored carefully.

Thus, both the architecture and the purpose of the Structure-Mapping Engine are quite different in spirit from those of Copycat. Although SME is meant to simulate human analogy-making, in that it models which types of structures people tend to map from one situation to another and which of the various possible mappings people tend to prefer, it does not attempt to model concepts or perceptual processes in the psychologically realistic manner that Copycat does. Certainly the exhaustive search SME performs through all consistent mappings is psychologically implausible (though some recent work on SME proposes ways of reducing the amount of search that must be done; see, for example, Forbus and Oblinger 1990). Rather, it seems that SME is meant to be an automatic way of finding what the structure-mapping theory would consider to be the best mapping between two given representations, and of rating various mappings according to the structure-mapping theory, which ratings can then be compared with those given by people.

In summary: Copycat has a store of knowledge about letter strings that is structured independently of any particular problem and that is adapted *by the program* to each new problem. SME has no permanent store of knowledge. For each new analogy between two situations, a new set of facts specific to the two situations is needed, and these facts must first be put into predicate-logic notation before being given to the program. These predicate-logic descriptions are fixed at the start of processing and cannot be altered by the program. In contrast, Copycat starts out with raw, unperceived situations, and it is in the process of describing these situations and their relations to one another that the concept network (the Slipnet) is modified dynamically and eventually settles into a certain pattern of activations and conceptual proximities. It is impossible for an analogy-maker to know ahead of time which concepts will be important and what reformulations and slippages will have to take place in the course of making an analogy. SME does not address these issues. The structure-mapping theory makes some very useful points about what features appealing analogies tend to have; however, in dealing only with the mapping process, while leaving aside the problem of how situations become understood and how this process of interpretation interacts with the mapping process, it leaves out some of the most important aspects of how analogies are made.

9.1.2 Holyoak and Thagard

Keith Holyoak and Paul Thagard (1989) have built a computer model of analogical mapping, based in part on theoretical and experimental work by Holyoak and his colleagues (Gick and Holyoak 1983; Holland, Holyoak, Nisbett, and Thagard 1986) and inspired in part by research by David Marr and Tomaso Poggio on constraint-satisfaction networks used to model stereoscopic vision. The computer model, ACME (Analogical Constraint Mapping Engine), is similar to SME in that it uses representations of a source situation and target situation given in sentences of predicate logic and makes an analogical mapping consisting of pairs of constants and predicates from the representations. In fact, ACME has been tested on several of the same predicate-logic representations of situations that SME was given, including the water-flow and heat-flow representations. For ACME, a mapping between two situations is based on the following three classes of constraints (not all of which must be fulfilled for a successful analogy):

- *Structural consistency*, which favors possible mappings in which the following hold:

  1. The elements of the target and source representations map one-to-one.

  2. A mapped pair has to consist of two elements of the same logical type. That is, constants are mapped onto constants and *n*-place predicates are mapped onto *n*-place predicates. For example, in the water-flow–heat-flow analogy, *water* could map onto *water* but not onto *flow*, because the former is a constant and the latter is a four-place relation.

  3. The various pairings making up a global mapping must support each other. For example, if *flow* in one situation maps onto *flow* in the other, then that supports a mapping between *water* and *heat*, since they play corresponding roles in the two different *flow* relations.

- *Semantic similarity*, which supports possible correspondences between elements that have similar meanings.

- *Pragmatic centrality*, which supports possible correspondences that are presumed ahead of time to hold or which involve objects that are deemed important ahead of time.

The model takes as input a set of predicate-logic sentences containing information about the source and target domains (e.g., water flow and heat flow), and it constructs a network of nodes in which each node represents a syntactically allowable pairing between one source element and one target element (a constant or a predicate). (Here, "syntactically allowable" means adhering to the structural-consistency constraint.) A node is made for every such allowable pairing. For example, one node might represent the *water* ⇒ *heat* mapping, whereas another node might represent the *water* ⇒ *coffee* mapping. Links between nodes in the network represent constraints: a link is weighted positively if it represents mutual support of two pairings (e.g., there would be such a link between the *flow* ⇒ *flow* node and the *water* ⇒ *heat* node, since *water* and *heat* are counterparts in the argument lists of the two *flow* relations), and negatively if it represents mutual disconfirmation (e.g., there would be such a link between the *flow* ⇒ *flow* node and the *water* ⇒ *coffee* node). The network also has a "semantic unit"—a node that has links to all nodes representing pairs of predicates. These links are weighted positively in proportion to the "prior assessment of semantic similarity" (i.e., assessed by the person constructing the representations) between the two predicates. In addition, the network has a "pragmatic unit"—a node that has positively weighted links to all nodes involving elements (e.g., *water*) deemed important ahead of time (again by the person constructing the representations), or to any nodes representing mappings that are presumed ahead of time to hold. Once the network is in place, activation is allowed to spread over links according to a relaxation algorithm, and the network eventually settles into a final state with a particular set of activated nodes representing the winning matches.

There are several points of agreement between the philosophy of this model and that of the Copycat program. They share the idea that analogy-making is closely related to perception and should be modeled with techniques inspired by models of perception. They also share the belief that analogies emerge out of a competition among pressures (or "soft constraints"), involving a large number of local decisions that give rise to a larger coherent structuring. And they agree that the pressure toward systematicity (as described by Gentner) emerges from other pressures. Copycat has counterparts to Holyoak and Thagard's three classes of constraints: structural consistency (Copycat's pressure toward compatible correspondences), semantic similarity (in Copycat, correspondences involving close concept mappings are strong), and pragmatic centrality (Copycat has certain *a priori* assumptions—e.g., string-position descriptions such as *left-most* are assumed *a priori* to be relevant—that affect the importance values of certain objects).

There are, however, deep differences between Copycat and ACME, related to Copycat's differences with SME (discussed in the previous section). First, ACME tries *all* syntactically plausible pairings—a method that is both computationally infeasible and psychologically implausible in any realistic situation. For example, in making an analogy between the Watergate and Iran-Contra scandals, do we consider a mapping between Nixon and every person involved in the Iran-Contra situation, including Fawn Hall, Daniel Inouye, Ed Meese, and Dan Rather? Even less plausibly, do we consider mapping Gerald Ford to the Contras' base camp in Honduras, or to the chair Oliver North sat in while testifying before Congress? Yet these are all plausible according to the structural-consistency constraint, in which semantics plays no role at all. The existence of this exhaustive (though parallel) search through all possible mappings shows that, like SME, ACME is not attempting to model how people search through such possibilities, whereas this is one of the Copycat project's main focuses. In Copycat, although any initial-string object can *in principle* be compared with any target-string object, an exhaustive search is avoided thanks to the parallel terraced scan, in which comparisons, if they are made at all, are made at different speeds and to different levels of depth, depending on estimates of their promise.

A major problem in the ACME system is the same problem I discussed with respect to SME: the representations of knowledge used are rigid, and are also tailored specially for each new analogy. ACME uses the same representation that SME used for the water-flow–heat-flow analogy, so the same issues discussed in the subsection on Gentner et al. apply here. Again, the program has no ability to restructure its descriptions or to add new descriptions in the course of making an analogy; the descriptions are constructed by a person ahead of time and are frozen. ACME differs from SME in that it has a "semantic unit" giving semantic similarities, which correspond in some sense to those embodied in Copycat's Slipnet; however, the similarities are also decided in advance by the programmer for the purposes of the given analogy, and are frozen. Unlike Gentner et al., Holyoak and Thagard recognize the necessity of considering semantics as well as syntax, but the problem is that it is impossible in general to have a "prior assessment of similarities" (as encoded in ACME's semantic unit). Rather, analogy-making is all about similarities being reassessed in response to pressures that were not apparent ahead of time.

ACME also leaves aside the question of how concepts come to be seen as important in response to pressures; this is taken care of by the pragmatic unit, which encodes the programmer's prior assessment of what is important in the given situations. The pragmatic unit could be said to correspond to the activation of Slipnet nodes and to the *importance* values of Workspace objects in Copycat. But again in contrast with Copycat, where these values emerge in response to what the program perceives, in ACME the pragmatic unit is set up by a person and then frozen for each new problem.

In summary: ACME, like SME, models only the "mapping stage" of analogy-making. In contrast, a philosophy underlying Copycat is that the mapping process cannot be separated from the processes of perceiving and reformulating perceptions and assessments of similarities in response to pressures. Holyoak and Thagard (1989) themselves point out that their model does not address this issue, which they call the issue of re-representation, and acknowledge that it will often be necessary to interleave mapping with manipulation of the representations, taking into account top-down pressures—which is essentially just what Copycat does.

9.1.3 How Real Are These "Real-World" Analogies?
One of the criticisms that has been made of Copycat (as well as of Evans' program, to be discussed in the next section) is that it makes analogies in an idealized microworld, whereas other analogy-making programs work in more complex real-world domains. On the surface it would seem that SME and ACME make real-world analogies that are much more complex than the "toy" problems Copycat deals with. But if one looks below the surface (as I did above for the water-flow–heat-flow example), one can clearly see that the knowledge possessed by these programs (that is, the knowledge given to them for each new problem, in the form of sentences of predicate logic), in spite of the real-world aura of words like "pressure" and "heat-flow", is even more impoverished than Copycat's knowledge of its letter-string microworld. The programs know virtually nothing about concepts such as *heat* and *water*—much less than Copycat knows about, say, the concept *successor group*, which is embedded in a network and can be recognized and used in an appropriate way in a large variety of diverse situations. For example, **abc, aabbcc, cba, abbbc, mrrjjj, mmrrrjjjj, jjjrrm, abbccc, xpqefg,** and **k** (a single-letter successor group) can all be recognized as instances of successor groups, under the appropriate pressures. In addition, myriad other examples of successor groups, of different degrees of abstruseness, can be formed in the letter-string domain. Many are beyond

Copycat's current recognition capabilities, though the same perceptual mechanisms the program has now could, I believe, be extended fairly readily to recognize more complex instances, such as **ace** (a "double-successor" group), **aababc** (which can be seen as a "coded" version of **abc** when parsed as **a-ab-abc**), **kmxxrreeejjj** (which could be described as "11-22-33"), **axbxcx** (where the x's form a ground for the figure **abc**), and **abcbcdcde** (which could be parsed **abc-bcd-cde**).

Copycat's concept of "successor group" is thus much richer than SME's and ACME's notion of, say, "heat" (as given for the purpose of making a water-flow–heat-flow analogy). There the notion of "heat" has essentially no semantic content and certainly cannot be adapted to any other situation. Nor can these programs recognize heat or a heat-like phenomenon. These programs are purported to make analogies involving the concepts *heat* and *water*, but the programs have absolutely no sense of "heat" and "water" themselves as categories and cannot make the very analogies required to recognize instances of these categories (as humans do) in a variety of contexts.

Thus, the claim that Copycat's microworld is a "toy domain" whereas these other programs are solving real-world problems is truly unfounded, and is based on the human tendency to attribute much more intelligence to a program than it deserves, on the basis of real-world-sounding words it uses (such as "heat")—concepts that are extremely rich for humans, but are almost completely empty as far as the program is concerned. (McDermott [1981] writes humorously and incisively about some related problems in AI research methodology.) Programs that use words which have real-world connotations but which are nonetheless completely devoid of semantic content as far as the program is concerned have great potential to be misleading. An "all the cards are on the table" quality is one of the advantages of using explicit microworlds for research in artificial intelligence.

9.1.4 Evans

Thomas Evans' (1968) ANALOGY program was written in the 1960s to solve IQ-test-like geometric-analogy problems, many of which were taken from actual examinations given to college-bound high school students by the American Council on Education. A sample problem is given in figure 9.3. The idea is to choose the box in the bottom row that has the "same" relation to box C as box A has to box B. ANALOGY is given as input the information that box A contains two simple closed curves, along with the coordinates of the vertices and the curvature of the lines; similar information is given for all the other boxes. The program then computes, for each box, properties of the figures inside it and relations among them, using a predetermined set of possible properties and relations and a "substantial repertoire of 'analytic geometry' routines." For example, for box A in the problem shown, the program would find the relation (INSIDE triangle2 triangle1). (I use the word "triangle" only for clarity. The program does not have the concept *triangle*, and has no notion of similarity at the conceptual level between, say, two different triangles. It was not able, therefore, to solve problems involving rules such as "Replace all triangles by squares.") In order to describe the change from box A to box B, the program uses a given set of possible transformations to make all possible mappings from the

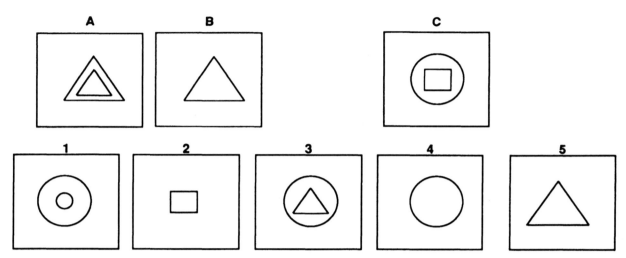

Figure 9.3
A sample problem from Evans' geometric-analogy domain.

figures in box A to those in box B. The repertoire of possible transformations contains: removal of objects, addition of objects, rotation of objects, uniform scale-change of objects, and horizontal and vertical reflection of objects. From this set of mappings the program creates a set of rules describing the change from A to B.

Next, the program tries to match box C with each of the numbered answer boxes, discarding an answer box if the matching does not agree with the A-to-B rules in terms of the number of objects added, removed, or matched. In the example, answers 1 and 3 are discarded for this reason. The program then does a (potentially huge) exhaustive search through all possible ways of mapping C to each of the remaining answers, given the possible A-to-B rules that have been formed. In this way, a set of possible C-to-answer rules is constructed (each one is a weakened form of one of the A-to-B rules, from which statements that are not true of the C-to-answer match are removed). Each of these C-to-answer rules is scored using a complicated procedure that values the amount of information the rule contains (roughly, the length of the rule). This reflects the heuristic that strong C-to-answer rules are ones requiring little alteration of the original A-to-B rule. The answer given by the rule with the highest score is chosen.

Evans' geometric-analogy problems are very much in the spirit of Copycat's letter-string problems, not merely because the analogies are in the form of "proportions" but also because they are abstract. Although such analogies have no conscious "purpose" (as in problem-solving), humans have definite feelings about what makes for a deep mapping and what makes for a shallow one. The fact that such abstract analogy problems are used without argument on intelligence tests (as requiring at least some aspect of intelligence) shows how generally accepted is the idea that people are able to bring to bear their perceptual and analogical abilities in an idealized domain; indeed, they are unable not to. This domain, like Copycat's, has the potential for very interesting and creative analogies, in spite of its limited number of concepts. Evans' domain is closely related to the extraordinarily rich domain of Bongard problems (Bongard 1970), which was one of the early inspirations for the Copycat project.

Although Evans' domain is potentially very rich, his program was able to solve only a very limited set of problems in this domain. For example, the transformations from box A to box B are restricted to those involving addition and removal of objects and Euclidean transformations (rotation, reflection, uniform-scale change). Therefore, the program would not be able to deal with a problem in which a triangle in box A was transformed into a square in box B, even if they both played the same role (say, "the outer object"). There is no notion of conceptual similarity or of similarity of roles.

The program also has no notion of grouping, and thus would not be able to solve the problem given in figure 9.4. The program would be stymied by the fact that the number of dots in A is different from the number of dots in C. The program is able to deal only with problems in which the number of parts added, removed, and matched in the A-to-B transformation is the same as in the C-to-answer transformation. All the problems that Evans' program attempted (he displays all 20 problems on which the program was tried) had the same number of objects in A as in C. In Copycat, the kinds of similarities possible between the initial and target strings can be much more complex. In addition, each of Evans' problems had exactly one strong answer, whereas many of Copycat's problems have more than one good answer. Such problems are among the most interesting, because they bring out very clearly issues of how various pressures compete.

ANALOGY is nonetheless more similar in many ways to Copycat than are the other analogy-making programs described in this subsection. As in Copycat, in Evans' system the situations as initially given to the program have only minimal descriptions attached, and the program itself has to perceive the relations among the various parts. The program also has a notion of adapting the A-to-B rule to fit the matchings between C and the various answers, which is roughly similar

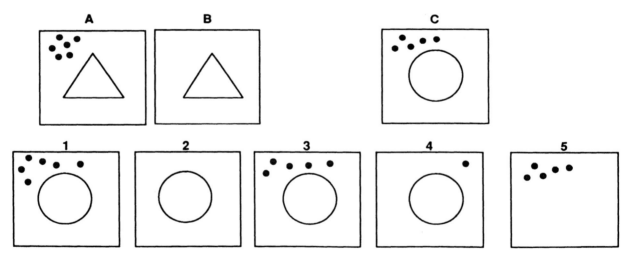

Figure 9.4
A problem that Evans' program would not be able to solve, because it requires grouping.

to rule translation in Copycat. In addition, in Evans' program context exerts top-down pressure on the way things are perceived. For example, given the boxes

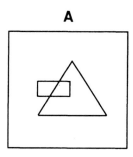

and

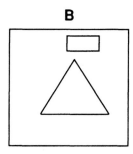

the program will decompose the figure in box A into a rectangle and a triangle, since these are the objects in box B (though, since the program has no concept of "rectangle" or "triangle," it would not be able to perceive the similarity between A and B if the corresponding figures happened to be of slightly different shapes). However, the role of context is limited. For example, the program's perception of box C has no effect on the perception of box A. In Copycat, such contextual effects can be very important (as they were in the problem **abd** ⇒ **abd, xyz** ⇒?, where the **a** can eventually get described as *first* in response to what is perceived in **xyz**). In general, the processes of description, mapping, and rule formation in ANALOGY do not interact as they do in Copycat. Evans saw the desirability of some kind of interaction among the various processes, but did not implement it. His program proceeds in stages in a strict serial fashion, with no backtracking for restructuring of perceptions.

Aside from the similarities mentioned above, the workings of Evans' program are very different from those of Copycat. ANALOGY has nothing like a Slipnet. There is no notion of conceptual similarity, only a rigid notion of geometric similarity. This, along with the fact that there must be a one-to-one correspondence between the objects changed in the A-to-B transformation and the objects changed in the C-to-answer transformation, severely limits the kinds of problems that ANALOGY is able to solve. Evans recognized that it is not always possible to adapt an A-to-B rule to a C-to-answer rule by weakening it; in some cases, translation with slippage is needed. In fact, he gave one example of a problem where this was needed; however, the great majority of his problems involved only identity concept mappings, so he was not very concerned by this issue. He did implement a very rough kind of slippage, in which one word in the A-to-B rule (e.g. ABOVE) is replaced by another word in the C-to-answer rule (e.g. LEFT). This is done only if, at the last stage, there is no single answer that is clearly stronger than the others. Then the program goes back to the A-to-B rule-building stage and generates some "variant rules" using this substitution technique. Evans does not explain exactly how this was done.

Another major difference is the lack in Evans' program of anything like a parallel terraced scan. Instead, his program adopts the brute-force method of making all possible relations, transformations, and rules, and then scoring them. This method has the usual problems of psychological implausibility and combinatorial explosion (though Evans cannot be faulted on the psychological implausibility, because his program was meant to be an AI program and not a cognitive model). ANALOGY was tried only on cases where there was no ambiguity and little competition, so there were only a few possibilities for the program to consider in each case. It would be impossible to use this method on more complex problems with more facets.

In summary: ANALOGY was an interesting early attempt at mechanizing analogy-making, and had some similarities in spirit to Copycat. However, it was significantly different from Copycat in many respects. It used a brute-force approach with a completely deterministic control structure that proceeded through stages in a fixed manner. It was not meant to be a cognitive model of concepts or perception. Its performance is in some ways impressive, since it was able to solve a number of problems considered hard enough to put on a college-entrance test; however, the range of problems it could solve was actually quite limited.

9.2 Comparisons with Related Artificial Intelligence Architectures

9.2.1 Seek-Whence

In addition to Jumbo (discussed in section 3.1), another precursor to Copycat was the Seek-Whence project. Douglas Hofstadter designed the domain and the original ideas for the architecture (Hofstadter, Clossman, and Meredith 1982), which was based on the architecture of Jumbo. The Seek-Whence program was developed by Marsha Meredith (1986). Seek-Whence is a discovery-and-extrapolation program: it tries to find the underlying regularity of a sequence of integers—in other words, to "seek whence" the sequence comes. The sequences it works on have patterns rather than mathematical functions underlying them, in which the major organizing concepts are successorship, predecessorship, sameness, and symmetry, and grouping based on those concepts. The following are some sample sequences given to the Seek-Whence program:

    1 2 3 4 5 6 . . .

1 1 2 2 3 3 ...

1 8 5 1 8 5 ...

1 1 2 1 2 3 1 2 3 4 ...

2 1 2 2 2 2 2 3 2 2 4 2 ...

Seek-Whence is given the terms of a sequence one by one, and it tries as soon as it can to propose a tentative hypothesis to explain the sequence. When a new term is presented that disagrees with its tentative hypothesis, it must then try to reformulate the hypothesis, or, failing that, to create from scratch an alternative new hypothesis.

Sequence-extrapolation programs in artificial intelligence (see, e.g., Pivar and Finkelstein 1964) have typically dealt with *mathematical* sequences, such as "1 2 4 8 16...," or "1 2 5 15 42..." (whose second differences are every third prime), and have approached them by trying out possible solutions from a standard repertoire of mathematical knowledge and tricks (e.g., primes, powers of 2, Fibonacci numbers), often recursively applying the same repertoire of techniques to derived sequences formed from the original sequence by taking every other term, every third term, first differences, ratios, etc. This is very different from the goal of the Seek-Whence project, which is to model a much more general sort of pattern-spotting ability: sequences in the Seek-Whence domain contain the essence of many central issues of pattern-recognition in general (Hofstadter, Clossman, and Meredith 1982). The sequences Meredith's program was able to tackle were more varied and general than the cyclical, fixed-length period sequences dealt with by a well-known program written by Simon and Kotovsky (1963), which will be discussed further in the next subsection. Analogy-making plays an essential part in solving these sequences. For example, to find a coherent interpretation for the sequence

"1 1 2 1 1 3 1 1 1 4 1 1 1 1 5 1 1 1 1 1 6..."

one must map hypothesized segments against one another, perceiving corresponding roles within segments (e.g., a reasonable parsing is "1-12-113-1114-11115-111116...," with the role played by the "2" in "1 2" corresponding to the role played by the "3" in "1 1 3", the role played by "1 1" in "1 1 2" corresponding to the role played by "1 1 1" in "1 1 1 3", and so on). What originally gave rise to the Copycat project was Hofstadter's desire to further isolate this essential role of analogy-making in Seek-Whence.

Like Jumbo, Seek-Whence has a nondeterministic parallel architecture involving codelets, and the program is based on many of the ideas Hofstadter first developed in the Jumbo project. As in Jumbo, a major part of the operation of Seek-Whence is the construction, destruction, and reformulation of groupings built out of the raw numerical data of the sequence (e.g., the program could parse the sequence "1 1 2 2 3 3..." into groups: "11-22-33..."). Seek-Whence proceeds by building such groupings, using the groupings to construct a hypothesis enabling it to predict the next number in the sequence, and reformulating that hypothesis via slippage when an unexpected piece of new evidence (i.e., an unexpected new term in the sequence) requires such action.

Such reformulation sometimes requires modifying or destroying the groupings the program has already made.

The Copycat and Seek-Whence projects deal with many of the same issues, and thus there are a number of correspondences between the Seek-Whence and Copycat programs. Some of my ideas for Copycat have come from Meredith's solutions to various implementation problems. Copycat further develops several of the mechanisms used in Seek-Whence (as it did with Jumbo) and includes a number mechanisms lacked by the Seek-Whence program, so there also are some major differences between the two programs.

Much of the implementation of Seek-Whence is admittedly *ad hoc*. For example, the program uses a large number of special-purpose domain-specific codelets and structures. In Copycat, I tried to avoid this problem by making codelets and perceptual structures as general and domain-independent as possible. Copycat's conceptual system is much richer than that of the current version of Seek-Whence. The latter's Slipnet has fewer nodes and no named relations—only undifferentiated "slipping links," with no notion of activation or conceptual distance. In contrast with Copycat, the dynamics of the Slipnet was not a central part of the Seek-Whence model. In Seek-Whence, slippage does not occur unless something goes wrong. It is not nearly as central a focus in the Seek-Whence program as it is in Copycat.

Another extremely important issue for both Copycat and Seek-Whence—how top-down pressures work to influence the program's conceptualization of the problem at hand—was dealt with by Meredith in only a limited way. For example, Seek-Whence could not solve the sequence

"1 2 2 3 3 3 4 4 4 4 ...,"

because of its lack of responsiveness to emerging top-down pressures. Since it was given the sequence one term at a time, the first two terms—1 and 2—put the program on the track of successorship and successor groups, and it could never recover enough to perceive the sequence's sameness groups. One shortcoming is that the program clings too tenaciously to its first organizing notion, and another shortcoming is that it lacks the kinds of top-down codelets that Copycat has (such as codelets that expressly look for sameness groups if several sameness relations have been spotted). The Copycat project has made considerable progress on this issue. The Seek-Whence program lacked much of the interaction between bottom-up and top-down pressures that is an essential part of Copycat, as well as many other architectural features that are present in Copycat (such as dynamically varying activation and link lengths in the Slipnet, different degrees of conceptual depth for different nodes, and temperature).

9.2.2 Tabletop and Letter-Spirit

In addition to the microworlds of Seek-Whence and Copycat, Hofstadter also designed the Tabletop domain, in which analogies can be made involving objects on a restaurant table. Robert French wrote the Tabletop program (French and Hofstadter 1991; French 1992; Hofstadter and French 1992), which uses an architecture similar in many ways to that of Copycat. A Tabletop analogy problem involves two people, "Henry" and "Eliza," sitting at opposite sides of a restaurant table, on which is an array of objects such as cups, glasses, dishes, etc., arranged in a natural-seeming way. Henry touches an object on the table and says "Do this!" The challenge for Eliza (the role played by the Tabletop program) is to find the analogous object on the table to touch (it may even be the same object that Henry touched).

Tabletop's analogy problems, like Seek-Whence's sequences and Copycat's letter-string problems, are idealized but can be set up to capture many central issues of high-level perception and analogy-making. Like Copycat's families of analogy problems (such as the families of variants presented in chapter 5), families of Tabletop problems can be formed that express minute variations in pressures, and the effects of these variations on the program's behavior can be studied. French (1992) presents a number of such families of problems and displays the program's performance on them.

The main purpose of the Tabletop project was to use the same basic architecture as Copycat but in a different, less abstract microworld, as a way of testing (and extending) the architecture's generality. Tabletop's domain is less abstract than Copycat's in a number of ways: (1) since Tabletop problems involve real-world objects (cups, glasses, etc.), the objects in a given problem can have richer descriptions and can have more complex conceptual relationships with one another than objects in Copycat problems; (2) the Tabletop world is two dimensional and continuous, so Tabletop problems can involve a more complex array of spatial pressures than can Copycat problems (e.g., one can measure the physical proximity of a particular cup on the table to Henry's side or to Eliza's side); and (3) since there are humans (Henry and Eliza) explicitly involved in the problem, the problems can involve human notions such as "ownership," "one's territory on the table," "the function of a cup," and so on. These various ingredients mean that the Tabletop domain has the potential to express issues in high-level perception and analogy-making in a more realistic way than does the Copycat domain, as well as to explore issues that the Copycat domain does not include.

The architecture of the Tabletop program is similar to Copycat's architecture in most respects. It includes all of the main features of Copycat's architecture, though the implementation of many of these features differs from that in Copycat. (For example, temperature in Tabletop differs in many significant respects from temperature in Copycat; this and other differences are described in French 1992.) French has also introduced some new architectural features to deal with new issues that come up in the Tabletop domain. One central new feature is allowing coherent sets of proposed structures to remain in memory even when a set of rival structures has been built instead. If the rival set is later broken, the proposed set, which has remained together in the background, can quickly be built as a whole, rather than having to be rediscovered piece by piece, as would be the case in Copycat. Another new feature is allowing Slipnet node activations to be associated with different global "contexts": when the program enters a new global context, node activations associated with the old context are erased but if the program re-enters the old context, the program attempts to use information present in the old context to restore the original Slipnet activations. Again, this allows the program to avoid "starting from scratch" when a global state is lost and then regained.

The fact that the same basic architecture can be used to solve problems in these two different microworlds gives evidence for the generality of the mechanisms being proposed. Future work on both Copycat and Tabletop that merges what has been learned in the two projects will lead to a more refined and general architecture.

Another, more ambitious project (which has not yet reached the implementation stage) is Hofstadter's "Letter Spirit" project (described in Hofstadter, Mitchell, and French 1987), which proposes to use an architecture related to Copycat's to produce "gridfonts" (typefaces in which all letters are designed on a specific grid, using discrete straight segments rather than continuously curving lines) in uniform styles. For example, the input to the program might be an A drawn on the grid by a person; the program's task would be to produce the rest of the alphabet in "the same style." As was discussed in chapter 1, the process of recognizing or producing certain styles (e.g., in music, art, or typography) is basically a process of analogy-making. Here the analogy problem is, given an A, to produce an analogous B, C, and so on.

In addition to projects that use the same basic architecture in these various microworlds, it should be possible to eventually use general ideas from this architecture (such as the notions of the parallel terraced scan, context-dependent concept activations and conceptual distances, probabilistically defined concepts with graded presence or relevance, temperature, etc.) in computer models of perception working in more complex domains. For example, it would be of great interest to attempt to use these ideas in computer models of real-world visual and auditory recognition processes, such as object recognition or speech understanding. All of the main mechanisms in Copycat and Tabletop were designed and implemented as much as possible with the idea that they could be eventually "scaled up"—in principle, they do not rely on the fact that there are only a small number of elements in each problem or a small number of nodes and links in the Slipnet. In practice, there will no doubt be difficulties in actually getting these mechanisms to work in more complex situations. However, it is essential to attempt to do so, because confronting these very difficulties is what will lead to new insights about the issues that the Seek-Whence, Copycat, Tabletop, and Letter-Spirit projects are meant to address.

9.2.3 *Simon and Kotovsky*

Herbert Simon and Kenneth Kotovsky's work on pattern perception and sequence extrapolation (Simon and Kotovsky 1963; Simon 1972; Kotovsky and Simon 1973) involves a domain similar in some ways to those of Seek-Whence and Copycat, though the approach is completely different. Meredith (1986) discusses Simon and Kotovsky's work with respect to Seek-Whence, and much of what she says also applies to a comparison with Copycat. Simon and Kotovsky studied human performance on understanding and extrapolating letter sequences such as

c d c d c d . . . ,

q x a p x b q x a . . . ,

and

r s c d s t d e t u e f . . . .

(The last consists of four interleaved sequences.) Their goal was to show that humans build a symbolic mental model of a given sequence based on a set of descriptions such as "successor," "predecessor," and "sameness," and that they use this model (or *rule*) to extrapolate the sequence. Part of the project was the construction of a computer program to model this process. There were actually two programs: one for producing a sequence given a pattern description and (more interesting) one for coming up with a pattern description given a sequence. The latter program first looked for two possible types of patterns in the sequence: (1) periodicity (e.g., "c d c d c d...," where the same symbol occurs in every second position, or "d e f g e f g h f g h i...," where the next symbol occurs at every fourth position) and (2) a relation that is interrupted at regular intervals by another relation (e.g., "a a b b c c d d...," where sameness relations are interrupted every second position by a successor relation). Once such a pattern was discovered, sameness, successor, and predecessor relations were explored between the successive terms within a period, or between terms in corresponding positions of successive periods.

Several variants of the program were written, with different degrees of success. The program (or at least some version of it) agreed with human subjects on which sequences were hard (as a function of which ones it could solve and how long it took).

Simon and Kotovsky's program was not a model of concepts or perceptual processes in the same way Copycat is. It searched through possible ways of describing a given sequence in a deterministic and exhaustive manner, trying out all the possibilities in its repertoire until one of them worked. There was no notion of top-down–bottom-up interaction and competition, no change in processing as a result of what had already been discovered, no notion of a parallel terraced scan, and no notion of fluid and adaptable concepts (rather, it had fixed concepts of successor, predecessor, sameness, and periodicity). Also, although the program worked in a domain that is similar in some ways to that of Copycat and Seek-Whence, Simon and Kotovsky were specifically studying *sequence* perception, whereas Copycat is not, at a deep level, about linear sequences; its focus is much broader. (The same can even be said of Seek-Whence.) Thus, though the Copycat project shares certain general goals and methodology with Simon and Kotovsky's work (i.e., investigating the mechanisms of pattern recognition by studying it in an idealized, abstract domain), *which* aspects of perception are being studied and *how* perception is modeled are vastly different for the two projects.

9.2.4 Hearsay-II
Many of the ideas for Copycat's architecture were originally inspired by the Hearsay-II speech-understanding system (Erman et al. 1980). The input to Hearsay-II is a waveform generated by a spoken utterance. Hearsay-II interprets this waveform through the cooperation of various "knowledge sources," each of which is able to perform a specific task, such as dividing the waveform into segments, creating phones and phonemes from segments, creating syllable-class hypotheses from phonemes, and creating word hypotheses from syllables. The knowledge sources build data structures representing various levels of interpretation of the utterance on a global blackboard. The blackboard

is the locus of communication among the various knowledge sources. The need for diverse knowledge sources to deal with different levels of description reflects the diversity of processes needed in perception. This is the intuition behind the various types of codelets in Copycat. But Copycat's codelets are somewhat different from Hearsay-II's knowledge sources: codelets perform small, very local tasks, whereas a knowledge source deals with large portions of the data at its level of abstraction (e.g., at the initial signal level, one knowledge source segments the entire waveform; at the word level, one knowledge source produces several "islands" of word-sequence hypotheses). As was discussed in previous chapters, the idea in Copycat is that early in a run the program does not have enough information to make large-scale intelligent decisions about which structures to build. Instead, structures are built via a large number of small, local decisions that allow many different possibilities to be scouted out and then looked at more deeply if more consideration seems warranted. Later in a run, when more structures have been built and the temperature is low, codelets tend to act more like Hearsay-II knowledge sources, building more global structures (e.g., a successor group comprising an entire string). The path for such a global structure has been laid both by the codelets that build the underlying structures that support it and by the codelets that scouted out (and perhaps rejected or slowed down consideration of) alternative pathways.

The various knowledge sources in Hearsay-II, in the process of moving from a raw waveform to a fully parsed utterance, build many levels of data structures, each based on hypotheses built at the immediate lower level. (Segments justify phones, phones justify phonemes, phonemes justify syllables, and so on.) This is similar to the way codelet chains in Copycat build various levels of perceptual structures, starting with three raw letter strings and ending with high-level descriptions and a coherent mapping. As in Copycat, an important part of Hearsay-II's architecture is an interaction between top-down and bottom-up processing, with structures built at lower levels providing evidence for higher-level hypotheses and vice versa.

In Hearsay-II, a knowledge source becomes activated through demons with various levels of conditions, preconditions, and pre-preconditions. This is roughly similar to the various stages of exploration and evaluation that take place in Copycat before a given structure is built. But although both programs perform a parallel exploration of different pathways, and both have competition between different interpretation hypotheses, there is a difference in method. In Hearsay-II, several rival hypotheses may coexist at each level (a hypothesis being a possible interpretation of the data at a given level), and the program evaluates all of them. This method suffers from a potential combinatorial problem: competing hypotheses can exist for different pieces of a whole, so the number of compound hypotheses at higher levels can become very large. Copycat constructs only one view at a time (for example, at any given time, the first **c** in the string **abccc** can be seen either as the rightmost letter of the group **abc** or as the leftmost letter of the group **ccc**, but not both); however, that view is malleable and can be easily reshaped under the right kinds of pressure. Humans cannot see the same high-level thing in two ways at once, but (as with the famous Necker cube) they can switch back and forth between coherent perceptions with varying degrees of ease. Thus, Copycat's method is more psychologically realistic than that of Hearsay-II, although Copycat's method is probably too extreme. It does not save any high-level coherent alternative views, although lower-level components of such views tend to be present in the form of proposed structures. A more psychologically plausible method might be to allow some kind of higher-level proposed structures representing an alternative "subconscious" view to "wait in the wings" (Keith Holyoak, personal correspondence). (As was mentioned above, a scheme of this sort is used in the Tabletop program [French 1992].)

There is also a difference between the control structures of Copycat and Hearsay-II. In Hearsay-II, a central scheduler assigns a "priority" to each active knowledge source, the priority being an estimate of the likely usefulness of the knowledge source's action in fulfilling the overall goal of recognizing the utterance. The notion of priority is somewhat different from that of codelet urgency in Copycat. There is no randomness in Hearsay-II; the scheduler always chooses the highest-priority knowledge source to run. This reflects a difference in philosophy between the two programs. At each point, Hearsay-II tries to make an intelligent decision about what to do next: it uses global knowledge about the current state of the interpretation to assign priorities, and chooses what seems to be the overall best thing to do next. The control structure of Copycat is simpler; since an individual codelet cannot see globally and cannot make very intelligent decisions, the urgencies it assigns are based on local information, and since individual codelets do very small jobs, no single decision is very important. What to do next is decided probabilistically, and Copycat's overall "intelligence" emerges from the statistics of this probabilistic control structure. As was described in chapter 3, Copycat's strategy of parallel and fine-grained exploration ensures fairness in deciding what should be explored, whereas always deterministically choosing the most promising pathway (even when very little information has been obtained and one thus has very little confidence in one's assessment of promise) does not allow alternative views the chance to be developed. This could be seen clearly in the results of experiment 6 in chapter 8, where the temperature was clamped at a very low value and Copycat's control strategy became similar to that of an agenda system. The program became very conservative in what possibilities it explored, and it was very rarely able to build the structures necessary to discover the interesting answer **mrrjjjj**.

9.2.5 Connectionist and Classifier-System Models, and Copycat's Place in the Symbolic-Subsymbolic Spectrum

In recent years, connectionism has become a broad field of research, with a number of different schools of thought producing a wide range of classes of connectionist models. The philosophy behind the Copycat project is similar in many ways to that of connectionism, so it is worth describing some of the more prominent classes in order to compare them with Copycat.

One major class is that of *PDP-style networks* (Rumelhart and McClelland 1986; McClelland and Rumelhart 1986). The PDP ("parallel distributed processing") school began by concentrating on feedforward networks, which consist of nodes connected by weighted links. Concepts and individual instances of concepts are represented as activation patterns distributed over large numbers of nodes. Typically, the nodes in the network are divided up into two or more layers, consisting of an input layer, possibly some internal "hidden" layers, and an output layer. These networks are generally used to perform recognition or classification tasks. The recognition process consists of presenting an activation pattern (representing an instance of something the network is supposed to recognize or categorize) to the input layer, and allowing this activation to spread forward from the input layer to the output layer through the hidden layers, with activation spreading via the links as a function of their weights. The "answer" (e.g., the category to which the input instance belongs) winds up being displayed as an activation pattern on the output nodes. As the network is given more and more input patterns, it gradually improves its performance as a result of a learning algorithm that adjusts the weights on the various links. There are many different such learning algorithms used in connectionist systems; the most common one for feedforward networks is known as *back-propagation* (Rumelhart, Hinton, and Williams 1986).

Recently, PDP-style networks have been extended to include networks with recurrent (feedback) connections (e.g., see Elman 1990). Such networks are thought to have the potential to perform more complex cognitive tasks than the simpler feedforward networks.

Another major class includes *Hopfield networks* and *Boltzmann machines* (Hopfield 1982; Hinton and Sejnowski 1986; also see Smolensky 1986 for a description of harmony theory, which proposes ideas similar to those proposed in Hinton and Sejnowski 1986). Many computational and cognitive tasks can be formulated as constraint-satisfaction problems, which these networks are designed to solve. In a Hopfield network, connections between nodes represent constraints, and the search for a solution proceeds by a relaxation algorithm in which an attempt is made to minimize the "energy" of the system (ACME, described in subsection 9.1.2, is one example of such a system). A Boltzmann machine is a Hopfield-type network in which the relaxation search is carried out with simulated annealing.

There has also been considerable research on so-called *connectionist symbol-processing models* (e.g., Touretzky and Hinton 1988; also see several articles in Hinton 1990). These are models in which connectionist techniques are used to implement symbolic structures such as production systems and semantic networks.

Finally, there is the class of *localist networks* (e.g., Feldman and Ballard 1982; Feldman 1986), in which each node stands for a separate concept. This class is in many ways different in spirit from the other classes, and it will not be discussed in detail here.

These are not the only classes, but together they represent the bulk of current research in connectionism. There is considerable overlap among these classes: many existing connectionist systems actually fall into two or more. Some modeling efforts concentrate on learning, others on representation, others on both. The purpose here is not to give a complete survey of connectionism, but to discuss some of the major ideas in the field and to compare them with the ideas underlying Copycat.

There are a number of features that are common to various subsets of these classes. The structure of most connectionist models is inspired (to greater or lesser degrees) by the structure of networks of neurons in the brain. In most connectionist systems, the network accomplishes its problem-solving tasks via spreading activation, cooperation, and competition among small units with no central controller. Most connectionist systems involve some form of parallelism, distributed representations, distributed learning, and reliance on "emergent" properties (e.g., emergent concepts). Some connectionist systems also involve probabilistic computation (sometimes controlled by temperature).

Classifier systems (Holland 1986; Holland et al. 1986) are another class of AI architectures related to connectionist networks. A classifier system is composed of a large number of simple agents called *classifiers*. The system has an input interface and an output interface. Into the input interface come "messages" about the current state of the environment and the system's relation to it. The job of the classifiers is to classify messages—that is, to decide what to do in response to them. Classifiers sometimes send messages to other classifiers, and sometimes perform some action on the environment. Environmental actions sometimes result in rewards from the environment. As in connectionist networks, the principles of self-organization and emergence are central to classifier systems: the representations of concepts and instances of concepts are at any time distributed over a number of classifiers. There is no central director controlling the actions of the system. Rather, all of the system's behavior arises from myriad cooperative and competitive interactions among the individual classifiers. Classifiers that produce beneficial messages for the system tend to get stronger (via a credit-assignment procedure known as the "bucket brigade" algorithm) and thus are more likely to win competitions with other classifiers (such competitions are probabilistically decided on the basis of strength). Another learning mechanism, known as the "genetic algorithm," effects a kind of natural selection among classifiers in which weak classifiers die out and strong classifiers thrive and, via reproduction (involving recombination with other strong classifiers), pass their "genes" on to offspring classifiers. The combination of the credit-assignment mechanism and the genetic algorithm should, in principle, allow the system to adapt (via reapportionment of strength, deletion of unhelpful classifiers, and creation of new classifiers) to the environment it faces.

Some forms of connectionist networks and classifier systems are examples of *subsymbolic* (also called *subcognitive*) architectures. Smolensky (1988) characterizes the difference between the symbolic and subsymbolic paradigms as follows: In the symbolic paradigm, descriptions used in representations of situations are built of entities that are *symbols* both in the semantic sense (they refer to categories or external objects) and in the syntactic sense (they are operated on by "symbol manipulation"). In the subsymbolic paradigm, such descriptions are built of *subsymbols*—fine-grained entities (such as nodes and weights in connectionist networks or classifiers in a classifier system) that give rise to symbols. In a symbolic system, the symbols used as descriptions are explicitly defined (e.g., a single node in a semantic network represents the concept "dog"). In a subsymbolic system, symbols are statistically emergent entities, represented by complex patterns of activation over large numbers of subsymbols. (Similar characterizations have been made by Hofstadter [1985d] and by McClelland, Rumelhart, and Hinton [1986].) Smolensky (1988, p. 7) makes the point that subsymbolic systems are not merely "implementations, for a certain kind of parallel hardware, of symbolic programs that provide exact and complete accounts of behavior at the conceptual level." Symbolic descriptions are too rigid or "hard," and a system can be sufficiently flexible to model human cognition only if it is based on the more flexible and "soft" descriptions that emerge from a subsymbolic system.

The faith of the subsymbolic paradigm is that human cognitive phenomena are emergent statistical effects of a large number of small, local, and distributed subcognitive events with no global executive. This is the philosophy underlying Copycat as well. Fine-grained parallelism, local actions, competition, spreading activation, and distributed and emergent concepts are essential to the flexibility of connectionist networks, classifier systems, and Copycat (although in classifier systems spreading activation is not explicit, but rather emerges from the joint activity of many classifiers). Some connectionist networks (e.g., Boltzmann machines [Hinton and Sejnowski 1986] and harmony-theory networks [Smolensky 1986]) have an explicit notion of temperature with some similarity to Copycat's (though, as was explained in chapter 3, there is a significant difference between the use of temperature in Copycat and in simulated annealing, which is essentially the temperature notion used by Hinton and Sejnowski and by Smolensky). In classifier systems, something akin to a parallel terraced scan emerges from probabilistically decided competitions among classifiers and from the genetic algorithm's implicit search through schemata (i.e., templates for classifiers) at a rate determined by each schema's estimated promise. (See Holland 1988 for a description of the dynamics of such searches in genetic algorithms.) In addition, the interaction of top-down and bottom-up forces is central in many connectionist systems (see, for example, McClelland and Rumelhart's [1981] model of letter perception or Touretzky and Hinton's [1988] Distributed Connectionist Production System) and in classifier systems (as discussed in chapter 2 of Holland et al. 1986).

The philosophy underlying the Copycat project is more akin to that of the subsymbolic paradigm than to that of the symbolic paradigm, but the actual program fits somewhere in between. As an oversimplified but useful characterization of the two ends of the spectrum, one could say that concepts in subsymbolic systems are highly distributed, being made up of individual nodes that have no semantic value in and of themselves, whereas in symbolic systems concepts are represented as simple unitary objects (e.g., Lisp atoms). Concepts in Copycat could be thought of as "semi-distributed," since a concept in the Slipnet is probabilistically distributed over only a small number of nodes—a central node (e.g., *successor*) and its probabilistic halo of potential slippages (e.g., *predecessor*).

The basic units of subsymbolic systems such as PDP-style connectionist networks are meant to model mental phenomena further removed from the cognitive, conscious level than those modeled by Copycat's Slipnet nodes and codelets. It may be that these systems are more neurologically realistic than Copycat, but their distance from the cognitive level makes the problem of controlling their high-level behavior quite difficult, and I don't think that at this point it would be possible to use such systems to model the types of high-level behavior exhibited by Copycat. Ideally, a model should be constructed in which a structure such as Copycat's Slipnet arises from such a low-level, distributed representation, but this is beyond the achievements of current research in connectionism. The connectionist symbol-processing school has made significant progress on implementing symbolic structures in connectionist networks (e.g., see Hinton 1990), but again the types of symbolic manipulations that have been achieved so far are not nearly complex enough to implement the types of processing performed by Copycat. Likewise, in classifier systems several properties implanted directly in Copycat (such as nodes, links, and spreading activation) would have to emerge automatically, which I believe would make a high-level task, such as Copycat's, quite difficult for classifier systems as they are currently conceived. Thus, Copycat models concepts and perception at an intermediate level in terms of the degree to which concepts are distributed and the extent to which high-level behavior emerges from lower-level processes.

A major difference between Copycat's architecture and that of most connectionist networks is the presence in Copycat of both a Slipnet, containing platonic concept *types*, and a working area, in which structures representing concept *tokens* (i.e., instances of concepts) are dynamically constructed and destroyed. Connectionist networks generally have no such separate working area; types and tokens are both represented in the same network. This has led to a great deal of research in connectionism on the "variable-binding" problem (see, e.g., Barnden 1984 and Touretzky and Hinton 1988), which is related to the larger question of the relationship between concept types and concept tokens. One reason many researchers in connectionism may hesitate to make such a separation is that neural plausibility is a very important part of their research program, and a structure like Copycat's Workspace—a mental region in which representations of situations are constructed—does not have a clear neural underpinning. In contrast, for the purposes of Copycat and related projects, my colleagues and I are influenced more by psychological than by neurological findings. We assume the existence of something like Copycat's Workspace even though we do not know its neural basis, and we investigate how a network with distributed concept *types* interacts with a working area in which ephemeral concept *tokens* can be arranged in complex structures. The lack of such a working area in many connectionist networks is another reason why it may turn out to be very difficult to use such systems to model concepts and high-level perception in the way Copycat does. (Some connectionist-symbol processing systems, such as Touretzky and Hinton's [1988] DCPS, carry out processing in some sort of working area, but as yet the types of operations that can be performed are quite simple. However, the next few years should see a great deal of progress in this field—some of it, we hope, inspired by ideas from Copycat.)

In classifier systems, the "message list" (on which all messages from the environment and from classifiers are posted) corresponds roughly to Copycat's Workspace; messages can serve as the tokens corresponding to concept types (classifiers). It is possible that structures similar to those built in Copycat could be represented in a classifier system as messages on a message list, though precisely how to do this is an open question.

Many connectionist networks and classifier systems learn from run to run. Copycat does not. Copycat is not meant to be a model of learning in this strict sense, though it does model some fundamental aspects of learning: how concepts adapt to new situations that are encountered, and how the shared essence of two situations is recognized.

The belief underlying the methodology of the Copycat project is that building a model at the level of Copycat's architecture is essential not only for the purpose of providing an account of the mental phenomena under study at its intermediate level of description, but also as a step toward understanding how these phenomena can emerge from even lower levels. The "subsymbolic dream" of modeling all of cognition using subsymbolic, neurally plausible architectures may be too ambitious at this point in the development of cognitive science. If there is any hope of understanding how intelligence emerges from billions of neurons, or even how it might emerge from connectionist networks, we need to understand the intermediate-level mechanisms underlying the structure of *concepts*, a term referring to mental phenomena of central importance in psychology that nonetheless still lack a firm scientific basis. The long-term goal of the Copycat project and related research is to use computer models to help provide such a scientific basis. The hope is that the understanding that results from this approach will not only in its own right contribute to answering long-standing questions about the mechanisms of intelligence, but will also provide a guide to connectionists studying how such intermediate-level structures can emerge from neurons or cell assemblies in the brain.

In summary: The architecture of Copycat is very different from the more traditional, "symbolic" AI systems, both in its parallel and stochastic processing mechanisms and in its representation of concepts as semi-distributed and probabilistic entities in a network. These features make it more similar in spirit to connectionist systems, though again there are important differences. As in Copycat, the high-level behavior of connectionist systems emerges statistically from a lower-level substrate. However, the fundamental processing units in most connectionist systems are more primitive, concepts in such networks are distributed to a much higher degree than in Copycat, and in most such systems concept types and tokens are required to reside in the same network. Consequently, there has not been much success so far in using connectionist systems as models of high-level cognitive abilities such as analogy-making (although there is currently a great deal of research on this topic; see, for example, Holyoak and Barnden, in press). Copycat thus explores a middle ground in cognitive modeling between high-level symbolic systems and low-level connectionist systems. The claim made by this research is that this level is at present the most useful for understanding the fluid nature of concepts and perception—central aspects of cognition that emerge with maximal clarity in analogy-making.

9.2.6 Copycat, Active Symbols, and Emergent Computation

Fundamental to Copycat is the notion of *statistical emergence*: the program's high-level behavior emerges from the interaction of large numbers of lower-level activities in which probabilistic decisions are made. Codelets, nodes, and links are all defined explicitly ahead of time, but their interaction gives rise to three types of statistically emergent entities: (1) emergent *concepts*, whose composition (in terms of the nodes that are included) and whose availability and relevance to the situation at hand are statistical properties (rather than being explicitly defined); (2) emergent *pressures*, which arise as statistical effects of large numbers of codelet actions; and (3) an emergent *parallel terraced scan*, which results statistically from a large number of probabilistic choices based on codelet urgencies and other factors (e.g., salience of objects, strengths of structures, etc.). These three types of emergent entities interact as well. The structure and activation of concepts influences both how codelets will evaluate possible structures (a codelet's evaluation of a structure almost always takes into account activations and conceptual distances in the Slipnet) and which top-down codelets will be posted. Concepts thus affect the population of codelets in the Coderack and their urgencies, out of which arise statistical pressures and a parallel terraced scan. In turn, the parallel terraced scan, by guiding the search through possible structurings of the problem, affects the activations of nodes and thus the conceptual distances encoded by links in the Slipnet. This interaction gives rise to a system in which concepts and perceptual exploration fluidly adapt to the situation at hand, and allow appropriate conceptual slippages to be made.

This interaction has the flavor of Hofstadter's vision of "active symbols" in the brain, in which the top level (the symbolic level) reaches back down toward the lower levels (the subsymbolic levels) and influences them, while at the same time being itself determined by the lower levels (Hofstadter 1979, chapter 11). This kind of system, in which explicitly defined entities (e.g., codelets, nodes, and links) give rise to implicit higher-level patterns (e.g., concepts, pressures, and the parallel terraced scan), which in turn reach back and influence the lower levels and thus each other, is an example of Forrest's (1990) characterization of "emergent computation."

Nondeterminism is an essential component of Copycat, and temperature is the mechanism for controlling the degree of nondeterminism in response to structures that have been built. This mechanism in principle allows the system to gradually shift from being parallel, random, and dominated by bottom-up forces to being more deterministic, serial, and dominated by top-down forces as the system gradually closes in on an appropriate way of conceiving the situation. (Some questions about the effectiveness of temperature in the current version of Copycat were discussed in section 8.7.)

The fact that the composition and activation of concepts, the type and strength of various pressures, and the parallel terraced scan emerge statistically from large numbers of probabilistic decisions imbues Copycat with both flexibility and robustness. Because of nondeterminism, no path of exploration is absolutely excluded *a priori*, but at the same time, the system has mechanisms that allow it to avoid following bad pathways, at least most of the time. A crucial idea is that the program has to have the *potential* to follow risky (and perhaps farfetched or even crazy) pathways in order for it to have the flexibility to follow subtle and insightful ones. This was strikingly illustrated by the results of experiment 6 in chapter 8, in which nondeterminism was suppressed to a large degree. The program almost never gave farfetched fringe answers to **abc ⇒ abd, mrrjjj ⇒ ?**, but it also almost never gave the insightful answer **mrrjjjj**. The program has to have the potential to bring in *a priori* unlikely concepts (such as group-length) into its interpretation of the problem, but should do so only in response to strong pressures. These pressures are what give shape to the program's concepts and guide the program's exploration.

By design, none of the mechanisms summarized above is specific to the letter-string microworld, and none depends on the size of the problems Copycat currently deals with or the size of its current conceptual repertoire. Copycat's mechanisms were designed to be general; our claim is that the same mechanisms will apply to more complex domains.

Chapter 10

Contributions of This Research

Until words like "concept" have become terms as scientifically legitimate as, say, "neuron" or "cerebellum," we will not have come anywhere close to understanding the brain.
(Hofstadter 1985b, p. 234)

No one knows how to represent a concept or thing on the subsymbolic microlevel, or even precisely what this means. If this ambition could be recognized, it would come close to cracking the cognition problem. And no one is close to accomplishing that.
(Pagels 1988, p. 141)

These sentiments reflect the view that underlies the research described in this book—that the understanding and explication of the psychological notion of "concept" is perhaps the most important problem facing cognitive science. Concepts can be said to be the fundamental units of thought, as genes are the fundamental units of heredity. And the present state of cognitive science is something like the state of biology before the recognition of DNA as the hereditary substance: the notion of a "gene" existed, but it was a vague and proto-scientific term awaiting an explanation in terms of lower-level biological entities and mechanisms. Likewise, the brain mechanisms underlying concepts are not currently known. It seems likely that a full account of these mechanisms will be much more complex and much more difficult to uncover than was the account of genes in terms of DNA.

The long-term goal of the Copycat project (and related projects) is to use computer models to help provide such a scientific basis for concepts. This goal is still quite distant. An early stage in this process is to make clearer what concepts are in a psychological sense (as opposed to a neurological sense) and to elucidate the issues surrounding them. As was mentioned in chapter 1, there has been much research in psychology on the internal structure of categories, and much light has been shed on that topic. The focus of the Copycat project is somewhat different. We are concentrating on investigating and clarifying the nature of conceptual slippage and the dynamics of the activation and association of concepts as they interact with perception. The hope is that the research described here has contributed to the understanding of these aspects of concepts.

As part of this process of elucidation, this book has described a set of ideas about concepts, perception, and analogy-making, and has shown that a computer program that implements these ideas exhibits rudimentary fluid concepts—the program's concepts are able to adapt to different situations in a microworld that, though idealized, captures much of the essence of real-world analogy-making. The main contributions of this research have been to develop and explicate these ideas, to show the extent to which they do indeed work, and also to examine the ways in which they are flawed or incomplete. The result is not yet a complete "theory" of high-level perception and conceptual slippage—at least, not in the standard sense of theories in physics or chemistry. These ideas have not yet been sufficiently developed or implemented to be predictive of human behavior on a large scale, or to be strictly "falsifiable" (though some of the results given in this book have demonstrated certain problems and incompletenesses in the program's mechanisms). Since we are investigating very general abilities (rather than domain-specific performance on letter-string analogy problems), and since we are trying to understand how high-level mental activities such as concepts emerge from lower levels, the phenomena that we are studying are too complex to allow the development of complete predictive theories at this stage of research. Rather, the process of developing these ideas and implementing them in computer programs allows us to clarify what it is we are studying, and to begin to see what components such complete theories might have. The ideas presented in this book are meant to act as stepping stones toward the development of more complex models and more complete theories.

For the purposes of this explication process, the importance of actually writing a computer program and getting it to work cannot be overemphasized. Many ideas for the Copycat program were originally set forth by Hofstadter (1984a) in a broad outline form before the program was written, but it was the process of writing the program—which required constant confrontation with the all-important "details"—that allowed the original ideas to become more fully developed by Hofstadter and myself. Along the way, vague ideas were clarified, wrong ideas were discarded, and new ideas were added. This parallel development of ideas and models is how cognitive modeling has to proceed. Many insights can come only through grappling face to face with the real issues, and it is certain that this same process of modification will occur in attempts to use ideas from Copycat in modeling perception in more complex domains. New insights often come when things go wrong. In the process of writing the Copycat program, many unanticipated problems (such as the problems with top-down forces, focus of attention, and self-watching discussed in chapter 7) guided the implementation and sometimes helped shed light on deep issues in perception and analogy-making. The appearance of unexpected strange answers (such as **abc ⇒ abd, hhwwqq ⇒ hhxxrr**, discussed in chapter 5) not only demonstrated that something was wrong with the program but also helped drive home the subtlety and complexity of the mental phenomena that we are studying. The process of writing a program such as Copycat brings up at least as many questions as it answers, and one of the points of writing the program was to find out what these questions *are*. There are many ways in which the current version of Copycat is lacking, and many problems with the mechanisms the program does have, and a result of writing the program is that these aspects and problems are uncovered and brought to light; they would have remained unseen and obscured if the program had never been written. (Some of these points concerning the advantages of writing AI programs have also been made by Longuet-Higgins [1981], among others.)

In summary: The main contributions of this work are clarifying and making explicit many central features of concepts, high-level perception, and analogy-making (e.g., emergent concepts, conceptual slippage, the interaction of bottom-up and top-down forces, commingling pressures, the parallel terraced scan, the role of nondeterminism in thought, etc.); presenting ideas for mental mechanisms underlying these features; and verifying and further developing these ideas by implementing them in a computer program. My hope is that the ideas and results described in this book have fulfilled what I have asserted to be the main criteria for success—to help us to better understand what concepts are and to broaden our intuitions on how to think about these issues. All of this serves to set the stage for the very long-term goal of developing more complete scientific theories that will explain how human cognition comes about in the brain and that will propose how human-like intelligence might be achieved in computers.

Afterword:

The Long Road from Copycat to Metacat

Melanie Mitchell has described with great precision and clarity the realization of a long-standing dream of mine—a working computer program that captures what, to me, are many of the central features of human analogy-making, and indeed of the remarkable fluidity of human cognition.

First and foremost, the Copycat computer program provides a working model of *fluid concepts*—concepts with flexible boundaries, concepts whose behavior adapts to unanticipated circumstances, concepts that will bend and stretch—but not without limit. Fluid concepts are necessarily, I believe, *emergent* aspects of a complex system; I suspect that conceptual fluidity can only come out of a seething mass of subcognitive activities, just as the less abstract fluidity of real physical liquids is necessarily an emergent phenomenon, a statistical outcome of vast swarms of molecules jouncing incoherently one against another. In previous writings I have argued that nothing is more central to the study of cognition than the nature of concepts themselves, and yet surprisingly little work in computer modeling of mental processes addresses itself explicitly to this issue. Computer models often study the *static* properties of concepts—context-independent judgments of membership in categories, for instance—but the question of how concepts stretch and bend and adapt themselves to unanticipated situations is virtually never addressed.

Perhaps this is because few computer models of higher-level cognitive phenomena take perception seriously; rather, they almost always take situations as static givens—fixed representations to work from. Copycat, by contrast, draws no sharp dividing line between perception and cognition; in fact, the entirety of its processing is properly called *high-level perception*. This integration strikes me as a critical element of human creativity. It is only by taking fresh looks at situations thought already to be understood that we come up with truly insightful and creative visions. The ability to *reperceive*, in short, is at the heart of creativity.

This brings me to another way of describing Copycat. Copycat is nothing if not a model, albeit incipient, of human creativity. When it is in trouble, for instance, it is capable of bringing in unanticipated concepts from out of the blue and applying them in ways that would seem extremely farfetched in ordinary situations. I am thinking specifically of how, in the problem **abc** $\Rightarrow$ **abd**, **mrrjjj** $\Rightarrow$?, the program will often wake up the concept "sameness group" and then, under that unanticipated top-down pressure, will occasionally perceive the single letter **m** as a *group*—which *a priori* seems like the kind of thing that only a crackpot would do. But as the saying goes, "You see what you want to see." It is delightful that a computer program can "see what it wants to see," even if only in this very limited sense—and doing so leads it to an aesthetically very pleasing solution to the problem, one that many people would consider both insightful and creative.

All these facets of Copycat—fluid concepts, perception blurring into cognition, creativity—are intertwined, and come close, in my mind, to being the crux of that which makes human thought what it is. Connectionist (neural-net) models are doing very interesting things these days, but they are not addressing questions at nearly as high a level of cognition as Copycat is, and it is my belief that ultimately people will recognize that the neural level of description is a bit too low to capture the mechanisms of creative, fluid thinking. Trying to use connectionist language to describe creative thought strikes me as a bit like trying to describe the skill of a great tennis player in terms of molecular biology. Even a description in terms of muscle-cell actions would be too low-level. What makes the difference between bad, good, and superb tennis players requires description at a high functional level. If thinking is a many-tiered edifice, connectionist models are its basement and the levels that Copycat is modeling are much closer to the top. The trick, of course, is to fill in the middle levels so that the mechanisms posited in Copycat can be justified (or "cashed out," as philosophers tend to say these days) in lower-level terms. I believe this will happen eventually, but I think it will take a considerable length of time.

Cognition is an enormously complex phenomenon, and people look at it in extremely different ways. One of the hardest things for any cognitive scientist to do is to pick a problem to work on, because in so doing one is effectively choosing to ignore dozens of other facets of cognition. For someone who wishes to be working on fundamental problems, this is a gamble—one is essentially putting one's money on the chosen facet to be the *essence* of cognition. My research group is gambling on the idea that the study of concepts and analogy-making is that essence, and the Copycat program represents our first major step toward modeling these facets of cognition. I think Copycat is an outstanding achievement, and I am very proud of this joint work by Melanie and myself.

But of course, this work, however good it is, falls short of a full explanation of the phenomena it is after. After all, no piece of scientific work is ever the last word on its topic—especially in cognitive science, which is just beginning to take significant strides toward unraveling the mind's complexity. In this afterword, I would like to sketch out some of my hopes for how the Copycat project will be continued over the next few years.

One of the prime goals of the Copycat project is, of course, to get at the central mechanisms of creativity, since creativity might be thought of as the ultimate level of fluidity in thinking. I used to think that the miniature paradigm shift in the problem **abc** $\Rightarrow$ **abd, xyz** $\Rightarrow$?, wherein **a** is mapped onto **z** and, as a consequence, a sudden dramatic perceptual reversal takes place, was really getting at the core of creativity. I still believe that this mental event as carried out in a *human* mind contains something very important about creativity, but it now seems to me that there is a significant quality lacking in the way this mental event is carried out in the "mind" of Copycat.

I would say that Copycat's way of carrying out the paradigm shift that leads to **xyz** $\Rightarrow$ **wyz** is too *unconscious*. It is not that there is no awareness in the program of the *problem* it is working on; it is more that Copycat has little awareness of the *processes* that it is carrying out and the *ideas* that it is working with. For instance, Copycat will try to take the successor of **z**, see that it cannot do so, go into a "state of emergency," try to follow a new route, and wind up hitting exactly the same impasse again. This usually occurs several times before Copycat discovers a way out of the impasse—not necessarily a clever way out, but just *some* way out. People working on this problem do not get stuck in such a mindless mental loop. After they have hit the **z**-snag once or twice, they seem to know how to avoid it in the future. Copycat's brand of awareness thus seems to fall quite short of *people's* brand of awareness, which includes a strong sense of what they themselves are doing. One wants a much higher degree of *self*-awareness on the program's part.

There is a clear danger, whenever one thinks about the "awareness" or "consciousness" of a computer model of any form of mentality, to be carried along by the intuitions that come from thinking about computers at the level of their arithmetical hardware, or even at the level of ordinary deterministic symbol-manipulating programs (such as word-processing and graphics programs). Virtually no one believes that a word processor is conscious, or that it has any genuine understanding of notions such as "word," "comma," "paragraph," "page,"and "margin." Although such a program *deals* with such things all the time, it no more *understands* what they are than a telephone understands what voices are. One's intuition says that a word processor is just a user-friendly but deceptive façade erected in front of a complex dynamic process—a process that, for all its complexity and dynamism, is no more alive or aware than a raging fire in a fireplace is alive.

This intuition would suggest that *all* computer systems—no matter what they might do, no matter how complex they might be—must remain stuck at the level of zero awareness. However, this uncharitable view involves an unintended double standard: one standard for machines, another for brains. After all, the physical substrate of brains, whether it is like that of computers or not, is still composed of nothing but inert, lifeless molecules carrying out their myriad minuscule reactions in an utterly mindless manner. Consciousness certainly seems to vanish when one mentally reduces a brain to a gigantic pile of individually meaningless chemical reactions. It is this *reductio ad absurdum* applying to *any* physical system, biological or synthetic, that forces thoughtful persons to reconsider their initial judgments about both brains and computers, and to rethink what it is that seems to lead inexorably to the conclusion of an in-principle lack of consciousness "in there."

Perhaps the problem is the seeming need that people have of making black-and-white cutoffs when it comes to certain mysterious phenomena, such as life and consciousness. People seem to want there to be an absolute threshold between the living and the nonliving, and between the thinking and the "merely mechanical," and they seem to feel uncomfortable with the thought that there could be "shadow entities," such as biological viruses or complex computer programs, that bridge either of these psychologically precious gulfs. But the onward march of science seems to force us ever more clearly into accepting intermediate levels of such properties.

Perhaps we jump just a bit too quickly when we insistently label even the most sophisticated of today's "artificial life" products as "absolutely unalive" and the most sophisticated of today's computational models of thought as "absolutely unconscious." (I must say, the astonishing subtlety of Terry Winograd's SHRDLU program of some 20 years ago always gives me pause when I think about whether computers can "understand" what is said or typed to them. SHRDLU always strikes me as falling in a very gray area. Similarly, Thomas Ray's computational model of evolution, "Tierra," can give me eerie feelings of looking in on the very beginnings of genuine life, as it evolved on earth billions of years ago.)

Perhaps we should more charitably say about such models of thought as SHRDLU and Copycat that they might have an unknown degree of consciousness—tiny, to be sure, but not at an absolute-zero level. Black-and-white dogmatism on this question seems as unrealistic, to me, as black-and-white dogmatism over whether to apply the label "smart" or "insightful" to a given human being.

If one accepts this somewhat disturbing view that perhaps machines—even today's machines—should be assigned various shades of gray (even if extremely faint shades) along the "consciousness continuum," then one is forced into trying to pinpoint just what it is that makes for *different* shades of gray.

In the end, what seems to make brains *strongly* conscious is *the special way they are organized*—in particular, the higher-level structures and mechanisms that come into being. I see two dimensions as critical: (1) the fact that brains possess *concepts*, allowing complex representational structures to be built that automatically come with associative links to all sorts of prior experiences, and (2) the fact that brains can *self-monitor*, allowing a complex internal self-model to arise, which gives the system an enormous degree of self-control and open-endedness. (These two key dimensions of mind are discussed in my articles "Variations on a Theme as the Crux of Creativity" [Hofstadter 1985b] and "On the Seeming Paradox of Mechanizing Creativity" [Hofstadter 1985c].) Now, Copycat is fairly strong along the first of these dimensions—not, of course, in the sense of having many concepts or complex concepts, but in the sense of rudimentarily modeling what concepts are really about. On the other hand, Copycat is very weak along the second of these dimensions, and that is a serious shortcoming.

One might readily admit that self-monitoring would seem to be critical for *consciousness* and yet still wonder why self-monitoring should play such a central role in *creativity*. The answer is: to allow the system to *avoid falling into mindless ruts*. The animal world is full of extremely complex behaviors that, when analyzed, turn out to be completely pre-programmed and automatized. (A particular routine by the *Sphex* wasp provides a famous example, and indeed forms the theme song of the second of the two articles cited above.) Despite their apparent sophistication, such behaviors possess almost no flexibility. The difference between a human doing a repetitive action and a more primitive animal doing a repetitive action is that humans *notice* the repetition and get bored, whereas most animals do not. Humans do not get caught in obvious "loops"; they quickly perceive the pointlessness of loopy behavior and *jump out of the system*. This ability of humans (humorously dubbed "antisphexishness" in my article) requires not just an *object-level* awareness of the *task* they are performing but also a *meta-level* awareness—an awareness of *their own actions*. Clearly, humans are not in the slightest aware of their actions at the *neural* level; the self-monitoring carried out in human brains is at a highly chunked *cognitive* level, and it is this coarse-grained kind of self-monitoring that seems so critical if one is to imbue a computer system with the same kind of ability to choose whether to remain *in* a given framework or to *jump out* of that framework.

In my article on self-watching I surprised myself by citing, in an approving manner, somebody with whom I had earlier thought I had absolutely no common ground at all: the British philosopher J. R. Lucas, famous for his strident article "Minds, Machines, and Gödel" (Lucas 1961), in which he claims that Gödel's incompleteness theorem proves that computers, no matter how they are programmed, are intrinsically incapable of simulating minds. Let me briefly give Lucas the floor:

> At one's first and simplest attempts to philosophize, one becomes entangled in questions of whether when one knows something one knows that one knows it, and what, when one is thinking of oneself, is being thought about, and what is doing the thinking....
>
> The paradoxes of consciousness arise because a conscious being can be aware of itself, as well as of other things, and yet cannot really be construed as being divisible into parts.... A machine can be made in a manner of speaking to 'consider' its performance, but it cannot take this 'into account' without thereby becoming a different machine, namely the old machine with a 'new part' added. But it is inherent in our idea of a conscious mind that it can reflect upon itself and criticize its own performances, and no extra part is required to do this: it is already complete, and has no Achilles' heel.

This passage suggests the need for what might be called "reflexivity" (i.e., the quality of a system that is "turned back" on itself, and can watch itself) if a mechanical system is to attain what we humans have. I am not at all sympathetic to Lucas' claims that machines can never do this—indeed, I shall give below a kind of rough sketch of an architecture that could do something of this sort; rather, I am sympathetic to the flavor of his argument, which is one that many laypeople would resonate with yet one that very few people in cognitive science have taken terribly seriously.

Another idea that resonates with the flavor of Lucas' article is captured by the title of a posthumous book of papers by the uniquely creative Polish-American mathematician Stanislaw Ulam: *Analogies between Analogies*. The obvious implication of the title is that Ulam delighted in meta-level thinking: thinking about his own thoughts, and thinking about his thoughts about his thoughts, etc. etc., *ad nauseam*, as Lucas might say. Spelling out the next level implied by this title would be superfluous—everybody sees where it is heading—and the feeling is of course that the more intelligent someone is, the more levels of "meta" that person is comfortable with.

This sets the stage for me to describe my long-term ambitions for Copycat. The goals to be described below have emerged in my mind over the past several years, as I have watched Copycat grow from a metaphorical embryo into a baby and then a toddler. At a lecture I was giving not long ago on Copycat as a model of creativity, somebody asked me point-blank if I thought that Copycat really captured the essence of creativity. Was there anything left to do? Of course I felt there was much more to do, and so, prompted by this question, I tried to articulate, in one short phrase, what I think the creative mind does, as opposed to more run-of-the-mill minds. Here is the phrase I came up with:

> Full-scale creativity consists in having a keen sense for what is interesting, following it recursively, applying it at the meta-level, and modifying it accordingly.

This was too terse and cryptic, so I then "unpacked" it a little. Here is roughly how that went. Creativity consists in:

- *Having a keen sense for what is interesting:* that is, having a relatively strong set of *a priori* "prejudices" —in other words, a somewhat narrower, sharper set of resonances than most people's, to various possibilities in a given domain. It is critical that the peak of this particular *individual's* resonance curve fall close to the peak of the curve representing the average over *all people*, ensuring that the would-be creator's output will please many people. An example of this is a composer of popular tunes, whose taste in melodies is likely to be much more sharply peaked than an average person's. This aspect of creativity could be summarized in the phrase *central but highly discriminating taste.*

- *Following it recursively:* that is, following one's nose not only in choosing an *initially* interesting-seeming pathway, but also *continuing* to rely on one's nose over and over again as the chosen pathway leads one to more and more new choice-points, themselves totally unanticipated at the outset. One can imagine trying to find one's way out of a dense forest, making one intuitive choice after another, each choice leading, of course, to a unique set of further choice-points. This aspect of creativity could be summarized in the term *self-confidence.*

- *Applying it at the meta-level:* that is, being aware of, and carefully watching, one's pathway in "idea space" (as opposed to the space defined by the domain itself). This means being sensitive to unintended patterns in what one is producing as well as patterns in one's own mental processes in the creative act. One could perhaps say that this amounts to sensitivity to *form* as much as to *content*. This aspect of creativity could be summarized in the term *self-awareness.*

- *Modifying it accordingly:* that is, not being inflexible in the face of various successes and failures, but modifying one's sense of what is interesting and good according to experience. This aspect of creativity could be summarized in the term *adaptability.*

Note that this characterization implies that the system must go through its own experiences, just as a person does, and store them away for future use. This kind of storage is called "episodic memory," and Copycat entirely lacks such a thing. Of course, during any *given* run, Copycat retains a memory of what it has done—the Workspace serves that role. But once a given problem has been solved, Copycat does not store memories of that session away for potential help in attacking future problems, nor does it modify itself permanently in any way. Amusingly, babies and very young children seem similarly unable to lay down permanent memory traces for episodes, which is why adults virtually never have memories of their infancy. If Copycat is to grow into an "adult," it must acquire an ability that adults have: the ability to commit episodes one has experienced to permanent memory.

The third point listed above concerns the importance of self-watching—making explicit representations not just of objects and relationships in a situation before one, but also of one's own actions and reactions. To a very limited extent, Copycat already has a self-watching ability. It is described in section 7.2 of this book. However, the degree of reflexivity that I envision goes far beyond this. Indeed, it would alter Copycat so radically that the resulting program ought probably to be given some other name, and for want of a better one I tentatively use the name "Metacat." Here, then, are several ways in which the hypothetical Metacat program would go beyond Copycat:

> • We humans freely refer to the "issues involved in" or "pressures evoked by" a given puzzle. For example, the problem **abc** $\Rightarrow$ **abd**, **xyz** $\Rightarrow$ **?** is about recovery from a snag, the bringing in of a new concept ("last") under pressure, perceptual reversal and abstract symmetry, simultaneous two-tiered reversal, and a few other things. However, Copycat has no explicit representation of issues or pressures. Although it makes conceptual slippages such as *successor* $\Rightarrow$ *predecessor*, it does not anywhere *explicitly* register that it is trying out the idea of "reversal". It does not "know what it is doing"—it merely *does* it. This is because, even though the concept of "reversal" (i.e., the node *opposite*) gets activated in long-term memory (i.e., the Slipnet) and plays a crucial role in guiding the processing, no explicit reflection of that activation and that guiding role ever gets made in the Workspace. A Metacat, by contrast, should be sensitive to any sufficiently salient event that occurs inside its Slipnet (e.g., the activation of a very deep concept) and be able to explicitly turn this recognition into a clear characterization, in its Workspace, of the issues that the given problem is really "about." Additionally, the program should be able to take note of the most critical actions that occur in its Workspace, and to create a *record* of those actions. This way, the program would leave an explicit coarse-grained temporal trail behind it. The way in which such self-monitoring would take place would roughly be this: Copycat, as it currently stands, is pervaded by numerical measures of "importance," roughly speaking. There are important objects, important concepts, important correspondences, and so on. We would simply add one further numerical measure—a rough-and-ready measure of the *import* of an action taken in the Workspace or of an activation occurring in the Slipnet. For actions in the Workspace, import would reflect such features as the *size* of the object acted upon (the bigger the better) and the *conceptual depth* of its descriptions; for actions in the Slipnet, import would reflect the *conceptual depth* of the node activated, among other things. The details don't matter here; the main thing is that events' import values would be spread out over a spectrum, allowing one to filter out all those events above some threshold, so that one gets a highly selective view of what has

happened. This high-level view of events taking place, once it is explicitly represented in some part of the Workspace (the "Lucas part," it might be called), would then itself be subject to perceptual processing by codelets looking for patterns. This would thus allow the system to become aware of regularities in its own actions, and perhaps to get a hold of the *pressures* in a given problem, which would lead to a characterization of what a given problem is "about." Of course, what a problem is considered to be about depends on what answer one comes up with, so in a sense this would be a description not of what the *problem* as a whole is about but of the issues that a given *answer* is about. Though this is but the crudest approximation to what people do, it is at least a first stab.

• We humans readily see how a given answer to a given analogy puzzle could make sense to someone else, even if we ourselves did not think of it and might well never have thought of it on our own. The current version of Copycat, however, has no such capability. It needs to be given the capacity to work backward from a given answer suggested by an outside agent. If the program has the capacity to see through to the issues that a given answer is about, this working-backward capacity would allow it to size up an answer quickly and to put it in mental perspective. From that point on, it would be able to engage in "banter" of sorts with a human about the merits and demerits of a given solution.

• We humans do not forget what we have done right after doing it. Rather, we store our actions in episodic memory. So too, Metacat should store a trace of its solution of a problem in an episodic memory. There are two important types of consequence of this ability. The first type of consequence is that, during a single problem-solving session, the program should be able to avoid falling into mindless loops, and to "jump out of the system" (meaning, for instance, that it should be able to make an explicit decision, based on its failures, to focus on previously ignored objects or concepts). The second type of consequence is that, over a longer time span, it should be able to be "reminded" of previously encountered problems by a new problem. At present, of course, Copycat does not in any way try to model retrieval of episodes in its past, because it simply does not *have* any past, no matter how many problems it has solved. (Of course, *during* a run, the current version of Copycat has a short-term past, but all that is lost once the run is over.) With an episodic memory, that would all be changed. The search for analogous episodes would be governed by many of the principles that already pervade Copycat's architecture: activation would spread from concepts involved in the current problem (e.g., "symmetry," "reversal") to problems in episodic memory that were indexed under those concepts. Needless to say, all of this would be heavily biased by conceptual depth, so that surface-level remindings would be kept to a minimum.

• We humans have a clear "meta-analogical" sense—that is, an ability to see *analogies between analogies*, as in the title of Ulam's book. An episode-retrieval ability as just described would endow Metacat with the capacity to map one Copycat analogy problem (and its answers) onto another—thus making, rather than an analogy between two letter strings, a meta-level analogy between two *puzzles*, based on issues and pressures that they evoke. Going even further, it would be hoped that the ability to make such meta-level analogies would automatically entail the ability to make meta-meta-analogies, and so forth. Thus, a Metacat program would, hopefully, be able to relate the way in which two specific analogy puzzles were early on noticed to resemble each other to the way in which two *other* analogy puzzles have *just now* been noticed to resemble each other. (Thus we are moving beyond the title of Ulam's book!) Achieving this multi-leveled type of self-reflectiveness would, I firmly believe, constitute a major milestone en route to a theory of how consciousness emerges from the interaction of many small subcognitive agents in a system.

• Finally, we humans not only enjoy *solving* these kinds of puzzles, but can enjoy *making up* new puzzles. It takes a keen explicit sense of the nature of pressures involved in problems to make up a really new and high-quality Copycat analogy puzzle. What makes a problem good is often the fact that it has two appealing answers, of which one is deep but elusive while the other is shallow but easy to see. An example of this is the puzzle **apc** $\Rightarrow$ **abc**, **opc** $\Rightarrow$?, which admits of the easy-to-find answer **opc** $\Rightarrow$ **obc** (based on a letter-by-letter imitation of what happened to **apc**) and the elusive answer **opc** $\Rightarrow$ **opq** (based on an abstract vision according to which the defect in a flawed successor group is removed). While both answers make perfect sense, the latter is clearly far more elegant than the former. Inventing a problem of this sort, delicately poised at the balance point between two rival answers, requires an exquisite internal model of how people will perceive things, and often requires exploration of all sorts of variants of an initial problem that are close to it in "problem space," searching for one that is optimal in the sense of packing the most issues into the smallest and "cleanest" problem. This is certainly a type of aesthetic sense. (Incidentally, I feel no need to apologize for the inclusion of aesthetic qualities, with all the subjectivity that they imply, in the modeling of analogy. Indeed, I feel that responsiveness to *beauty* and its close cousin, *simplicity*, plays a central role in high-level cognition, and I expect that this will gradually come to be more clearly recognized as cognitive science progresses.) Needless to say, Copycat as it currently stands has nothing remotely close to such capabilities.

Work toward this type of Metacat program is just beginning at the Center for Research on Concepts and Cognition at Indiana University. If the effort to impart these sorts of abilities and intuitions to a Metacat program is a success, then, I would say, Metacat will be *truly* insightful and creative. I make no pretense that the above description is a clear recipe for an architecture, although, to be sure, what is in my mind is considerably more fleshed out than this vague sketch. These wildly ambitious ideas are unlikely ever to be realized in full, but they can certainly play the role of a pot of gold at the end of the rainbow, pulling me and my co-workers on toward a perhaps chimerical goal.

I have been privileged to travel a long ways in search of the pot of gold in the company of Melanie Mitchell. Her beautiful work has deeply inspired me, and I hope that it will similarly inspire a new generation of questers after the mysteries of mind. As we go forward, the more clearly we see how long a road remains ahead of us.

Douglas R. Hofstadter
Center for Research on Concepts and Cognition
Indiana University

Appendix A

A Sampler of Letter-String Analogy Problems Beyond Copycat's Current Capabilities

Problems

The following is a collection of analogy problems in the letter-string domain that are beyond Copycat's current abilities. The purpose of presenting them is to give readers a better feel for the breadth and richness of this microworld, as well as a better feel for the limits of Copycat's current abilities. These problems also point to a number of issues for future work on Copycat.

The problems are arranged in seven "families," each having a common idea or theme among its problems. In many of the families, several problems in a row are based on a single example. In those cases, the example is given only once, and the various targets are listed below it. (In the next section, the problems given here are discussed, and reasons are given for why Copycat cannot currently solve them.)

1. **abc ⇒ abd**
   - a. **ace ⇒ ?**
   - b. **aababc ⇒ ?**
   - c. **pxqxrxsx ⇒ ?**
   - d. **aaabbbcck ⇒ ?**
   - e. **bcdacdabd ⇒ ?**

2. **abcd ⇒ abcde**
   - a. **ijklm ⇒ ?**
   - b. **ijxlm ⇒ ?**
   - c. **mlkji ⇒ ?**
   - d. **iiii ⇒ ?**
   - e. **iiiijjjj ⇒ ?**

3. a. **mmmkooeeeeefqxx ⇒ kfq**
      riipppppplooyg ⇒ ?
   - b. **rrccmmkppbb ⇒ k**
      ljooooosrezv ⇒ ?

4. a. **abcde ⇒ xxxxx**
      pqr ⇒ ?
   - b. **xxh ⇒ fgh**
      pxxx ⇒ ?

    c. **pqrxxxx ⇒ pqrstuv**
        efghmm ⇒ ?

    d. **amcmemg ⇒ abcdefg**
        wxyx ⇒ ?

5. a. **eeeeqee ⇒ eeeeree**
        sosss ⇒ ?

    b. **eeeqee ⇒ qqqeqq**
        sabsss ⇒ ?

    c. **eqe ⇒ qeq**
        abcdcba ⇒ ?

    d. **eqe ⇒ qeq**
        aaabccc ⇒ ?

6. a. **abcdde ⇒ abcde**
        pqstu ⇒ ?

    b. **abced ⇒ abcde**
        ppqqrrs ⇒ ?

7. a. **a ⇒ z**
        b ⇒ ?

    b. **pqr ⇒ rqp a ⇒ ?**

Discussion

1

1a. **abc ⇒ abd, ace ⇒ ?**
As was discussed in chapter 2, the target string in this problem can be understood as a "double successor" group, yielding answer **acg**. Copycat currently can perceive relations and make slippages involving only nodes separated by one link in the Slipnet, so it cannot perceive a double-successor relation. In order to solve this problem, Copycat would have to perceive such relations and use them to create a new concept—*double successor*—on the fly. This new concept would have the same properties as the program's other concepts. It would be used by codelets to calculate strengths of structures involving it; when active, it would post top-down codelets to look for instances of it; and so on. The program does not currently have any mechanism for creating a new concept such as this.

1b. **abc ⇒ abd, aababc ⇒ ?**
As was discussed in chapter 2, if the target string is parsed as **a-ab-abc**, then a strong, though abstract, similarity to the initial string **abc** emerges, where the "rightmost letter" of **aababc** is the group **abc**, and its "successor" is **abcd**, yielding the answer **aababcd**. Copycat can solve this problem *in principle* in the same way it solves **abc ⇒ abd, xpqdef ⇒ ?**. However, in practice it tends to be too hard for the program to arrive at this solution: in 1000 runs the program got this solution only once. The program usually very quickly constructs a sameness group consisting of the leftmost two **a**'s, and cannot break it in order to come up with the parsing **a-ab-abc**. The program usually answers **aababd**, using the rule "Replace the rightmost letter by its successor", though it sometimes constructs

an **abc** successor group from the rightmost three letters in the target string and maps the **c** in the initial string onto this group, answering **aabbcd**. On occasion, the program gives the answer **aababcd** for a strange reason (figure A.1). The **aa** group is constructed and then it is bonded together with the adjacent **b**, and a two-element successor group is formed: **Ab**. The program also forms the three-element group **abc**, and then notices a successor relation between the lengths of these two groups. It thus parses the string as **2-3** (i.e., **Ab-abc**) and answers **2-4**—that is, **aababcd**.

The difficulty Copycat has with this problem has to do with the lack of adequate top-down forces (discussed in chapter 7). Once the **abc** successor group is made in the target string, the combination of top-down forces and high temperature should ideally combine to make it more likely for a proposed **ab** group (i.e., one containing the second and third letters) to successfully compete with the intrinsically strong **aa** group. Once the string has been parsed as **a-ab-abc**, then the same kinds of forces as are present in **abc** ⇒ **abd**, **mrrjjj** ⇒ **?** should make it possible for the leftmost **a** to be seen as a single-letter *successor* group and for length relations to be noticed. This is all possible for the current version of Copycat. What is not possible for the current program, and what would make the desired solution much stronger, is to see letter-category relations between the groups **a**, **ab**, and **abc**, or concept mappings based on letter categories between the letters in the initial string and these three groups. These relations and concept mappings would be based on the view that **a-ab-abc** is basically **A-B-C** in *code*, in the same way that **ii-jj-kk** is basically **I-J-K** in code. However, Copycat does not currently give letter-category descriptions to successor and predecessor groups in the way it does to sameness groups (e.g., the group **ii** is given the description *"letter-category: I"*, but the group **abc** is not given any letter-category description), so such bonds and concept mappings cannot be made. However, I believe that such structures are in part what make the solution **aababcd** seem very strong to many people.

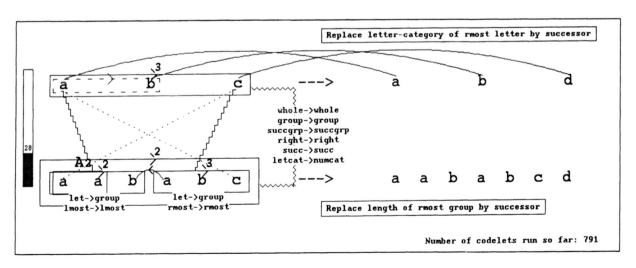

Figure A.1
Final configuration of the workspace for a strange route to the answer **aababcd**.

1c. **abc ⇒ abd, pxqxrxsx ⇒ ?**

To solve this problem, one must separate the "figure" (the successor group **pqrs**) from the "ground" (the interleaved **x**'s). If this figure and ground are perceived, then the answer is **pxqxrxtx**. A more literal answer is **pxqxrxsy**. Copycat cannot get the former solution for several reasons. For instance, it cannot build bonds between letters that are not spatially adjacent (e.g., the **p** and the **q** here are separated by an **x**), and it can only make groups that are based on relations in the Slipnet (thus it could not group the **p** and its neighbor **x** together as one unit).

1d. **abc ⇒ abd, aaabbbcck ⇒ ?**

Here the question is what to do about that pesky **k**. Some possible answers are **aaabbbddd**, **aaabbbddl**, **aaabbbddk**, and **aaabbbccl**. The present version of Copycat can produce the last two (as well as the usual "Replace the rightmost letter by *D*" answer, **aaabbbccd**), but it is not flexible enough to do what humans can do: assume that the **k** "really should have been a **c**", because then the analogy would make more sense, and give the answer **aaabbbddd**.

1e. **abc ⇒ abd, bcdacdabd ⇒ ?**

This problem looks chaotic and senseless, but one way of solving it is the following: The target string can be parsed as **bcd-acd-abd**, where each triplet is a code for the "missing" letter. When the string is thus decoded, it is simply **abc**, so the answer is **abd**, but once again in code: **bcd-acd-abc**. This is a very hard problem for people, and I don't know if Copycat will ever be sophisticated enough to get this answer.

2.

This family of problems shows various ways of extending a group. The current version of Copycat cannot deal with any of these problems, since it cannot yet form a rule like "extend the successor group."

2a. **abcd ⇒ abcde, ijklm ⇒ ?**

The most straightforward answer is **ijklmn**.

2b. **abcd ⇒ abcde, ijxlm ⇒ ?**

There are several possible answers, including **ijxlmn** (ignore the **x** and the lack of a **k**), **ijkxlmn** (view the target string as two successor groups separated by an **x**, both of which should be extended), and **ijklmn** (view the **x** as "the space into which to extend the group"). The last answer requires a kind of flexibility that is far beyond Copycat's current abilities.

2c. **abcd ⇒ abcde, mlkji ⇒ ?**

The main rival answers here are **mlkjih** (extending the predecessor group to its right) and **nmlkji** (extending the successor group to its left). These are similar to the rival answers to **abc ⇒ abd, kji ⇒ ?**.

2d. **abcd ⇒ abcde, iiii ⇒ ?**

If the concept of *successor group* is slipped to the concept of *sameness group*, or is generalized to the more general concept of *group*, then the answer is **iiiii** (that is, the group length is incremented by 1). Another reasonable answer is **iiiijjjj,** with the string **iiii** perceived as a successor group of length 1 (consisting only of the chunk **iiii**), and extended by one "letter" (here a group of four **j**'s). These answers (in my opinion) are much better than more literal-minded answers such as **iiiij** ("Tack on the successor of the rightmost letter"), **iiiie** ("Add on an **e** at the right"), or **iiii** ("Do nothing, since the target string **iiii** contains no successor groups").

2e. **abcd** ⇒ **abcde**, **iiiijjjj** ⇒ *?*
Two good answers are **iiiiijjjjj** (extending both sameness groups at once) and **iiiijjjjkkkk** (extending the successor group seen at the group level).

3.

These problems involve *extracting* letters from a string, a notion Copycat does not currently have.

3a. **mmmkooeeeeefqxx** ⇒ **kfq**, **riipppppplooyg** ⇒ *?*
A plausible rule is "extract all single letters," yielding the answer **rlyg**.

3b. **rrccmmkppbb** ⇒ **k**, **ljooooosrezv** ⇒ *?*
Here there is competition between the rule "Extract all single letters" (yielding the answer **ljsrezv**) and the even more abstract rule "Extract the 'oddball' or 'black sheep'" (yielding **ooooo**). Giving Copycat the flexibility to recognize instances of the concept "oddball" (or "objects in the situation that are different from all the other objects") in a psychologically plausible way would be extremely challenging. This is the kind of commonsense notion that people can use very easily and flexibly, but that would be very hard to impart to a computer program.

4.

4a. **abcde** ⇒ **xxxxx**, **pqr** ⇒ *?*
A plausible rule is "Replace all letters by *X*'s." This would yield the answer **xxx**. Copycat cannot currently construct rules describing changes of more than one letter, so it cannot solve this problem.

4b. **xxh** ⇒ **fgh**, **pxxx** ⇒ *?*
This problem is easy for people, who answer **pqrs**. However, Copycat is quite far away from being able to perceive the relation between **xxh** and **fgh** or to deal with the abstract concept of "filling in the spaces."

4c. **pqrxxxx** ⇒ **pqrstuv**, **efghmm** ⇒ *?*
A reasonable way of solving this problem is to see the **m**'s in **efghmm** as playing the same role as the **x**'s in **pqrxxxx**. This view would yield the answer **efghij**.

4d. **amcmemg** ⇒ **abcdefg**, **wxyx** ⇒ *?*
This problem has an amusing twist: the **x**'s in **wxyx** play the same "mask" or "placeholder" roles as the **m**'s in **amcmemg**, but what replaces the leftmost **x** in the desired answer (**wxyz**) is another copy of **x**, this time playing the role of itself! This problem, like the previous two, is far beyond Copycat's current capabilities.

5.

5a. **eeeeqee** ⇒ **eeeeree**, **sosss** ⇒ *?*
A reasonable rule here is "Replace the isolated letter by its successor," yielding answer **spsss**. Copycat cannot currently describe something as "the isolated letter," so it cannot at present form this rule.

5b. **eeeqee** ⇒ **qqqeqq**, **sabsss** ⇒ *?*
One very abstract rule is "Switch the letters" (or "flip the bits"). If the **a** and the **b** in the target string are grouped as a single unit, then the answer is **absababab**. Another way to describe the change is "Turn the string inside-out." In this case, **assbbb** is a plausible answer. This problem is, of course, beyond Copycat's current capabilities, since it has no notion of switching letters or turning things inside-out.

5c and 5d. **eqe** ⇒ **qeq**, **abcdcba** ⇒ *? and* **eqe** ⇒ **qeq**, **aaabccc** ⇒ *?*
Both these problems explore the concept of "turning a string inside-out." One possible answer to part c is **dcbabcd**. Some possible answers for part d are **baaacccb**, **bbbacbbb**, and **abbbc**. The last answer expresses an extremely abstract view in which the letters themselves are ignored and "turning the string inside-out" is done at the level of group length. That is, the pattern 3-1-3 (**aaabccc**) corresponds to **eqe** and the pattern 1-3-1 (**abbbc**) corresponds to **qeq**.

6.

6a and 6b. **abcdde** ⇒ **abcde**, **pqstu** ⇒ *? and* **abced** ⇒ **abcde**, **ppqqrrs** ⇒ *?*
Both problems could be seen to be about "fixing up" or "cleaning up" a structure—a quite abstract concept (it would be very challenging to enable Copycat to recognize instances of it). A good answer to part a is **pqrstu**, and a good answer to part b is **ppqqrrss**. This is, in my opinion, somewhat better than the answer **pqrs**, since it reflects the idea that the initial and target strings had "just a little bit wrong with them," rather than a massive defect requiring global rewriting.

7.

7a. **a** ⇒ **z**, **b** ⇒ *?*
If the **a** and the **z** are seen as "mirror images" of each other, then the answer should be **y**—that is, the **b**'s mirror image. For this answer, the rule would be something like "Replace the first letter by the last letter," and the translated rule would be something like "Replace the next-to-first letter by the next-to-last letter." Copycat cannot get this answer because it cannot presently describe a **b** as "next-to-first" or a **y** as "next-to-last."

7b. **pqr** ⇒ **rqp**, **a** ⇒ *?*
One answer is **a**. A very abstract answer is **z**, which might come about as a result of seeing the essential relation between **pqr** and **rqp** as *opposite* and asking "What is *A*'s opposite?" This would involve something like the "coattails" effect discussed in chapter 8. The **pqr** ⇒ **rqp** correspondences might involve the slippage *right* ⇒ *left* or, alternatively, *successor* ⇒ *predecessor*. Then the slippage *first* ⇒ *last* might come on the coattails of the other slippage, since the two slippages are conceptually related. Copycat currently has no mechanism implementing such an effect.

Appendix B

Parameters and Formulas

This appendix lists the values of the parameters used in Copycat, and gives more detailed descriptions of some of the formulas used in the program.[1]

All values in Copycat (parameter values, structure strengths activation values, temperature, and so on) are in the range from 0 to 100.

There are many parameters in the program whose values were assigned by me. In general, the values were decided by a combination of intuition, trial and error, and some arbitrariness, and are not necessarily optimally tuned in the current version of the program. They should thus not be thought of as cast in concrete; they are very much open to further testing and refinement.

Values Used in Setting Up the Slipnet

Conceptual-Depth Values

    A, B, . . . , Z: 10
    1, 2, . . .5: 30
    leftmost, rightmost, middle, single, whole: 40
    left, right: 40
    letter: 20
    group: 80
    first, last: 60
    predecessor, successor, predecessor-group, successor-group: 50
    sameness, sameness-group: 80
    letter-category: 30
    length: 60
    string-position: 70
    direction: 70
    object-category: 90
    alphabetic-position: 80
    bond-category: 80
    group-category: 80
    identity, opposite: 90

Link Lengths
The length of a link in the Slipnet is determined by its label, if it has one, and otherwise remains at a fixed value, set ahead of time by me. The labels on various links were shown in figure 3.4.

Lengths of Labeled Links
The length of a labeled link is equal to the *intrinsic link length* of its label node (e.g., *opposite*) if the label node is not fully active, and is equal to the *shrunk link length* of its label node if the label is fully active.

The intrinsic link lengths assigned to the various label nodes are the following:

predecessor: 60

successor: 60

identity: 0

opposite: 80

The shrunk link length for each label node is 0.4 times the intrinsic link length.

Lengths of Fixed-Length Links
For all links from nodes to their superordinate category nodes (e.g., $A \Rightarrow$ *letter-category*, or *last* $\Rightarrow$ *alphabetic-position*), the length is the difference in conceptual depth between the two nodes. That is, the closer they are in conceptual depth, the shorter the link. The idea here is that the amount of activation that spreads from a concept to a superordinate category should depends on how abstract the superordinate category is with respect to the concept. For example, neither *A* nor its superordinate *letter-category* are very abstract, and once *A* is activated, it should be fairly easy to "wake up" the notion that letter categories are relevant to the given situation. On the other extreme, the concept *last* is rather abstract (and thus harder to perceive than, say *A*), and so is its superordinate *alphabetic position*. But once *last* is perceived to be relevant, the more general notion of *alphabetic position* should fairly easily be brought into the picture as well. In contrast, the notion of *letter* is not very abstract, but its superordinate, *object-category* is quite abstract. We don't want the very abstract idea of "objects in general" to be brought into the picture every time the ubiquitous notion of, say, *letter* is being perceived. However, *group* is a much more abstract type of object, and it is more plausible that, once groups are perceived, the system have some chance of considering "generalized objects" to be part of the picture. Using the difference in conceptual depth values as the degree of association between a node and its superordinate is a rough way of implementing this idea.

For other fixed-length links, the lengths are set by hand. The values are:

$A \Rightarrow$ *first*: 75

$Z \Rightarrow$ *last*: 75

letter-category $\Rightarrow$ *length*: 95

length $\Rightarrow$ *letter-category*: 95

letter $\Rightarrow$ *group*: 90

group $\Rightarrow$ *letter*: 90

predecessor $\Rightarrow$ *predecessor-group*: 60

successor ⇒ *successor-group*: 60
sameness ⇒ *sameness group*: 30
predecessor-group ⇒ *predecessor*: 90
successor-group ⇒ *successor*: 90
sameness-group ⇒ *sameness*: 90
single ⇒ *whole*: 90
whole ⇒ *single*: 90
left ⇒ *leftmost*: 90
leftmost ⇒ *left*: 90
right ⇒ *rightmost*: 90
rightmost ⇒ *right*: 90
successor-group ⇒ *length*: 95
predecessor-group ⇒ *length*: 95
sameness-group ⇒ *length*: 95
sameness-group ⇒ *letter-category*: 50

At present, all types of groups can have *length* descriptions, but only sameness groups can have letter-category descriptions. This is why there are no *successor-group* ⇒ *letter-category* or *predecessor-group* ⇒ *letter-category* links.

In addition to the links listed above, it was necessary to add certain links for the purpose of making certain concept mappings compatible and internally coherent (e.g., *first* ⇒ *last* should support *leftmost* ⇒ *rightmost*). Each of the following links has a fixed length of 100, which means that no activation spreads over them even though the program considers the nodes to be related for the purpose of calculating the strengths of correspondences. This mechanism is not ideal, and should probably be modified in future work on Copycat.

right ⇒ *leftmost*: 100
leftmost ⇒ *right*: 100
left ⇒ *rightmost*: 100
rightmost ⇒ *left*: 100
leftmost ⇒ *first*: 100
first ⇒ *leftmost*: 100
rightmost ⇒ *first*: 100
first ⇒ *rightmost*: 100
leftmost ⇒ *last*: 100
last ⇒ *leftmost*: 100
rightmost ⇒ *last*: 100
last ⇒ *rightmost*: 100

Other Slipnet Parameters

Number of codelets run before a Slipnet update: 15
Number of Slipnet updates for initially clamped nodes (i.e., *letter-category* and *string-position*) to remain clamped: 50

Slipnet Formulas

Activation: The probability of a node discontinuously becoming fully active (100%) is 0 if the node is less than 50% active, and $(activation/100)^3$ otherwise.

Activation decay: Each node loses (100 − conceptual depth) percent of its activation at each Slipnet update.

Activation spread: If a node is fully active, it spreads activation to each of the nodes it is linked to. Each neighboring node gets a percent of the original node's activation equal to 100 minus the length of the link from the original node to the neighboring node. The current version of the program always uses the intrinsic link length rather than the shrunk link length for this calculation, even when the label node for this link is active. Shrunk link lengths are used only by codelets in evaluating slippages, bonds, etc. When shrunk link lengths were used for spreading activation, the network tended to become too active. It is possible that a different mechanism (e.g., some kind of inhibition technique) should be used to control activation in the network. This is a topic for future work on Copycat.

Temperature Formulas

The temperature is updated along with the Slipnet, every 15 codelet steps. The formula for calculating the temperature is

(0.8 * [the weighted average of the unhappiness of all objects, weighted by their relative importance]) + (0.2 * [100 − strength(rule)]).

The factors 0.8 and 0.2 are the weights given to the two components (the unhappinesses of objects in the Workspace and the complement of the strength of the rule) in this calculation. As was discussed in chapter 4, there are some problems with this weighting scheme, which result in implausible temperature values for some answers.

The following describes how the temperature-controlled probabilistic choice of codelets works. There are a fixed number of possible "urgency bins" to which codelets can be assigned (currently 7), and each of those bins is given a new numerical value each time the temperature is updated. The bins are numbered 1, 2, . . . , *highest-bin-number*. The function for the value of each bin is

$$\text{Urgency} = \text{Bin number}^{\frac{(100 - temperature) + 10}{15}}.$$

The constants 10 and 15 are for scaling purposes and were determined by trial and error. The calculated urgency values are then used to directly make a probabilistic choice of the next codelet to run.

In addition to affecting the choice of which codelet to run next, temperature affects several probabilistic choices made by codelets. This is implemented as follows.

Before a codelet makes a probabilistic choice based on probability p (e.g., the probability of a strength-tester codelet deciding to post a builder codelet—a function of the proposed structure's strength), it adjusts p (a number between 0 and 1) according to the current temperature by sending it through a filter. The filter adjusts probabilities lower than 0.5 upwards and probabilities higher than 0.5 downward by an amount that depends on the temperature. (The higher the temperature, the closer probabilities are brought to 0.5.) The filter is at present a fairly complicated formula, arrived at partially by trial and error, and is inelegant. The whole formula should eventually be simplified. The formula, written in Common Lisp, is given below (*temperature* is the global temperature variable):

```
(defun adjust-probability (p)
      (cond ((= p 0) 0)
            ((≤ p .5)
             (let* ((term1 (max 1 (truncate (abs (log p 10)))))
                    (term2 (expt 10 (- (- term1 1))))
                (min .5 (+ p (* (/ (- 10 (sqrt (- 100 *temperature*))) 100)
                           (- term2 p)))))))
            ((> p .5)
             (max .5 (- 1 (+ ( - 1 p)
                          (* (/ (- 10 (sqrt (- 100 *temperature*))) 100) p)))))))).
```

Temperature also affects the degree of randomness with which fights between competing structures are decided. A fight is decided probabilistically on the basis of the respective strengths of the structures involved, but these strengths are first sent through a filter that adjusts them according to the current temperature, enhancing differences in strength more and more as the temperature falls. The filter is

$$\text{Adjusted strength} = \text{Strength}^{\frac{(100 - temperature) + 15}{30}}.$$

The constants 30 and 15 are for scaling purposes and were determined by trial and error.

Coderack Parameters and Formulas

The Coderack is limited to a certain size (currently 100). If this limit is exceeded by new codelets being posted, codelets are chosen probabilistically (as a function of their urgency and their age on the Coderack) to be deleted until the limit is again reached. The following value is first assigned to each codelet c in the Coderack:

Age(c) * [Highest urgency − Urgency(c)],

where Highest urgency is the current highest possible urgency value in the Coderack. These values are then converted into probabilities that are used to decide which codelets to delete. Thus, the older the codelet and the lower its urgency, the more likely it will be chosen to be deleted.

Appendix C

More Detailed Descriptions of Codelet Types

This appendix describes the various codelet types in more detail than was given in chapter 3. The various probability values detailed in these descriptions are the values *before* the adjustment for temperature (described in appendix B) is applied.

Description-Building Codelets

Bottom-up description scout (no arguments)
1. Choose an object in the Workspace probabilistically as a function of salience.

2. Choose a relevant description from the object's description list probabilistically as a function of the activation of the descriptors.

3. See if this descriptor has any *property* links in the Slipnet that are short enough. This is decided probabilistically, with the probability equal to

(100 − link-length) / 100.

4. If not, then fizzle. Otherwise, choose one of the properties probabilistically as a function of degree of association and activation.

5. Propose a description of the object, based on this property, and post a description strength-tester codelet whose urgency is a function of the activation of the description type. For example, if the proposed descriptor is *first*, then the urgency is a function of the activation of *alphabetic-position*.

Top-down description scout (argument: a description-type node)
1. Choose an object in the Workspace probabilistically as a function of salience.

2. Test all the possible descriptors of the given description type to see if any can be applied to this object. For example, if the description-type is *alphabetic-position*, then *first* and *last* will be tested.

3. If no descriptors of this type can be applied to the chosen object, then fizzle. Otherwise, choose one of the descriptors probabilistically (as a function of activation) and post a description strength-tester codelet whose urgency is a function of the activation of the description type.

Description strength-tester (argument: a proposed description)
1. Activate the proposed descriptor in the Slipnet (i.e., give it full activation).
2. Calculate the proposed description's strength.
3. Decide probabilistically whether to continue, as a function of the proposed description's strength. If no, then fizzle. Otherwise, post a description-builder codelet whose urgency is a function of the proposed description's strength.

Description builder (argument: a proposed description)
If this description is already attached to the given object, then fizzle. Otherwise build the description, and activate the descriptor and the description type in the Slipnet.

Bond-Building Codelets

Bottom-up bond scout (no arguments)
1. Choose an object in the Workspace probabilistically as a function of salience.
2. Choose an adjacent object probabilistically as a function of salience.
3. Choose a "bonding facet" for this potential bond. A bonding facet describes which aspect of the objects to look at in making a bond. At present the only possible bonding facets are *letter-category* and *length*. This choice is made probabilistically as a function of the possible facets' local support (i.e., a function of how many objects in the string have this type of description) and activation.
4. See if each chosen object has a descriptor of the chosen bonding facet (e.g., *letter-category*). If not, then fizzle.
5. If so, then see if there is a relationship in the Slipnet between these two descriptors. If not, then fizzle.
6. If so, then propose a bond between these two objects, and post a bond strength-tester codelet whose urgency is a function of the proximity of the two descriptors in the Slipnet.

Top-down bond scout: category (argument: a bond-category node)
1. Choose a string to work in probabilistically, as a function of both the support of the given bond category in each string (e.g., if the bond category is *successor*, then the string with more successor bonds is more likely to be chosen) and the average unhappiness of objects in the string (the string with more unhappy objects is more likely to be chosen).
2. Choose an object in that string probabilistically as a function of salience.
3. Choose an adjacent object probabilistically as a function of salience.
4. Choose a bonding facet.
5. See if each chosen object has a descriptor of the chosen bonding facet (e.g., *letter-category*). If not, then fizzle.

6. If so, then see if there is a link in the Slipnet of the given bond category between these two descriptors. If not, then fizzle.

7. If so, then propose a bond between these two objects, and post a bond strength-tester codelet whose urgency is a function of the proximity of the two descriptors in the Slipnet.

Top-down bond scout: direction (argument: a direction node)

1. Choose a string to work in probabilistically, as a function of both the support of the given direction in each string (e.g., if the direction is *right*, then the string with more right-going bonds is more likely to be chosen) and the average unhappiness of objects in the string (the string with more unhappy objects is more likely to be chosen).

2. Choose an object in that string probabilistically as a function of salience.

3. Choose an adjacent object in the given direction.

4. Choose a bonding facet.

5. See if each chosen object has a descriptor of the chosen bonding facet (e.g., *letter-category*). If not, then fizzle.

6. If so, then see if there is some link in the Slipnet between these two descriptors, when they are looked at in the given direction. (For example, if the two objects are **a** and **b** in the string **abc**, with descriptors *A* and *B* respectively, and if the given direction is **left**, then this codelet sees if there is a link in the Slipnet from *B* to *A*. If the given direction is *right*, then this codelet sees if there is a link in the Slipnet from *A* to *B*.) If not, then fizzle.

7. If so, then propose a bond between these two objects, and post a bond strength-tester codelet whose urgency is a function of the proximity of the two descriptors in the Slipnet.

Bond strength-tester (argument: a proposed bond)

1. Calculate the proposed bond's strength.

2. Decide probabilistically whether or not to continue, as a function of the proposed bond's strength. If no, then fizzle. Otherwise, post a bond-builder codelet whose urgency is a function of the proposed bond's strength, and activate (in the Slipnet) the two descriptors being related (e.g., *A* and *B*) and the bonding facet (e.g., *letter-category*).

Bond builder (argument: a proposed bond)

1. If a bond of this type has already been built between the two objects, then fizzle.

2. Otherwise, fight with any incompatible bonds, groups, and correspondences. If any fight is lost, then fizzle. Otherwise, destroy all incompatible structures, build the proposed bond, and activate (in the Slipnet) the new bond's category and direction.

Group-Building Codelets

Any time a new group is proposed, the proposed group is automatically given a number of descriptions, including a group-category description, an object-category description (i.e., *group*), a letter-category description if it is a sameness group, and a string-position description if applicable. There is also some probability that it will be given a *length* description. This probability is a function of the length of the group (the shorter, the more likely) and the activation of *length* (the higher, the more likely).

Top-down group scout: category (argument: a group-category mode)
1. Choose one of the strings probabilistically as a function of the support in the string for the bond category associated with the given group category (e.g., if the group category is *successor-group*, then the string with more successor bonds is more likely to be chosen) and the average unhappiness of objects in the string (the string with more unhappy objects is more likely to be chosen).
2. Choose an object in that string probabilistically as a function of salience.
3. Choose a window in the string (with the chosen object at one end) in which to look for adjacent bonds of the given category and all in the same direction. That is, the bonds in the window must all have the same direction—either left, right, or no direction (as in the case of sameness bonds). The choice is probabilistic, with larger windows being more likely to be chosen.
4. Starting from the chosen object, scan through the chosen window until no more adjacent bonds of the given category are found. If no bonds are found at all, then decide probabilistically whether or not to propose a single-letter group. The probability is a function of local support in the string for the given group category and the activation of *length*.
5. If no bonds are found, and a single-letter group is not being proposed, then fizzle.
6. Otherwise, propose a group based on the bonds found, and post a group strength-tester codelet whose urgency is a function of the group's bond category (e.g., *successor*, if the proposed group is based on successor bonds), and its activation.

Top-down group scout: direction (argument: a direction node)
1. Choose one of the strings probabilistically as a function of support for the given direction (e.g., if the direction is *right*, then the string with more right-going bonds is more likely to be chosen) and the average unhappiness of objects in the string (the string with more unhappy objects is more likely to be chosen).
2. Choose an object in that string probabilistically as a function of salience.
3. Choose a window in the string in which to look for adjacent bonds of the given direction and all of a single category. That is, all the bonds in

the window must have the same category. The choice is probabilistic, with larger windows being more likely to be chosen.

4. Start from the chosen object, and scan through the chosen window until no more adjacent bonds of the given direction are found.

5. If no bonds are found, then fizzle.

6. Otherwise, propose a group based on the bonds found, and post a group strength-tester codelet whose urgency is a function of the group's bond category (e.g., *successor*, if the proposed group is based on successor bonds) and its activation.

Group-string scout (no arguments)

1. Choose a string at random.

2. See if there is a set of adjacent bonds of the same type and direction spanning the string.

3. If not, then fizzle. Otherwise, propose a group based on these bonds, and post a group strength-tester codelet whose urgency is a function of the group's bond category (e.g., *successor*, if the proposed group is based on successor bonds) and its activation.

Group strength-tester (argument: a proposed group)

1. Calculate the proposed group's strength.

2. Decide probabilistically whether to continue, as a function of the proposed group's strength. If no, then fizzle. Otherwise, post a group-builder codelet whose urgency is a function of the proposed group's strength, and activate (in the Slipnet) the group's bond category and direction (e.g., *successor* and *right*).

Group builder (argument: a proposed group)

1. If the proposed group already exists, then fizzle.

2. Otherwise, fight with any incompatible bonds, groups, and correspondences. If any fight is lost, then fizzle. Otherwise, destroy all incompatible structures, build the proposed group, and activate (in the Slipnet) all the descriptions given to the new group, including the new group's category.

Correspondence-Building Codelets

Bottom-up correspondence scout (no arguments)

1. Choose two objects, one from the initial string and one from the target string, probabilistically as a function of salience.

2. Take all the relevant descriptions of each object and make a list of all possible concept mappings between the descriptors. A concept mapping is possible if the two descriptors are identical or if they are linked in the Slipnet by a single Slip link. (See section 3.3 for a discussion of the different types of links in the Slipnet.)

3. See if there is any concept mapping on the list that warrants proposing a correspondence between the two objects. Such a concept mapping has

to consist of *distinguishing* descriptors (e.g., the concept mapping *letter* ⇒ *letter* does not warrant a correspondence on its own) and has to represent a "close enough" relationship in the Slipnet. Identity mappings are always considered to be close enough, so if there is a distinguishing identity mapping (i.e., a mapping with distinguishing descriptors, such as *rightmost* ⇒ *rightmost*) then it is a sufficient basis for a correspondence. For slippages, the probability of being considered close enough is a function of both the conceptual depth of the descriptors and the length of the link between them. The shorter the link, the more likely it is for the the concept mapping to be judged close enough, and (as was explained in chapter 3) the deeper the descriptors, the more resistance there is to slippage, so the less likely it is for the descriptors to be considered close enough for a slippage to be made.

4. If there is no concept mapping that warrants proposing a correspondence, then fizzle. Otherwise, propose a correspondence with all the possible concept mappings that were found in step 2. Once one concept mapping (e.g., *rightmost* ⇒ *rightmost*) has been determined to be sufficient, all the others (e.g., *letter* ⇒ *letter*) come along for the ride. Post a correspondence strength-tester codelet whose urgency is a function of the strengths of the proposed correspondence's *distinguishing* concept mappings.

Important-object correspondence scout (no arguments)

1. Choose an object from the initial string probabilistically as a function of importance.

2. Choose a descriptor (from that object's relevant descriptions) probabilistically as a function of conceptual depth (e.g., it might be the descriptor *rightmost*).

3. Search through the target string for an object with the same descriptor, possibly taking into account a slippage that has already been made (e.g., if the chosen descriptor is *rightmost*, and if the slippage *leftmost* ⇒ *rightmost* has already been made, then that implies the slippage *rightmost* ⇒ *leftmost*, so this codelet will look for the *leftmost* object rather than the *rightmost* object).

4. If no object in the target string with that descriptor is found, then fizzle. Otherwise, proceed as in steps 2–4 of the bottom-up correspondence scout to propose a correspondence.

Correspondence strength-tester (argument: a proposed correspondence)

1. Calculate the proposed correspondence's strength.

2. Decide probabilistically whether or not to continue, as a function of the proposed correspondence's strength. If no, then fizzle. Otherwise, post a correspondence-builder codelet whose urgency is a function of the proposed correspondence's strength, and activate (in the Slipnet) the description types and descriptors of all of the proposed correspondence's concept mappings.

Correspondence builder (argument: a proposed correspondence)
1. If the proposed correspondence has already been built, then fizzle.

2. Otherwise, fight with any incompatible bonds, groups, and correspondences, and with the rule if an incompatible one has been built. If any fight is lost, then fizzle. Otherwise, destroy all incompatible structures, build the proposed correspondence, and activate (in the Slipnet) the nodes representing the labels of any slippage in the new correspondence's concept mappings. For example, if one of the concept mappings is *rightmost* ⇒ *rightmost*, then activate *identity*; if one of the concept mappings is *rightmost* ⇒ *leftmost*, then activate *opposite*.

Rule-Building Codelets

Rule scout (no arguments)
1. Find the letter in the initial string that has been changed—that is, whose replacement in the modified string does not have the same letter category. (The program assumes that exactly one letter will have changed.)

2. Get a list of the possible descriptors of the changed letter (e.g., the **c** in **abc**) that can be used in filling in the rule template. These descriptors have to be taken from relevant and distinguishing descriptions, but there are sometimes some other restrictions. If a correspondence has been built from this letter to an object in the target string, then the possible descriptors have to be part of the concept mappings underlying the correspondence. For example, in **abc** ⇒ **abd**, **ijk** ⇒ ?, if a correspondence has been built from the **c** to the **k**, then this codelet would not propose the rule "Replace C by *D*," since the descriptor *C* is not part of that correspondence. Likewise, in **abc** ⇒ **abd**, **xcg** ⇒ ?, if a correspondence has been built between the two **c**'s, then this codelet would not propose the rule "Replace the rightmost letter by its successor," since the descriptor *rightmost* is not part of that correspondence. If there is no correspondence attached to the changed letter, then all the relevant, distinguishing descriptors are eligible.

3. Choose a descriptor from the list of eligible descriptors probabilistically, as a function of conceptual depth.

4. Find the letter in the modified string corresponding to the changed letter in the initial string (e.g., the **d** in **abd**) and choose a descriptor of this letter. The choice is made probabilistically, as a function of conceptual depth. When a replacement structure has been built between the initial-string letter and the modified-string letter, the modified-string letter is given a description corresponding to the relationship between the two letters, if there is one. For example, for **abc** ⇒ **abd** the **d** would be given the description "successor of the **c**," but for **abc** ⇒ **abq** no such description would be given, since there is no relationship in the Slipnet between *C* and *Q*.

5. Propose a rule with the two chosen descriptors, and post a rule strength-tester codelet whose urgency is a function of the conceptual depths of the two descriptors.

Rule strength-tester (argument: a proposed rule)
    1. Calculate the proposed rule's strength.

    2. Decide probabilistically whether or not to continue, as a function of the proposed rule's strength. If no, then fizzle. Otherwise, post a rule-builder codelet whose urgency is a function of the proposed rule's strength.

Rule builder (argument: a proposed rule)
    1. If the proposed rule already exists, then fizzle.

    2. Otherwise, if there is a different existing rule, fight with it. If the fight is lost, then fizzle. Otherwise, destroy the incompatible rule, build the proposed rule, and activate (in the Slipnet) the two descriptors making up the rule.

Rule translator (no arguments)
    1. Decide whether the temperature is too high to translate the rule. To do this, choose a threshold probabilistically as a function of the amount of structure that has been built so far (this is described in subsection 3.4.3), and see if the temperature is above the chosen threshold. If so, fizzle.

    2. Otherwise, construct a translated rule by applying the slippages that have been made in the various correspondences to the descriptors in the original rule. Once the translated rule has been built, the program will stop running codelets, and will produce an answer by applying the translated rule to the target string.

Other Codelets

Replacement finder (no arguments)
    1. Choose a letter at random in the initial string. If this letter already has a replacement structure attached to it, then fizzle.

    2. Otherwise, get the letter in the corresponding position in the modified string.

    3. Build a replacement structure between the two letters.

    4. If the two letters have different letter categories, then, if their letter categories are related in the Slipnet, add a description to the modified-string letter describing the relation (e.g., add "successor of the **c**" to the **d**'s list of descriptions).

Breaker (no arguments)
    1. Decide probabilistically, as a function of temperature, whether to fizzle immediately (the lower the temperature, the more likely this codelet is to decide to fizzle).

    2. If the decision was made to continue, choose a structure at random. Decide probabilistically, as a function of the structure's strength, whether to destroy it (the weaker it is, the more likely it is to be destroyed). If the decision is made to destroy the structure, then destroy it.

Notes

Chapter 1

1. David Moser (personal communication) has pointed out that much of the trouble a few years ago between Nancy Reagan and Raisa Gorbachev may have been due to a bad analogy on the part of Americans—namely, that Mrs. Gorbachev was the first lady of the Soviet Union. This view caused many people (in particular, Mrs. Reagan) to be offended when Mrs. Gorbachev did not act in the way they felt a first lady should properly act. However, it seems that Mrs. Gorbachev did not see herself as playing the same role in the Soviet Union that Mrs. Reagan played in the United States, and thus their encounters were rife with misunderstandings. (As it turned out, Mrs. Reagan, in her memoirs, acknowledged that the analogy was imperfect, noting—though perhaps inaccurately—that "there isn't even a Russian word for 'first lady'" [1989, pp. 337–338].)

2. There has been much research in psychology and linguistics on error-making; see, for example, Fromkin 1980 and Norman 1981. A large collection of interesting speech and action errors is presented and discussed in Hofstadter and Moser 1989. The examples given above come from these three references.

3. The word "concept" is used differently here than in some of the psychological literature. For example, Barsalou (1989, p. 93) defines "concept" as "simply a particular individual's *conception* of a category on a particular occasion." He uses the word "concept" to refer to a temporarily constructed representation in working memory. I will refer to such representations as "perceptual structures." When I use the word "concept," I am referring to longer-term memory structures. This is more in keeping with the meaning of "concept" in, for example, Smith and Medin 1981.

Chapter 4

1. The bar graphs given in this and the following chapter are slightly different from those given in Mitchell 1990 and in Hofstadter and Mitchell, in press; a set of new runs was performed in order to collect more detailed statistics. There are no significant qualitative differences from the earlier set of bar graphs, although there are some differences in the "fringe" answers that appear.

2. The differences between the frequencies given in this figure and those given for the same problem in Mitchell and Hofstadter 1990 are due to several improvements in the program—in particular, improvements in the way groups and correspondences are constructed.

Appendix B

1. The detailed formulas for the importance, happiness, and salience of objects and for the strengths of structures are not given here (they were described in general terms in chapter 3). There are also other, less central details of the program that are not described in appendixes B and C. Readers interested in these and other details may request the source code for Copycat (written in Common Lisp) from the author, c/o Santa Fe Institute, 1660 Old Pecos Trail, Suite A, Santa Fe, New Mexico 87501.

Bibliography

Barnden, J. A. 1984. On short-term information processing in connectionist theories. *Cognition and Brain Theory* 7: 25–59.

Barsalou, L. W. 1989. Intraconcept similarity and its implications for interconcept similarity. In S. Vosniadou and A. Ortony (eds.), *Similarity and Analogical Reasoning*. Cambridge University Press.

Bongard, M. 1970. *Pattern Recognition*. Hayden Book Co. (Spartan Books).

Burstein, M., and Adelson, B. 1987. Mapping and integrating partial mental models. In *Proceedings of the Ninth Annual Conference of the Cognitive Science Society*. Erlbaum.

Chalmers, D. J., French, R. M., and Hofstadter, D. R. 1992. High-level perception, representation, and analogy. *Journal of Experimental and Theoretical Artificial Intelligence* 4: 185–211.

deGroot, A. 1965. *Thought and Choice in Chess*. Mouton.

Elman, J. L. 1990. Finding structure in time. *Cognitive Science* 14: 179–211.

Erman, L. D., Hayes-Roth, F., Lesser, V. R., and Raj Reddy, D. 1980. The Hearsay-II speech-understanding system: Integrating knowledge to resolve uncertainty. *Computing Surveys* 12(2): 213–253.

Evans, T. G. 1968. A program for the solution of a class of geometric-analogy intelligence-test questions. In M. Minsky (ed.), *Semantic Information Processing*. MIT Press.

Falkenhainer, B., Forbus, K. D., and Gentner, D. 1989. The structure-mapping engine. *Artificial Intelligence* 41(1): 1–63.

Farmer, J. D., Packard, N. H., and Perelson, A. S. 1986. The immune system, adaptation, and machine learning. *Physica D* 22: 187–204.

Feldman, J. A. 1986. Neural Representation of Conceptual Knowledge. Technical report 189, Department of Computer Science, University of Rochester.

Feldman, J. A., and Ballard, D. H. 1982. Connectionist models and their properties. *Cognitive Science* 6(3): 205–254.

Forbus, K. D., and Oblinger, D. 1990. Making SME greedy and pragmatic. In *Proceedings of the Twelfth Annual Conference of the Cognitive Science Society*. Erlbaum.

Forrest, S. 1990. Emergent computation: Self-organizing, collective, and cooperative phenomena in natural and artificial computing networks. *Physica D* 42: 1–11.

French, R. M. 1992. Tabletop: An Emergent, Stochastic Computer Model of Analogy-Making. Doctoral dissertation, University of Michigan, Ann Arbor.

French, R. M., and Henry, J. 1988. La traduction en français des jeux linguistiques de *Gödel, Escher, Bach*. *Méta* 33(2): 133–142.

French, R. M., and Hofstadter, D. R. 1991. Tabletop: An emergent, stochastic model of analogy-making. In *Proceedings of the Thirteenth Annual Conference of the Cognitive Science Society*. Erlbaum.

Fromkin, V. (ed.) 1980. *Errors in Linguistic Performance: Slips of the Tongue, Ear, Pen, and Hand*. Academic Press.

Gentner, D. 1983. Structure-mapping: A theoretical framework for analogy. *Cognitive Science* 7(2): 155–170.

Gick, M. L., and Holyoak, K. J. 1983. Schema induction and analogical transfer. *Cognitive Psychology* 15: 1–38.

Hall, R. P. 1989. Computational approaches to analogical reasoning. *Artificial Intelligence* 39: 39–120.

Hebb, D. O. 1949. *The Organization of Behavior*. Wiley.

Hinton, G. E. (ed.) 1990. Special issue on connectionist symbol processing. *Artificial Intelligence* 46(1–2).

Hinton, G. E., and Sejnowski, T. J. 1986. Learning and relearning in Boltzmann machines. In D. E. Rumelhart and J. L. McClelland (eds.), *Parallel Distributed Processing* volume 1. MIT Press.

Hofstadter, D. R. 1979. *Gödel, Escher, Bach: an Eternal Golden Braid*. Basic Books.

Hofstadter, D. R. 1982. The Search for Essence 'twixt Medium and Message: What Is the Essence of an Idea? Report 4, Center for Research on Concepts and Cognition, Indiana University, Bloomington.

Hofstadter, D. R. 1983. The architecture of Jumbo. In Proceedings of the International Machine Learning Workshop, Monticello, Illinois.

Hofstadter, D. R. 1984a. The Copycat Project: An Experiment in Nondeterminism and Creative Analogies. AI Memo 755, Artificial Intelligence Laboratory, Massachusetts Institute of Technology.

Hofstadter, D. R. 1984b. Simple and Not-So-Simple Analogies in the Copycat Domain. Report 9, Center for Research on Concepts and Cognition, Indiana University, Bloomington.

Hofstadter, D. R. 1985a. Analogies and roles in human and machine thinking. In Hofstadter, *Metamagical Themas*. Basic Books.

Hofstadter, D. R. 1985b. Variations on a theme as the crux of creativity. In Hofstadter, *Metamagical Themas*. Basic Books.

Hofstadter, D. R. 1985c. On the seeming paradox of mechanizing creativity. In Hofstadter, *Metamagical Themas*. Basic Books.

Hofstadter, D. R. 1985d. Waking up from the Boolean dream: Subcognition as computation. In Hofstadter, *Metamagical Themas*. Basic Books.

Hofstadter, D. R. 1987. Fluid Analogies and Human Creativity. Report 16, Center for Research on Concepts and Cognition, Indiana University, Bloomington.

Hofstadter, D. R., Clossman, G., and Meredith, M. J. 1982. SEEK-WHENCE: A Project in Pattern Understanding. Report 3, Center for Research on Concepts and Cognition, Indiana University, Bloomington.

Hofstadter, D. R., and French, R. M. 1992. Probing the emergent behavior of Tabletop, an architecture uniting high-level perception with analogy-making. In *Proceedings of the Fourteenth Annual Conference of the Cognitive Science Society*. Erlbaum.

Hofstadter, D. R., and Gabora, L. M. 1990. Synopsis of the workshop on humor and cognition. *Humor* 2(4): 417–440.

Hofstadter, D. R., and Mitchell, M., in press. The Copycat project: A model of mental fluidity and analogy-making. In Holyoak, K. J., and Barnden, J. A. (eds.) 1992. *Advances in Connectionist and Neural Computation Theory*, volume 2. Ablex.

Hofstadter, D. R., Mitchell, M., and French, R. M. 1987. Fluid Concepts and Creative Analogies: A Theory and Its Computer Implementation. Technical report 10, Cognitive Science and Machine Intelligence Laboratory, University of Michigan, Ann Arbor.

Hofstadter, D. R., and Moser, D. J. 1989. To err is human; to study error-making is cognitive science. *Michigan Quarterly Review* 28(2): 185–215.

Holland, J. H. 1975. *Adaptation in Natural and Artificial Systems*. University of Michigan Press.

Holland, J. H. 1986. Escaping brittleness: The possibilities of general-purpose learning algorithms applied to parallel rule-based systems. In R. Michalski et al. (eds.), *Machine Learning: An Artificial Intelligence Approach*, volume 2. Morgan Kaufmann.

Holland, J. H. 1988. The dynamics of searches directed by genetic algorithms. In Y. C. Lee (ed.), *Evolution, Learning, and Cognition*. World Scientific Press.

Holland, J. H., Holyoak, K. J., Nisbett, R. E., and Thagard, P. R. 1986. *Induction*. MIT Press.

Holyoak, K. J. 1984. Analogical thinking and human intelligence. In R. J. Sternberg (ed.), *Advances in the Psychology of Human Intelligence*, volume 2. Erlbaum.

Holyoak, K. J., and Barnden, J. A. (eds.), in press. *Advances in Connectionist and Neural Computation Theory*, volume 2. Ablex.

Holyoak, K. J., and Thagard, P. 1989. Analogical mapping by constraint satisfaction. *Cognitive Science* 13(3): 295–355.

Hopfield, J. J. 1982. Neural networks and physical systems with emergent collective computational abilities. *Proceedings of the National Academy of Sciences* 79: 2554–2558.

James, W. 1890. *The Principles of Psychology*. Holt. Reprinted by Dover, 1950.

Johnson-Laird, P. 1989. Analogy and the exercise of creativity. In S. Vosniadou and A. Ortony (eds.), *Similarity and Analogical Reasoning*. Cambridge University Press.

Kahneman, D., and Miller, D. T. 1986. Norm theory: Comparing reality to its alternatives. *Psychological Review* 93(2): 136–153.

Kaplan, S., and Kaplan, R. 1982. *Cognition and Environment*. Praeger.

Kedar-Cabelli, S. 1988a. Analogy—from a unified perspective. In D. H. Helman (ed.), *Analogical Reasoning*. Kluwer.

Kedar-Cabelli, S. 1988b. Towards a computational model of purpose-directed analogy. In A. Prieditis (ed.), *Analogica*. Morgan Kaufmann.

Kirkpatrick, S., Gelatt, C. D., Jr., and Vecchi, M. P. 1983. Optimization by simulated annealing. *Science* 220: 671–680.

Kotovsky, K., and Simon, H. A. 1973. Empirical tests of a theory of human acquisition of concepts for sequential patterns. *Cognitive Psychology* 4: 399–424.

Lakoff, G. 1987. *Women, Fire, and Dangerous Things*. University of Chicago Press.

Lakoff, G., and Johnson, M. 1980. *Metaphors We Live By*. University of Chicago Press.

Lewenstein, M., and Nowak, A. 1989. Fully connected neural networks with self-control of noise levels. *Physical Review Letters* 62(2): 225–228.

Longuet-Higgins, H. C. 1981. Artificial intelligence: A new theoretical psychology. *Cognition* 10: 197–200.

Lucas, J. R. 1961. Minds, machines, and Gödel. *Philosophy* 36: 112.

McClelland, J. L., and Rumelhart, D. E. 1981. An interactive activation model of context effects in letter perception: Part 1. An account of basic findings. *Psychological Review* 88: 375–407.

McClelland, J. L., and Rumelhart, D. E. (eds.) 1986. *Parallel Distributed Processing*, Volume 2. MIT Press.

McClelland, J. L., Rumelhart, D. E., and Hinton, G. E. 1986. The appeal of parallel distributed processing. In D. E. Rumelhart and J. L. McClelland (eds.), *Parallel Distributed Processing*, Volume 1. MIT Press.

McDermott, D. 1981. Artificial intelligence meets natural stupidity. In J. Haugeland (ed.), *Mind Design*. MIT Press.

Meehan, J. 1976. The Metanovel: Writing Stories by computer. Technical report 74, Computer Science Department, Yale University.

Meredith, M. J. 1986. Seek-Whence: A Model of Pattern Perception. Technical report 214, Computer Science Department, Indiana University, Bloomington.

Mitchell, M. 1990. Copycat: A Computer Model of High-Level Perception and Conceptual Slippage in Analogy-Making. Doctoral dissertation, University of Michigan, Ann Arbor.

Mitchell, M., and Hofstadter, D. R. 1990. The right concept at the right time: How concepts emerge as relevant in response to context-dependent pressures. In *Proceedings of the Twelfth Annual Conference of the Cognitive Science Society*. Erlbaum.

Moser, D. J. 1991. Sze-chuan pepper and Coca-Cola: The translation of *Gödel, Escher, Bach* into Chinese. *Babel* 37(2): 75–95.

Norman, D. A. 1981. Categorization of action slips. *Psychological Review* 88(1): 1–15.

Pagels, H. R. 1988. *The Dreams of Reason*. Simon and Schuster.

Pivar, M., and Finkelstein, M. 1964. Automation, using LISP, of inductive inference on sequences. In E. C. Berkeley and D. Bobrow (eds.), *The Programming Language LISP: Its Operation and Applications*. Information International.

Reagan, N., with Novak, W. 1989. *My Turn: The Memoirs of Nancy Reagan*. Random House.

Rosch, E., and Lloyd, B. B. 1978. *Cognition and Categorization*. Erlbaum.

Rumelhart, D. E., Hinton, G. E., and Williams, R. J. 1986. Learning internal representations by error propagation. In D. E. Rumelhart and J. L. McClelland (eds.), *Parallel Distributed Processing*, volume 1. MIT Press.

Rumelhart, D. E., and McClelland, J. L. (eds.) 1986. *Parallel Distributed Processing*, volume 1. MIT Press.

Schank, R. C. 1983. *Dynamic Memory*. Cambridge University Press.

Schank, R. C., and Leake, D. B. 1989. Creativity and learning in a case-based explainer. *Artificial Intelligence* 40(1–3): 353–385.

Simon, H. A. 1972. Complexity and the representation of patterned sequences of symbols. *Psychological Review* 79(5): 369–382.

Simon, H. A., and Kotovsky, K. 1963. Human acquisition of concepts for sequential patterns. *Psychological Review* 70(6): 534–546.

Skorstad, J., Falkenhainer, B., and Gentner, D. 1987. Analogical processing: A simulation and empirical corroboration. In *Proceedings of the American Association for Artificial Intelligence, AAAI-87*. Morgan Kaufmann.

Smith, E. E., and Medin, D. L. 1981. *Categories and Concepts*. Harvard University Press.

Smolensky, P. 1986. Information processing in dynamical systems: Foundations of harmony theory. In D. E. Rumelhart and J. L. McClelland (eds.), *Parallel Distributed Processing*, volume 1. MIT Press.

Smolensky, P. 1988. On the proper treatment of connectionism. *Behavioral and Brain Sciences* 11(1): 1–14.

Thagard, P. 1989. Explanatory coherence. *Behavioral and Brain Sciences* 12(3): 435–467.

Thagard, P., Holyoak, K. J., Nelson, G., and Gochfeld, D. 1990. Analog retrieval by constraint satisfaction. *Artificial Intelligence* 46(3): 259–310.

Touretzky, D. S., and Hinton, G. E. 1988. A distributed connectionist production system. *Cognitive Science* 12: 423–466.

Turner, M. 1988. Categories and analogies. In D. H. Helman (ed.), *Analogical Reasoning*. Kluwer.

Wilson, S. W. 1987. Classifier systems and the animat problem. *Machine Learning* 2: 199–228.

Woods, A. 1975. What's in a link: Foundations for semantic networks. In D. G. Bobrow and A. Collins (eds.), *Representation and Understanding: Studies in Cognitive Science*. Academic Press.

Yukawa, H. 1973a. Creative thinking in science. In *Creativity and Intuition: A Physicist Looks at East and West*. Kodansha International.

Yukawa, H. 1973b. Meson theory in its developments. In *Creativity and Intuition: A Physicist looks at East and West*. Kodansha International.

Index

CPSIA information can be obtained at www.ICGtesting.com
Printed in the USA
243756LV00011B/176/P